MW01251131

Palgrave Studies in the History of Finance

Series Editors
D'Maris Coffman
Institutional Research Information Service
University College London
London, United Kingdom

Tony K. Moore
University of Reading
Crewe, United Kingdom

Martin Allen
University of Cambridge
Cambridge, United Kingdom

Sophus Reinert
Harvard Business School
Cambridge, Massachusetts, USA

The study of the history of financial institutions, markets, instruments and concepts is vital if we are to understand the role played by finance today. At the same time, the methodologies developed by finance academics can provide a new perspective for historical studies. Palgrave Studies in the History of Finance is a multi-disciplinary effort to emphasise the role played by finance in the past, and what lessons historical experiences have for us. It presents original research, in both authored monographs and edited collections, from historians, finance academics and economists, as well as financial practitioners.

More information about this series at
http://www.springer.com/series/14583

Nigel Edward Morecroft

The Origins of Asset Management from 1700 to 1960

Towering Investors

Nigel Edward Morecroft
Edinburgh
United Kingdom

Palgrave Studies in the History of Finance
ISBN 978-3-319-51849-7   ISBN 978-3-319-51850-3 (Ebook)
DOI 10.1007/978-3-319-51850-3

Library of Congress Control Number: 22017934437

Cover illustration © HultonArchive / Getty

Printed on acid-free paper

This Palgrave Macmillan imprint is published by Springer Nature
The registered company is Springer International Publishing AG
The registered company address is: Gewerbestrasse 11, 6330 Cham, Switzerland

Acknowledgements

Charley Ellis and Gill Hollis suggested I should 'have a go' when I was first mulling over the idea of a book, while both Amanda Fisher and my daughter Heather read the first draft chapter and made encouraging comments, so they all bear some responsibility for what has followed, though the errors are all my own. Huge appreciation is due to the people who directly contributed by providing specific information, lines of enquiry and ideas. My old colleagues at Foreign & Colonial have been very useful: Hugh Potter sent me various documents and gave me access to the remaining papers and pamphlets that are retained in-house; Jeremy Tigue also offered early thoughts and insights which prompted me to consider embarking on a more ambitious project. Having reached a dead-end on Keynes, David Chambers produced a portfolio for me to use and this, in combination with his own excellent work on Keynes' investment performance in particular, has been invaluable. The Bursar at Kings College, Keith Carne, enabled me to gain a much broader appreciation of Lord Keynes and his lasting impact at Kings, while visiting the archives there was a real joy. Information about unit trusts is thin on the ground but both Anthony Ashplant and Richard Miles at M&G provided me with much needed material about unit trusts in general and M&G in particular. James Wragg and James Hughes-Hallett at the Esmée Fairbairn Foundation were generous with their time; John Fairbairn, Ian Fairbairn's nephew, not only provided insights and anecdotes but also was also extremely knowledgeable and entertaining in conversation about his uncle. Peter Dunscombe was exceptionally patient dealing with a long string of separate requests for information about George Ross Goobey and the Imperial Tobacco pension fund. Many others provided useful guidance or specific information too, namely Professor Graeme Acheson, Theresa and Georgie Booth, Dr. Adam Fox, Professor Richard ('Dick') Kent, Chris Lewin, Mike Redwood, Richard Schuster, Bill Smith, Mike Staunton and Gervais Williams. I also thank the small number of people who were very helpful and asked to remain anonymous.

Anybody writing a book needs support and I needed quite a lot so I am absolutely indebted to all those who have got me through this undertaking including Fiona and Gavin. Apologies to those that I have failed to mention but I do wish to record my particular appreciation to Richard Burns, John Carson, Pat Harkin, Peter Hollis, Howard ('Mitch') Mitchell, Claire Oxenham, Leslie Robb and Robert Ross. Over the last couple of years working on the book, one thing I have come to appreciate is that we have the most wonderful libraries, librarians and archivists in this country for which we should all be grateful. Their continuing geniality, efficiency and knowledge are, surely, one sign of a truly civilised country and the Reading Room at the National Library of Scotland has been a particularly pleasant place to spend time. The British Library in London and the Guildhall Library (Valerie in particular) have been of immense assistance, as has David Hood at the Library of the Institute & Faculty of Actuaries in Edinburgh. Also in Edinburgh, the Library of Mistakes deserves a special mention, owing to a combination of its usefulness combined with its quirkiness; Russell Napier, 'The Keeper', provided excellent early guidance on the broad shape of my manuscript, while several of my fellow 'Errorists' there have been immensely useful either by sending me information or acting as critical friends. Various archivists have been delightful to deal with and deserve special mention as follows: Lydia at the Borthwick Institute for Archives at the University of York; the Archive Centre, Kings College, Cambridge (Peter and Patricia); and the Dundee City Archives (Ian and Martin). The London Metropolitan Archives is now a tremendously useful resource housing amongst other things, the Pensions Archive Trust. Finally, in Edinburgh, the Lloyds Banking Group Archives (which contains comprehensive material on Scottish Widows) is well organised and Sian Phillips was exceptionally cooperative.

Mistakes and all, I trust this book goes some small way to broadening knowledge of the asset management profession and how, and why, it started. It is written in a serious tone but I hope my mother, bless her, who never had money to invest, would have enjoyed reading it, so this is for her.

Contents

List of Figures

List of Tables

1

Introduction and Overview

This is a story about investment – why and how an asset management profession developed and became established in Britain. The role of asset management within the broader financial services sector is not well understood because, while much is known in Britain about the City of London and individual financial services businesses, mainly banks, very little has been written about asset management, particularly its early days.[1] In the US scholarly academic research, articles and a variety of books about asset management abound, and some investors such as Warren Buffett are revered. In addition, the redoubtable Wellington Fund which started in 1928, Benjamin Graham, the legendary US investor and writer from the 1930s, and Fidelity, which was established in the 1940s are all very well known and highly respected. Britain, however, had investment gurus and successful asset management institutions equivalent to those in the USA and they pre-dated their American cousins. Foreign & Colonial Investment Trust, born in

---

[1] As an example, David Kynaston's magnificent four volumes about *The City of London* from 1815 to 2000 (Pimlico 1995) make only passing reference to asset management.

© The Author(s) 2017   1
N.E. Morecroft, *The Origins of Asset Management
from 1700 to 1960*, Palgrave Studies in the History of Finance,
DOI 10.1007/978-3-319-51850-3_1

1868, has outlived them all; John Maynard Keynes, the economist, was a prolific investor who wrote insightfully about investing; and M&G was managing unit trusts, or mutual funds, long before Fidelity. Asset management may not have started in Britain but by the end of the nineteenth century it had become fully established here, as a sustainable and discrete activity. Why, how it began, survived and grew has largely been ignored which is why this book considers the institutions and individuals who made significant contributions to the profession in Britain after 1700 and up to 1960.

There is an important distinction to be made within financial services between asset management, which is a long-term investment activity, and deposit-taking, a shorter-term need satisfied by banks. The widespread problems created by banks and bankers, particularly over the last 10 years, but going back to the nineteenth century, produce a warped and distorted view of the broader financial services industry which has many specialised segments, of which asset management is one. Deposits placed with banks should be short-term, low risk and low return, whereas asset management should offer clients a professional service that is longer term, higher risk and higher return. Banking differs from asset management because 'bankers lend other people's money not their own. This creates an incentive problem because bankers get most of the benefit if the risky loans they make do well, whereas depositors, not bankers, incur most of the costs if loans go bad'.[2] With asset management, there is not the same incentive problem because when the assets increase in value then most of the benefit goes to the client. The essence of asset management is that it is, or should be, a professional service provided as part of a long-term relationship based on recycling excess savings over and above deposits. Banks provide capital directly and operate as principals, whereas asset management companies are agents, charging fees: there is a fundamental difference.

In terms of purpose, this is not another book about 'great investors' nor does it explain how to get rich quick nor how to turn a small fortune into a large one. Rather, it considers how financial markets have changed

---

[2] John Turner, *Banking in Crisis* (Cambridge University Press 2014) 6.

over a long period of time and it concentrates on the building blocks of asset management – the underlying securities in an investment portfolio. This work looks at these first portfolios, describes them and, in some cases, analyses how they may have changed to highlight the thought processes of early investors and the prevailing financial thinking and economic ideas of their time. It gives a sense of the investment performance over long-term periods produced by these investment strategies, but it deliberately eschews detailed calculation and analysis of investment performance statistics and benchmarks, nor is there a detailed assessment of style factors or risk measures: the investment pioneers in this book did not think in such terms, nor did the people who gave them money to invest. Rather, this is the story of ideas and behaviours and the organisations and people who moulded the asset management profession in Britain and made it a discrete activity within financial services, distinct from banking, insurance and stockbroking. Most of the time, asset management is exceptionally transparent and should benefit, more than many activities, from the perspective of history. As George Santayana allegedly said, 'Those who cannot remember the past are condemned to repeat it.' This book is intended to fill a gap and help us to understand the origins of asset management as a profession and, possibly, to learn from some of the individuals and institutions who were responsible for its development. More generally, over this period, asset management was socially useful; it had a beneficial impact on the development of securities markets and savings were recycled effectively. At a practical level, having an alternative route for savings and investment through an asset management channel independent of banks is a good thing.

**

In eighteenth-century Britain, borrowing became better organised and financial markets developed in important directions based around the Bank of England and the government's better management of finances. An orderly government bond market created the bedrock of an efficient system whereby British governments could borrow at economic rates and this provided Britain with an important structural advantage compared to other European countries. The year 1752 was a particularly important date for borrowing when the British government created a risk-free asset which investors, particularly insurance companies, could confidently utilise.[3] A regulated single London Stock Exchange came into being in 1801 and in conjunction with the 'financial revolution' of the preceding century, enabled London to achieve a leadership position in global capital markets after 1815. Throughout the nineteenth century, London was the dominant centre for listing and trading international bonds. Domestic bond and money markets were equally vibrant in the nineteenth century owing to the demand for capital arising from industrialisation and urbanisation. Overall therefore, by the middle of the nineteenth century, debt markets in Britain were wide and deep. Britain also influenced market practices in the foreign exchange markets when it formally adopted the Gold Standard in 1819 (though as Master of the Mint, Sir Isaac Newton had introduced it in practice in 1717) and other countries followed suit.[4] Currencies did not float freely but instead were fixed to gold for most of this period. In theory, this meant that notes were backed by, and could be exchanged into, gold. During periodic crises, countries would come off the Gold Standard: the USA, for example during the Civil War in the 1860s (only returning to it in 1879), most European countries abandoned convertibility during the First World War and the Gold Standard system crumbled during the 1930s as a result of the Depression.

Equity markets also developed but at a much slower, almost glacial, pace. Joint stock companies in the shape of the chartered mercantile businesses such as the East India Company had been important institutions during the seventeenth century, but after 1720, further progress was limited, owing to restrictive government legislation. For a century thereafter equity financing was barely used, which seems incongruous given that the industrial revolution was in full flow in Britain. Laws associated with company formation were relaxed during the nineteenth century but only towards the end of it did the limited liability company,

[3] Gerard Caprio, *Handbook of Key Global Financial Markets, Institutions, and Infrastructure* (Academic Press 2012) 245.
[4] Michael Bordo, *The Concise Encyclopaedia of Economics, Gold Standard* (www.econlib.org, website accessed 24 May 2016).

underpinned by ordinary shares, become the norm. Guinness was the first major commercial company to list in London in 1886, though even as late as 1900, the quoted equity of railroad companies dominated the market in terms of market capitalisation. Nevertheless, the direction of travel was clear and in the twentieth century many businesses would choose to list on the London Stock Exchange and this, in parallel with the growth of dedicated investment companies independent from banks and insurance companies, had wide-ranging implications for the capitalist system. The public listing of ordinary shares on the stock market led to significant changes in the nature of the business corporation in two areas. First, ownership and control became separated. Second, ownership, and particularly stewardship, resided increasingly with institutional asset management businesses. Importantly, these structural changes in the nature of the company, in terms of limited liability, public listing and ownership, were not primarily to fund industrialisation but instead represented a widening and deepening of the capitalist system. Consequently, over the 250 years or so up to 1960, there has been a natural progression from the partnership, to the small-scale business or speculative endeavour funded by individuals, to the rise of the business corporation or private company, and then to the modern limited liability corporation listed on publicly traded markets, now largely owned by asset management companies as agents on behalf of their underlying clients.

Institutionalised saving had its beginnings around 1700 when the earliest insurance companies were formed. Insurance companies were the first investment institutions in Britain and they expected to meet their liabilities by generating an appropriate level of income from their assets. At this juncture, insurance companies functioned like cautious banks and were central cogs at the heart of the financial system. In practice, these early British insurance companies were hybrid financial institutions that both supplied credit or capital where needed, and also invested surplus assets – they operated at a time when the banking system was small, local and fragmented. Gradually, and particularly as life assurance grew, the balance of their activity moved towards longer-term investing and away from the provision of bank finance. Over a long period of time, about 150 years between 1720 and 1870, they proved that financial markets could be trusted and they developed rudimentary investment expertise, though their primary activity was the business of insurance so in that respect, and perfectly naturally, investment was always a secondary focus. In 1862, A.H. Bailey, an actuary, mapped out rudimentary principles of investment for life offices which were cogent, albeit risk-averse, with an emphasis on investment into assets with stable market values and security of capital. This was perhaps the first application of portfolio theory to institutional investments and clearly demonstrated the increasing importance of investing. While insurance companies were large, influential investors, occasionally they come across as institutions that appear slightly impersonal or rather dull. This was deliberate on their part and was reflected very clearly in the understated titles that they bestowed on their most senior executives such as the Secretary, or the Actuary (in England) and the Manager (in Scotland). This has meant that insurance companies, as discussed in Chapter 2 and in the context of this book, are dealt with at a corporate level as businesses, whereas the rest of the book focuses on individuals in addition to the organisations in which they worked.

The 100 years from the mid-nineteenth century to the middle of the twentieth century represents the principal emphasis of this book because during this period saving and investment became more sophisticated. Over this period, the growth of investment companies, unit trusts, life offices and pension funds represented a long-term trend for aggregating and channelling investment in the modern economy. If borrowing was changing after 1700, as mentioned above, then so was saving, particularly after 1850. As the nineteenth century progressed, owing to a combination of industrialisation and the British Empire, Britons were becoming wealthy and a new middle class was springing up with money to invest, but the question was, what to do with it? For savers who were purely interested in income rather than capital gain, just about anything was better than placing hard-earned money in British government bonds whose yields fell for most of the century after 1815. Worse still, banks had the habit of failing on an alarmingly regular basis – in 1825, 1847, 1866, 1873, 1878 and 1890 to name just a few banking crises. The City of Glasgow Bank's failure in 1878, in particular, had major ramifications with widespread media coverage across Britain and not least because several directors of the bank were imprisoned and some shareholders were bankrupted. Arguably, the public demise of this bank highlighted the benefits of a discrete non-banking channel for savings that could be provided by dedicated asset management companies.

In the latter part of the nineteenth century, asset management changed fundamentally with dedicated investment companies being established in their own right, forming a discrete sector within financial services. These investment companies sought higher returns over the long-term by embracing risk, rather than avoiding it, and investing internationally.[5] From 1868, the Foreign & Colonial Government Trust, a pooled fund, provided access to professional investment services for a wide spectrum of society. Philip Rose was the driving force behind the Foreign & Colonial Government Trust in the first 15 years of its existence. It had some notable features: it invested in marketable securities and its own certificates (not shares until 1879) were tradable. Second, it had a dedicated group of individuals, the Trustees, who were responsible for the investments and they operated with various checks and balances to ensure probity. Third, it not only survived but during the 1870s and 1880s it was accompanied by other investment companies employing different strategies, meaning that asset management became embedded in financial services in England and Scotland. As an activity, it was distinct from banking and it was more accessible, specialised and visible than the investment activities of insurance companies.

By the late nineteenth century, solid foundations had been established so it was unlikely that asset management would fade away in Britain, as the mutual funds of the Netherlands had done around 1800.[6] Investment companies were cost-effective, diversified investment vehicles which enabled middle-class savers to invest in the stock market with confidence that their money was being handled with integrity. The basic idea of

---

[5] I have generally used the term 'investment company' rather than 'investment trust' or 'closed-end fund' for a couple of reasons. Legally, some early investment trusts were trusts while others were incorporated as companies but all of them were investment companies. Second, 'investment company' is the description used in the USA and the term is, therefore, more consistent.

[6] A 'mutual fund' is an open-ended fund or unit trust. Current examples of mutual funds are OEICs, SICAVs and Exchange Traded Funds.

the investment company has survived to the present day and the Foreign & Colonial Investment Trust PLC, now approaching its 150th anniversary, rivals many august British institutions in terms of its longevity and has outlived most industrial corporations. After 1873, Robert Fleming and other Scottish investors did much to ensure that the investment management profession continued to evolve in a coherent direction in both Scotland and more widely in Britain. His investment company, the Scottish American Investment Trust (known as the 'First Scottish'), identified the USA as the great investment opportunity of the nineteenth century and Fleming, in conjunction with its Trustees, added an important element of professionalism to asset management. The Scottish investment companies, operating out of Dundee and Edinburgh, undertook detailed research and engaged with company managements, thus developing the idea of using information advantageously to achieve a competitive advantage. Working diligently in small decision-making teams and investing internationally, Scottish asset managers quickly acquired a distinctive and enduring personality which shaped active asset management and took it in a different direction from the Foreign & Colonial Government Trust. Whereas Foreign & Colonial essentially administered its investments with a 'buy and hold' approach, investing in sterling-denominated assets via the London Stock Exchange, the First Scottish made its investments directly into the USA in dollars so it was genuinely invested overseas and could therefore explore wider investment opportunities. Technological change helped the First Scottish because the cable telegraph under the Atlantic became a cost-effective method of faster communication from the 1870s onwards. Telegraphic communication was almost instantaneous whereas prior to its introduction, letters were sent across the Atlantic by boat: the round-trip took weeks. The telegraph made the pricing of securities more efficient between London and New York while it also reduced costs by, for example, making money transfers quicker. Finally, at a personal level Fleming demonstrated that someone with intelligence and application could rise to be a success in the world of asset management despite coming from a humble background.

After the First World War, Maynard Keynes applied his idiosyncratic intellect to asset management. He is best known as an economist; but he was also a prolific investor. As a general observation, Keynes' contribution to the advancement of asset management in Britain is more difficult to assess than the other individuals and institutions in this book. He was involved in a range of investment activities, some of which failed while others succeeded and he changed his own investment philosophy fundamentally after about 1930. While he wrote engagingly about asset management, with the exception of Chapter 12 of the *General Theory* published in 1936, most of his insights about institutional investing only appeared long after his death in 1946. On balance, he deserves recognition owing to his role after 1921 as the prescient chairman of the National Mutual, a life assurance company. He provided life assurance companies with a blueprint for success in asset management which some of them followed in the 1920s and 1930s; and he was an advocate for investing into ordinary shares, advice which most of them followed in the fullness of time. But even at the National Mutual where he was largely successful over 17 years, Keynes had financial problems in the early 1930s that were largely self-inflicted, which led to the postponement of the annual bonus to policyholders. In order to provide a rounded view of Keynes as an investor, Chapter 5 analyses his activities at the National Mutual while Chapter 6 also explores his roles at the Independent Investment Company, and at the Discretionary Fund at Kings College Cambridge where he created a very sophisticated investment framework and achieved remarkably strong investment returns over 25 years. Keynes was years ahead of his time as an asset manager, which made it difficult for many of his contemporaries to grasp what he was really doing. For example, he was writing about 'behavioural finance', the psychology of markets and investors, more than 40 years before the term was widely understood.

The Great Crash of 1929 was a major market event which led to innovative thinking about markets and investment, as well as soul-searching, particularly in the USA. Owing to misdemeanours during the late 1920s, American investment companies fell into disrepute. Mutual funds with limited investment discretion became a popular alternative, providing a means to limit the power of directors and to control abuse. George Macaulay Booth imported the mutual fund idea and he launched a unit trust, the First British Fixed Trust at the bottom of the market, and in the midst of a depression in 1931. It invested in British equities, mainly industrial shares. Booth, and his lifelong business partner Ian Fairbairn, shared similar values with Rose from 1868: they wished to broaden participation in wealth generation by making investment available to a wider constituency. They needed to be patient and determined: unit trusts enjoyed only modest growth during the 1930s and did not become fully established in Britain until the early 1960s. The pattern of development was completely different in the USA where mutual funds eclipsed investment companies within a very short space of time. In Britain, the occasional disreputable behaviour of some practitioners, the complete absence of regulation and the Second World War severely restricted the development of unit trusts. Booth and Fairbairn used Municipal and General Securities, a finance company, as the vehicle to manage the first unit trusts. It exists today in the shape of its successor organisation, M&G Investments, the asset management arm of the Prudential Assurance Company PLC, one of the few surviving unit trust managers from the middle of the twentieth century. M&G excepted, the lack of longevity among asset management groups in this sector may explain the dearth of information and historical data relating to the unit trust industry but the absence of material means that there are major gaps in our knowledge. This ignorance about unit trusts contrasts sharply with the many dignified and informative histories written about investment companies.

Fortunately, information is more widely available about British pension funds which were formed in large numbers during the early part of the twentieth century. Similar to the life companies of the nineteenth century, initially they aimed to achieve a monetary rate of interest linked to their liabilities until George Ross Goobey explained that pension fund investment should be approached differently. After 1950, he argued against the orthodox investment thinking of the time, as Keynes had with life office investment, and he understood that ordinary shares and property were most likely to produce acceptable real returns during periods of rising inflation. As a consequence, he argued that bonds ought to yield more than equities in an inflationary environment. At a practical level, Ross Goobey started investing in equities in the 1950s, when they yielded 2% more than government bonds. By 1960, this yield relationship had reversed. Rather than matching liabilities with assets, he was interested in producing high, real returns which logically, he argued, implied having 100% of assets invested in ordinary shares. He also held that volatility of market values was largely irrelevant for long-term investors who did not need immediate access to liquidity. By around 1960 and with Ross Goobey's revolutionary impact on investment, the institutional asset management profession had a recognisably modern appearance. Therefore, 1960 appears to be a sensible place to draw a line under this first phase of its development.

Bibliography (Restricted)

Books

Gerard Caprio, *Handbook of Key Global Financial Markets, Institutions, and Infrastructure* (Academic Press 2012)
David Kynaston, *The City of London 1815 to 2000*, in four volumes (Pimlico 1995)
John Turner, *Banking in Crisis* (Cambridge University Press 2014)

Articles, Journals, Pamphlets, Websites, etc.

Michael Bordo, *The Concise Encyclopaedia of Economics, Gold Standard* (www.econlib.org)

2

Markets and Insurance Company Investments, 1700–1900

After 1700, financial markets in Britain developed slowly but in important new directions, influenced partly by the insurance companies who were the first, sizeable institutional investors in Britain. The historian Dickson has argued convincingly that a 'financial revolution' occurred in Britain in the eighteenth century which placed public borrowing on a sound footing. Specifically, in 1752 with the introduction of the Consol, an irredeemable British government bond, an 'investment revolution' also took place because this created a risk-free asset for savers. A combination of financial stability and maritime dominance gave Britain a powerful position in the world, and from the early part of the nineteenth century onwards, Britain was the dominant nation-state, politically and economically. In turn, this created wealth, enabling London to become the global centre for the listing and trading of international securities built on the solid financial foundations put down in the eighteenth century. The insurance companies, and their investment portfolios, were an integral component of this financial revolution for several reasons: they were

© The Author(s) 2017   **13**
N.E. Morecroft, *The Origins of Asset Management
from 1700 to 1960*, Palgrave Studies in the History of Finance,
DOI 10.1007/978-3-319-51850-3_2

embedded in the credit markets, like banks; they were a major participant in the fledgling government bond market; and increasingly, they were long-term investors in a wide range of different asset classes. In practice, as a group of large, stable investing institutions, insurance companies helped to develop British money markets in the eighteenth century and securities markets in the nineteenth century. Bonds, loans and land mortgages were important constituents of their portfolios and as Britain industrialised, they funded much urban development and industrial infrastructure, particularly in the nineteenth century.[1] Although their investment portfolios were conservatively managed to meet liabilities rather than to produce high returns, this did not mean that investment activity was static. In practice, investment policy was actively managed and changed significantly over time: the most notable asset allocation move was the reduction in UK government bond holdings from very high to negligible levels during the nineteenth century as yields fell from 5% to 2% and other investment opportunities were seized. From their beginnings, insurance companies were directly involved in the money markets and operated like banks, but more prudently perhaps, because they had the useful discipline of needing to use their assets to meet expected, specific liabilities. They made short-term loans and provided mortgages, lending against collateral, usually land. With the exception of the Bank of England, which essentially had a banking monopoly after the Bubble Act of 1720, British banking was small-scale and very fragmented until the middle of the nineteenth century, and insurance companies, with their large asset base, partly filled this gap in the banking sector.[2] The Bubble Act of 1720 restricted new company

---

[1] 'Mortgage' tends to be a general term covering more than one aspect of lending. The specific meaning in the eighteenth century referred to lending against the freehold land of country estates. But in the nineteenth century, the terms mortgages had much wider application and the words 'mortgages' and 'loans' became interchangeable until 1870 when they were required to be separately classified.

[2] The Bank of England had a banking monopoly and was effectively a metropolitan London bank. Local country banks became established but these were often small-scale family firms. By contrast, banking in Scotland was much more flexible and effective. The Bubble Act was repealed in 1825 largely because approximately 300 private banks had failed in the 30 years prior.

formation by requiring larger companies of more than six partners or directors to be approved (chartered) by Parliament. The full name of the act was 'An Act for better securing certain Powers and Privileges, intended to be granted by His Majesty by Two Charters, for Assurance of Ships and Merchandise at Sea, and for lending Money upon Bottomry; and for restraining several extravagant and unwarrantable Practices therein mentioned' which partly explains why 'Bubble Act' became the short-hand description.[3] Specifically this act granted charters to two insurance companies, the Royal Exchange and London Assurance, to be discussed later in this chapter, and the Act was passed into law before, not after, the collapse of the South Sea Company.

As insurance companies built up surplus funds, particularly the life assurance companies, they began to invest for the long-term and their assets supported major urban developments in both the provinces and London, such as building Regent Street after 1814 and Belgravia between the 1830s and 1860. In practice, the insurance companies had a dual function – like banks, with surplus capital they provided short-term credit finance through the provision of personal loans but they also made longer-term investment decisions, for example, based around mortgages secured on agricultural land. Over time, and particularly as life assurance, with its longer-term horizon for investment, developed rapidly during the early nineteenth century, insurance companies moved more towards behaving like investing institutions and less like banks: increasingly, rather than being principal suppliers of credit, they became long-term investors in quoted securities. In 1861, an influential paper by A.H. Bailey, an actuary, highlighted the evolution of their investment thinking. He articulated several important principles of investment that should underpin life office investing and Bailey's ideas, particularly his first investment principle, based on security, held sway long into the twentieth century. Therefore, over this period of 200 years, financial markets experienced transformational change while, in parallel, insurance companies grew and developed as important investing institutions.

---

[3] Ron Harris, *Industrializing English Law* (Cambridge University Press 2000) 67/68.

2.1   Money and Markets After 1700

Immediately prior to 1700, government borrowing was haphazard; investment choice was limited because the legal structure of the company was
evolving and the London Stock Exchange was still 100 years away from
coming into existence. The chartered, mercantile joint stock companies,
beginning with the Muscovy Company of 1555, were the dominant
businesses.[4] Despite their fascinating history, a detailed analysis of joint
stock companies is beyond the scope of this work but three of them – the
East India Company, the South Sea Company and, in particular, the
Bank of England – will be discussed briefly because they were deeply
embedded within the financial system in the eighteenth and nineteenth
centuries. The Bank of England was the most important institution
because it improved the operation of money markets and it played a key
role at the heart of the government bond market, eventually achieving a
dominant position. The foundation of sound money in the eighteenth
century enabled cash and bond markets, principally in London, to develop
and improve more or less continuously during the nineteenth century.
Conversely, between 1700 and 1900, equity markets developed very
slowly: equity-related financing did not power the industrial revolution
in Britain. Between 1720 and 1825 new company formation was severely
restricted by the Bubble Act; while between 1825 and 1862, although the
legislative framework applicable to company creation was relaxed, the law
remained very fluid and iterative. The birth of the quoted limited liability
business corporation was a long slow process but the death of the joint
stock company was even slower. The next four sub-sections therefore will
consider the nature of the East India Company and similar entities; the
role of the Bank of England within financial markets; the ownership and
management structures of joint stock companies with particular reference
to the modern-day business corporation and the gradual evolution of
equity markets during the nineteenth century.

---

[4] 'Chartered' means the English Crown granted them a royal monopoly; 'mercantile' means they
had commercial trading operations; 'joint stock' means there was equity-funding, transferable
stock and ownership rights.

2.1.1 The East India Company and Others

Established in 1599 and granted its royal charter in 1600, the East India Company experimented with different financial models during the seventeenth century, occasionally with several models co-existing simultaneously.[5] In practice this meant that there were different methods of financing individual projects and distributing profits or dealing with specific losses: generalisations therefore about the business models of joint stock companies are not straightforward. This company became a commercial leviathan responsible for all trade east of Africa ('from the Cape of Good Hope to the Straits of Magellan', according to its charter) and it accounted for approximately 14% of all British imports between 1699 and 1774.[6] The privileges were more than just commercial for these joint stock companies: political and even military obligations were incumbent on them in their particular geographic areas of operation. By the late eighteenth century, the East India Company employed 100,000 soldiers within India, more than the British government's entire standing army.[7] It retained a monopoly of trade with India until 1813, China until 1834, and was only wound up in 1858 after the Indian Mutiny.[8] In the context of government finance specifically, the East India Company was important: sporadic large loans to government between 1669 and 1678 were superseded by a continuous credit relationship after the 1690s: £2 million was lent in 1698; £1.2 million in 1708.[9] Clearly, this type of funding to the state from business strengthened the relationships between the chartered joint stock companies and government. It was desirable for the British government that some joint stock companies were big, strong and powerful: the more successful the East India Company became, the better it could fulfil its quasi-judicial and military functions and the

---

[5] Ron Harris, *Industrializing English Law* (Cambridge University Press 2000) 25.

[6] Nick Robins, *The Corporation That Changed the World* (Pluto Press 2012) 29.

[7] GJ Bryant, *Asymmetric Warfare* (Journal of Economic History 68/2, 2004).

[8] The South Sea Company and the East India Company were both wound up in the 1850s. This coincided with legislation in Britain which effectively changed the characteristics of commercial and financial businesses ushering in the limited liability company as the main corporate structure.

[9] Ron Harris, *Industrializing English Law* (Cambridge University Press 2000) 57.

more money it could lend to the state. It was in the government's interest to have successful joint stock companies that could operate with wide remits beyond simple commerce and, very importantly, provide financial assistance too. The problem with monopoly rights was that ultimately this worked against the interest of the consumer by restricting competition. As Adam Smith explained in 1776,

> Since the establishment of the East India Company . . . the other inhabitants of England, over and above being excluded from the trade . . . must have paid [more] in the price, of East India goods . . . not only for the extraordinary profits which the company may have made . . . but for all the extraordinary waste, which the fraud and abuse . . . must necessarily have occasioned.[10]

The South Sea Company was founded in 1711. Whereas the Bank of England and the East India Company developed over centuries, the South Sea Company had a very different trajectory: within a decade it was essentially just an administrative shell having suffered a spectacular share price boom and then bust. Initially, it was expected to make money from its trading monopoly with South America but, in its first years, it was severely hampered by continuing hostilities between Britain and Spain.[11] Its first ship sailed only in 1717, and with slavery at the company's commercial heart, its main contract was to supply 4,800 slaves each year to Spanish colonies in South America.[12] From the outset, perhaps not unnaturally, the South Sea Company was as much interested in financial engineering as it was in trade: in 1713, £9.2 million of heavily depreciated short-term British government debt had been converted into long-term South Sea stock.[13] This was a debt for equity swap: government bonds were converted into stock of the South Sea Company, which

---

[10] Adam Smith, *An Inquiry into the Nature and Causes of the Wealth of Nations* (Wordsworth 2012) 628.

[11] In the War of the Spanish Succession which lasted from 1701 to 1714 England, Holland and Austria waged war against France and Spain with much of the conflict in and around the Iberian Peninsula.

[12] PGM Dickson, *The Financial Revolution in England* (Macmillan 1993) 48.

[13] John Giuseppi, *The Bank of England* (Evans 1966) 42.

in turn raised equity from the public giving it the funds to execute the transaction. Ironically, much of this debt had been produced by the War of the Spanish Succession: a war that stopped the company from pursuing its *raison d'être* of trading with the Spanish colonies in South America. At this juncture the South Sea Company had two revenue streams. The first, and most lucrative, was the interest paid by the government to the South Sea Company on its bond portfolio; the second was attributable to the trade monopoly it had been granted. In 1720, it tried to acquire the remaining government debt, about £31 million, not owned by the Bank of England and the East India Company. Here the company was in direct competition with the Bank of England, and although it had agreed to pay the Government £7.5 million to acquire the debt, when the stock price of the South Sea Company collapsed from £1000 to £100, the deal unravelled.[14] During 1720, one of the most famous victims, Sir Isaac Newton, allegedly bemoaned, 'I can calculate the movement of the stars but not the madness of men.' After 1732 the South Sea Company became an administrative entity: its commercial activities, slavery and Arctic whaling ceased and it simply managed the bond assets that it owned.[15] The story of the South Sea Bubble itself is not relevant to this narrative but the contrast between this company and the East India Company is instructive. The former was created at the wrong time and never achieved commercial credibility showing that a monopolistic charter had its limitations. Significantly, many other joint stock companies had failed during the first 20 years of the eighteenth century with numbers dropping from about 150 in 1695 to around 12 in 1717 meaning that the South Sea Company may have been the most spectacular joint stock story of that era but its demise was not an isolated incidence.[16] Indeed Lewis, the legal historian, argues that the joint stock company construct was failing and that the Bubble Act of 1720 simply

---

[14] Ron Harris, *Industrializing English Law* (Cambridge University Press 2000) 63.

[15] Bryan Taylor, *Complete Histories, The South Seas Company, The Forgotten ETF* (www.globalfinancialdata.com, website accessed on 14 May 2016). Taylor describes the South Sea Company after 1732 as the first Exchange Traded Fund because its dividends and profits were entirely based on the income from its government bond portfolio.

[16] Ron Harris, *Industrializing English Law* (Cambridge University Press 2000) 57.

postponed its demise. Despite the bursting of the bubble, the South Sea Company continued as a business until 1855. During the eighteenth century, it was the third-most actively traded stock in London after the Bank of England and the East India Company, with its share price typically moving inversely relative to bond yields and in a price range between £50 and £100.[17]

2.1.2 The Bank of England and Government Borrowing

In the 1690s, methods of raising debt finance began to change in significant ways. English kings had always needed money for military adventures, generally fighting the French. The Crown had borrowed, usually via short-term loans, from various entities such as the Corporation of London, merchants, private banks and the goldsmiths, or had simply levied taxes, sold land or organised state lotteries. Generally, the King and Parliament muddled along though King Charles II tarnished the credit-worthiness of the Crown after 1672 by his moratorium on debt repayments.[18] In the 1690s, ideas for long-term borrowing, guaranteed by parliament, emerged and one of these was rolled out in 1694: a lottery raised £1 million in 1694 at an estimated interest rate of 14%, and with a 16-year life, it would operate until 1710.[19] Another scheme for long-term borrowing, also established in 1694, involved a Bank of England. The Bank, corporately and legally, was very similar to the East India Company. Both possessed specific monopoly privileges subsequently enshrined as charters and both organisations were entwined with the public finances of the state. The Bank, a joint stock company, privately owned by its stockholders, was granted its charter in 1694. It raised equity from over 1,000 subscribers, including the King, and this was completed briskly between June and July 1694, and, the £1.2 million raised was then lent to the state at an interest

---

[17] Bryan Taylor, *Complete Histories, The South Seas Company, The Forgotten ETF* (www.globalfinancialdata.com, website accessed on 14 May 2016).
[18] PGM Dickson, *The Financial Revolution in England* (Macmillan 1993) 44.
[19] PGM Dickson, *The Financial Revolution in England* (Macmillan 1993) 48.

rate of 8% over 12 years.[20] The transaction can be summarised as follows: money was raised from individuals who received stock in the Bank of England, with the proceeds then loaned to the government who, in turn, paid back the loan to the Bank at 8% per annum based on revenue raised from taxes. Monopoly rights subsequently followed in 1697 when the Bank's charter was extended for another 13 years. This debt was secured by new customs and excise revenues on shipping and alcohol, specifically on 'Beer, Ale and other Liquors' raised by the government and paid to the Bank.[21] This loan to the government from the Bank of England in 1694 was effectively the start of structured borrowing by the UK state and so was an important event in British finance.[22] At the time, it would not, however, have felt like a pivotal moment in finance given it was born out of expediency, by a desperate King William willing to pay handsomely for the privilege. An interest rate of 8% may have been a necessary price to pay to fight that particular war at that time against France, but it represented an unsustainable cost of borrowing on any long-term perspective. Inflation was essentially non-existent until the latter part of the eighteenth century, when the Napoleonic Wars pushed up prices.[23] In addition to lending the government money, the Bank of England also had the ability to issue Bills – 'Running Cash Notes'. These were transferable because they were in bearer form, so an important credit facility was also created at this juncture. Although created in 1694, it would be another 40 years before the Bank of England moved to permanent, purpose-built premises in Threadneedle Street in 1734, at which point it had put down firm

---

[20] The English monarch regularly invested in Joint Stock Companies. This was partly to make a profit, hopefully, but recognition also that these organisations had a foreign policy role that was much broader than commerce. Their activities encompassed building and maintaining forts, supporting foreign embassies and paying for Royal Navy protection, for example.

[21] J. Lawrence Broz & Richard. Grossman, *Paying for the privilege: the political economy of the Bank of England charters, 1694–1844* (Explorations in Economic History 41/1, 2002).

[22] John Giuseppi, *The Bank of England* (Evans 1966) 11.

[23] Helen Macfarlane & Paul Mortimer-Lee, *Inflation Over 300 years* (Bank of England Quarterly Bulletin, May 1994). Note that foodstuff accounted for most of the inflationary basket of goods in the seventeenth and eighteenth centuries so in turn these items could have been sensitive to particular shortages or a failure of the grain harvest for example thus creating sporadic inflation.

foundations in more ways than one. By this date, the Bank had also taken over the administration of shorter-term state debt from the Exchequer, a government department, by playing the central role subscribing, circulating and holding these bills and bonds.[24]

With borrowing and money markets on a sounder footing, the government bond market could also develop. By 1730, government and related debt was starting to be graded, in a rudimentary fashion, based on negotiability and risk of capital loss.[25] Exchequer Bills, for example, were treated as 'loans on call', meaning they were short-term paper instruments yielding about 1% less than the main body of government debt showing that the pricing of debt was becoming more sophisticated. In the middle of the eighteenth century, the British government consolidated all redeemable government debt into a single bond. In 1752, it created a perpetual bond, the Consol, initially paying 3.5% but then reduced to 3% in 1757, materially lower than the 14% interest rate paid in the 1690s. Henry Pelham, the British prime minister, pushed through this major change, in the face of concerted opposition from the joint stock companies because it weakened their financial influence and ties with government.[26] The Consol was the first, single, highly marketable bond and henceforward, the British government would be able to utilise structured borrowing raised directly from institutions – over the 50 years from 1752, the government issued £315 million of Consols. In conjunction with this increased issuance, liquidity also improved with arrangements to buy bonds back in the open market via a sinking fund. With the increasing professionalism and dominance of the Bank of England, the government bond market was firmly established by the second half of the eighteenth century. British governments now had the means to raise long-term finance, while investors could purchase what was to become accepted as a risk-free asset. Apart from enabling Britain to finance and fight several major wars – the Seven Years War, the American War of Independence and the

---

[24] Ron Harris, *Industrializing English Law* (Cambridge University Press 2000) 56.

[25] AH John, *Insurance Investment and the London Money Market of the Eighteenth Century* (Economica Vol 20, May 1953).

[26] Perry Gauci, *Emporium of the World: The Merchants of London 1660–1800* (Hambledon Continuum 2007) 158.

Napoleonic Wars - Consols provided a natural home for insurance company assets. By 1754 and for the following 100 years, the Royal Exchange Assurance and other insurance companies held most of their investments in UK government bonds. While East India Bonds had been one of the principal forms of collateral for the merchant community for most of the eighteenth century, they diminished in importance after 1780, supplanted by the Consol, now accepted by the market as an improved form of security.[27] As an indication, by 1800, nine major insurance companies had more than 80% of their assets invested in government bonds, or 'Public Funds' as they were called at the time.[28] Debt markets became firmly established in eighteenth-century Britain and provided an increasingly reliable conduit for government borrowing and offered a secure home for savings. This latter development was very useful for insurance companies, who became large and loyal investors in the government bond market, but only as long as yields remained attractive.

2.1.3 Ownership and Management by Stockholders

Joint stock companies provided investment opportunities for investors in two areas: stocks (shares) and bonds. Theoretically, stocks had unlimited liability but the nature of the potential risks varied by institution. The Bank of England, for example, had monopoly banking rights and was quasi-governmental in that Parliament would stand behind it, probably just by raising more taxes. The likelihood of the Bank defaulting therefore was relatively small. By comparison, The Company of Royal Adventurers Trading in Africa, founded in 1660, was a much riskier investment proposition. Basically established to transport slaves from Africa to the West Indies it was also obliged, under the terms of its charter, to maintain a series of forts along the West African coast. It was prone to making losses, particularly when England's wars disrupted its

---

[27] AH John, Insurance *Investment and the London Money Market of the Eighteenth Century* (Economica Vol 20, May 1953).

[28] Clive Trebilcock, *Phoenix Assurance and the Development of British Insurance: Vol 1, 1782–1870* (Cambridge University Press 1985) 620.

trading routes, and it had frequent revisions to its charter. The joint stock companies also differed from one another in their treatment of profits, capital and losses. Profits could be fully or partially distributed; capital deployed could be permanent or fluctuating; and losses could be covered by existing shareholders, or raised from external shareholders or by loans instead of equity. Finally, the nature of unlimited liability varied. In 1720, when the Royal African Company raised new capital, it was called an 'engraftment', primarily to cover debts and it took the form of issuing new shares to new shareholders.[29] This, therefore, was one example where liability was transferred, or at least, diluted. In a historical context, the early joint stock companies were closer to partnerships than today's corporations, as the following description makes clear: 'Shareholders became partners in a company and by signing the partnership deed, or taking over shares by transfer deed from those who had been parties to the partnership deed, they became subject to the obligations of the partnership and were liable to calls made by directors on the shareholders.'[30] Stockholder liability within the joint stock companies remains a complex area and, while unlimited liability existed in theory, it may have been difficult to enforce in practice, not least because at that time there was no body of company law. The risks, rights and obligations of owning equity or stock in these entities varied enormously from company to company.

In broad terms, stockholders in joint stock companies enjoyed, along with their unlimited liability, the right to share profits, not just dividends, and the opportunity to be an owner-manager. Only larger shareholders could vote for directors; and a shareholder could only become a director, if that individual had a very large shareholding; even larger ownership was required to be eligible for the position of Governor. At the Bank of England, for example, a personal shareholding of £4,000 was required to be eligible for the top job, the Governorship.[31] These

---

[29] Gary Shea, *(Re)financing the Slave Trade with the Royal African Company in the Boom Markets of 1720* (Centre for Dynamic Macroeconomic Analysis, 11/14, October 2011).

[30] Harold Raynes, *A History of British Insurance* (Pitman 1948) 339.

[31] Ann Carlos, et al, *Share Portfolios and Risk Management in the Early Years of Financial Capitalism* (Center for Economic Institutions, September 2012). The voting hurdles at the East India Company were similar to the Bank of England: a minimum shareholding of £500 was required

businesses were a curious mixture of owner-managed, profit-sharing, quasi-partnerships utilising equity capital. The fundamental difference with the traditional partnership structure was that interest was transferable in a joint stock company whereas in a partnership it was not. Compared with today's limited liability companies, stockholders had more control and owned these businesses much more directly than ordinary shareholders in modern-day quoted limited liability companies.

2.1.4 Equity Markets and Ordinary Shares in the Nineteenth Century

In the context of the development of the business corporation, joint stock companies represented an interim step between the early forms of corporate organisation, namely partnerships or private, family-run business and today's limited liability companies. As noted, the Bubble Act of 1720 restricted new company formation by requiring larger companies of more than six partners or directors to be approved (chartered) by Parliament. Specifically, the Act constrained banking activity and protected the monopoly rights given to the Bank of England, which may have been unhelpful during the early stages of industrialisation by restricting the flow of risk capital. After 1720 the equity market stagnated, or at least failed to develop materially for 100 years. Gradually, during the nineteenth century, legislative changes made company formation more straightforward and limited liability emerged as the preferred legal form of the business corporation. The Bubble Act was repealed in 1825; limitation on the formation of joint stock companies was relaxed in 1834 by dispensing with the need for a parliamentary Charter; company incorporation by registration rather than statute was introduced in 1844; limited liability status had been introduced in 1855 and was extended to banks and insurance companies by 1862 at which point the legislation was consolidated and simplified, meaning that the Companies Act of 1862 was a particularly significant milestone. Despite these changes, ordinary shares did not immediately become a meaningful asset class for institutional investors,

---

to have a (one) vote and £2,000 to be considered eligible for a directorship; £4,000 to be a potential Governor. Also see Robin, *The Corporation That Changed the World* (Pluto Press 2012) 27.

though the perceived attractiveness of the limited liability structure increased sharply when the failure of the City of Glasgow Bank in 1878 bankrupted many of its shareholders. Still, in 1883, the nominal value of industrial ordinary shares on the London Exchange represented less than 1% of its turnover: 93% of business was in British, overseas government and railway bonds.[32] This began to change, but only slowly, during the last two decades of the century. Ordinary shares in Guinness became available in 1886. This was a seminal event because it marked the beginning of large, commercial enterprises issuing long-term equity but as late as 1900, by value the ordinary shares of railway companies still dominated trading on the London Stock Exchange, so the equity market remained narrow and insurance companies did not seriously consider investment in them. By 1900, holdings of ordinary shares by insurance companies were insignificant, amounting to less than 3% of their entire investments. Investing in ordinary shares was to be a twentieth-century phenomenon not a nineteenth.[33]

2.2   Insurance Companies and Their Investments

2.2.1 The Growth of Insurance Companies

Having discussed borrowing and changing nature of financial markets, the remainder of this chapter will consider the development of insurance companies and their investment activities up to the end of the nineteenth century. Later in the book, Chapter 5 highlights the investment activities of insurance companies after 1900, and particularly from 1918, when they began to make significant changes to their investment approach, influenced by Keynes, Raynes and external factors.

---

[32] Francois Crouzet, *The Victorian Economy* (Routledge 2005) 329.

[33] Mae Baker and Michael Collins, *The Asset Composition of British Life Insurance Firms, 1900–1965* (Financial History Review 10, 2003). Baker and Collins calculated that 3% was invested in ordinary shares in 1913 but do not give a comparable figure for holdings of ordinary shares in 1900 given data was not sub-divided in this manner.

After the Great Fire of London in 1666, fire insurance became widely available and the early fire insurance companies even employed their own firemen, quite rationally, to try and extinguish fires as quickly as possible before they spread. The Fire Office was the first fire insurance company (established sometime between 1667 and 1680) and was followed by a number of others: The Friendly Society (1684), The Hand-in-Hand (1696), The Sun (1710), The Union (1715) and The Westminster (1717). These non-life insurance companies would charge annual premiums and potentially build up reserves over time, dependent on the nature of the claims. Given the nature of their short-term risks, liquidity was very important within their investment portfolios, so they had limited scope for long-term investing. Life offices providing life assurance had extended liabilities linked to mortality, so they could approach investment much more as a longer-term opportunity than their non-life counterparts. The first company offering life assurance with longer-term investable assets was The Worshipful Company of Mercers (the 'Mercers' Company', a livery company), its annuity scheme was established in 1699.[34] The Mercers' Company, one of the 12 original livery companies of the City of London, was crippled by debts at the end of the 1690s and hoped to make some fast profits and improve its cash flow by offering annuities to the widows of clergymen. Essentially this entailed swapping short-term debt into long-term obligations linked to life contracts. But by 1750, the scheme had failed owing to a mixture of financial inadequacy and a poor understanding of life expectancy, described as follows:

In the short-term the money raised did provide the funds necessary to deal with some of the Company's most pressing debts, though it left it in debt (a shortfall or deficit) to the annuity fund. Unfortunately, no one had properly calculated the potential pay-outs or considered that many of the wives of clergymen were much younger than their husbands so would be collecting payments for many years. The fund was paying out more than it was taking in.[35]

---

[34] *The Mercers' Company* (www.mercers.co.uk/700-years-history, website accessed on 24 August 2016).

[35] *The Mercers' Company* (www.mercers.co.uk/700-years-history, website accessed on 24 August 2016).

By 1725 the annuity scheme was failing; in 1745 it had debts of over £110,000 whereas the income of the livery company was only in the region of £7,000 per annum; Parliament was petitioned and in 1748 a special act of Parliament was passed to help with the relief of the plaintiffs; finally, the debts were cleared but only by 1803.[36] The Mercers' had shown a distinct lack of prudence, financial acumen and no understanding of linking assets to liabilities so this was an inauspicious beginning for the nascent life assurance sector. In 1706 on the other hand, The Amicable owned by its 2000 policyholders, had a slightly better appreciation of the underlying principles of life assurance and was 'the first insurance company to offer long-term life cover, building up funds to meet claims in later years'.[37] The much larger Royal Exchange Assurance and the London Assurance were founded in 1720, initially as marine insurers under the Bubble Act. As chartered joint stock companies, the two businesses were granted privileged marine insurance rights on condition of paying £300,000 each into the government's finances. Robert Walpole, generally regarded as the first British Prime Minister, concocted the scheme to extract £600,000 from the two insurance companies in order to pay off the debts of the King, which had been accumulated on the Civil List.

The parliamentary charters of 1720 granted to the Royal Exchange Assurance and the London Assurance followed in the well-trodden footsteps of the chartered mercantile companies and the Bank of England. In addition to marine insurance, where they were granted a duopoly, the Royal Exchange and the London Assurance could also offer life assurance but in competition with other providers. Despite the mistakes of the Mercers', lessons had not been learned and life assurance remained unsophisticated. For example, the Royal Exchange Assurance initially charged equal premiums irrespective of age and only imposed an upper age limit of 60 for any new life assurance policy in 1752.[38] In some respects, given the failure at the Mercers' and the evident incompetence of the Royal Exchange Assurance, it is surprising that life assurance in Britain survived as long as it did until the Equitable Life

---

[36] *The Mercers' Company* (www.mercers.co.uk/700-years-history, website accessed on 24 August 2016).

[37] Chris Lewin, *Pensions & Insurance before 1800* (Tuckwell Press 2004) 321.

[38] *Practical History of Financial Markets, History of Institutional Investment* (Pearson 2004) 5.38.

2 Markets and Insurance Company Investments, 1700–1900   29

Assurance Society put it onto a much more solid and scientific footing. Established in 1762, the Equitable was the first insurance company to offer life assurance in a form recognisable today, based on age-related premiums, mortality tables and with the amount payable on death from the life policy guaranteed. The Equitable was also the first life assurance company to identify the position of Actuary when William Morgan, regarded as the father of the profession, was appointed to the post in 1775. He 'had exceptional qualifications for the post of Actuary because he was an able mathematician with medical qualifications and an interest in experimental science'.[39] Following in the footsteps of the Equitable, the Royal Exchange Assurance finally moved onto a proper mathematical basis for pricing life policies and introduced premiums suitably graduated for age and period of assurance in 1783.[40] By 1800, with the entry of The Westminster in 1792 and the Pelican Life Office in 1797 there were six entities that provided life assurance and from this point onwards, life assurance companies and their assets grew very rapidly, as did surplus funds for investment.

After 1815, growth was taking place in many parts of the country so this was not just about the history of the metropolis: Scottish Widows was founded in 1815 and Standard Life in 1825, both based in Edinburgh. Scottish Widows was established to provide a 'General Fund for securing provision to widows, sisters and other females', it expanded rapidly opening agencies in Glasgow in 1819, Perth in 1823 and within 50 years, its assets exceeded those of the Royal Exchange Assurance, and it had become the largest mutual life office by the turn of the twentieth century. It is argued by Pearson that expansion of insurance companies in the provincial areas of Britain was important because they were often closely linked with local businessmen and politicians which, in turn, facilitated de-centralised investment in local projects rather than just London-centric activity.[41] By 1850 almost 200 life offices existed and most of these had been established during the first half of the nineteenth century. The sharp growth in the assets of life

---

[39] Maurice Ogborn, *The Professional Name of Actuary* (Journal of the Institute of Actuaries 82, 1956).

[40] Maurice Ogborn, *The Professional Name of Actuary* (Journal of the Institute of Actuaries 82, 1956).

[41] Robin Pearson, *Insuring the Industrial Revolution* (Ashgate 2004) 341/2.

assurance companies – from £28 million in 1837 to almost £300 million by 1900 – in conjunction with the increasing sophistication of life offices, created the opportunity to have more expansive investment policies.[42] Insurance companies themselves were beginning to specialise and diversify – the Royal Exchange Assurance created a 'with-profits' life policy in 1841, which placed a greater emphasis on future returns for policyholders than on security and liquidity.[43] In 1853, Standard Life was 'confident that it could reserve over half its annual £200,000 in premium income for long-term investment' though its investment strategy remained conservative and as late as 1869, Standard Life held 69% in mortgages; Gordonstoun House, now Gordonstoun School, being one of the mortgages granted in 1869 to Gordon Cumming for £110,762 to cover the gambling debts of the owner's grandfather from the 1830s![44] Occasionally commercial loans were made (£25,000 to the Aberdeen Railway Company in 1846) and there were sporadic property acquisitions (the estate of Lundin and Aithernie near Leven in Fife was purchased for £90,000 in 1852) but these were exceptions.[45] The broad picture, highlighted by Standard Life's lending both to railways and poor aristocrats, was that in parallel with the increasing funds accumulated by life offices came the demand for capital from a rapidly growing industrial economy and the continuing need for credit from an impoverished landed gentry. Life assurance, specifically, started earlier in Britain than in other European countries and it developed much more quickly. France, for example, only granted full statutory recognition to life assurance in 1850 and had declared the activity as morally repugnant in 1793 owing to its role in undermining societal values built around the family.[46] Compared to other European countries therefore, and particularly countries of a similar size such as the German and Italian states, insurance developed earlier and more rapidly in Britain which in turn provided Britain with a head start in the

---

[42] Barry Supple, *The Royal Exchange Assurance: A History of British Insurance 1720–1970* (Cambridge University Press 1970) 5, 309.

[43] Barry Supple, *The Royal Exchange Assurance: A History of British Insurance 1720–1970* (Cambridge University Press 1970) 314.

[44] Michael Moss, *Standard Life, 1825–2000* (Mainstream 2000) 79, 106.

[45] Michael Moss, *Standard Life, 1825–2000* (Mainstream 2000) 73,77.

[46] Geoffrey Clark, *Betting on Lives* (Manchester University Press 1999) 10.

field of institutional investment. From the early/mid-eighteenth century onwards, insurance was an established activity in Britain with these institutions collecting premiums and investing the proceeds. For more than 200 years from 1720, these general insurance companies and life offices dominated the investment landscape in the UK owing to the size of their assets.

2.2.2 The Dawn of Institutional Investment: A Portfolio from 1734

Owing to excellent historical data about the Royal Exchange Assurance, we can obtain useful insights into both the longer-term investment policy of one insurance company and also the changing nature of securities markets.[47] The investment portfolio of the Royal Exchange Assurance was worth a sizeable £351,759 in 1734 (the equivalent of £50.7 million inflation adjusted to 2015). The initial asset distribution is summarised in Table 2.1 and the information is of more than just financial interest because it provides a social commentary on the period. Since the number of merchants active in and around the City at this time was probably in the region of only about 1,000 individuals, this band of influential merchant-financiers was a tightly knit group.[48] In the small world of eighteenth-century business, the directors of the Royal Exchange Assurance had strong relationships with other leading commercial organisations of the time: 'Twelve [individuals] were at some time directors of the Bank of England, six of the East India Company, and six of the South Sea Company. Most of the Royal Exchange Assurance's directors were merchants.'[49] The merchant community represented a close network of interlocking interests held together by family ties, passed down through

---

[47] Barry Supple, *The Royal Exchange Assurance* (Cambridge University Press 1970).

[48] Perry Gauci, *Emporium of the World: The Merchants of London 1660–1800* (Hambledon Continuum 2007) 3. Gauci refers to a cohort of merchants numbering 850 in 1690 rising to 1,250 in 1763. Various sources estimate London's population to be about 650,000 in the first half of the seventeenth century. So, London was populous but the business and merchant community was very small.

[49] David Kynaston, *The City of London, Volume 1: A World on Its Own, 1815 to 1890* (Pimlico 1995) 12.

Table 2.1 Royal Exchange Assurance portfolio 1734

	Allocation %
Property	
Mortgages	
Loans (private)	5.1
Loans (public)	19.5
UK gov't bonds	23.1
Other bonds[a]	29.3
Debentures	
Preference shares	
Ordinary shares[b]	23.0
Other	
Total	100
Value £	351,759

[a]Only East India Company bonds in 1734
[b]Joint stock equity holdings as follows:
Royal Exchange Stock 17.9%
Bank of England Stock 4.3%
South Sea Co. Stock 0.8%
Data in Table 2.1 is taken from Barry Supple, *The Royal Exchange Assurance* (Cambridge University Press 1970) 74

generations and the most influential City magnates were the increasingly wealthy merchant-financiers 'probably numbering only a few dozen at any one time'.[50] Given this relationship-based way of merchant life, it was natural for them to invest in each other's businesses, which is exactly what the Royal Exchange Assurance did. The portfolio shown below is intrinsically interesting given that it is almost 300 years old. However, an analysis of the underlying holdings shows that it is not particularly informative about securities markets because it merely highlights that the Royal Exchange had very little choice in 1734. Table 2.2, on the other hand, shows how investment opportunities changed over time and were much broader after the middle of the nineteenth century.

The investment holdings in Table 2.1 can be described and understood as follows:

---

[50] Perry Gauci, *Emporium of the World: The Merchants of London 1660–1800* (Hambledon Continuum 2007) 154.

Table 2.2 Royal Exchange Assurance asset allocation 1734–1900

	1734 allocation (%)	1754 allocation (%)	1854 allocation (%)	1871 allocation (%)	1900 allocation (%)
Property					5.5
Mortgages			36.2	29.1	22.9
Loans (private)	5.1	1.8	18.0	3.9	4.7
Loans (public)	19.5		21.4	23.8	10.8
UK gov't bonds	23.1	57.4	22.7	21.4	4.6
Other bonds[a]	29.3			3.1	14.0
Debentures				16.1	21.7
Preference shares[b]					10.9
Ordinary shares[c]	23.0	31.4		1.7	
Other		9.3	1.7	0.8	4.9
Total	100	100	100	100	100
Value £	351,759	621,791	2,457,000	3,342,000	4,327,000

[a] Only East India Company bonds in 1734; overseas government bonds in 1871 and 1900

[b] In 1900, a small allocation to ordinary shares would have been included within this category

[c] Joint stock equity holdings in 1734 (see Table 2.1) and 1754 as follows: 10.1% Royal Exchange; 21.3% South Sea Co

The data in Table 2.2 is sourced from Supple, *The Royal Exchange* (Cambridge University Press 1970) 74, 315 and 333

Other Bonds: These were *East India Company Bonds* and traded at very similar interest rates to government paper. After 1715, East India bonds generally yielded between 3% and 5% and followed the path of government bond yields very closely not least because the East India Company was owed such large sums by the British government so these two entities had many overlapping financial interests.[51] These bonds were redeemable

---

[51] AH John, *Insurance Investment and the London Money Market of the Eighteenth Century* (Economica Vol 20, May 1953).

fixed-coupon corporate bonds and were highly regarded because they could be used effectively as cash proxies. The bonds were transferable by endorsement so were widely used by the merchant community and this instrument, rather than bank finance, was the principal method of facilitating credit and loans between merchants. One account described East India Bonds as being sufficiently marketable that they could be turned into money at an hour's notice.[52] These bonds, issued by a successful trading company enjoying monopolistic privileges, were the equal of government bonds at the time and almost certainly more transparent than most forms of government debt. Shorter-term government debt was referred to generically as Exchequer Bills and came in many forms, but much of the borrowing was in the guise of Navy Bills – the Royal Navy was costly and it was much more willing to use credit than the British army.[53] These government bonds had their drawbacks: they often had no redemption date; payment of interest was uncertain; and while they were assignable, they were not divisible.[54] In their later form, Exchequer Bills had a 5-year life with interest payable every six months; Treasury Bills with a fixed life of 1 year with the interest taking the form a discount in the price of issue only came into existence in 1877. [55]

Loans (public): This is indicative of the close ties to government that existed between the chartered companies and the state, not least because the government had the power to withdraw a charter. It is unclear whether this particular loan was part of the original loan from 1720 of £300,000 (subsequently reduced to £150,000) when the Royal Exchange was established or a different loan. But, effectively as arms of government and dependent on parliament for their charters, the joint stock companies had little alternative but to provide credit to the government when called upon to do so.

---

[52] AH John, *Insurance Investment and the London Money Market of the Eighteenth Century* (Economica Vol 20, May 1953).

[53] PGM Dickson, *The Financial Revolution in England* (Macmillan 1993) 399.

[54] AH John, *Insurance Investment and the London Money Market of the Eighteenth Century* (Economica Vol 20, May 1953).

[55] Jeremy Wormell, *National Debt in Britain 1850–1930 Vol 1* (Routledge 1999) xxvii.

Ordinary shares: Royal Exchange Stock and *Bank of England Stock* would have been equity (joint stock so not ordinary shares) though in the case of the latter, it was perhaps more bond-like than equity because much of the Bank's revenue was secure and predictable. The tiny holding in *South Sea Stock* seems somewhat incongruous although, as mentioned earlier, the company remained a viable business and the stock was heavily traded in London, priced at a little under £100 throughout the 1730s.[56]

Loans (private): These were short-term loans of less than 12 months to individuals and operated almost like a bank overdraft.

UK Gov't bonds were (probably) short-term Exchequer Bills, simply notes of credit, because the government had no formal mechanism for raising longer-term debt on its own account at this date.

Overall, this was a simple portfolio, predominantly invested in debt securities with a small equity component, mainly its own stock. It had some basic diversification but not very much because government bond yields would have determined the price of the East India bonds and the interest payable on the loans. In practical terms, therefore, the fortunes of this portfolio would have been dependent on the whims of the government of the day, so in practice and despite the spread of investment holdings, the portfolio was a lot less diversified than it appears.

2.2.3 The Need for Capital and a Changing World of Investment

The changes to Britain's financial markets in the eighteenth century received a further spur after 1800 owing to the increasing need for capital investment associated with urbanisation, industrialisation and internationalisation. In parallel, asset allocation by insurance companies changed radically over time. Although they remained focused on solvency and liabilities, their portfolios, while conservatively managed, were

---

[56] Bryan Taylor, *Complete Histories, The South Seas Company, The Forgotten ETF* (www.globalfi nancialdata.com, website accessed on 14 May 2016).

organised to achieve an appropriate level of income. Extracting data from the Royal Exchange Assurance in Table 2.2, its investment portfolios went through the following phases: first, from the middle of the eighteenth century, government bonds became the dominant asset class for almost a century; these were superseded by mortgages of various types, including loans to public bodies, around the middle of the nineteenth century; finally, by the end of the nineteenth century, the aggregate asset allocation of life company portfolios, became better diversified with a broad range of complementary holdings, in areas such as debentures and foreign bonds. Requiring income, it is noteworthy that the Royal Exchange had largely sold out of British government bonds by 1900 having held 72% in the asset class in 1839. In 1900, it had only 4.6% invested in the asset class (the average life company held 2% at the same date) as yields fell from just over 5% in 1816 to a little over 2% in 1898.[57]

As mentioned earlier, since banking in England remained very small scale and fragmented until well into the nineteenth century, insurance companies filled a much-needed gap in the provision of credit, and subsequently capital. In England outside of London, country banks, constituted as partnerships or small family firms and largely organised by provincial businessmen, became widely established and numbered 119 by 1784.[58] The capital city relied on the Goldsmiths and private banks such as Coutts (founded in 1692), together with the monopolistic Bank of England which retained its privileged position as the only joint stock bank until 1826. Banking in Scotland was better organised than in England.[59] 'By 1825 the Scottish banking system, in all its parts, had achieved a level of maturity which was far ahead of what had been

---

[57] Sally Hills, Ryland Thomas & Nicholas Dimsdale, *The UK Recession in Context – What Do Three Centuries of Data Tell Us?* (Bank of England Quarterly Bulletin, Q4 2010).

[58] British Banking History Society, *A History of English Clearing Banks* (www.banking-history.co.uk, website accessed 15 May 2016).

[59] Scottish commercial banks – the Royal Bank, the Bank of Scotland and the British Linen Bank – could issue notes, lend, pay interest and they also had branch networks throughout the country. The Savings Bank movement then started in 1810 with the Reverend Dr. Henry Duncan which made banking available to savers with less than £10 to deposit; this movement blossomed, based on management by Trustees and a mutual ownership structure.

achieved in other parts of the United Kingdom' at which point Scotland began exporting its banking expertise to the rest of Britain.[60] In effect, during much of the eighteenth century, insurance companies operated as quasi-banks and offered unsecured, short-term (up to 12 months) personal loans, typically between £5,000 and £10,000, to a range of clients and their members. The London Assurance held £356,180 in loans (the majority of its assets) at the end of 1761; these loans would have been expensive to administer owing to the small unit sizes and not very productive given that the Usury Laws limited the amount of interest that could be earned.[61] Lending money as mortgages on the security of owned property and land to the landed gentry became more important as the eighteenth century progressed which meant that the provision of unsecured loans to individuals diminished.[62] As an example, the Equitable and the Sun showed sharp increases in their mortgage lending against landed property after 1750.[63] The Sun typically lent up to about 70% of the value of an estate and repayments were generally made over a 20-year period. It was very thorough with its procedures for establishing mortgage quality by inspecting the assets, checking rental flows, methods of collecting rents and requiring guarantors.[64] Most borrowing by mortgagees was needed for liquidity purposes though some was utilised to support development such as the £35,000 in 1769, which was lent to the Duke of Bridgewater to help build his eponymous canal.[65] The extensive role of insurance companies, in broadening and deepening money markets in the UK, was important given the limited role of

---

[60] Charles Munn, *Historical Context Within Banking, Henry Duncan and the Banks* (pdf. presentational material for the Henry Duncan Bicentenary Conference, June 2010) 18–21.

[61] AH John, *Insurance Investment and the London Money Market of the Eighteenth Century* (Economica Vol 20, May 1953).

[62] AH John, *Insurance Investment and the London Money Market of the Eighteenth Century* (Economica Vol 20, May 1953). John states that the London Assurance had loans of £356,000 in 1761 but that was the high point and by 1770 the amount of personal loans was virtually negligible.

[63] AH John, *Insurance Investment and the London Money Market of the Eighteenth Century* (Economica Vol 20, May 1953).

[64] Robin Pearson, *Insuring the Industrial Revolution* (Ashgate 2004) 333.

[65] Robin Pearson, *Insuring the Industrial Revolution* (Ashgate 2004) 333.

banks. Investment behaviour began to change in the nineteenth century for a variety of reasons: life assurance assets and new providers grew rapidly; investment theory received a helpful prod from the actuarial community; investment choice increased and government bond yields fell persistently throughout the century which prompted the search for different sources of investment income.

Urbanisation

From the beginning of the nineteenth century, there was direct investment by insurance companies into urban development and infrastructure in areas such as Regent Street (1814–1825) for retail and Belgravia (1835–1860) for residential building, provided by loans to large-scale building contractors.[66] Owing to the parlous state of government finances at the end of the Napoleonic Wars, private funding was essential so the Royal Exchange Assurance lent £300,000 at 5% to fund the development of Regent Street in 1816.[67] The buildings were to be let on 99-year leases and income would be recouped in the form of ground rent; the Royal Exchange Assurance, enterprisingly, also sold fire insurance to new residents as part of their lease obligations. Regent Street was one of the first planned developments in London and the scale of the development was unprecedented. John Nash, the architect responsible for much of Regency London (he also designed parts of Buckingham Palace), drew up the plans in 1811 under the auspices of a government department, the 'Office of Woods, Forests and Land Revenues', and such was the scale of the development that it needed approval by an Act of Parliament in 1813. Nash hoped to offer better facilities than currently existed further west in London. Basically he wanted Regent Street to be more attractive than Bond Street, so he called for 'the stream of London fashion [to] be diverted to a new street,

---

[66] Clive Trebilcock, *Phoenix Assurance and the Development of British Insurance: Vol 1, 1782–1870* (Cambridge University Press 1985) 738.
[67] Barry Supple, *The Royal Exchange Assurance: A History of British Insurance 1720–1970* (Cambridge University Press 1970) 313.

where the footpath will be 15 feet wide, instead of 7 feet, and the carriageway double that in Bond Street'.[68] The development was undertaken between 1814 and 1825 with individual buildings also designed by Charles Cockerell and Sir John Soane. The Equitable similarly lent about £300,000 for building improvements in The Strand in 1829, so many iconic parts of London were developed at this time with capital supplied by British insurance companies.[69]

During the eighteenth and earlier part of the nineteenth centuries, the typical mortgage was for agricultural land linked into freehold country estates but as the century progressed, mortgages became more varied, larger and more aligned with the needs of the Victorian economy and consequently urban mortgages became a larger component within portfolios.[70] This was partly driven by new legislation from government: the New Poor Law of 1834 placed obligations on local government to improve conditions, such as sanitation and housing, in the teeming cities. Insurance companies could therefore lend money to local government, sometimes with lending covenants underwritten by central government, which possessed attractive guarantees and income streams repayable over periods of 20–30 years. Unsurprisingly, owing to the security of an extended income stream, some life companies had very high exposure to this type of asset – in June 1857, London Life had 79% of its funds invested in mortgages and Eagle Life 72%, while two major Scottish life companies had similarly high percentage exposure to mortgages even 20 years later.[71] In addition to land, during the nineteenth century, mortgages also covered the following areas: loans to urban developers engaged in housing; loans to local authorities obliged to make physical improvements and loans to commercial and industrial

---

[68] Mathew Green, *Revolutionary Road* (*The Financial Times*, 2 October 2015).

[69] AH John, *Insurance Investment and the London Money Market of the Eighteenth Century* (Economica Vol 20, May 1953).

[70] Barry Supple, *The Royal Exchange Assurance: A History of British Insurance 1720–1970* (Cambridge University Press 1970) 317.

[71] George May, *The Investment of Life Assurance Funds* (Journal of the Institute of Actuaries 46/2, 1912).

firms.[72] By 1854 the Royal Exchange Assurance had lent £880,000 to builders and contractors, mainly in the west end of London, typically advancing between 50% and 66% of the cost. Such high advances were required because much housing was built in anticipation rather than built to order.[73] The direct demand for capital by local government from insurance companies was therefore high after the 1830s but this subsided in the latter part of the century, when local councils and municipal authorities began to make their own public issues of bonds, raising money from the wider market rather than through specific financial institutions. In turn this encouraged insurance companies to move away from providing capital directly to particular borrowers towards investing more broadly in quoted securities traded on the market.

Industrialisation

Mortgages and loans were also secured against urban development in towns and cities or income-streams associated with transport infrastructure, in areas where local authorities had responsibility for both provision and physical improvements.[74] Examples include the construction of the first docks at Newport, Monmouthshire, in 1841, financed by the Palladium Insurance Company.[75] In 1851, Liverpool Corporation borrowed £10,000 from Standard Life so it could build a new prison.[76] While some insurance companies allocated assets to the development of the country's railways they were selective with their investments, preferred debt to equity and avoided the excesses of the boom and bust after 1845. During the 1840s, the Royal Exchange Assurance invested about 10% of its portfolio in railways in a variety of

---

[72] Prior to the Life Assurance Act 1870, insurance companies did not need to distinguish between 'loans' and 'mortgages'.

[73] Robin Pearson, *Insuring the Industrial Revolution* (Ashgate 2004) 340.

[74] Clive Trebilcock, *Phoenix Assurance and the Development of British Insurance: Vol 1, 1782–1870* (Cambridge University Press 1985) 648.

[75] AH John, *Insurance Investment and the London Money Market of the Eighteenth Century* (Economica Vol 20, May 1953).

[76] Michael Moss, *Standard Life, 1825–2000* (Mainstream 2000) 78.

securities covering loans, mortgages, bonds and debentures but not equi-ties.[77] Its exposure to railway securities peaked in 1842, whereas in 1856, Rock Life had 14.3% invested in Railway debentures and Metropolitan Life had 24.7% in 'Railway and other Debentures'.[78] Other insurance companies however showed less enthusiasm for this sector: Standard Life dabbled with railways in only a minor way; whereas the ultra-conservative Equitable adopted a haughty stance because, 'railway debentures were then [in 1853] considered to be too speculative for respectable life offices'.[79] There is no evidence that insurance companies invested material amounts of money in the share boom and busts of 1825 and the 1840s, largely owing to their risk-aversion; rather the investors in these early, more speculative ventures funded by equity capital were mainly wealthy indivi-duals and to a lesser extent, entrepreneurial businessmen, not financial institutions and definitely not the insurance companies.[80]

Internationalisation

By 1800, certainly after 1815 and the Battle of Waterloo, Britain was firmly established as the dominant maritime power and it soon became the financial powerhouse of the world. Geopolitically, Spain was about to lose its empire in South America, Holland its hegemony in the Far East and France was embroiled in revolution and counter-revolution. London supplanted Amsterdam as the prin-cipal financial centre in the world, a position it would retain for the next 100 years. Britain, and particularly London, had a network of financial services that was established, reliable and relatively stable, so geopolitical dominance and global financial leadership came together

---

[77] Barry Supple, *The Royal Exchange Assurance: A History of British Insurance 1720–1970* (Cambridge University Press 1970) 327.

[78] George May, *The Investment of Life Assurance Funds* (Journal of the Institute of Actuaries 46/2, 1912).

[79] Maurice Ogborn, *Equitable Assurances, The story of life assurance in the experience of The Equitable Life Assurance Society 1762 to 1962* (Routledge 1962) 243.

[80] Graeme Acheson et al, *Who financed the expansion of the equity market? Shareholder clienteles in Victorian Britain* (QUCEH Working Paper 2015-07, October 2015).

at this juncture. The London Stock Exchange was established in 1801 and began operating as a self-regulating, central exchange with its own capital provided by members. It also moved into its own building having previously operated from more than one location, though primarily Jonathan's Coffee House.[81] Supported by a network of financial services firms, the Bank of England and a strong legal system, London established a position of prominence in issuing and controlling a range of financial instruments, which included overseas bonds, issued and also traded in London. For example, in 1863 the paid up value of securities quoted on the London Stock Exchange was £1,601 million, of which £373 million represented foreign bonds from overseas borrowers.[82] Later in the century, horizons expanded geographically with direct overseas investments; the new breed of investment companies launched in the latter part of the nineteenth century offered a new spectrum of international investment opportunities and between 1868 and 1874, 20 investment trusts were launched in England and Scotland.[83] Most of these investment companies specialised in overseas investments in asset classes such as: bonds, railways, overseas mortgages and international infrastructure: investment by life offices in foreign securities, mainly bonds and loans, increased from 2.7% in 1871 to 13.5% by 1900.[84] So, a broader opportunity set produced very significant changes in the structure of insurance company and life office portfolios during the nineteenth century. There was a complex interplay between the insurance companies growing their funds so having to search for investment opportunities, while at the same time securities markets were becoming deeper and wider as borrowing became more sophisticated.

---

[81] Harold Raynes, *Insurance Companies' Investments* (Pitman 1935) 127.

[82] Ranald Michie, *The London and New York Stock Exchanges* (Allen & Unwin 1987) 52.

[83] John Newlands, *Put Not Your Trust in Money* (Association of Investment Trust Companies 1997) 103.

[84] *Practical History of Financial Markets, History of Institutional Investment* (Pearson 2004) 5/48.

2.2.4 Actuaries and Investment

The development of the actuarial profession from around 1800 is an interesting example of how highly specialised financial skills advanced alongside the growth of insurance companies. One reasonably clear description of the role of the actuary is 'the ability to combine probability with financial techniques to produce long-term forecasts and cost estimates'.[85] Mostly numerate and learned individuals, actuaries expend much energy on estimating returns on asset classes and the relationship with future liabilities. Naturally therefore, it was only a matter of time before this expertise was applied to the investment portfolios of insurance companies. The Institute of Actuaries, the English arm of the actuarial profession, had been established in 1848; Scotland's Faculty of Actuaries followed in 1856, though the formative period of the actuarial profession dated from slightly earlier during the first quarter of the nineteenth century, 'in England, the name of actuary became customary for members' by 1827.[86] Up until the middle of the nineteenth century, the investment policies of insurance companies were built on personal contacts, the search for income and meeting liability obligations, with the occasional opportunistic investment described as 'empirical' by one commentator – a polite way of saying that investment policy was at the behest of the individual companies.[87] There was no conventional wisdom or theoretical basis about how a long-term investment portfolio should be structured and managed. In 1861, A.H. Bailey, a future president of the Institute of Actuaries 1878–1882, correctly identified there was a gap which he described in the following terms, 'the finances of Life Assurance Societies ought to be managed on some clear general principles, and not as is sometimes the case, left to depend on the passing impulses of the day, or on ideas derived from other and very

---

[85] Chris Lewin, *Pensions & Insurance before 1800* (Tuckwell Press 2004) 426.

[86] Maurice Ogborn, *The Professional Name of Actuary* (Journal of the Institute of Actuaries 82, 1956).

[87] AH John, *Insurance Investment and the London Money Market of the Eighteenth Century* (Economica Vol 20, May 1953).

different pursuits'.[88] Bailey was thinking about the financial future of life assurance and in his '*Principles on which the funds of life assurance societies should be invested*', he argued that the primary objective of the investment strategy of a life office was security of capital.[89] Addressing the Institute of Actuaries in 1862, Bailey enunciated five investment principles which, in condensed form, are

- security of capital was of paramount importance;
- the highest rate of interest should be sought, consistent with security;
- a small proportion of assets should be available to meet short-term liquidity needs;
- a proportion of assets could be invested in less liquid assets and
- all the capital should be employed to support the life assurance business.[90]

Although risk-averse and conservative, nevertheless Bailey had produced an extremely cogent investment framework that was useful and influential. His ideas held sway for many years until challenged by two things: first, the market dislocation of the First World War; and second, the arguments of Keynes and Raynes who extolled the benefits of ordinary shares (Chapter 5).[91] In translating his principles into practice, Bailey recommended mortgages as the most suitable investments, together with loans backed by collateral and bank deposits but he considered government bonds to be unsuitable owing to their fluctuations in market value. As of 1870 life offices, on average, had 48% of their assets invested in mortgages which represented the largest single asset class but, inevitably, individual life office experience varied

---

[88] AH Bailey, *Principles on Which the Funds of Life Assurance Societies Should Be Invested* (Assurance Magazine X, 1861).

[89] AH Bailey, *Principles on Which the Funds of Life Assurance Societies Should Be Invested* (Assurance Magazine X, 1861).

[90] The last principle is incongruous and is more business related, so not really an investment principle in the sense of framing investment beliefs. I think it means that profits from life assurance should be applied only to the life assurance business and not used to cross-subsidise other business activities associated with general insurance, for example.

[91] Bailey's investment ideas were treated with great reverence and deference by many of his actuarial colleagues and his principles were referred to as 'Bailey's canons'.

and the Royal Exchange Assurance for example had only 29% invested therein.[92] On the other hand, Standard Life was holding about 70% of its investments in mortgages at this date and, from 1870 to 1890, Scottish Widows had between 60% and 80%. Both began to diversify away from mortgages only in the final decade of the century.[93] Mortgages, of course, were not exempt from market forces and agricultural land prices plummeted in value by almost 50% in Britain in the latter part of the nineteenth century. This made mortgages on farm property, for example, less attractive and much riskier than Bailey might have expected in 1861.

Bailey's fourth principle was the most interesting from the perspective of expected rates of return and portfolio theory. Bailey said a 'proportion may be safely invested in securities that are not readily convertible; and it is desirable that it should be so invested, because such securities, being unsuited to private individuals and Trustees ... command a higher rate of interest in consequence'. He argued that institutional investors, in this instance life offices, could harvest an illiquidity premium because a proportion of investments should be invested longer term and need not be allocated to readily realisable holdings. With strong cash flow and improved actuarial forecasting techniques, Bailey proposed that life offices needed to rely less on immediate liquidity provided by, for example, British government bonds. This represented a major shift in thinking. In 1815, the Equitable had held 93% of its investment portfolio in Consols while the more adventurous Royal Exchange Assurance held 72% in government bonds as late as 1839.[94] While Bailey approached investment strategy from a theoretical perspective and disliked government bonds for their price fluctuations rather than their current yield, there was a looming practical problem with

---

[92] Barry Supple, *The Royal Exchange Assurance: A History of British Insurance 1720–1970* (Cambridge University Press 1970) 332/333.

[93] Dorian Mormont, *Performance and Analysis of the Oldest Mutual Fund, the Scottish Widows Fund from 1815 to 2000* (PhD, ULB Solvay Brussels School, 2012).

[94] W. Palin Elderton, *Investments a Hundred Years Ago* (Journal of the Institute of Actuaries Vol 51, April 1918) & Barry Supple, *The Royal Exchange Assurance: A History of British Insurance 1720–1970* (Cambridge University Press 1970) 315.

government bonds caused by the prolonged fall in bond yields during the nineteenth century. Bond yields had stood at 5.9% in 1798 but fell to 2.0% by 1896, effectively a 66% reduction in income.[95] Standard Life highlighted the problem in 1891 as follows, 'It being hardly possible, as in former times to obtain investments in which the principal was secure with a reasonable rate of interest, insurance companies... must be prepared to run risks of fluctuations in value.'[96] The actuary of the Royal Exchange Assurance in 1901 warned his Directors, 'the welfare of the Life Department may really be said to largely depend on the skill of the investing department in producing the highest return consistent with safety'.[97]

2.2.5   The Pelican Life Office: The First Asset Management Company?

In the annals of asset management, the Pelican Life Office, 1797–1908, deserves an honourable mention.[98] It was probably the first institution to be organised as an asset management company given that it was established in 1797 explicitly, to make money from its investing activities. In practice, this helpfully subsidised its poor claims record as a life assurer. In that respect, the Pelican was reverse-engineered because other British life offices had life assurance at their heart and regarded investing as a means to an end, so secondary to the core activity. At the Pelican, asset management expertise needed to compensate for weaknesses in life assurance because 'the suspicion that [the] Pelican was primarily an investment trust [company] with a subsidiary interest in life assurance is difficult to resist. Its vital signs do not indicate a business surviving in its declared area of commerce

---

[95] Sally Hills et al, *The UK Recession in Context – What Do Three Centuries of Data Tell Us?* (Bank of England, Quarterly Bulletin, Quarter 4 2010).

[96] *Practical History of Financial Markets, History of Institutional Investment* (Pearson 2004) 4/49.

[97] Barry Supple, *The Royal Exchange Assurance: A History of British Insurance 1720–1970* (Cambridge University Press 1970) 335.

[98] Clive Trebilcock, *Phoenix Assurance and the Development of British Insurance: Vol 1, 1782–1870* (Cambridge University Press 1985) 524. The legal structure of the Pelican was an 'extended partnership with unlimited liability'.

[life assurance]'.[99] It struggled continually with in its core business and it suffered two major deficits in 1825 and 1840 which threatened its solvency. According to one Board paper (a 'Private Minute') from 1840, the Pelican 'admits that Life Assurance had been imperfectly understood since the inception of the Office' which was a remarkable admission after 43 years providing life assurance policies to its customers![100] But despite this self-awareness of past failings, it did not get any better at writing life policies because the claims record was very high for decades to come 'after 1840, the office encountered an avalanche of mortality [claims], due, no doubt, to a combination of poor risk selection in its early years and indifferent actuarial practice' and even as late as 1870 the Pelican 'never achieved an adequate separation of the actuarial and administrative roles of the Secretary; the function of actuary was not given a sufficiently defined or authoritative position'.[101]

Clearly, this company was incompetent as a life office but was it any better at asset management? In this respect it had been established at a beneficial juncture because government bond yields peaked at 5.9% in the two years 1797 and 1798, and its founders had an opportunistic eye on making-money. The catalyst for establishing the Pelican as a discrete business, after 12 years of dithering by the Phoenix Board, was that 'the Public Funds [government bonds].... were at an unusually low price... and this afforded a favourable opportunity for the remunerative investment of the premiums'.[102] A similar account of the initial impetus behind the establishment of the Pelican by its founders runs as follows:

The desire of the Phoenix Board to take advantage of the exceptionally favourable opportunities for speculation in Government stock afforded by the war economy of the 1790s and 1800s. At this point calculations of investment advantage clearly bulked larger in their minds than any

---

[99] Clive Trebilcock, *Phoenix Assurance and the Development of British Insurance: Vol 1, 1782–1870, 1782 to 1870, Vol 1* (Cambridge University Press 1985) 752.

[100] George Hurren, *Phoenix Renascent* (Phoenix Assurance 1973) 39.

[101] Clive Trebilcock, *Phoenix Assurance and the Development of British Insurance: Vol 1, 1782–1870* (Cambridge University Press 1985) 747 & 607.

[102] George Hurren, *Phoenix Renascent* (Phoenix Assurance 1973) 32.

considerations for diversification into [life] insurance. . . . the emphasis on investment objectives as against [life] insurance objectives was with Pelican from the beginning and remained a feature of the company for many years.[103]

The backers of the Pelican in 1797 were a mixture of City types and not just insurance men from the Phoenix: 'There was a notable consensus between the Phoenix interest and the banking interest as to the purpose of the new venture. The Phoenix men saw it primarily as a means of augmenting their investment power without hazarding their fire funds. And the bankers were more than content to view the company primarily as an investment vehicle.'[104] The Pelican made its first investments into government debt in 1797 – this was perfect timing given that yields on 3% Consols had reached their high point and then, for much of the following century, it made a series of sensible investment decisions as it moved into different asset classes. In 1812, having created the Annuity Loan, it widened its own investment powers with a new Deed of Settlement.[105] The Annuity Loan was a method of circumventing the Usury Laws that limited interest payments to a maximum of 5%. Annuity Loans typically paid between 8% and 10% though one historian (Trebilcock) estimated the cost of the loan to one borrower was in the region of 16% per annum.[106] By 1820 these Annuity Loans comprised the majority of its investment activity, possibly approaching 80% of its assets but in due course there were superseded by mortgages, initially on agricultural and then subsequently mortgages, loans and debentures for urban development after the 1840s.[107] Specific mortgages were granted to the Gloucester Canal

---

[103] Clive Trebilcock, *Phoenix Assurance and the Development of British Insurance: Vol 1, 1782–1870* (Cambridge University Press 1985) 523.

[104] Clive Trebilcock, *Phoenix Assurance and the Development of British Insurance: Vol 1, 1782–1870* (Cambridge University Press 1985) 531.

[105] Clive Trebilcock, *Phoenix Assurance and the Development of British Insurance: Vol 1, 1782–1870* (Cambridge University Press 1985) 631.

[106] Clive Trebilcock, *Phoenix Assurance and the Development of British Insurance: Vol 1, 1782–1870* (Cambridge University Press 1985) 636/7.

[107] Clive Trebilcock, *Phoenix Assurance and the Development of British Insurance: Vol 1, 1782–1870* (Cambridge University Press 1985) 633–652.

(£60,000 in 1850) and the Birkenhead Dock Company (£30,000 undated).[108] Between 1848 and 1870, Pelican's extensive lending activities in the area of Victorian urbanisation reads as follows: 12 councils, 11 health boards, 10 boards of guardians and 5 local health boards.[109] In monetary terms, the Pelican's mortgage activity had peaked by 1856, a few years before Bailey had propounded his principles extolling the usefulness of mortgage investments. From the late 1850s, investment into higher yielding overseas bonds gathered pace, particularly during the 1870s, so that in 1879, out of the Pelican's 28 investment holdings, 18 of these were overseas.[110] By 1900, the Pelican had completely disinvested from British government bonds so even with this decision it went one small step further than most of the other life companies in the sector.

From its birth in 1797, the Pelican had an explicit interest in making investment decisions and this was given further expression in 1826, when it established a dedicated investment committee of five, called the 'Standing Committee of Accounts'. Henceforth, this committee would deal with all investment matters because the directors were worried that they were spending too much time discussing investment 'owing to the great increase in money transactions of this office' rather than life assurance at the board meetings, another indication about the real interests of this organisation.[111] In terms of investments, the Pelican moved relatively quickly into new areas of investment. It was much more successful than its sister company, the Phoenix, and it was more adventurous and innovative than say the Equitable, Scottish Widows and Standard Life. Rather disappointingly however, the Pelican was something of an exception among insurance companies because it does not appear that it inspired other life offices to develop their investment capabilities in a similar manner. In 1877, the Sun Life

[108] Phoenix Renascent, George Hurren (Phoenix Assurance 1973) 65.

[109] Clive Trebilcock, *Phoenix Assurance and the Development of British Insurance: Vol 1, 1782–1870* (Cambridge University Press 1985) 648.

[110] George Hurren, *Phoenix Renascent* (Phoenix Assurance 1973) 65.

[111] Clive Trebilcock, *Phoenix Assurance and the Development of British Insurance: Vol 1, 1782–1870* (Cambridge University Press 1985) 645.

Assurance Society created a 'Standing Committee' with powers to make decisions about the society's non-mortgage investments but there is little evidence that it made a great deal of progress and even by 1900, despite being granted the authority in 1889, the Sun had not made any direct investments into ordinary shares. In practice, most insurance companies relied on a Management Committee or the Board of Directors to set investment policy but this was just one of their many responsibilities and in practice, with its investment decision-making structure, the Pelican was unusual if not unique. Unlike Bailey who was influential, and had a cogent investment philosophy, the Pelican lacked any rational basis for its approach apart from opportunism. It may have been effective at making money but it was ineffective in explaining how it approached investment. This is analogous to the Rowntree pension fund in the twentieth century (Chapter 8) which was also good at investing but other pension funds only changed their investment behaviour when Ross Goobey articulated a coherent approach which they could understand and emulate. The Pelican example is interesting in that it highlighted that, while increasingly important, investment and asset management remained a subsidiary activity and not a primary one at most life insurance companies.

2.3   Summary

From the early eighteenth century onwards, insurance companies were the first institutional investors and their investment portfolios not only survived into the nineteenth century but grew and changed. They weathered various financial crises and several major conflicts – the Seven Years War, the American War of Independence, the Napoleonic Wars, the Crimean War and the US Civil War. There was a rapid expansion of British government debt after 1750 and subsequently falling bond yields for much of the nineteenth century. Their achievement in navigating through these very stormy waters and survived should not be underestimated. They were helped by, and in turn supported, a liquid and efficient government bond market from the second half of the eighteenth century. Meeting liabilities with assets by achieving an acceptable rate of interest underpinned their investment thinking but in time they began to diversify and the life offices in particular were prepared to invest in a broad range of asset classes as the nineteenth century progressed. Critically, the early insurance companies helped the development of money markets and securities markets in the UK owing to the breadth and size of their investments. They made very large shifts in asset allocation within their portfolios through significant moves away from British government bonds into mortgages in particular, but also into debentures, loans, property, overseas bonds and on a smaller scale into equities. These were conscious decisions to produce higher returns, particularly to achieve an appropriate level of income as government bond yields dropped.

From the mid-1700s, and after the Mercers' debacle, life offices proved that they were reliable as custodians and administrators of financial assets. Over time, these institutions became important participants in securities markets, supplying capital and exhibiting rudimentary skills in asset management – very important building blocks for a new area of financial services. In the 1860s, Bailey established a body of investment principles that were embraced by most life assurance companies. He showed that the actuarial profession was starting to think more about assets in addition to the liabilities even if investment policy was risk-averse and focused on security of capital with a preference for assets with stable values. Over almost 200 years, insurance companies operated as hybrid institutions supplying credit or capital directly where it was needed and investing surplus assets into securities markets. By 1900 they were doing more investing and providing less credit so in that respect, they looked less like banks and more like long-term investing institutions. The investment activities of the UK insurance companies were an important first step in the evolution of institutional asset management in Britain. The underlying principles of life assurance were that long-term risks could both be estimated and understood and that assets could be invested for the long-term to meet obligations. Consequently, life assurance demonstrated an optimistic belief in planning for the future and in the trustworthiness of financial markets; both essential pre-conditions for long-term investment decision-making. They proved that investment was viable in difficult market conditions and paved the way for the more imaginative investment policies of the first investment companies which blossomed after 1868.

Bibliography

Geoffrey Clark, *Betting on Lives* (Manchester University Press, 1999)
Francois Crouzet, *The Victorian Economy* (Routledge 2005)
PGM Dickson, *The Financial Revolution in England* (Macmillan 1993)
Perry Gauci, *Emporium of the World: The Merchants of London 1660–1800* (Hambledon Continuum 2007)
John Giuseppi, *The Bank of England* (Evans 1966)
Ron Harris, *Industrializing English Law* (Cambridge University Press 2000)
George Hurren, *Phoenix Renascent* (Phoenix Assurance 1973)
David Kynaston, *The City of London, Volume 1: A World on Its Own, 1815 to 1890* (Pimlico 1995)
Chris Lewin, *Pensions & Insurance Before 1800* (Tuckwell Press 2004)
Ranald Michie, *The London and New York Stock Exchanges* (Allen & Unwin 1987)
Michael Moss, *Standard Life, 1825–2000* (Mainstream 2000)
John Newlands, *Put Not Your Trust in Money* (Association of Investment Trust Companies 1997)
Maurice Ogborn, *Equitable Assurances, The Story of Life Assurance in the Experience of Equitable Life Assurance Society 1762 to 1962* (Routledge 1962)
Robin Pearson, *Insuring the Industrial Revolution* (Ashgate 2004)
Harold Raynes, *A History of British Insurance* (Pitman 1948)
Harold Raynes, *Insurance Companies' Investments* (Pitman 1935)
Nick Robins, *The Corporation That Changed the World* (Pluto Press 2012)
Adam Smith, *An Inquiry into the Nature and Causes of the Wealth of Nations*, ed. Tom Griffith (Wordsworth 2012)
Barry Supple, Introduction, in *The Historian and the Business of Insurance*, ed. Oliver Westall (Manchester University Press 1984)
Barry Supple, *The Royal Exchange Assurance: A History of British Insurance 1720–1970* (Cambridge University Press 1970)
Clive Trebilcock, *Phoenix Assurance and the Development of British Insurance: Vol 1, 1782–1870* (Cambridge University Press 1985)
Jeremy Wormell, *National Debt in Britain 1850–1930 Vol 1* (Routledge 1999)

Articles, Journals, Pamphlets, Websites etc.

Graeme Acheson, Gareth Campbell & John Turner, *Who Financed the Expansion of the Equity Market? Shareholder Clienteles in Victorian Britain* (QUCEH Working Paper, 2015-07 October 2015)

AH Bailey, *Principles on Which the Funds of Life Assurance Societies Should Be Invested* (Assurance Magazine X 1861)

Mae Baker and Michael Collins, *The Asset Composition of British Life Insurance Firms, 1900–1965* (Financial History Review 10, 2003)

British Banking History Society, *A History of English Clearing Banks* (www.banking-history.co.uk)

J. Lawrence Broz and Richard Grossman, *Paying for the Privilege: The Political Economy of the Bank of England Charters, 1694–1844* (Explorations in Economic History 41/1, 2002)

GJ Bryant, Asymmetric Warfare (*Journal of Economic History* 68/2, 2004)

Ann Carlos, Erin Fletcher and Larry Neal, *Share Portfolios and Risk Management in the Early Years of Financial Capitalism* (Center for Economic Institutions September 2012)

Mathew Green, *Revolutionary Road* (*The Financial Times*, 2 October 2015)

Sally Hills, Ryland Thomas and Nicholas Dimsdale, *The UK Recession in Context – What Do Three Centuries of Data Tell Us?* (Bank of England, Quarterly Bulletin, Quarter 4 2010)

AH John, Insurance Investment and the London Money Market of the Eighteenth Century (*Economica* Vol 20, May 1953)

Helen Macfarlane and Paul Mortimer-Lee, *Inflation Over 300 years* (Bank of England Quarterly Bulletin, May 1994)

George May, The Investment of Life Assurance Funds (*Journal of the Institute of Actuaries* 46/2, 1912)

The Mercers' Company (www.mercers.co.uk/700-years-history)

Dorian Mormont, *Performance and Analysis of the Oldest Mutual Fund, the Scottish Widows Fund from 1815 to 2000* (Phd, ULB Solvay Brussels School, 2012)

Charles Munn, *Historical Context Within Banking, Henry Duncan and the Banks* (pdf. presentational material for the Henry Duncan Bicentenary Conference, June 2010)

Maurice Ogborn, The Professional Name of Actuary (*Journal of the Institute of Actuaries* 82, 1956)

W. Palin Elderton, Investments a Hundred Years Ago (*Journal of the Institute of Actuaries* 51, April 1918)

Practical History of Financial Markets (Pearson 2004)

Gary Shea, *(Re) financing the Slave Trade with the Royal African Company in the Boom Markets of 1720* (Centre for Dynamic Macroeconomic Analysis 11/14, October 2011)

Bryan Taylor, *Complete Histories, The South Seas Company, The Forgotten ETF* (www.globalfinancialdata.com)

3

Philip Rose and the First Investment Company, 1868–1883

The Foreign and Colonial Government Trust ('Foreign & Colonial'), an investment company created on 19 March 1868, was instrumental in shaping today's asset management profession.[1] Foreign & Colonial, as a pure investment company (an investment trust or closed-end fund) with a stand-alone investment strategy, was different to the insurance companies that preceded it because their investment activity was secondary, essentially a by-product of their insurance business.[2] For life companies and their investments, as we have seen, the actuary Bailey advocated security of capital as his main investment principle whereas Foreign & Colonial was prepared to challenge this thinking in the search for higher returns unfettered by liability considerations. Foreign & Colonial offered savers an indicative

---

[1] The Foreign and Colonial Government Trust was an investment company. It was created in 1868 under trust law and only became incorporated as a company in 1879. At that date it had most of the recognisable features of an investment trust company. In US terminology this would be referred to as a 'closed-end fund'.

[2] The name Foreign and Colonial Government Trust applied from 1868 to 1891 at which point it changed to Foreign & Colonial Investment Trust when its powers of investment were widened. The name 'Foreign & Colonial' has been used throughout the remainder of the book.

© The Author(s) 2017
N.E. Morecroft, *The Origins of Asset Management*
from 1700 to 1960, Palgrave Studies in the History of Finance,
DOI 10.1007/978-3-319-51850-3_3

return of 7% based on a willingness to exploit risk, and accepting that security prices could be volatile: an investment approach with a different starting point from Bailey's. Foreign & Colonial not only provided investors with a yield more than double that on British government bonds, but it also aimed to achieve it over a very long period, 24 years, creating an investment channel that was quite different from the deposit channel offered by the banking sector. Before Foreign & Colonial, asset management simply did not exist as a discrete activity within financial services. After Foreign & Colonial, and in conjunction with other investment companies that had been established by 1890 (Chapter 4), asset management in Britain had firm foundations with an investment objective to produce a return significantly higher than the yield on government bonds or bank deposits by long-term investing and diversification. Foreign & Colonial borrowed, adapted and improved the original idea of the investment company invented by the Dutch 100 years earlier.[3] However, asset management withered and died in Holland in the early part of the nineteenth century whereas it survived and thrived in Britain, to the extent that Foreign & Colonial Investment Trust PLC still exists today. Foreign & Colonial had a number of interesting features but its main significance resided in the pooled fund structure which made investment available to a wide spectrum of society: it enabled multiple investors to invest relatively small sums into the pooled fund which, in turn, held a diversified portfolio within a tightly controlled governance arrangement. Consequently, middle-class and lower-middle-class individuals, not just the very wealthy, could access it, thus making investing available to the burgeoning middle classes of Victorian Britain. Foreign & Colonial's most important features were captured in the clear prose of its Prospectus:

The object of the Trust is to give the investor of moderate means the same advantages as the large Capitalists, in diminishing the risk of investing in Foreign and Colonial Government Stocks, by spreading the investment over a number of different Stocks, and reserving a portion of the interest as a Sinking Fund to pay off the original capital.[4]

---

[3] The Napoleonic Wars killed off the Dutch unit trusts.

[4] *Foreign and Colonial Government Trust, Prospectus March 1868* (Guildhall Library).

The basic investment ideas were accessibility, global investing, diversification and the accumulation of a cash reserve. In addition, the investment company was managed with high standards of governance and probity. Five prominent Trustees with distinguished professional backgrounds were appointed to administer it and further checks and balances were incorporated to provide comfort and security to investors. A strong investment idea was combined with a pooled fund structure underpinned by high levels of oversight. The respectability offered by Foreign & Colonial was a breath of fresh air in the context of many and varied financial scandals running from the South Sea Bubble crisis in 1720, dubious joint stock companies, speculative railway companies in early Victorian Britain and unstable banks. Market crashes and company failures were not uncommon: about 37% of 4859 companies formed in the UK between 1856 and 1865 failed owing to combinations of fraud and mismanagement.[5] The 1825 stock market crash in the UK had been the first modern-day financial crash when the banking system malfunctioned and it was subsequently reformed by legislation while in the 1840s there was a more traditional speculative boom-to-bust based on railway companies.

As recently as 1866, the collapse of the bank Overend, Gurney & Co., Ltd. sent tremors through financial markets. Not only did Overend, Gurney's failure create a more general run on banks but because the equity funding had been only partly paid by the new shareholders, they remained liable for further calls on their assets: £50 shares were £15 partly paid.[6] In this respect Overend, Gurney was not unusual because 'many of the finance companies created in the early 1860s had issued shares with low proportions of paid-in capital, with the intention of making calls on shareholders as the company expanded but also leaving a proportion uncalled as a buffer to protect their depositors'.[7] Shareholders could be required to stump up more capital either to support the growth of the

---

[5] Neil McKendrick and John Newlands *A History of Foreign & Colonial Investment Trust* (Chappin Kavanagh 1999) 26.

[6] Neil McKendrick and John Newlands *A History of Foreign & Colonial Investment Trust* (Chappin Kavanagh 1999) 26.

[7] John Turner, *Banking in Crisis* (Cambridge University Press 2014) 80.

bank or to act as a buffer to protect depositors.[8] Effectively this operated as an early form of depositor insurance but with the shareholders picking up the liability rather than government in the form of the taxpayer. As such, when the bank failed, the shareholders were required to invest more capital to cover the debts.[9] Overend, Gurney had become a 'limited liability' company on paper as recently as July 1865, when it raised fresh equity capital from unsuspecting new shareholders. In practice, the liability proved to be not very limited owing to the partly paid nature of the shares and their contingent nature. This bank failed owing to reckless lending after 1857 and inadequate capital but it was in trouble, apparently, well before the placing of new shares.[10]

> Overend, Gurney & Co ultimately failed because it had taken too many risks in the late 1850s . . . [it] made considerable advances to companies of questionable creditworthiness on the basis of dubious security. . . . it made advances to 13 borrowers totalling £3.5 million, which were worth only an estimated £711,500 by the time the partnership converted to a limited liability company.[11]

The failed Overend, Gurney took down six other UK banks, the largest of which was the Birmingham Banking Company,[12] This was a high-profile failure which led to a wider run on banks; bank rate rose to 10%; and sterling was very weak in the futures market.[13] The directors of Overend, Gurney were prosecuted at the Old Bailey and reprimanded for errors of judgement but escaped without being fined or imprisoned.

---

[8] John Turner, *Banking in Crisis* (Cambridge University Press 2014) 80.

[9] Neil McKendrick and John Newlands *A History of Foreign & Colonial Investment Trust* (Chappin Kavanagh, 1999) 26. The authors quote a figure of £25 rather than the full obligation of £35 as the additional payment required from shareholders.

[10] Ashraf Mahate, *Contagion Effects of Three Late Nineteenth Century British Banking Failures* (Business and Economic History 1994).

[11] John Turner, *Banking in Crisis* (Cambridge University Press 2014) 81.

[12] John Turner, *Banking in Crisis* (Cambridge University Press 2014) 81.

[13] Marc Flandreau & Stefano Ugolini, *The Crisis of 1866* (Graduate Institute of International and Development Studies, working paper 10, 2014).

Appearing immediately after this major banking collapse and, as a financial services business, Foreign & Colonial needed to demonstrate that it was, or would be, safer than the banks that had failed around that time: it needed to prove itself.

In 1868, savings opportunities were relatively limited out with land, corporate bonds, and UK and overseas government bonds. While insurance companies were well established in Britain, and life assurance had grown rapidly during the nineteenth century, they did not offer products with specific investment content. Therefore, Foreign & Colonial with a limited life restricted to 24 years and a 7% yield offered savers a very attractive, long-term investment opportunity different from anything else currently available. Philip Rose, lawyer and occasional financial adviser to Benjamin Disraeli, twice prime minister, was the key man behind the creation and development of this first investment vehicle. This is Rose's story more than anybody else's and he deserves to be acknowledged as the founding father of today's asset management profession. Rose both created Foreign & Colonial and steered it through its early years. Importantly, by the time of his death in 1883, Foreign & Colonial was in a strong position; sufficiently robust to continue functioning up to the present day. This chapter therefore focuses on the period between 1868 and 1883 covering the creation of the first investment company and up to Philip Rose's death. The following section considers the particular role and contribution of Philip Rose while the remainder of the chapter explains the investment proposition.

3.1   Philip Rose

Philip Rose was the guiding light behind Foreign & Colonial during its first years; he was one of the three key people who created the investment company along with James Thomson Mackenzie and Samuel Laing, his business partners. He was an inaugural Trustee, one of five, whereas neither Laing nor Mackenzie were Trustees; his legal firm, Baxter, Rose & Norton were legal advisers to it; his son William was its first secretary; and it was Philip who guided it through its first crises during in 1879. In the minutes of the AGM from 24 April 1883, a week after Rose's death, he was described as ' . . . the colleague, to whom more than anyone else, the Company's foundation and success are due'.[14] In due course, Rose became an archetypal member of the middle classes in nineteenth century Britain as a successful businessman and lawyer. In later life he was also made a baronet and a member of the British establishment but his own family circumstances were modest. Born in 1816, Rose's father was an assistant surgeon in the British Army. Rose left school aged 17 to become a trainee solicitor and was made partner in the firm of Barker & Rose (subsequently becoming Baxter, Rose & Norton in the 1840s) aged 22. He possessed considerable financial acumen combined with a strong social conscience. In 1841, in order to treat diseases of the chest, he established the committee that would build the now world famous Royal Brompton Hospital. Shocked to discover that he was unable to obtain treatment for one of his legal clerks suffering from tuberculosis, Rose decided to raise funds for a specialist hospital. With no government support, the Brompton Hospital was founded entirely as a charitable endeavour and received a considerable boost in 1842 when Queen Victoria granted the new 'Hospital for Consumption', her royal patronage.[15] Rose was an interesting mixture of a bright, motivated lawyer with a strong social conscience as described by one of the members of his Royal Brompton Hospital committee in 1841 when Rose was still only 25 years old: 'Mr. Rose was a solicitor, young in the profession and life, he had little power except that which was given him by a sagacious mind, large intelligence, thorough integrity, and a nature purely philanthropic.'[16] By the middle of the 1840s, aged only 30, Rose was becoming well connected in both business and political circles. Rose made money in the railway boom of the 1840s as a lawyer and, Disraeli, the Conservative politician, also retained him as an adviser after 1846. The caricature of Rose in Fig. 3.1 even refers to 'Lord Beaconsfield', Disraeli's official title after 1876. Famously Disraeli coined the phrase 'climbing the greasy pole' on becoming Prime Minister in 1868 but Rose also did some climbing up his own greasy pole. Rose was

---

[14] Neil McKendrick and John Newlands *A History of Foreign & Colonial Investment Trust* (Chappin Kavanagh 1999) 63.
[15] Neil McKendrick and John Newlands *A History of Foreign & Colonial Investment Trust* (Chappin Kavanagh 1999) 26.
[16] Andrew St George, *A History of Norton Rose* (Granta 1995) 45.

Fig. 3.1   Philip Rose, 1816–1883, cartoon, Vanity Fair, 1881

made a baronet in 1874 and, with suitable recognition of his lowly upbringing, he wrote to his friend Corry, 'Such an honor (sic) for such an 'umble (sic) individual.'[17] Rose was extremely energetic and had achieved a great deal professionally by the mid-1840s. He was also well-travelled but suffered recurrent bouts of illness owing to overwork and the demands of his large family of 10 children. Chapter 7 explains that unit trusts were established to enable smaller savers, particularly lower middle class and the working classes to invest for their futures. In 1868, Philip Rose, solidly embedded in middle-class Britain, had similar ideas when he established Foreign & Colonial with the objective of making it available to 'the investor of moderate means'.

The other key person most closely associated with Foreign & Colonial in its early years was Richard Bethell, First Baron Westbury ('Westbury'). Westbury was the first chairman of Foreign & Colonial and his presence certainly helped to raise its profile and standing when it was being launched. Westbury was also influential in writing, or at least editing, the excellent Prospectus that accompanied the launch of Foreign & Colonial. Westbury was 'the most cherished individual from its [Foreign & Colonial's] early beginnings in 1868 . . . he is in consequence the most easily identifiable symbol of Foreign & Colonial's early history . . . and deservedly so'.[18] As the chairman of Foreign & Colonial it appears that Westbury was mainly an important figurehead rather than somebody who was either knowledgeable about investments or involved in operational matters associated with the company. This is not to diminish his role because without his presence, Foreign & Colonial may not have got off the ground at all. But, anecdotally, Westbury devoted little of his time and attention to Foreign & Colonial and he died in 1873, just 5 years after the creation of the investment company, and before it had faced any major challenges. Additionally, chairing Foreign & Colonial did not appear to have been a major part of Westbury's daily life. In the two-volume Nash biography of Westbury, only

---

[17] Mary Millar, *Rose, Sir Philip, First Baronet 1816–1883* in Oxford Dictionary of National Biography (Oxford University Press 2004).
[18] Neil McKendrick, *The Birth of Foreign & Colonial: The World's First Investment Trust* (Foreign & Colonial 1993) 56.

one sentence touches on Westbury's role as chairman of Foreign & Colonial.[19] According to Nash's account, the bulk of his time in the late 1860s appears to have been devoted to the House of Lords and working on legal policy. Specifically, Westbury was involved in legal bills such as the Status of the Church in the Colonies, the Privy Council together with enquiries into the expediency of a Digest of Law and the Colonial Bar. Compared to John Guild (Chapter 4), for example, who was Chairman of the First Scottish American Trust in Dundee, Westbury's role appears to have been completely passive. Guild was very much an executive hands-on investor whereas in comparison, Westbury was a non-executive chairman. Despite this, Westbury was an extremely interesting and able person in his own right – he attended Wadham College Oxford at the age of 14 and graduated with a top class degree (a first in Classics and a second in Maths) aged only 17 years old. The impressive Westbury was summarised as follows:

> Not only the most brilliant barrister of his generation, a Fellow of Wadham, a member of parliament, a member of the Cabinet, a Privy Councillor, a former Solicitor General, a former Attorney General, and a celebrated Lord Chancellor. . . . a man who was respected for his integrity as he was feared for his intellect.[20]

With Foreign & Colonial, it was possibly Westbury but probably mainly Rose, along with James Thompson Mackenzie and Samuel Laing, who came up with the investment company idea in the first place.[21] Both of these men were long-time business partners of Rose: he worked with Laing on various railway companies and, in 1863, they had created the General Credit and Finance Company. This operated as an early investment bank, acting as a principal on investment deals, similar to Societe Generale in France. Laing was Chairman while Rose and Mackenzie were fellow directors. During 1868, Mackenzie provided the initial portfolio of stocks for

---

[19] Thomas Nash, *A Life of Richard Lord Westbury Vol 2* (London 1888) 189.

[20] Neil McKendrick, *The Birth of Foreign & Colonial: The World's First Investment Trust* (Foreign & Colonial 1993) 55.

[21] Samuel Laing (see Thomas Seccombe, in the Oxford Dictionary of National Biography) was a lawyer, barrister, businessman, senior Liberal politician, civil servant and in his later years a prolific author. Born in 1812, a few years older than Rose, they were kindred spirits.

Foreign & Colonial. According to Rose's son Frederick, 'I am not able to say whether the original idea of the Trust originated with Mr. Mackenzie, Mr. Laing or my father. It was probably a combination of all three . . . my father brought it to the attention of Lord Westbury who took it up at once.'[22]

Rose had a good working knowledge of financial instruments, particularly bonds both for international companies and overseas governments. Within the firm of solicitors of Baxter, Rose & Norton in the 1860s, Rose dealt with institutional business and was active in arranging loans for companies from France, Belgium and Australia; he had also arranged Russian and Turkish bond issues, all London-listed securities.[23] He visited Constantinople in 1866 to renegotiate the terms of Turkish bonds and must have done a good job because he was subsequently invited back by to Constantinople the Turkish Sultan to receive an honour, The Order of the Mejidie.[24] Philip Rose's legal firm, Baxter, Rose & Norton, helped to establish the Association (later renamed the Corporation) of Foreign Bond Holders in September 1868, to represent and to protect British owners of foreign bonds.[25] One of its tasks was to limit or prohibit new loans being raised by an existing borrower if it had an existing issue that was in default, which demonstrated the rudimentary, albeit evolving, nature of bond markets at that date.[26] Significantly, it was Rose, along with Robert Fleming (Chapter 4), who was co-opted to the committee fighting for better terms for the bondholders in the infamous case of the Erie Railroad. Finally, as an aide to Disraeli he had managed the latter's financial affairs from the mid-1840s as Disraeli's 'confidential man of business' and was also an Executor of Disraeli's will in 1881.[27] Given that Disraeli was a

---

[22] Neil McKendrick and John Newlands *A History of Foreign & Colonial Investment Trust* (Chappin Kavanagh 1999) 12.

[23] Andrew St George, *A History of Norton Rose* (Granta 1995) 87.

[24] Andrew St George, *A History of Norton Rose* (Granta 1995) 88. The name of a military and knightly order of the Ottoman Empire, The Order of the Mejidie, was instituted in 1851 by Sultan Abdülmecid I.

[25] Andrew St George, *A History of Norton Rose* (Granta 1995) 88.

[26] Victor Morgan & W. Thomas, *The Stock Exchange: Its History and Functions* (Elek 1962) 93.

[27] Mary Millar, *Rose, Sir Philip, First Baronet 1816–1883* in Oxford Dictionary of National Biography (Oxford University Press 2004). Disraeli was leader of the Tory Party and prime minister twice, first in 1868 and then between 1874 and 1880.

notoriously difficult individual with somewhat parlous financial affairs, his trust in Rose was testament both to Rose's financial acumen and also his interpersonal skills. Rose thus had financial experience and a good working knowledge of both foreign and domestic bonds together with high level contacts in politics and business. All of these attributes were used advantageously in the creation, organisation and management of Foreign & Colonial during its early years.

Foreign & Colonial was also a family affair for the Roses. Baxter, Rose & Norton were lawyers to the investment company and continue in that capacity even today as Norton Rose Fulbright. In 1868, Philip's son William was the first secretary of the original investment company, and when he died in 1872 his younger brother, Robert, succeeded him. His eldest son, Philip Frederick, followed in his father's footsteps: in 1883, he too became a Trustee and subsequently after 33 years on the board, the temporary Chairman in 1919.[28] The Rose family thus had extensive involvement in Foreign & Colonial throughout the first 50 years of its existence, with the elder Philip being the dominant personality at the outset. In 1879, Philip Rose steered Foreign & Colonial through its first major crisis and ensured its survival by avoiding liquidation. He was responsible for changing its legal status from a trust, established under Common Law, to a limited liability company established under Company Law. This change not only ensured the survival of Foreign & Colonial but it also made it a more effective investment vehicle. In February 1879 Sir George Jessel, Master of the Rolls, one of the most senior judges in England and Wales, ruled that all trusts formed under Common Law were illegal. In his view investment trusts were 'Associations of more than 20 persons for the acquisition of gain and as such, not registered under the Joint Stock Companies Acts 1862-67.'[29] Jessel also ruled that the annual draw system – the lottery element (3.2.3 below) – for redeeming share

---

[28] Similar to his father, the eldest son, Philip Frederick Rose, was also close to the Conservative party and the Disraeli family. He sanitised source material about Disraeli in the official biography by Moneypenny and Buckle, published in 1920. Consequently, there was no mention of Disraeli's financial problems, mistresses and marital difficulties (see Oxford Dictionary of National Biography).
[29] Neil McKendrick and John Newlands *A History of Foreign & Colonial Investment Trust* (Chappin Kavanagh 1999) 50.

certificates was illegal under the existing Lottery Acts too.[30] The initial legislative test case had been brought against 'The Governments and Guaranteed Securities Permanent Trust' but this legal judgement meant that all other investment trusts formed under Common law, including Foreign & Colonial, were also illegal. The problem for Foreign & Colonial was then immediately exacerbated when a lawyer, Edmund Lewis, served a writ threatening to wind it up but according to Andrew St George's account of the crisis in 1879, it was Rose who 'saved the day'. Not only did he return from Pau in southern France, about 800 miles from London, in order to resolve the problem, but also in transit he drew up the legal terms to enable the five investment companies to be consolidated into a single limited liability company.[31] Also, he persuaded two of his fellow Trustees, Currie and Cecil, to accept Lewis as a Trustee on the board of the re-constituted corporate entity. The board minutes of the meeting of 17 March 1879 indicate that it was Rose who highlighted the complexity of combining the five issues (see Section 3.2.3 'Investment Performance' for a fuller description of the different issues of Foreign & Colonial certificates) of the different investment companies into a single entity.[32] He understood that the volume of work was too much for the current staff and the solution agreed was to appoint Price Waterhouse & Co to undertake the task and to perform the conversion calculations. Owing to Rose's decisiveness and energy therefore, Foreign & Colonial moved from a trust structure with five separately constituted trusts to an incorporated company with a single portfolio of securities, and most importantly, most of the original investors were retained during the transition process too. Given the very high conversion rate of these certificate holders to shareholders in March 1879 – over 80% converted – into the new limited liability vehicle, it appears that a large majority of them maintained a belief that investing through an asset management company remained an attractive proposition.

---

[30] The lottery aspect was more than just an oddity because it materially influenced actual investment returns. Its impact on investment performance is discussed in detail later in the chapter.

[31] Andrew St George, *A History of Norton Rose* (Granta 1995) 98.

[32] *Foreign & Colonial Government Trust, Minute Book* (F&C Asset Management).

With hindsight, 1879 was a pivotal moment for the asset management profession in Britain. It could have folded ignominiously. The majority of investment companies that were established around 1870, such as Foreign & Colonial and the First Scottish, had been created as trusts not limited companies. At this juncture, these two were the highest profile investment companies: they were the first to be launched in England and Scotland respectively; and both had multiple issues of certificates, nine separate issues in total between them. Prior to March 1873, 13 investment companies had been established, 12 of them under trust law and only 1 under corporate law.[33] By 1875, 16 investment companies had adopted the trust format and only 9 the limited liability corporate structure. Following the Jessel legal judgement, these trusts needed to move to a different legal form to continue as going concerns, and they also had to persuade their investors that they should transfer their holdings from certificates to shares. Retaining the loyalty of Foreign & Colonial's investors was not a trivial task because its investment performance had been patchy during the 1870s. One Scottish newspaper, no doubt with considerable *schadenfreude* and during the conversion process, described problems at Foreign & Colonial in the following terms:

> The Trusts formed in London under the auspices of Lord Westbury and other great names have not turned out so well. From the fact of so much less care having been exhibited in the choice of securities. The result is that the promised rates of interest have not been paid, and the certificates are now at a considerable discount.[34]

Why, therefore, did most of these certificate holders choose to convert certificates into shares rather than just take the cash available? It certainly required an act of faith to transfer holdings from the old to the new

---

[33] By end 1872, the Government Stock Investment Company Limited was the only English investment company to have been established as a company rather than a trust. The first Scottish investment trust established as a company was the confusingly named Scottish American investment Company, dated April 1873. Confusing owing to a similarity of name with the Scottish American Investment Trust launched in February 1873.

[34] *The Dundee Advertiser*, 7 March 1879.

corporate structure, not least because the re-configured investment companies no longer included the lottery feature that had produced the highest returns. On the other hand, the reconstruction proposal by Foreign & Colonial in March 1879 explained to shareholders that a starting yield of between 5%, for preferred shareholders, and 6.5%, for deferred shareholders, remained attractive.[35] But these yields of 1879 were considerably lower than the proffered returns in 1868. The underlying explanation for the high conversion rates in 1879 appears attributable more to reasons of fear rather than greed and, fear took at least two forms. First, the reconstruction proposal explained clearly that investors would suffer greater capital losses, owing to forced sales in the market, if they did not convert: this was one strand of concern. The other large fear factor in 1879 was that the British banking system had just suffered another crisis. In October 1878, the City of Glasgow Bank, with the third largest branch network in the country, failed. This was the largest commercial banking failure in the UK prior to the recent crisis of 2008.[36] Apart from the size of the failure which also led to other bank failures in December 1878, namely the West of England Bank and the South Wales District Bank, there were two aspects of this bank failure that intensified its impact at the time: first, the imprisonment of the directors of the City of Glasgow Bank; and second, the consequences of unlimited liability on over 1000 shareholders. The trial was widely reported in the press and six directors plus the general manager of the bank received prison sentences of between 8 and 18 months for fraudulently falsifying the accounts: this failure was very much in the public eye. Fraud and incompetence were on a grand scale with the City of Glasgow Bank: liabilities had been deliberately understated while assets had been consciously overstated; four unreliable borrowers accounted for 75% of all the loans. Arguably, the impact on shareholders had an even more significant effect on public perception. As a joint stock company with unlimited liability, shareholders were responsible for the debts of £5.2 million (£472 million inflation adjusted to 2016). Shareholders, not depositors, were on the hook meaning that an

---

[35] *Foreign and Colonial Government Trust, Plan of Consolidation, March 1879* (Guildhall Library).
[36] John Turner, *Banking in Crisis* (Cambridge University Press 2014) 88.

investor could lose multiples of the initial investment, not just 100%. The press typically covered the story as bringing about the financial ruin of vulnerable shareholders with small holdings so this created huge popular interest and awareness.[37] The impact was very real: of the 1,500 shareholders in the City of Glasgow Bank, 1,200 faced bankruptcy. In the event, one-third of the shareholders paid three-quarters of the cash calls because the remaining shareholders had insufficient assets.[38] In early 1879, the City of Glasgow Bank failure was the major financial story at a time when Foreign & Colonial was putting its reconstruction proposals to certificate holders. This was almost a case of history repeating itself, given that Foreign & Colonial had been launched in 1868 shortly after the banking disaster of Overend, Gurney of 1866.

The demise of the City of Glasgow Bank was the nail in the coffin of unlimited liability and the consequences were thus far more significant than the failure of Overend, Gurney in 1866, which had failed, albeit with even larger liabilities of £11 million.[39] While Overend, Gurney was a large, important bank it was essentially a corporate City bank, a 'bankers bank' and the Bank of England allowed it to fail.[40] The City of Glasgow Bank had 133 branches and national reach so it was much more visible.[41] Recently, the Bank of England has argued that the City of Glasgow Bank failure shaped the future structure of the UK banking system. In a broader historical context, it represented another clear step towards limited liability as the preferred structure and vehicle for equity investors.[42] Starkly,

---

[37] Thomas A. Lee, *A Helpless Class of Shareholder: Newspapers and the City of Glasgow Bank Failure* (Accounting History Review 22/2, 2012).

[38] Richard Button et al., *Desperate Adventurers and Men of Straw: The Failure of the City of Glasgow Bank* (Bank of England Topical Paper, 2015).

[39] Generalising and making comparisons with the twenty-first century, Overend, Gurney was relatively specialised and London-centric so more akin to the failure of Lehman Brothers whereas the failure of the City of Glasgow Bank was the equivalent to the Royal Bank of Scotland.

[40] Marc Flandreau & Stefano Ugolini, *The Crisis of 1866* (Graduate Institute of International and Development Studies, working paper 10, 2014). Ashraf Mahate, *Contagion Effects of Three Late Nineteenth Century British Banking Failures* (Business and Economic History 1994).

[41] University of Glasgow, *City of Glasgow Bank* (www.gla.ac.uk/services/archives, website accessed on 19 April 2016).

[42] Richard Button et al., *Desperate Adventurers and Men of Straw: The Failure of the City of Glasgow Bank* (Bank of England Topical Paper 2015).

the events of 1878 highlighted the skewed risk that remained with an unlimited liability obligation as the following statement explains:

> As was common at the time, City of Glasgow Bank's shareholders had unlimited liability. Shareholders in an unlimited liability company are jointly liable to cover a company's debts. This means that if the value of a company's assets falls below the value of its debts, shareholders are called to inject additional funds to cover the gap. Thus, unlike shareholders in a limited liability company, shareholders in an unlimited liability company can lose more than their initial investment.[43]

By 1879, and in terms of shareholder capitalism; much had changed over more than 300 years to reach this point in the evolution of the company: it had begun with the mercantile joint stock companies of the mid-sixteenth century and, it was ending with limited liability corporations as the preferred form. As discussed in Chapter 2, the Bubble Act of 1720 tried to preserve the privileges of charter companies and limit the formation of competitors; its repeal in 1825 acknowledged that more flexible corporate forms were required. The Companies Act of 1844 had made incorporation much more straightforward in terms of standardisation and simplification of procedures, and the updated version of 1862 created the blueprint for unlimited liability to become the norm. Henceforward, the financial benefits of investing in ordinary shares would be tilted more in favour of shareholders whereby a successful investment could return a multiple of the initial investment but the maximum loss would be limited to 100%. In Chapter 4, the advent of large industrial and commercial corporations, issuing ordinary shares in limited liability form, will be discussed more fully. Coincidentally, in 1879 Foreign & Colonial itself was about to adopt that very same structure: limited liability supported by different classes of risk capital from shareholders. By the end of the 1870s, limited liability was about to become the norm owing to a combination of government legislation after

---

[43] Richard Button et al., *Desperate Adventurers and Men of Straw: The Failure of the City of Glasgow Bank* (Bank of England Topical Paper, 2015).

1825, the failure of the City of Glasgow Bank and the conversion of the leading investment companies from trusts to limited liability companies.

3.2 Foreign & Colonial

3.2.1 Foreign & Colonial Portfolio in 1868

The initial portfolio consisted of 18 stocks representing government bonds from 15 different countries: it was a concentrated portfolio but reasonably well-diversified geographically. This diversification in a risky portfolio was very important, not least because three of these bonds were trading at less than £0.50 in the £1 which explains the very high yield, 15.4% of the Turkey 5% coupon for example.[44] Therefore, these were holdings that would have failed to meet Bailey's first investment principle for life assurance investment based on the primacy of capital security – he even felt British government bonds had values that fluctuated excessively. Table 3.1 shows the geographic distribution of the portfolio in 1868 combined with data on estimated yields from 1875.

The portfolio was very eclectic with a high yield: it begs the question about how it was constructed and the source of the investment ideas. Victorian Britain at this time was an extremely confident outward-looking nation and there was a very strong international ethos to business at that time. The British Empire was vast, incorporating Canada, India, Australia, various African countries and effective economic control over many parts of South America. This gave Britain unrestricted trading rights, including the sale of opium, in China. This was an Empire based on trade and finance rather than physical domination but geographical control combined with commercial expertise proved to be very powerful. The rapid growth of wealth in Britain after 1815, and the subsequent investment of much of this overseas, made London the undisputed financial centre of the world in terms of securities markets.[45] The pound sterling was also the

---

[44] Neil McKendrick and John Newlands *A History of Foreign & Colonial Investment Trust* (Chappin Kavanagh 1999) 33.
[45] Victor Morgan & W. Thomas, *The Stock Exchange: Its History and Functions* (Elek 1962) 88.

Table 3.1 Foreign & Colonial portfolio and yields 1868/1875

Issue	Allocation (%)	Implied yield (%)	Coupon (%)
Argentina	4	8.6	6
Austria	6	8.3	5
Brazil	3.5	7.5	5
Chile	5	6.8	6
Chile	5	7.1	7
Danube	6	11.7	8
Egypt	5	8.0	7
Egypt Railways	5	7.6	7
Italy	10	11.5	5
New South Wales	1.5	5.1	5
Nova Scotia	3.5	5.8	6
Peru	10	6.8	5
Portugal	5	9.7	3
Russian (Anglo Dutch)	8	11.5[a]	n/a
Spain	10	10.4	3
Turkey	6	15.4	5
Turkey	4	11.5	6
USA	2.5	7.5[b]	n/a

[a]Russian bond yield is estimated and assumed to be similar to yields in Austria/Hungary and Italy
[b]The US bond yield is estimated based on a combination of prevailing US money rates of 5.9% and also 6% US bonds trading at 70c in March 1868
n/a – not available
This table combines data from the initial Prospectus (% allocation) in the left-hand column with yield information taken from Elaine Hutson's article 'The early managed fund industry: investment trusts in nineteenth century Britain' in *Handbook of research on stock market globalization, ed. Poitras (Elgar, 2012) Chapter 5,* September 2003, who extracted yield information from Scratchley (1875)
In terms of the names shown in the table:
'Danube' bonds would be some combination of Austria or Hungary, probably both
'New South Wales' is a state within Australia
'Nova Scotia' is a province of Canada
'Russian Anglo Dutch' in the 1868 Prospectus appear to be Russian bonds quoted in Dutch Florins and listed in the UK!

international reserve currency just as the US dollar is today. Sterling was backed by gold, which meant that currencies were fixed and, in theory, paper money was translatable into gold. The financial stature of the UK in turn attracted many overseas countries, states and cities to raise money in London by way of bond issues. Between 1860 and 1876, more than 150 foreign government loans were issued in London with a nominal value of £720 million by 36 different countries and other entities.[46] Owing to London's dominance as a financial centre for issuing and trading bonds, it provided a large liquid pool of investable securities. Almost certainly, the initial Foreign & Colonial portfolio from 1868 consisted of securities that were entirely issued and traded in London in sterling given that the original holdings and prices were quoted in sterling in the Prospectus and, that the 'Money Market & City Intelligence' section of *The Times* reported prices, again in pounds sterling for virtually all of these bonds. Being London-listed, the portfolio was a clear expression of the dominance of Britain's, particularly London's, financial system in the mid-Victorian era. It is also likely that the initial portfolio was sourced from a private portfolio and not bought in the open market. Rose's eldest son suggested that William Mackenzie, one of his father's main business partners, created it by transferring his own personal holdings into the first issue of Foreign & Colonial certificates. The following statement, interesting as it is, perhaps raises more questions than it answers:

No doubt Mr Mackenzie held a great many of the Securities which were acquired by the Trust, and out of these Securities the Trust afterwards made enormous profits . . . and although he doubtless made a handsome profit on the Securities he sold to the Trust, at the prices set forth in the Prospectus, he could by judiciously feeding the Markets, have realized quite as good prices if he had desired to part with his holdings in the ordinary manner through brokers.[47]

The main issue arising from this passage is, of course, whether Mackenzie received better prices by transferring the securities into the fledgling investment company than he would have by selling them in the open market. It is doubtful that we shall ever know what Mackenzie personally got out of this deal. Viewing it less cynically than a handy personal transaction for

---

[46] Victor Morgan & W. Thomas, *The Stock Exchange: Its History and Functions* (Elek 1962) 88.
[47] Andrew St George, *A History of Norton Rose* (Granta 1995) 95. This passage refers to a 'Memoir' written by Rose's son Philip Frederick. Sadly, despite contacting Norton Rose Fulbright, the Bodleian and the British Library, I have been unable to find this document which may shed more light on this intriguing assertion.

Mackenzie, perhaps the practical reason for creating the portfolio in this manner was that it enabled the promoters of the investment company to show prospective investors how the funds would be invested in practice, so they could see the actual portfolio that they would be buying into.

London may have dominated securities trading but even in the world's largest securities market, standards were lax. Some of the loans raised by foreign governments were of dubious provenance and the fund-raising practices smacked of market manipulation and insider trading. This was unsurprising: banks and brokers dominated the market, which meant there was no institutional asset management framework on the 'buy side' to provide the disciplines of valuation and governance. One infamous bond issue placed in London between 1867 and 1872, on behalf of the State of Honduras serves to highlight some of the problems.[48] The Honduran government was allegedly trying to build a railway track between the Caribbean Sea and the Pacific Ocean. The final iteration of the project in 1872 was based on a proposal to lift ships out of one ocean, hoist them on to the railway, transport them across country and then take them off the railway at the other end returning them to the sea. This was a good, old-fashioned scam: the transoceanic railway was not built; nor did the technology exist to lift large ships on and off trains in this manner. In due course institutional investors such as Robert Fleming would come to exert an additional level of scrutiny on the new issues market but even before that could happen, prices of the underlying securities needed to be more accurate. Prior to 1865, prices were written down on brokerage slips and sent to brokerage houses by courier boys employed by the telegraph companies. Apart from obvious problems such as loss and forgery of these brokerage slips, it meant there was very little pricing consistency, 'On the London Stock Exchange, only Consols prices were published in standardised form at the beginning of the 1860s.'[49] Therefore, quoted prices of stocks were opaque because it was often unclear if prices were opening, closing or something else.

---

[48] Victor Morgan & W. Thomas, *The Stock Exchange: Its History and Functions* (Elek 1962) 90.
[49] Alex Preda, *Rational Investors,* in Pioneers of Financial Economics Vol 1, ed. Geoffrey Poitras (Elgar 2006) 157.

Increasingly newer forms of technology would have a beneficial impact helping to improve disclosure and prices because price transmission improved rapidly during the late 1860s and 1870s: a stock exchange ticker which could transmit names and prices in real time was installed in London in 1872, having been established in New York in 1867.[50] The first telegraphic cable between the UK and the USA became operational in 1858 though it was destroyed after only 3 weeks and it took until July 1866 to lay a reliable replacement cable. For financial markets, the telegraph had the immediate effect of reducing price discrepancies between London and New York (Chapter 4). The telephone was introduced in 1878 with, allegedly, Queen Victoria receiving the first British phone call on the Isle of Wight and subsequently, telephone exchanges were opened around Britain after 1879.[51] While the telephone improved intra-country communications, transatlantic communication was still reliant on the cable telegraph (and letters) until after the First World War. At the end of the nineteenth century, the telegraph rather than the telephone was the main form of technology enabling international investment and, in particular, was crucial for direct investment into the USA.

In 1868, Foreign & Colonial's investment strategy was deliberately positioned to invest in higher-yielding non-UK government bonds and in today's language this would have been called a portfolio of junk bonds or perhaps emerging market debt. The emphasis on yield is highlighted by the absence of any exposure to lower-yielding securities in other European countries such as France and Germany with the latter's bonds yielding 4.6% in 1870.[52] Additionally, owing to the after effects

---

[50] Alex Preda, *Rational Investors*, in Pioneers of Financial Economics Vol 1, ed. Geoffrey Poitras (Elgar 2006) 157.

[51] *Queen Victoria Tries the Telephone* (www.queen-victorias-scapbook.org, website accessed 19 April 2016). The story is recorded as follows: 'In January 1878, Alexander Graham Bell demonstrated his new invention, the telephone, to Queen Victoria at Osborne House on the Isle of Wight. The Queen recorded in her journal that the telephone "had been put in communication with Osborne Cottage & we talked with Sir Thomas & Mary Biddulph, also heard some singing quite plainly" and that she found the whole process "most extraordinary"'.

[52] *National Bureau for Economic Research, Chapter 13*, Interest Rates (www.nber.org/databases/macrohistory/contents/chapter13).

of internal strife, very little was invested in the USA. The American Civil War had finished in 1865 but from an investment perspective the USA still had several drawbacks. The Confederate South had been very successful selling 'Cotton Bonds' to overoptimistic English investors as a means of financing the war. These bonds were denominated in sterling and sold in London. Additionally, these 'Cotton Bonds' were theoretically convertible into physical cotton but on the proviso that the commodity had to be collected by the bondholder in one of the blockaded confederate ports, usually New Orleans. But owing to a combination of inflation amounting to 9,000% and the collapse of a worthless confederate currency (the 'greyback') by the end of the war, 'Cotton Bonds' were worthless.[53] The greyback was not the only currency concern. There were also questions about the convertibility and value of the US dollar which were not resolved until 1879 when the USA finally returned to the Gold Standard. Surprisingly perhaps, given that the British Empire covered almost a quarter of the globe, not much was invested in parts of the world that were British possessions such as India and the Cape Colony in southern Africa while there were only small allocations to Canada and Australia. Therefore, and perhaps unexpectedly, the actual Foreign & Colonial portfolio of 1868 was much more 'foreign' than it was 'colonial'. Within the portfolio, Europe was the largest area in percentage terms, understandable in the context of Continental European proximity to London together with the political and industrial dominance of the Old World. In the nineteenth century, as today, Turkey and Russia had one foot in Europe and the other in Asia, for the purposes of this exercise therefore, Turkey and Russia, are classified as 'European'. While broadly supportive of Foreign & Colonial, *The Economist* had reservations about the country allocations and criticised several of the investments.[54] It referred to Danubian, Egyptian and Turkish bonds as 'loans to semi-civilised states' and then '...as to Turkey and Egypt especially, our opinion...is well known that these

---

[53] Marc Weidenmier, *Money and Finance in the Confederate States of America* (www.eh.net, website accessed 18 April 2016).
[54] *The Economist*, 27 March 1868.

countries will go on borrowing as long as they can, and when they cease to borrow, they will also cease to pay interest'.[55] Nor was *The Economist* feeling very optimistic about mainland Europe, asserting, '[with] Italy, you lend to an inchoate state; in lending to Austria, you lend to a dishevelled State; and in both there is danger'.[56] That newspaper emphasised the financial problems of these countries but equally, it could have stressed diplomatic and political problems because this was a period when a changing world faced many challenges arising from nationalism, imperialism and conflicting political ideologies.

Geographically, the holdings can be categorised as follows: British Colonies, Europe, Egypt and South America.

British Colonies past and present as of 1875: Only 7.5% of the portfolio was invested in countries either with a linguistic or a colonial connection to Britain such as Canada (Nova Scotia) and Australia (New South Wales). The USA was just emerging from the Civil War which explains why there is so little invested, only 2.5%.

Europe: European countries had the largest allocation of assets, 55% considering Turkey and Russia as part of Europe, spread across a diverse collection of high-yielding countries. Rose had previous knowledge of European debt in 1864 having visited St Petersburg, Russia and he also re-negotiated Turkish government debt in 1865 so he would have had familiarity with both of these bond markets.[57] Yields were high and often exceeded 10%.

Ten per cent was allocated to *Egypt*. The country was part of the Ottoman Empire's sphere of influence but Egypt was also well known to British merchants owing to its importance as a source of cotton during the American Civil War. It was also important geographically owing to a combination of political instability within the country and strategic importance given the construction of the Suez Canal by the French. The canal was one of the great capital projects of the nineteenth century,

---

[55] *The Economist*, 27 March 1868.

[56] *The Economist*, 27 March 1868.

[57] Andrew St George, *A History of Norton Rose* (Granta 1995) 87.

alongside the Trans Continental Railroad in the USA, and both of these huge engineering projects acted as a great stimulus to the movement of people, goods and trade. The canal halved the journey time between Britain and India since ships no longer needed to sail around the Cape of Good Hope. Building work had commenced in 1859, and the canal was opened to shipping in 1869. The British government was hostile to the original idea of the canal, owing to fears it might threaten Britain's power in India. In due course, the Suez Canal increased British influence in Africa, India and the Far East so perhaps the initial opposition by Britain was based on traditional Francophobic pique given that the canal had been a French project. Much of the initial financial and technical support for the canal came from France and a French-owned canal company had a 99-year lease. In 1875 Britain acquired a substantial financial stake in the endeavour – shares worth £4 million, 45% of the equity, were purchased, allegedly overnight, by the British prime minister Disraeli, funded by his local banker, Rothschild, rather than the British government when the Egyptian government needed to sell assets in order to raise short-term funds. Although French shareholders remained the majority owners, British influence increased permanently in 1882 when Britain bombarded the port of Alexandria invaded Egypt, stationed troops there and took control of the finances, administration and armed forces of the country.

South America: 17.5% was invested in securities across four different countries. Britain was not only the major overseas investor in South America at the time but it was also South America's largest trading partner. Spain had been driven out of the continent in 1824 at which point Britain partially stepped into Spanish shoes, commercially if not politically and economic growth in some South American countries subsequently improved. In the latter part of the nineteenth century for example, the railway network in Argentina increased dramatically, financed by British capital, enabling the development of trade in new bulk commodities such as beef and coffee.[58] For a period into the early

---

[58] John Newlands, *Put Not Your Trust in Money* (Association of Investment Trust Companies 1997) 127. The Argentinean rail network expanded from 836 km in 1870 to 9,400 km by 1890.

twentieth century Argentina enjoyed steady growth and became a wealthy country in its own right but this was short-lived. South America had too many problems. Political instability, income inequality and lack of representative rights – particularly in contrast to North America – would weigh heavily on South America's economic growth for more than 150 years.[59] Given the Spanish legacy and the inability of South America to build sustainable, political institutions, the quoted yields which were all below 10% appear relatively low compared to most other bonds in this portfolio.

Individual bond yields ranged between 5% (New South Wales) to a little over 15% for Turkish. All of the bonds were much higher yielding than British government bonds which stood at 3.2% in 1868. The Foreign & Colonial Prospectus referred to an expected dividend of 7% for investors with the actual portfolio earning a yield of 6%. Using information from Scratchley and based on comments at the time by Jellicoe, the redemption yield was probably in the region of 8%.[60] Therefore, this was a product driven by the objective of achieving high investment returns over a long period rather than any idea of offering a small premium to government bonds or bank deposits. While investors saw this 7% dividend as attractive compared to the alternatives, *The Economist* was less than convinced,

> The Prospectus promises a clear 7 per cent, and if people get as much as that while sitting still and doing nothing, they are very lucky.... and make it unlikely that 7 per cent can be cleared in it [Foreign & Colonial] except by a discreet (sic) first selection and unceasing watching.[61]

Owing to advances in refrigeration technology, frozen beef was successfully transported from Argentina to France after 1877.

[59] Niall Ferguson, *Civilisation* (Penguin 2012) 127.

[60] Charles Jellicoe was appointed to estimate returns in 1868 and subsequently thereafter, to verify returns produced by Foreign & Colonial. He was a past president of the Institute of Actuaries. In 1868 he estimated an 8% return assuming no defaults. In 1875, Scratchley in his book, *On Average Investment Trusts,* calculated individual redemption yields on 16 of the bonds assuming a 20-year life for each bond shown in Table 3.1. The weighted average yield is higher than 8% so perhaps Jellicoe was being cautious with his initial estimate.

[61] *The Economist,* 27 March 1868.

The idea of 'unceasing watching' however was not the intention at Foreign & Colonial because it was envisaged as a 'buy-and-hold' strategy. There was no expectation of regular trading nor was there an appointed fund manager. Thus *The Economist* was quite accurate when it said the portfolio was 'sitting still and doing nothing' because Foreign & Colonial essentially had a quasi-passive approach to investing. The founders of Foreign & Colonial did not see a role for a dedicated fund manager of the assets *per se;* instead, day-to-day administration was the responsibility of the company secretary. In this instance, the first secretary was William Barker Rose, Philip's son. Of note, it was not until 1924 that Foreign & Colonial subdivided the role of secretary between administrative and asset management duties: the first dedicated asset manager to be appointed was Arthur Crichton in June 1924.[62] Therefore, while Foreign & Colonial exhibited certain characteristics of a modern asset management company in 1868, it would take another 50 years to recognise that the activity of asset management itself was a discrete activity and more than just a book-keeping task.

With Foreign & Colonial, all receipts from investments were to be treated as distributable income, including both the paid coupons on the bonds and potentially redeemed bonds. It had the power to re-invest but this was more theoretical than practical because it was described as follows in the Prospectus: 'On the unanimous decision of all Trustees supported by the approval of Certificate holders, at a Special General Meeting, the proceeds might be invested.' As drafted, this was an extremely cumbersome way to make new investment decisions, and if a bond was redeemed early then the number of holdings would shrink in what was already a very concentrated portfolio of 18 securities. It was assumed that the proceeds from a sold security would be used to redeem certificates but this limited the flexibility to change or improve the standing portfolio. As an example, Westbury reported in March 1873 that 13% of the certificates had been redeemed 'mainly caused by the compulsory payment at par of the Peruvian 5 per cents, 1885'.[63]

---

[62] Neil McKendrick and John Newlands *A History of Foreign & Colonial Investment Trust* (Chappin Kavanagh 1999) 84.
[63] Neil McKendrick and John Newlands *A History of Foreign & Colonial Investment Trust* (Chappin Kavanagh 1999) 45.

Insightfully *The Economist* explained that this decision-making structure was ineffective: 'Though, therefore, we approve of the essential idea of the Foreign & Colonial Trust Company, we disapprove of its machinery, and believe that its prospectus contains promises far too sanguine to be ever performed.'[64] *The Economist* was absolutely correct to point out that this investment decision-making structure – 'machinery' – was poor because it was both unwieldy and slow. *The Economist*'s other negative prediction concerned the expected future investment performance of Foreign & Colonial. While the paper was partially correct in its judgement, as shown later, generalisations about investment performance were complicated for a number of reasons (Section 3.2.3).

3.2.2 Structure of the Investment Company and the Lottery

In 1868, the investment proposition by Foreign & Colonial was very closely based on the ideas underpinning the Dutch fund, Eendragt Maakt Magt, established in 1773.[65] Hutson has provided a detailed comparison of the features of the two funds and there are marked similarities.[66] Both funds had the following shared characteristics: a limited life; overseas bond investments with clear rules about diversification; low annual management fees and a front-end charge; high initial yield; excess income or an investment reserve to redeem certificates; certificates redeemed at par value and not market value; and a lottery component (more of which below). When it was launched in 1868, Foreign & Colonial may have appeared as a radical, new idea in financial services in a British context and the media, at the time, responded to it in that manner. In reality, and less prosaically, it was a re-packaged Dutch investment product from 100 years earlier.

---

[64] *The Economist*, 27 March 1868.

[65] Eendragt Maakt Magt can be translated as 'unity makes strength'.

[66] Elaine Hutson, *The Early Managed Fund Industry: Investment Trusts in 19th Century Britain* in *Handbook of research on stock market globalization*, ed. Geoffrey Poitras (Elgar 2012) Chapter 5. *There is a particularly good table (5.1) on page 142 comparing the main aspects of the Foreign and Colonial Government Trust with Eendragt Maakt Magt.*

Eendragt Maakt Magt was wound up in 1824 so it survived for 50 years, which was longer than many of the other Dutch investment funds that had sprung up in the late eighteenth century.[67] In a similar manner, Foreign & Colonial spawned a host of imitators during the 1870s and 1880s in Britain. The really important difference however was that in Britain these investment companies became the kernel of the asset management profession, which then developed in innovative directions during the first half of the twentieth century. By comparison, in Holland, asset management withered away and died out in the nineteenth century. The reasons for these different patterns of development in Britain and Holland will be discussed in more detail at the end of the chapter.

Foreign & Colonial had two main features: it offered higher returns than domestic equivalents and a pooled fund structure to limit costs and spread risks. As noted, in practice the underlying investments, while they looked exciting, were not particularly innovative since all of the bonds could be bought via the London Stock Exchange. For British savers therefore, the pooled fund structure based on diversification, probity and safety, rather than the underlying investment portfolio, was the principal innovation introduced by Foreign & Colonial. A pooled fund enabled a range of investors to invest collectively, thus spreading risk in a vehicle that had safeguards offering investor protection. Prominent Trustees were appointed of whom the most notable was Westbury: a lawyer, previously Lord Chancellor; and heavily involved in piloting anti-fraud legislation through Parliament in the form of The Fraudulent Trustees Bill (1857) and the Bankruptcy & Insolvency Bill (1861). The share certificates were deposited with the bank Glyn, Mills, Currie & Co.; Price Waterhouse was appointed as accountants; and, as mentioned earlier, an actuary Charles Jellicoe was enlisted to validate and estimate returns. The checks and balances were important, not least because the foreign bonds held in the portfolio were all in bearer form, so not registered in the name of a specific holder, meaning that an unscrupulous person might, potentially,

---

[67] K. Geert Rouwenhorst, *The Origins of Mutual Funds* in The Origins of Value, ed. William Goetzmann & K. Geert Rouwenhorst (Oxford University Press 2005) 269.

steal the certificates and sell them. One of the annual duties of the Trustees was to make an annual inspection of the certificates at Glyn, Mills, Currie & Co, to confirm that they were all still there. This diligent activity proved its worth in 1879 when it was discovered that some of the stock had been embezzled by one of the Foreign & Colonial clerks. The clerk was sent to prison for 12 months while his boss, the chief accountant Mr. Bailey, was required to provide an indemnity of £1,000 to cover potential losses incurred by his clerk.[68] While the governance structure may have been less than perfect it had however worked in this case. Compared to other financial scandals of the time, such as the failure of the City of Glasgow Bank, this unfortunate incident was a relative minor infraction. Finally, superficially at least, ongoing fees looked reasonable as they were fixed at less than £2,500 per investment company, per annum, which amounted to about 0.5% of the asset value for the first issue of certificates in 1868. According to the Prospectus: 'The ordinary expenses of management of the Trust are limited to a sum not exceeding £2,500 per annum. No other expenses can be undertaken without the assent of the certificate holders' committee.'[69] Had Foreign & Colonial raised the entire expected amount of £1 million then the initial fees would have been only 0.25% per annum. But, although ongoing expenses were controlled, there was also a hefty front-end charge of 2.5%.[70] With specific reference to the ongoing management charges, an annual fixed monetary fee was sensible because the fee covered the running costs of the investment vehicle and charges were capped. Consequently, investors would benefit if the assets increased in value because the monetary fee to the asset manager is unchanged but the percentage fee would reduce. The modern method of charging fees is to

---

[68] Neil McKendrick and John Newlands *A History of Foreign & Colonial Investment Trust* (Chappin Kavanagh 1999) 61.

[69] *Foreign and Colonial Government Trust, Prospectus March 1868* (Guildhall Library). The 1868 prospectus hoped to raise £1 million and set the annual management charge at £2,500 which would have been 0.25%; in practice, a little over £0.5 million was raised so the annual fee was in the region of 0.5%.

[70] CH Walker *Unit Trusts* (unpublished PhD LSE Library, 1938). Walker describes this front-end charge as a 'preliminary charge' and it varied: it was 2.5% for the first issue of certificates, 1.5% for the next three issues and 2% for the fifth issue.

levy a percentage charge, which means the revenue to the asset management company is uncapped and the asset manager benefits as assets increase in value because their revenues also increase. Therefore, the main incentive for the directors and Trustees of Foreign & Colonial in 1868 was to produce satisfactory returns for the certificate holders rather than grow funds under management.

At launch the Foreign and Colonial Government Trust raised £500,085, net of expenses, which today equates to about £40 million adjusting for inflation.[71] According to The Standard newspaper, '... the majority (of investors) however, vary from £15,000 to £30,000'.[72] This implied a median-sized initial investment of £22,500, equivalent to £2 million in today's money. In turn, this would have equated to about only 25 initial investors. This large holding size across a small number of wealthy investors was the means by which the investment company was established, so the very first investors in 1868 were a small group of rich men and not 'the investor of moderate means' as envisaged in the Prospectus. But during the course of the 1870s the shareholder base became much broader and it changed significantly: in 1879, across all five issues of Foreign & Colonial, the average size of shareholding was only £570.[73] By 1881, Foreign & Colonial had finally reached the middle and lower middle classes in Britain given that the shareholders included several tradesmen, with occupations such as 'leather cutter', 'slater', 'warehouseman', 'flax spinner' and 'farmer'.[74] As an interesting window on social attitudes, the list of shareholders had two other interesting features: aristocrats were not given occupations but simply referred to by their title; nor were women given occupations either being classified only by their marital status as in 'married' 'spinster' or 'widow'.[75] In

---

[71] Neil McKendrick and John Newlands A History of Foreign & Colonial Investment Trust (Chappin Kavanagh 1999) 40.
[72] Neil McKendrick and John Newlands A History of Foreign & Colonial Investment Trust (Chappin Kavanagh 1999) 40.
[73] CH Walker Unit Trusts (unpublished PhD LSE Library, 1938) 49.
[74] Neil McKendrick and John Newlands A History of Foreign & Colonial Investment Trust (Chappin Kavanagh 1999) 62.
[75] As late as the 1930s, women were not given occupations and were still classified by marital status on unit trust registers.

1868, each certificate of the first issue was priced at £85 and issued on a partly paid basis: £10 up front; £5 on allotment and then £25 in each of the following three months. The investment company was then closed to new money and had a maximum life of 24 years so it would be liquidated by 1892 at the latest. As a trust with Trustees, so not a company, it could not raise new money by resorting to a rights issue, for example, meaning that any further fund-raising had to be done by means of creating a new investment company, which is what the Trustees did. By December 1872, four additional Foreign & Colonial investment companies had been launched and had raised a total of £3.5 million of new money to invest. There was a large drop in the expected dividend yield from the first issue of certificates in 1868, with an expected portfolio yield of a little over 6%, to the fifth issue of certificates in December 1872 with an expected yield of only 5%.[76]

From today's perspective, one of the most interesting and unusual features of Foreign & Colonial was its lottery component, which operated on the basis of an annual random draw of certificates. The lottery component was essentially a mechanism for early redemption of certificates over the life of the investment company but it may also have been a simple marketing ploy by Foreign & Colonial. Lotteries linked to investments were not unusual in Holland and Britain from the seventeenth century onwards: and, as today, these lotteries offered a small chance of high gains and were designed to appeal to unsophisticated savers. It was a form of gambling really and had been used as a feature in the Eendragt Maakt Magt.[77] In England lotteries were occasionally organised by individuals, but mainly by governments, and they were widely advertised being open to anybody who wanted to participate.[78] Lotteries at that time were popular, and would have been seen as more akin to betting then investing. The idea of drawn bonds, or a

---

[76] Neil McKendrick and John Newlands *A History of Foreign & Colonial Investment Trust* (Chappin Kavanagh 1999) 42.

[77] K. Geert Rouwenhorst, *The Origins of Mutual Funds* (ICF Working Paper, 2004).

[78] PGM Dickson, *The Financial Revolution in England* (Macmillan 1993) 54 & 80.

version of it, also persisted into the second half of the twentieth century as retired Baillie Gifford partner Richard Burns explained:

> This lottery, or drawings, feature still existed in some of the bond issues that I bought for Scottish Mortgage [an investment trust] in the early 1980s mostly from European issues dating from the 1960s. Drawings were a method of increasing the redemption yield and hastening the overall maturity of the issue. It was not considered unusual.[79]

In terms of the lottery based on an annual draw, Foreign & Colonial used surplus funds to repay share certificates at par, so £100. The investment company was conceived as having a maximum life of 24 years, thus implying that approximately 4–5% of the shares would be redeemed each year. In practice, the number of certificates drawn depended on the investment reserve. Winning certificate holders via the lottery had their share certificates redeemed early thus making an early capital gain of almost 18% based on an £85 subscription price and £100 par value. Randomly, if named in the annual draw, then the investor was re-paid early with a capital uplift and would have achieved a higher return than the remaining investors, albeit with re-investment risk given falling yields. This early redemption process may have been open to abuse by unscrupulous individuals but the Trustees had a duty of care and there is no recorded instance of malpractice though a contemporary account at the time considered the basic process unfair because it was arbitrary.[80] The lottery, based on an annual draw, was removed in 1879 when the legal status changed. Given the strong governance structure that was established at the very outset, the lottery component of Foreign & Colonial may have been an improvement on the Dutch version from 100 years earlier but it was still an oddity by the standards of today where there is a greater focus on treating all investors equally. But it might be wrong simply to consider a drawn certificate as a 'winner' and those not drawn as 'losers' as explained in the following paragraph.

---

[79] Richard Burns, comments on lotteries and drawn bonds (conversation, 14 January 2016).
[80] Arthur Scratchley, *On Average Investment Trusts* (Shaw 1875) 41.

Investors in the nineteenth century were interested in yield and income rather than capital appreciation and there was no apparent understanding of total returns based on capital plus income. Therefore, as noted, because yields were still falling through the 1870s, a redeemed certificate in one of the Foreign & Colonial investment companies could only be reinvested at lower yields. Consequently, there was potentially a re-investment problem with an early redemption. Second, at times the certificates traded above their par value of £100, reaching £108 in both 1873 (McKendrick & Newlands) and 1875 (Walker). So, if investors had bought the first issue at £85 on a yield of 7%, it is possible that they may have been unhappy both to lose their income stream and also to have their certificate redeemed at £100, potentially below the market price. Thus, the lottery aspect of drawing certificates annually was a very subtle mechanism and it is difficult to know how investors reacted to being drawn, or not being drawn. In the context of the 1870s, investors were on a journey and learning about asset management as events unfolded and probably had few pre-conceptions. The initial motivation to invest was probably to achieve a higher yield but increasingly, both the prospect and attractiveness of earning a capital gain would have become apparent. Above all, it would have become clear, relatively quickly, that investment via an investment company would produce a very different pattern of returns from a bank deposit or a government bond. Additionally, different investors would experience varying rates of return depending on when their certificates had been redeemed. For example, redemption at the end of the first year would have resulted in a capital uplift of 17.6% (100/85) with an assumed income payment of 7% resulting in an annual return (capital plus income) of nearly 25%. Alternatively, the certificate redeemed after 6 years would have achieved an annualised return of about only 8.5% These were still very handsome returns of course but higher returns would have been earned by being at the front of the redemption queue than at the end, albeit with reinvestment at lower yields having foregone future income. But clearly, the underlying point is that the structure generated a wide range of returns, which complicates the analysis of investment performance. Despite the reinvestment problem of being drawn early, most Foreign & Colonial lottery winners would have been delighted with their good fortune and in addition, probably enjoyed the excitement of the annual draw.

3.2.3 Investment Performance

Investment performance from 1868 to 1883 was mixed but in practical terms it was strong enough to convince a large proportion of investors that Foreign & Colonial provided a viable alternative to investing in British government bonds and bank deposits. This outcome was critical for a fledgling branch of financial services which needed to prove its worth. In reality and in aggregate, between 1868 and 1883, Foreign & Colonial produced adequate investment returns for certificate holders and shareholders although different groups of investors experienced very variable returns. Investment performance was reasonable until 1876; patchy in the latter part of the 1870s and strong between 1879 and 1883. A more detailed evaluation of the investment performance becomes more challenging for two reasons. First, there was not one single Foreign & Colonial investment company in the early years but five separate issues of certificates between 1868 and 1872. Therefore, there were five Foreign & Colonial investment companies and each was constituted as separate legal entity, and the holdings were not common across the different investment companies. Second, the calculation is complicated because, some certificates could be redeemed, or 'drawn', early by virtue of the lottery arrangement which meant that different investors, the certificate holders, would achieve very different returns depending when or if their shares were redeemed. In order to understand the investment returns, it is necessary therefore to consider the underlying returns of each investment company and then include the impact of the drawings. In practice, investors experienced two streams of investment returns: one from the income produced by the underlying holdings and a second from a capital gain in the event of success in the lottery. Scratchley, in his book of 1875, provided details about the Annual General Meetings (AGM) of 1874 for the various investment companies which provides a good snapshot on progress up to that date.[81] His contemporary writing indicates that Foreign & Colonial's performance had been very much

---

[81] Arthur Scratchley, *On Average Investment Trusts* (Shaw 1875) 18/19.

as expected during the first 6 years of its existence for investors who subscribed to the first issue of certificates. According to the Foreign & Colonial Chairman, G W Currie, his précised report of the first issue ran as follows:

– Interest had been regularly paid on the certificates.
– 1,745 of the total outstanding number of certificates (5,883) from the First Issue had been 'drawn or paid off'. [This meant that 30% of the total number of certificates had been redeemed after 25% of the lifetime of the investment company.]
– There had been only a little evidence of bond defaults from the initial portfolio from 1868. The 'Spain 3%' government bond had missed payments during 1874 and the terms of this bond were being renegotiated with an expectation that between 50% and 60% of the initial investment would be recouped.[82]

The Foreign & Colonial first issue paid a reliable income during its first 10 years: it distributed 6% dividends every year until 1876, dropping to 5.3% in 1877 and then paying 5.7% in 1878.[83] The price of the Foreign & Colonial first issue of certificates was however surprisingly volatile for a vehicle basically paying a level income each year and with limited trading.[84] Certificates had been issued at £85 in 1868, and they touched a high of £108 at end 1875 and a low in 1877 of £55 so a 49% fluctuation.[85] In 1879, the certificates of the first issue were priced at £75.5 when they were consolidated representing a capital reduction of 11% on the initial investment. When Foreign & Colonial became a listed company on the London Stock Exchange, the initial investors

---

[82] Arthur Scratchley, *On Average Investment Trusts* (Shaw 1875) 18/20.

[83] CH Walker *Unit Trusts* (unpublished PhD LSE Library, 1938).

[84] It is unclear what trading took place in certificates of Foreign & Colonial prior to 1879 when it became a quoted company. Prices were available as we can see from the Walker thesis and *The Times* newspaper. Hutson refers to the stock being listed on the London Stock Exchange, which is possible, but it wasn't a company. It is probable that there was a grey market in the certificates. The question is perhaps more hypothetical than practical given that most holders of certificates would have held the investment for its yield and would not have expected to trade.

[85] CH Walker *Unit Trusts* (unpublished PhD LSE Library, 1938) 35.

from the first issue in 1868 who still remained invested in 1879 would have earned a total return of about 6.5% per annum. All investors therefore achieved acceptable returns while a minority of investors would have achieved outstanding returns if they had their certificates redeemed through the lottery. By comparison, British government bonds yielded around 3% over this period (3.22% in March 1868 dropping to 3.10% in March 1879) so Consols produced a total return in the region of 3.5% per annum over this 11-year period (7% capital increase and yield of about 3.15%).[86] These first Foreign & Colonial investors from 1868 should have been very satisfied with the results.

But, as mentioned, there were five different issues of certificates by Foreign & Colonial between 1868 and 1872 holding a range of different bonds in different portfolios. Additional certificates were issued at different prices and lower yields compared to the first ones. These subsequent issues of certificates did not perform as well as the first issue. In March 1879 the five investment companies were finally consolidated into a single company with limited liability status and the respective investment company certificates were valued as shown in Table 3.2.[87] At the time of conversion, the first issue was valued at about 89% of its initial value and had produced the best returns of the five; while the second issue, the worst, valued disappointingly at only 71% of its initial value. This second issue would have produced a return broadly in line with government bonds, so about 3% per annum over its 10-year life. A broad-brush summary of investment performance would be as follows:

- Very good returns for any investor drawn in the lottery
- Strong performance from the first issue
- Disappointing performance from the second issue
- Acceptable returns from issues three, four and five

According to the Plan of Consolidation issued by the Trustees in March 1879, the document argued that the proposed conversion prices were

---

[86] *Foreign and Colonial Government Trust, Plan of Consolidation, March 1879* (Guildhall Library).
[87] *Foreign and Colonial Government Trust, Plan of Consolidation, March 1879* (Guildhall Library).

Table 3.2   Foreign & Colonial: investment companies 1868–1879

Certificate	Date issued	Issue price (£)	Coupon (%)	Dividend yield (%)	1879 price (£)	Price change (%)
First issue	March 1868	85	6	7.1	75.50	−11.18
Second issue	March 1870	80	5	6.3	56.89	−28.89
Third issue	April 1871	92	6	6.5	77.85	−15.38
Fourth issue	January 1872	95	6	6.3	72.96	−23.20
Fifth issue	December 1872	88	5	5.7	72.46	−17.66

Note that this table excludes the American Investment Trust, managed by Foreign & Colonial from March 1873, because it is not directly comparable owing to its different geographic remit
Source: Foreign & Colonial Plan of Consolidation (March 1879) and Walker, *Unit Trusts* (unpublished PhD, LSE 1938)

appropriate in the circumstances because the alternative to converting would be worse. It stated:

> If these stocks had to be realised under compulsory liquidation by order of the Court of Chancery, there would be a large depreciation below the price at which they are now valued, independently of the costs of liquidation, the amount of which we are unable to estimate.[88]

This clause was written in italics in the offer document either to frighten investors or to stress the importance of converting and it clearly had the desired effect as it persuaded most of the existing certificate holders to transfer to the new vehicle. Of the 30,245 outstanding certificates from the first five issues, 25,943, or 86%, had been returned by the beginning of April 1879 for conversion. In total, 3,628 people held these certificates, an average holding of £570

---

[88] *Foreign and Colonial Government Trust, Plan of Consolidation, March 1879* (Guildhall Library).

per person.[89] In mid-1879, the five separate issues of certificates in Foreign & Colonial were consolidated into one limited liability investment company with two share classes and with almost 90% of existing investors converting. How did the merged portfolio look and where did it differ from the first incarnation from 1868? There were just over 90 securities in the amalgamated portfolio of 1881.[90] This was much higher than the 18 securities in the original 1868 portfolio, but it remained highly concentrated given that the 10 largest holdings accounted for 76% of the assets.[91] Geographically in 1880, the portfolio was similar to the initial one from 1868: it had a preponderance of its assets in Europe, 51% and only 15% in British Empire or Colonial stocks.[92] In terms of sector allocation, the 1880 portfolio had a little more in railways compared to 1868, 14% versus 5%, but it remained predominantly invested in overseas government bonds. Up until the time of Rose's death in 1883, Foreign & Colonial remained true to its initial idea of holding big positions in a small number of securities. Therefore, while there were some differences between the first Foreign & Colonial portfolio of 1868 and the combined one of 1880, these differences were marginal and importantly, it remained a concentrated portfolio given the size of the largest holdings. Therefore, the more mature Foreign & Colonial of the early 1880s retained many similarities to its younger sibling from 1868.

Between 1879 and 1883, re-constituted as a limited liability company, Foreign & Colonial had two shares classes so investors could choose between safer and riskier assets. After 1879, there were safer preferred

---

[89] CH Walker *Unit Trusts* (unpublished PhD LSE Library, 1938) 49.

[90] David Chambers and Rui Esteves, *The First Global Emerging Markets Investor: Foreign & Colonial Investment Trust 1880–1913* (Explorations in Economic History 2013). This paper by Chambers & Esteves was the first forensic study of a British closed-end fund and it highlighted that Foreign & Colonial provided the first wholesale diiversified investment vehicle for the wider public.

[91] David Chambers and Rui Esteves, *The First Global Emerging Markets Investor: Foreign & Colonial Investment Trust 1880–1913* (Explorations in Economic History 2013).

[92] David Chambers and Rui Esteves, *The First Global Emerging Markets Investor: Foreign & Colonial Investment Trust 1880–1913* (Explorations in Economic History 2013).

shares or more risky deferred shares, but no lottery. Fundamentally, Foreign & Colonial's two classes of shares highlighted that capital markets had made a major step forward whereby shareholders should be rewarded for risk rather than by just being lucky. The preferred shares yielded 5% and had a prior claim on income with the balance of income then allocated to the deferred share class, which was expected to yield 6.5%.[93] For the subsequent 5 years, the preferred shareholders received their 5% income annually and the average dividends paid out to the deferred shareholders during the 5 years 1879 to 1883 was 6.65%.[94] The company also performed very strongly in share price terms.[95] According to one commentator, 'Four years after the reorganisation, Foreign & Colonial Government stocks had a high rating in the market, both the Preferred and the Deferred being quoted at £115.'[96] At 30 April 1883, shortly after Philip Rose passed away, the preferred shares traded at £115.25 and the deferred were priced at £116.50.[97] In percentage terms, the increase in value from summer 1879, in just less than 4 years was approximately 15% for the preferred shares and 37% for the deferred.[98] Unquestionably therefore, the certificate holders who transferred in 1879 from the original trust into the new limited company had their good faith rewarded because the revamped company performed as expected in income terms for both classes of shareholder and very well in share price terms. Preferred shareholders would have achieved an annual

---

[93] *Foreign and Colonial Government Trust, Plan of Consolidation, March 1879* (Guildhall Library).

[94] *Foreign & Colonial Government Trust AGM Reports for 1883 and 1884* (Guildhall Library).

[95] I was unable to confirm or validate a specific price at which the new shares began trading. Based on *The Times* from 27 August 1879, prices of £103.50 (preferred) and £88 (deferred) were quoted. This is the first mention of the new share classes. Implicitly therefore, the preferred shares were priced at £100 and the deferred at £85. The last reference to the old certificates appeared on 16 August when there was a sharp £3 rise in the price of the fifth issue of certificates, suggesting perhaps that the conversion was about to be formally announced.

[96] Donald Last, *A Centenary Review 1868–1968* (Shenvel Press, undated).

[97] *The Times* 30 April 1879.

[98] My estimated returns cover a different time period and are a little higher than the returns in the paper by David Chambers and Rui Esteves, *The First Global Emerging Markets Investor: Foreign & Colonial Investment Trust 1880–1913*, Explorations in Economic History, 2013. They calculate a 4-year return of just below 26% for 1880–1883. The broader point is that the trust performed well in the period immediately after it converted to limited liability status and up to the time of Rose's death.

total return (share price appreciation plus dividend income) of just under 10% whereas deferred shareholders achieved about 15% per annum. The appreciation in the share price after 1879 appears to have been driven by a couple of factors. First, the 1880s was a period of better growth and optimism for the world economy as the depressed conditions and financial crises of the 1870s were left behind, particularly as the US economy emerged from its prolonged recession of the 1870s and returned to the Gold Standard in 1879. Second, investment companies had become established as a popular savings vehicle with British investors so demand remained strong and a steady supply of these vehicles came to the market from the early 1880s onwards. By 1886, 28 companies were in existence, nearly all of them operating under company law, while in the subsequent 3 years to 1889, 56 new investment companies were created.[99] Asset management in the form of closed-end investment companies was booming in Britain and had become an important part of the investment landscape within 20 years of Foreign & Colonial's creation.

3.3   Concluding Remarks

Compared to the original projections in 1868 and the subsequent expectations after 1879, Foreign & Colonial largely achieved its performance objectives, particularly in terms of income. Compared to the yield of approximately 3% on British government bonds in the 1870s, it was demonstrably superior. Prices of the five different classes of share certificates were surprisingly volatile during the 1870s and significantly depressed by March 1879 at the consolidation date. But the share prices, both, preferred and deferred, of the reconstructed limited liability company then rose strongly between 1879 and 1883. Investors, by and large, would have been very satisfied with their financial returns over the first 15 years of Foreign & Colonial's existence.[100] Its resilience and success led

---

[99] John Newlands, *Put Not Your Trust in Money* (Association of Investment Trust Companies 1997) 124, 128.

[100] David Chambers and Rui Esteves, *The First Global Emerging Markets Investor: Foreign & Colonial Investment Trust 1880–1913* (Explorations in Economic History, 2013) estimate that

to many imitators, some of whom were charlatans, but enough were serious asset management undertakings such as the Scottish trusts in Dundee and Edinburgh. By 1883, asset management was firmly established in England and Scotland as a discrete activity.

Fortuitously, far from being a disaster for investment companies in general and Foreign & Colonial in particular, the Jessel legal judgement of 1879 had a galvanising impact. Forced to change legal structure and become limited liability companies, these investment companies were able to adopt more flexible capital structures, including the ability to use gearing (borrowings) together with the creation of separate share classes.[101] Also, Foreign & Colonial in 1868 had been created with a limited life of 24 years so if the original legal form had been unchanged it would have been liquidated in 1892 at the latest. The move to limited liability status removed the fixed term life of the original investment company which is one reason of course that the Foreign & Colonial Investment Trust still exists today. In practice therefore, with the change of legal status these investment companies became stronger.[102] The short-term impact of the requirement to incorporate in the UK led to a boom in the growth of investment trusts in the 1880s; the more lasting and longer-term impact is that investment trusts remain an important part of the British investment landscape, even today. Foreign & Colonial was the first asset management product to be brought to the attention of a wider public and thus

---

from 1880 to 1913 FCIT Preference Shares produced a total return of 4.5% per annum with the Deferred Shares returning 6.9% per annum. Beating Consols (by 2.2% p.a.) and with a better risk adjusted return.

[101] For completeness, it should be noted that the Jessel judgement was over-ruled on appeal in 1880 by the Submarine Cables Trust. This trust continued to operate very successfully under trust law until 1926. Nevertheless, virtually all British investment trusts adopted the legal structure of the limited liability company under Company Law after 1880.

[102] The Securities & Exchange Commission in the USA determined that investment trusts should be called investment companies in 1940. This was an eminently sensible decision because the word 'trust' is both misleading and confusing. It was used initially in 1868 partly because Foreign & Colonial had 'Trustees' but also as a marketing ploy to distinguish it from the word 'company' which had developed a bad name owing to the large number of bankruptcies. However, after 1879 virtually all trusts were companies and the use of the words 'investment companies' clearly distinguishes these entities from Unit Trusts. Unit Trusts are required to appoint an external entity to act as Trustee so this is accurate; Investment Trusts have no requirement to use a trust or a Trustee.

the investment company, investment trust or closed-end fund, was a pure investment management idea in a distinctive niche separate from insurance and banking.

Looking back almost 150 years, some aspects of the original idea from Foreign & Colonial were absolutely outstanding. The investment concept based on diversification was strong; also the idea of a pooled savings vehicle allowing middle-class people to invest in risky assets with some confidence was excellent; and offering an alternative to bank deposits and UK government bonds was attractive and, arguably, much needed. Perhaps the most important achievement was that Foreign & Colonial survived. As a product, it was very closely modelled on the Dutch investment fund, Eendragt Maakt Magt which had been established in 1774. Both were closed-end funds with a limited life invested, mainly invested in international government bonds offering a yield premium, and with a lottery component. But Eendragt Maakt Magt did not form the bedrock of an asset management profession in Holland whereas Foreign & Colonial, and subsequent British investment companies from the 1870s and 1880s, did. Three factors appear to explain Foreign & Colonial's lasting impact. First, Foreign & Colonial, and other investment companies established at the beginning of the 1870s, achieved sufficient success in the first 10 years that enabled it, and others, to continue after 1879, albeit in a different legal form. Almost 90% of certificate holders converted to shareholders in 1879 when Foreign & Colonial changed its legal status although the assets were trading at a discount to par in 1879, dividends had been strong and the concept of a pooled fund had largely proven itself. The first investors were sufficiently happy to continue investing after 11 years even though they had the opportunity to get out at that juncture had they so wished. By contrast, the Eendragt Maakt Magt and other Dutch mutual funds enjoyed less investment success in their early years owing to losses on plantation loans in the Napoleonic Wars.[103] Second, Foreign & Colonial had demonstrated that it could

---

[103] K. Geert Rouwenhorst, *Early Financial Contracts: Long Term Returns and Survivorship* (presentation, Cambridge Judge Business School, 23 July 2015).

survive through a period when the largest bank in the USA had gone bankrupt, Jay Cooke in 1873, as had one of the largest in Britain, the City of Glasgow Bank, in 1878. These unfortunate bank failures had demonstrated that alternative outlets for investing savings were useful. The resilience of Foreign & Colonial solidified the view that there was a fundamental difference between banks acting as principals with shorter-term deposits on the one hand and investment companies investing for the long-term as agents, on the other. There was a third factor at work here too: the British not only copied but they also refined and improved the initial idea that the Dutch had formulated a century earlier. It has been argued (Neal) that sometimes financial ideas succeed at the second attempt and in different circumstances 'precisely because the follower adopts the purer form of the innovation, stripping away the incrustations of local practices and encumbrances acquired in the era and country of origin'.[104] As an example, for safety and security the Dutch mutual fund Concordia, established in 1779, had held its stock certificates in an iron chest which needed three separate key holders to unlock it, thus offering re-assurance to their investors.[105] Foreign & Colonial on the other hand appointed lawyers, bankers and accountants together with an independent actuary to verify procedures, assets and annual calculations. So, while this level of re-assurance and professional scrutiny was much more sophisticated, it also reflected the broader development of financial and professional services in a different country and at a later juncture. In terms of checks and balances together with review and control, Foreign & Colonial was a better product than its Dutch predecessor. Perhaps the Concordia and the Eendragt Maakt Magt were a little unlucky too, because Foreign & Colonial also had better timing – the 1870s may have been a difficult decade economically and geo-politically but it was not as traumatic as the 25 years from 1790 covering the French Revolution and the subsequent Napoleonic Wars.

---

[104] Larry Neal, *Venture Shares of the Dutch East India Company*, in The Origins of Value, ed. William Goetzmann & K. Geert Rouwenhorst (Oxford University Press 2005) 175.

[105] K. Geert Rouwenhorst, *Early Financial Contracts: Long Term Returns and Survivorship* (presentation, Cambridge Judge Business School, 23 July 2015).

Foreign & Colonial was far from perfect, however, and the initial proposition needed to be improved. At the outset in 1868, it would have been better to establish Foreign & Colonial as a company under company law rather than as a trust. The company structure was more flexible than a trust-law one, subsequent certificate holders in the later trusts achieved poorer performance and it was messy when Foreign & Colonial was obliged to change its legal form in 1879. Also, the annual draw – based on a lottery element so that only some certificate holders got re-paid early – was potentially unfair and introduced the element of gambling, or betting, to the endeavour. The role of the secretary was purely administrative and it would be another 50 years before the actual practice of investment management was seen as a distinct activity separate from bookkeeping. In its early years, the decision-making structure for buying and selling investments was cumbersome because the Trustees did not expect to buy and sell securities. Asset management was seen as purely administrative at Foreign & Colonial with the Trustees acting as guardians rather than investment professionals so the *modus operandi* lagged the more dynamic investment decision-making process of some of the Scottish trusts (Chapter 4) established from the early 1870s.

Despite these imperfections, the benefits outweighed the problems. With Foreign & Colonial, investors had an alternative route for their longer-term savings which was independent of banks and very different from British government bonds. The basic theoretical and structural foundations of the investment trust – a closed-end pooled fund – was attractive to new strata of increasingly wealthy savers, particularly among the middle classes. These investment companies were flexible and enabled a large number of investment trusts to invest internationally in bonds, mortgages, property, land, railways and other asset classes. Having survived the first turbulent 15 years, investment trusts provided solid foundations on which an asset management profession could be built. Best of all, for UK savers not only was the investment product securely organised according to high standards of probity but the investment performance was more than adequate during a period of low and falling rates of interest on domestic bonds, political upheaval in Europe and economic slowdown. Asset management had begun to function as a distinct activity separate from banking giving savers better and longer-term alternatives, with Foreign & Colonial the vehicle and Philip Rose the pioneer.

Bibliography

Primary Sources

F&C Asset Management retains some original source material from the late nineteenth century including Minute Books of meetings

The Guildhall Library, London is an excellent source of data such as information on company prospectuses, including the following:

–*Foreign and Colonial Government Trust, Prospectus, March 1868*

–*Foreign and Colonial Government Trust*, Plan of Consolidation, *March 1879*

Books

PGM Dickson, *The Financial Revolution in England* (Macmillan 1993)

Niall Ferguson, *Civilisation* (Penguin 2012)

Elaine Hutson, The Early Managed Fund Industry: Investment Trusts in 19th Century Britain, in *Handbook of Research on Stock Market Globalization*, ed. Poitras (Elgar 2012)

Neil McKendrick, *The Birth of Foreign & Colonial The World's First Investment Trust* (Foreign & Colonial 1993)

Neil McKendrick and John Newlands, *A History of Foreign & Colonial Investment Trust* (Chappin Kavanagh 1999)

Victor Morgan and W. Thomas, *The Stock Exchange: Its History and Functions* (Elek 1962)

Thomas Nash, *A Life of Richard Lord Westbury, Vol 2* (London 1888)

Larry Neal, Venture Shares of the Dutch East India Company, in *The Origins of Value,* ed. William Goetzmann and K. Geert Rouwenhorst (Oxford University Press 2005)

John Newlands, *Put Not Your Trust in Money* (Association of Investment Trust Companies 1997)

Alex Preda, Rational Investors, in *Pioneers of Financial Economics Vol 1,* ed. Geoffrey Poitras (Elgar 2006)

K. Geert Rouwenhorst, The Origins of Mutual Funds in *The Origins of Value*, ed. William Goetzmann and K. Geert Rouwenhorst (Oxford University Press 2005)

Arthur Scratchley, *On Average Investment Trusts* (Shaw1875)

Andrew St George, *A History of Norton Rose* (Granta 1995)

John Turner, *Banking in Crisis* (Cambridge University Press 2014)

Articles, Journals, Pamphlets, Websites, etc.

Richard Button, Samuel Knott, Conor Macmanus and Mathew Willison, *Desperate Adventurers and Men of Straw: The Failure of the City of Glasgow Bank* (Bank of England Topical Paper, 2015)

David Chambers and Rui Esteves, *The First Global Emerging Markets Investor: Foreign & Colonial Investment Trust 1880–1913* (Explorations in Economic History, 2013)

The Dundee Advertiser

The Economist

Marc Flandreau and Stefano Ugolini, *The Crisis of 1866* (Graduate Institute of International and Development Studies working paper 10, 2014)

Donald Last, *A Centenary Review 1868–1968* (Shenvel Press, undated pamphlet)

Thomas Lee, *A Helpless Class of Shareholder: Newspapers and the City of Glasgow Bank Failure* (Accounting History Review 22/2, 2012)

Neil McKendrick, *The Birth of Foreign & Colonial: The World's First Investment Trust* (Foreign & Colonial 1993)

Ashraf Mahate, *Contagion Effects of Three Late Nineteenth Century British Banking Failures* (Business and Economic History 1994)

Mary Millar, *Rose, Sir Philip, first baronet 1816–1883* in Oxford Dictionary of National Biography (Oxford University Press 2004)

National Bureau for Economic Research, Chapter 13, Interest Rates (www.nber.org/databases/macrohistory/contents/chapter13)

Queen Victoria Tries the Telephone (www.queen-victorias-scapbook.org)

K. Geert Rouwenhorst, *The Origins of Mutual Funds* (ICF Working Paper, 2004)

K. Geert Rouwenhorst, *Early Financial Contracts: Long Term Returns and Survivorship* (presentation, Cambridge Judge Business School, 23 July 2015)

Thomas Seccombe, *Laing, Samuel 1812–1897* in Oxford Dictionary of National Biography (Oxford University Press 2004)

The Times

University of Glasgow, *City of Glasgow Bank* (www.gla.ac.uk/services/archives)

CH Walker *Unit Trusts* (unpublished PhD London School of Economics Library, 1938)

Marc Weidenmier, *Money and Finance in the Confederate States of America* (www.eh.net)

4

Robert Fleming and Scottish Asset Management, 1873–1890

After Foreign & Colonial had laid the keystone of asset management in Britain, during the 1870s the Scottish investment companies significantly improved the initial proposition and professionalised the process based on fundamental analysis and thoughtful, team-based investment decision-making. These Scottish investors were also handsomely rewarded for investing into the USA at an early stage prior to that country achieving rapid economic growth and prosperity. This was a classic example of taking Foreign & Colonial's good initial idea and then enhancing it so that asset management in Britain embarked on a virtuous circle of progress. Robert Fleming, in particular, made a very significant contribution and in the process imbued Scottish asset management with a distinctive personality. He was a man from an impoverished background in the east of Scotland and after starting work as an office boy aged 13 years old for the meagre sum of £5 (sic) a year, he became the dominant personality in asset management during the last 25 years of the nineteenth century. He also made Dundee, an industrial town, then of 120,000 people, a financial centre, and home to a cluster of asset management businesses with its own stock exchange. In the process Fleming helped to establish firm foundations for asset management in Scotland at the end

© The Author(s) 2017   **103**
N.E. Morecroft, *The Origins of Asset Management*
from 1700 to 1960, Palgrave Studies in the History of Finance,
DOI 10.1007/978-3-319-51850-3_4

of the nineteenth century and it continues to be an important activity today, though the hub is now in Edinburgh as Dundee's importance has diminished. The Scottish American Investment Trust (the 'First Scottish') was a pooled investment company with a limited life but no lottery component: although there were structural similarities, its investment approach was very different to the Foreign & Colonial Government Trust of 1868. The founders of the First Scottish were provincial merchants and self-made men interested in the operational aspects of their company and they were closely involved in day-to-day decision-making. They demonstrated great attention to detail; meeting in Dundee on an almost daily basis during the first few months of the trust's existence, and in a typically Scottish manner, the First Scottish charged even lower fees than Foreign & Colonial. These hard-working, self-made businessmen from Dundee were very different in style from the professional men and aristocratic individuals who established Foreign & Colonial in London and gave asset management a Scottish dimension. While the chapter concentrates on Fleming and the First Scottish, two additional Scottish investment companies are also covered in this chapter, the Scottish American Investment Company ('SAINTS') and the Edinburgh Investment Trust because they established an asset management capability in Edinburgh and deepened investment expertise more generally in Scotland. The former had a similar remit and approach to the First Scottish while the latter adopted an innovative investment strategy based around allocating assets to ordinary shares and international corporate bonds.

Fleming, in conjunction with the Trustees of the First Scottish, contributed to the development of asset management in a number of different ways. He was one of the first people to identify and exploit the great investment opportunity of the nineteenth century, the USA. Whereas Foreign & Colonial invested in London-listed securities denominated in pounds sterling, the First Scottish initiated cross-border investing: it was the first institutional investor purely invested overseas using local currency. This was made possible largely by the evolving nature of technology in the communication sector owing to the reliable operation of the cable telegraph under the Atlantic between the USA and Britain after 1866. Furthermore, Fleming understood the importance of fundamental research, as a means to establish an information advantage, so he applied rigour to investing whereas Foreign & Colonial operated largely as an administrative entity. He recognised that because investors are part owners of the businesses, shareholders needed to be actively involved as stewards in the governance of the businesses in which they invested. In practice, Fleming built on the idea of Foreign & Colonial and ensured that the investment management profession developed in a beneficial direction – savers were offered attractive investment opportunities that were professionally, actively managed. This was a sustainable approach built on hard work, attention to detail, low fees and an optimistic view of financial markets and the fledgling economy in the USA. By way of contrast, at the turn of the eighteenth century in the Netherlands, asset management activities had been established in the guise of Eendragt Maakt Magt and other mutual funds, but then had largely petered out. It was a very different pattern of development in the UK: across Britain, asset management built strong foundations in the 1870s and 1880s so that by the turn of the twentieth century it was securely established as a high-quality, professional activity. Robert Fleming, along with like-minded Scots in Dundee and Edinburgh, was an integral part of this process.

4.1   Fleming and the Scottish American Investment Trust (the 'First Scottish')

The First Scottish raised funds from native Dundonians and was managed locally in Dundee, despite Edinburgh and Glasgow being much larger cities: Edinburgh in particular had a more established network of professional services firms such as lawyers and accountants. But nineteenth-century Dundee, certainly its top social strata, was exceptionally prosperous with an international outlook. From the early nineteenth century Dundee was a centre for textile manufacture and had strong trading links with the USA. These links expanded rapidly during the American Civil War as Dundee became a very important manufacturer of products based on jute, imported from India. Dundee was also a whaling port, the largest in Britain, and the whale oil was used to soften raw jute for spinning fibre into yarn. At the height, there were 60 jute mills and works in Dundee employing over 50,000 people and Dundee was the largest producer of jute-based products in the world.[1] As an example of scale, the Camperdown Works in Lochee was the biggest textile factory in Europe: it employed 6,000 people and even had its own railway station.[2] Impartially, the Dundee merchants then sold these jute-based products – sacks, wrapping material for grain and other foodstuffs, tents, sandbags, tarpaulins and wagon-covers – to both sides fighting the US Civil War between 1861 and 1865. British textile manufacturers in general and Dundee in particular then received another commercial fillip with the Franco-Prussian War of 1870–1871, which closed the main continental European ports to shipping and generated further demand for Dundee's jute products. A businessman associated with textiles and drapery, Sir George Williams, subsequently pointed out, 'The trade of the civilised globe passed, of necessity, through British hands, for the United States was only then feeling its way into outside markets, French and German ports were closed to commerce, and all British stocks of drapery goods... increased immensely in value'.[3] In this way, war reduced competition, made Dundee wealthy and handed its merchants a great commercial advantage by expanding trade, particularly with the USA (Fig. 4.1).

Into this concatenation of textiles, wars and wealth stepped Robert Fleming. From 1866, Robert Fleming worked for the textile firm, Edward Baxter & Son and, in his own words: 'At twenty one [years of age] I was bookkeeper to Edward Baxter & Son, and private clerk to the senior, Edward Baxter, a very rich man who had investments in various countries, especially in American railway bonds. This was really what started the Scottish American Trust Companies'.[4] Baxter's, the firm, was the largest textile company in Dundee and had strong links with the USA; Edward Baxter had first visited the USA in 1826 and he also had some of his own personal investments there. Edward Baxter took Fleming under his wing and

---

[1] *Dundee's Jute Mills* (www.educationscotland.gov.uk, website accessed 29 May 2016).
[2] Norman Watson, *Dundee: A Short History* (Black & White 2006) 117.
[3] David Kynaston, *The City of London Vol 1, A World of Its Own 1815–1890* (Pimlico 1995) 303. Kynaston was quoting Sir George Williams in 1906.
[4] Speech by Robert Fleming on being made a Freeman of Dundee, 2 May 1929 (Dundee City Archive).

Fig. 4.1   Robert Fleming, 1845–1933, photo c. 1900

according to one account, 'Robert Fleming had a good deal to do with the management of Mr Baxter's American securities and it was from Mr Baxter that he obtained a grounding in a branch of financial business'.[5] Fleming first visited the USA in 1870, aged only 25, on a business trip representing his employer. He returned from this visit enthused by the opportunities for investing in the USA. The Civil War was over and the first transcontinental railway had just been constructed in 1869 from Omaha to Sacramento, The Union Pacific and the Central Pacific Railroads. The US railroads were seen as both an important spur to economic growth and a method of creating greater unity, both political and geographic, in a large and diverse country. Securities of railroad companies were also the largest sector quoted on the New York stock exchange: in 1870, of the 43 listed securities, 30 were railroads.[6] Unsurprisingly therefore, it was the railroad companies that attracted the majority of foreign capital that flowed into the USA and this remained the case up until 1914. In terms of USA's industrialisation, the more than fivefold increase in the railway network between 1860 and 1890 helped 'the United States was the first country of continental proportions to develop in the nineteenth century. This result was largely the consequence of the development of internal transportation.'[7] This meant Fleming was in exactly the right place at an opportune moment but he still needed to translate his investment idea into practice. This he achieved at the beginning of 1873 as the minutes of the first meeting of the First Scottish noted that, 'Mr. Fleming had previously brought the subject under consideration of the gentlemen present individually, giving them a sketch Prospectus of the nature of the business and the working of the proposed trust.'[8]

Launched in February 1873, legally and structurally, the First Scottish was similar to Foreign & Colonial – it was a trust not a company; it had a

---

[5] JC Gilbert, *A History of Investment Trusts in Dundee* (PS King & Son 1939) 13.
[6] Lance Davis & Robert Cull, *International Capital markets, Domestic Capital Markets and American Economic Growth 1820–1914*, in Cambridge Economic History of the US Vol 2 ed. Engermann & Gallman (Cambridge University Press 2000) 767.
[7] Albert Fishlow, *Internal Transportation in the Nineteenth and Early Twentieth Centuries*, in Cambridge Economic History of the US Vol 2 ed. Engermann & Gallman (Cambridge University Press 2000) 543.
[8] John Newlands, *Put Not Your Trust in Money* (Association of Investment Trust Companies 1997) 59.

limited life of 10 years; it had an initial portfolio yield of 7% and offered investors a return of 6% with the excess to go into a reserve fund. In one crucial area, the First Scottish improved on the Foreign & Colonial offering however, because it further developed the operational aspects and the underlying process of asset management. The Trustees had the power to sell and buy securities. Unlike Foreign & Colonial, this was a dynamic investment approach, based on a conscious policy of active management, rather than a static 'buy-and-hold' strategy. Additionally, the investment emphasis of the First Scottish was very different in terms of geography and type of securities. The Prospectus explained that it would invest in 'the Bonds of States, cities, railroads and other corporations in the United States but chiefly in the mortgage bonds of railroads' which, in practice, offered little diversification but the prospect of high returns.[9] The 10 largest holdings are shown in Table 4.1: the entire portfolio consisted of 30 securities, all corporate or municipal bonds, split approximately 80% railroads; 10% city

Table 4.1 First Scottish portfolio 1873: 10 largest holdings

Issue	Coupon (%)	Yield (%)	Price ($)	Holding (%)	Type
Michigan Central	7	7.1	99.3	7.5	Railroad
St Louis & Iron Mountain	7	7.4	95.0	6.6	Railroad
New York & Harlem	7	7.0	100.0	6.3	Railroad
Philadelphia & Reading Coal & Iron Co	7	7.8	90.0	6.0	Industrial
Pacific of Missouri	6	7.0	86.3	5.5	Railroad
Detroit & Bay City	8	8.0	99.5	5.0	Railroad
Cincinnati, Richmond & Fort Wayne	7	7.4	94.0	4.9	Railroad
Dunkirk, Warren & Pittsburg (sic)	7	6.8	103.5	4.9	Railroad
St Louis City	6	6.2	97.0	4.3	State/city
Cleveland & Pittsburg (sic)	7	7.5	93.0	4.1	Railroad

Data as in July 1873
Source: Extract taken from Claire Swan, *Dundee as a Centre of Financial Management* (University of Dundee, PhD 2009)

---

[9] *Scottish American Investment Trust Prospectus*, 1 February 1873 (Dundee City Archive).

and state; and 10% held in non-railroad industrial bonds. All the holdings had US dollar values apart from one investment in the 'Erie Railroad' (its full name was the New York & Erie Railroad), which suggests this particular security, which had dual listing, may have been London-listed.[10] This highlights another difference with Foreign & Colonial which invested entirely in London-listed pound sterling-denominated securities and was relatively simple to put together; the First Scottish was directly invested in the USA in US dollars. Technology made this possible: in particular the building of a reliable, cost-effective, cable telegraph between the USA and Britain after 1866: 'Prior to the telegraphic connection a minimum eight day voyage by steamship linked the capital markets of the United States and Europe. Thereafter information flowed across the Atlantic at the speed of an electrical impulse.'[11] In practice it was not quite that simple because the cost of using the first telegraph was high: £20 per word in 1866 but falling rapidly to £0.1 per word by 1906.[12] With the telegraph costing only £1 per word in the 1870s, this ensured that the First Scottish was not at a material information or trading disadvantage compared to local investors in the USA. Analysis of the price of the dual-listed Erie Railroad between 1864 and 1868 showed that prices regularly diverged in London and New York by more than 5% up to 1866 but subsequently traded in a much tighter range, generally about only 1–2%, after the introduction of the telegraph.[13] This same piece of analysis also showed that prior to 1866 foreign investors would have been disadvantaged because local investors drove the price of Erie Railroad, despite large foreign ownership, so that 'information generally flows from the home market to the foreign market but not the other way around'.[14] With the introduction of the telegraph, transactions became

---

[10] According to the *New York Times* of 28 October 1865, 60% of $100 Erie common shares were held in foreign, mainly British, ownership.

[11] Christopher Hoag, *The Atlantic Telegraph Cable and Capital Market Information Flows* (The Journal of Economic History 66/2, 2006).

[12] Ranald Michie, *The London & New York Stock Exchanges 1850–1914* (Allen & Unwin 1987) 42. In real terms, £20 would be worth almost £1,700 today.

[13] Christopher Hoag, *The Atlantic Telegraph Cable and Capital Market Information Flows* (The Journal of Economic History 66/2, 2006).

[14] Christopher Hoag, *The Atlantic Telegraph Cable and Capital Market Information Flows* (The Journal of Economic History 66/2, 2006).

easier to implement and transaction costs reduced as communication was simplified and inter-bank payments to distant locations became possible.[15] As a general observation, despite the introduction of the telegraph, at the time it would have been very difficult, though not impossible, for an individual British investor to create a portfolio similar to the First Scottish owing to the complexity both of currency management and also direct foreign investment: currency required sterling to be moved into gold and then into the US greenback; direct holdings required access to international brokerage services and a banking network to deal both in stocks and then hold them in custody. By 1873 therefore, enabled by the telegraph, cross-border international investment was an institutional proposition.

4.2   America

Perhaps Fleming and the Dundee merchants had an element of good fortune with the timing of their fund launch despite the severe economic and financial problems that emerged after 1873. This was not the first time that British investors had invested in the Americas. Several US states had defaulted on their bonds in the 1840s while the Confederate South had proved to be a disastrous investment for many English investors who bought 'Cotton Bonds' out of London during the Civil War. By 1870 the USA had a population of 40 million (3.1% of the world), rising to 98 million (5.5% of the world) by 1913.[16] The equivalent figures for Western Europe were 188 million people in 1870 and 261 million in 1913.[17] In population terms therefore, the USA was considerably smaller than Western Europe, though the population was growing steadily as it had done throughout the nineteenth century. In 1870, US GDP represented just 8.9% of the global economy whereas Western European GDP accounted for 33.6%. At

---

[15] Kenneth Garbade & William Silber, *Technology, Communication and the Performance of Financial Markets: 1840–1975* (The Journal of Finance 33/3, 1978).

[16] University of Groningen, Madison Project (www.ggdc.net/maddison/maddison-project, website accessed 15 June 2016).

[17] University of Groningen, Madison Project (www.ggdc.net/maddison/maddison-project, website accessed 15 June 2016).

this point the US economy was about to change gear. US GDP increased by 3.9% per annum between 1870 and 1913, so by 1913 the USA represented 19.1% of the world economy.[18] At this point it had become the world's largest economic power and future economic domination, always likely, became a certainty when Europe went on to destroy its economic base in two world wars.

Against this background, American railroads grew rapidly through the late nineteenth century. The scale of that growth was enormous and required significant amounts of capital to finance it. Railroad mileage in the USA increased from about 53,000 miles in 1870 to 250,000 in 1910, by which date Germany had 26,000 miles of track and the UK 23,000. Of course, the USA is geographically much larger than either Germany or Britain but the key point here is not the absolute numbers but the speed and magnitude of the growth in the USA after 1870. The US historian Paul Romer explains that this growth in the USA, at this particular period, was attributable to a combination of factors – infrastructure, technology, free trade between the states, the ability to exploit natural resources and scale.[19] Specifically, Romer argues that the 'scale' factor was critical and generally underappreciated, pointing out that even in 1870, the US population of 40 million was bigger than the UK's 30 million and that while Western Europe was much larger in terms of people, it did not form a homogenous economic area. As he says, 'Even at this early date [1870] the United States had a transportation system and a commercial infrastructure that effectively linked most of its citizens into a truly national market'.[20] So, the proposition is that the USA had huge economic potential in 1870 even after the Civil War and that it simply needed some catalysts to make that potential a reality; one of the catalysts was railroads which Fleming and the First Scottish spotted.

The Dundee merchants, and some professional counterparts in Edinburgh, were excited by the growth opportunity in the USA and were happy to provide finance. Several investment companies with varying legal

---

[18] University of Groningen, Madison Project (www.ggdc.net/maddison/maddison-project, website accessed 15 June 2016).

[19] Refrigeration was a very important new technology which enabled the transportation of food and hence the westward expansion of the US.

[20] Paul Romer, *Why, Indeed in America?* (NBER January 1996).

structures were created in both Dundee and Edinburgh to invest in railroad, state and municipal bonds or to buy mortgages on property and land. Ten of the investment companies shown in Table 4.2 were focused on the USA, while the eleventh company was the somewhat exotically named 'Hawaiian Investment & Agency Company'. Of the Hawaiian, it was said: 'Dundee's fascination with American railroad stocks, and then with mortgage lending in the Wild West, might seem excitement enough for one Scottish city, but Dundee's most globally challenged land mortgage company has not yet been mentioned. This was The Hawaiian.'[21] Despite its unlikely geographic remit, the Hawaiian performed extremely well and became part of the Alliance Trust stable of companies in 1923, renamed rather unimaginatively the 'Second Alliance' at that date.[22] The 1870s and 1880s was the heyday for Dundee as a centre of asset management but sadly for the city it was to be relatively short-lived. Fleming moved to London around 1890 and Dundee's loss was London's gain owing to his ability, entrepreneurial drive and

Table 4.2 Scottish investment companies 1873–1880

Name	Location	Date
First Scottish American Trust ('First Scottish')	Dundee	1873
Scottish American Investment Company ('SAINTS')	Edinburgh	1873
Second Scottish American Trust	Dundee	1873
The Oregon & Washington Trust	Dundee	1873
Scottish American Mortgage Company	Edinburgh	1874
Third Scottish American Trust	Dundee	1875
Dundee Mortgage & Trust	Dundee	1876
The American Mortgage Company of Scotland	Edinburgh	1877
Dundee Land Investment Company	Dundee	1878
The Edinburgh American Land Mortgage Company	Edinburgh	1878
The Hawaiian Investment & Agency Company	Dundee	1880

Sources: Claire Swan (*Dundee as a centre*), Charles Munn (*Alliance Trust*) and John Newlands (*Put Not Your Trust*)

---

[21] John Newlands, *Put Not Your Trust in Money* (Association of Investment Trust Companies 1997) 65. Hawaii became a US territory only in 1900 following many decades of prevarication by US authorities.

[22] John Newlands, *Put Not Your Trust in Money* (Association of Investment Trust Companies 1997) 66.

influence: in 1929, towards the end of his life Fleming was linked to 66 investment companies – a remarkable number.[23] His successors went on to create a very successful London-based international financial services business in the shape of Robert Fleming Holdings Limited, a company employing more than 7,500 people when it relinquished its independence in 2000. Towards the end of the twentieth century, asset management activities also began to drift south from Dundee towards Edinburgh and London. The First Scottish moved its professional asset management staff to Edinburgh in 1984 and the administrative staff followed subsequently; and, while the Alliance Trust is still headquartered in Dundee, the asset management work is now done elsewhere. Perhaps the remarkable point about Dundee is not that it lost its asset management expertise but that it had so much of it in the first place.

4.3   Scotland

In Scotland, Edinburgh was also an important centre for asset management from the late nineteenth century onwards though it lacked the wealth of Glasgow, London and Manchester in 1880.[24] Two trusts in particular are worthy of mention, the Scottish American Investment Company (1873), and the Edinburgh Investment Trust, established in 1889. For the avoidance of doubt, the Scottish American Investment Company ('SAINTS') based in Edinburgh was an entirely different investment company from the Scottish American Investment Trust (the 'First Scottish') established earlier that year in Dundee by Fleming. Founded in late 1873, SAINTS was one of the very first investment trusts structured as a limited company rather than a trust. Compared to the trust law structures of Foreign & Colonial, discussed in Chapter 3, and the First Scottish, limited company status provided greater flexibility with the capital structure, in particular, the ability to borrow and to organise rights

---

[23] Janette Rutterford, *Learning from one another's mistakes: investment trusts in the UK and US, 1868–1940* (Financial History Review 16/2, 2009).
[24] K. Theodore Hoppen, *The Mid-Victorian Generation, 1846–1886* (Clarendon Press 2000) 524.

issues, as evidenced by SAINTS which had six rights issues between 1874 and 1891.[25] In terms of the process of asset management, SAINTS operated in a very similar area to the First Scottish focusing on American railroads as its main sphere of investing despite the original Prospectus giving it a much broader investment remit in North America. William Menzies, the founder and a director of SAINTS, believed in visiting companies and established his own network of information in a similar manner to Fleming. Menzies created an Advisory Board of four US-based professionals in New York to support SAINTS' investment decisions so he was also thinking about methods of gaining an information advantage in order to have an investment edge. Additionally, similar to the First Scottish, SAINTS established safety-first criteria for any investment: 'That the net revenue of the Company [in which SAINTS might invest] is more than sufficient to pay the interest on the mortgage, that the mortgage itself is in proper terms and in the hands of competent and honest men.'[26] SAINTS was very successful: it declared an annual dividend on its ordinary shares of 15% in 7 years (1881–1884 and 1890–1892) and not lower than 10% in any one year (apart from 1873).[27] These were huge returns in a non-inflationary period and with British government bond yields hovering around 3%. This SAINTS record was even better than the First Scottish which produced an annual return of about 10% between 1873 and 1891. But, the important point is that together, these two investment vehicles proved that British investors could make money investing in the USA, a developing country, and also that active asset management based on fundamental research and analysis was effective. SAINTS still exists today, with a remit to grow dividends in real terms, mainly through investment in global equities, and is managed by Baillie Gifford & Co.

While SAINTS in 1873 was built on similar investment foundations to the First Scottish, in 1889 the Edinburgh Investment Trust invested

[25] Ronald Weir, *A History of the Scottish American Investment Company Limited, 1873–1973* (Scottish American Investment Company 1973) 11.

[26] Ronald Weir, *A History of the Scottish American Investment Company Limited, 1873–1973* (Scottish American Investment Company 1973) 11.

[27] Ronald Weir, *A History of the Scottish American Investment Company Limited, 1873–1973* (Scottish American Investment Company 1973) 11.

in different asset classes and was one of the first institutions in the nineteenth century to invest significant proportions in equities, particularly ordinary shares.[28] By the end of its first year, March 1890, 52% of its assets were invested in equities.[29] The remainder of the portfolio was held in a broad geographic spread of international railroad bonds. This was an interesting mix – equities and global corporate bonds – and much more innovative than many of the other trusts of that time. For example, the Alliance Trust, established in 1888, was invested rather narrowly in land and mortgages in the USA.[30] In March 1889, within the equity portfolio of the Edinburgh Investment Trust, ordinary shares were held in the Distillers Company (today part of Diageo which also owns Guinness), Hong Kong & Shanghai Bank and various companies that no longer exist, such as Dalmeny Oil, London & North Western Railway and the North British Rubber Company.[31] In terms of investment policy, therefore, the Edinburgh Investment Trust broke new ground by investing into ordinary shares owing to a combination of innovative thinking and the changing nature of capital markets. For the first 75 years of the nineteenth century, it was not possible to invest in a broad spread of corporate equities, or ordinary shares, of established commercial businesses because they were not widely available apart from the occasional banking stock or railway company. Most securities traded in London were foreign bonds, corporate bonds or limited amounts of preference shares. Joint stock companies began to be formed by enterprises issuing equity in the 1860s and 1870s, but these were often small businesses, tightly held by family and regional (listed on provincial stock exchanges rather than

---

[28] The Share Investment Trust in England was also a very early investor into ordinary shares according to Janette Rutterford in *Learning from one's mistakes*. I have used the words 'ordinary shares' as much as possible to distinguish between pure equity investments and 'preference shares'. Preference shares were probably considered equity-type investments over the period of this book but today they would be more normally regarded as debt instruments.

[29] John Newlands, *Put Not Your Trust in Money* (Association of Investment Trust Companies 1997) 87.

[30] David Luck, *Scotland's 100 Oldest Companies, The Edinburgh Investment Trust* (Business Archives Council of Scotland, May 2011).

[31] David Luck, *Scotland's 100 Oldest Companies, The Edinburgh Investment Trust* (Business Archives Council of Scotland, May 2011).

London), so neither widely traded nor very liquid. As of 1883 industrial ordinary shares represented only 1% by value of the securities quoted on the London Stock Exchange, with over 90% represented by Government and railroad bonds.[32]

However, the nature of capital markets in the UK changed fundamentally in the 1880s with large and established businesses, commercial and manufacturing, coming to the stock market in the form of limited liability companies to raise outside equity, specifically ordinary shares.

The majority of the companies which floated on the London and provincial stock markets prior to the 1880s were companies which floated from scratch i.e., the founders sought finance from the capital markets right from the company's inception. However, in the last two decades of the nineteenth century, there was an increasing number of companies which were viewed as "conversions" i.e., long-established private companies or partnerships which went public by raising capital. There was a transformational shift from private or partnership-based ownership structures to limited liability joint stock companies.[33]

This was partly to fund improved methods of production to meet large-scale demand but in Britain this was a second phase of industrialisation, not the first. The legal form of the company and securities markets were changing therefore, 'to carry through the "deepening and widening" of the capitalist system once the capitalist system had been accepted'.[34] The brewing industry was the most conspicuous example of companies adopting the limited liability form in the last 15 years of the nineteenth century as almost 300 brewers raised external shareholder capital.[35] Guinness, founded in 1759, and with net profits of more than £0.5 million in 1885, was

---

[32] Francois Crouzet, *The Victorian Economy* (Routledge 2005) 329.

[33] Graeme G. Acheson et al, *Happy Hour Followed by Hangover: Financing the UK Brewery Industry, 1880–1913* (Business History 58/5, 2016).

[34] James B. Jefferys, *Business Organisation in Great Britain 1856–1914* (PhD University of London, 1938; Arno 1977).

[35] Graeme G. Acheson et al, *Happy Hour Followed by Hangover: Financing the UK Brewery Industry, 1880–1913* (Business History, 58/5, 2016).

one of the first major companies to do so.[36] The Guinness Prospectus of October 1886 planned to raise £4.5 million in equity capital and £6 million in total split between debentures, preference shares and ordinary shares. The ordinary shares, worth £2.5 million, were the largest component of the Guinness fund-raising orchestrated by Barings, a bank. *The Economist* referred to it under the heading of '*A Unique Prospectus*' and was rather shocked that 'the company is thus to start operations without a farthing in its pocket and whatever may be the result of this method of operation, it is certainly peculiar'.[37] *The Economist* highlighted the innovative nature of the Guinness share offer and that the resulting capital structure of the business was unusual, though the comments did not curb speculative enthusiasm. It was massively oversubscribed, by more than 20 times, and there was also a major administrative mistake whereby partly-paid shares were issued in bearer form. The London Stock Exchange refused to grant it a quotation.[38] But these were mere teething troubles in the new issues market, and ordinary shareholders received a glimpse of the potential returns of equities after the Guinness board meeting of August 1887: the first dividend payment amounted to 12% plus a 2% bonus.[39] A 14% dividend payment in 1887 was followed by a 15% dividend in 1888 and a tripling of the share price to £3.15 by the end of September 1888.[40] It should be noted that the quoted dividend percentage was based on the initial issue value of the shares of £1 so the actual running yield was in the region of 5% in September 1888. The overwhelming success of the Guinness listing started a trend – drinks companies began raising outside equity finance and during 1888 *The Times* began showing the stock exchange prices for 'Brewers and Distilleries' as a discrete sector in their daily report on share prices. By 1890, there were 87 quoted brewing companies with issued share capital of £50 million valued at £70 million.[41] But the

---

[36] Ranald Michie, *The London Stock Exchange, A History* (Oxford University Press 1999) 94.

[37] *The Economist*, 23 October 1886.

[38] SR Dennison & Oliver McDonagh, *Guinness 1886–1939* (Cork University Press 2000) 22.

[39] SR Dennison & Oliver McDonagh, *Guinness 1886–1939* (Cork University Press 2000) 23.

[40] Dividend information taken from Guinness Annual Report dated 10 August 1888; share price taken from *The Times* for 29 September 1888.

[41] SR Dennison & Oliver McDonagh, *Guinness 1886–1939* (Cork University Press 2000) 23.

Guinness share offer also highlighted that the modern structure of companies whereby, in most case, ownership (by shareholders) is separate from control (by management) still had some way to go. At flotation in 1886, one-third of the ordinary shares had been reserved for Sir Edward Guinness, the chairman, but by February 1887 he had re-acquired his controlling interest by buying shares in the market, effectively taking back control of the company he had just floated.[42]

Although the securities market was changing only slowly, the direction of travel was very clear – as of 1893, ordinary shares of industrial companies represented only 2.5% of London Stock Exchange securities by value rising to 8% by 1913. At a broader level, this listing activity of the brewers in general and Guinness in particular provided a clear example of the development of capitalism as it moved from a system of private or family ownership to one which split entrepreneurship between ownership and control. Increasingly external shareholders would own a business but internal managers would run it. At the same time, investment companies had become firmly established with almost 50 in existence at the end of the 1880s. Most of these companies were investing in the secondary market so they were not supplying new capital direct to businesses. This represented a further tweak to capitalism by clearly subdividing ownership between partners, entrepreneurs or founding families and investment organisations. Chapter 2 showed that the early insurance companies oscillated between bank-related activities based on the direct supply of capital and gradually they shifted towards longer-term investing of surplus assets in quoted securities. The investment companies, on the other hand, were pure investing organisations. This separation between the supply of capital from the decision to invest represented a significant change in the operation of finance and this change ran in parallel with splitting control of companies between external ownership and internal management (Fig. 4.2).

The Edinburgh Investment Trust was one of the earliest institutional investors in ordinary shares. As mentioned, the first of many ordinary share purchased in 1889 by the Edinburgh Investment Trust was

---

[42] SR Dennison & Oliver McDonagh, *Guinness 1886–1939* (Cork University Press 2000) 23.

PROSPECTUS.

Messrs. BARING BROTHERS & CO. offer for Subscription the Capital under-
mentioned. The Subscription List will open on Monday, the 25th instant,
and will close on or before Tuesday, the 26th, at 4 p.m.

ARTHUR GUINNESS, SON & CO., LIMITED.

(Incorporated under the Companies' Acts, 1862 to 1886.)

SHARE CAPITAL, £4,500,000,

Debenture Stock, £1,500,000,

TO BE ISSUED AS FOLLOWS :—

Ordinary Shares (of £10 each)	£2,500,000
Preference Six per Cent. Shares (of £10 each) ...	2,000,000
Total Share Capital	£4,500,000
Debenture Stock, bearing Interest at Five per Cent. ...	1,500,000
(Redeemable at the Company's option after the expiration	
of 20 years from 1st January, 1887, at 110 per Cent.)	£6,000,000

Interest on the Debenture Stock will be payable 1st May and 1st November, the
first payment on 1st May, 1887. The Company will receive the profits of the business
from 1st October, 1886.

One-third of the present issue of Ordinary Share Capital (being about £800,000) is
reserved for the Vendor, who agrees to hold this amount for not less than five years, and
the remainder, together with the Preference Shares and the Debenture Stock, are now
offered severally for public subscription at par.

The payments for each class of security will be as follows :—

£5 per Cent	...	on Application.
£20 „	...	„ Allotment.
£25 „	...	„ 14th December, 1886.
£25 „	...	„ 10th January, 1887.
£25 „	...	„ 8th February, 1887.
£100 per Cent.		

The instalments may be paid up under discount at the rate of 4 per cent. per
annum on Allotment, or on any subsequent Tuesday or Friday.

The Allotment will be made as early as possible after the Subscription is closed,
and in cases where it is not practicable to make any allotment, the amount deposited
on application will be returned as soon as possible.

The failure to pay any instalment when due forfeits all previous payments.

Provisional Certificates will be issued as early as possible after Allotment, and
the Definitive Certificates when the payments have been completed.

The Debenture Stock will be secured by a Mortgage over the whole of the undertaking.

Trustees for Debenture Stockholders :—

THE RIGHT HONBLE. LORD REVELSTOKE. | THE RIGHT HONBLE. LORD HILLINGDON.
THE RIGHT HONBLE. D. R. PLUNKET, Q.C., M.P.

The Preference Shares will be entitled to a cumulative preferential dividend of
6 per cent., payable out of the profits of the Company, and will also be entitled to rank
on the property and assets of the Company, in preference to the ordinary shares.

DIRECTORS.

*SIR EDWARD CECIL GUINNESS, BART., *Chairman.*
CLAUDE GUINNESS, ESQ., *Managing Director.*
REGINALD B. GUINNESS, ESQ., Dublin.
VISCOUNT CASTLEROSSE, Killarney House, Ireland.
HENRY R. GLYN, ESQ., 67, Lombard Street, E.C.
HERMAN HOSKIER, ESQ., Director of the Union Bank of London, Limited.
JAMES R. STEWART, JUN., ESQ., (Messrs. STEWART & KINCAID), Dublin.
* Will join the Board after Allotment.

BANKERS.
MESSRS. GLYN, MILLS, CURRIE & CO.

SOLICITORS.
MESSRS. MARKBY, STEWART & Co., 57, Coleman Street, London, E.C.

AUDITORS.
MESSRS. TURQUAND, YOUNGS & Co., 41, Coleman Street, London, E.C.

SECRETARY.
C. THEOBALD, ESQ.

TEMPORARY OFFICES.
8, BISHOPSGATE STREET WITHIN, LONDON.

Fig. 4.2   Guinness Prospectus (front page), 1886

The Distillers Company.[43] Distillers was formed in 1877, based in Edinburgh, out of a disparate collection of Scotch distilleries. The initial attempt at a share placing and stock exchange listing in 1880 was largely unsuccessful and only about 10% of the initial shares were allotted. A London Stock Exchange listing was finally achieved in 1886 and the decision to invest in 1889 by the trust was well timed, or fortuitous. Profits at Distillers rose rapidly, by 9.9% per annum between 1890 and 1898, on the back of strong domestic consumption of spirits and gradually rising exports. The Edinburgh Investment Trust also had large holdings in the Holts Brewery Based in Manchester (still in existence today) and Parker Burslem Brewery (ceased brewing in 1963). So 'Brewers and Distillers' featured prominently among the early investments, all three stocks being among the ten largest equity holdings.[44] There were also some international equity investments, notably the overseas mining stocks, De Beers Diamond Mining and the Broken Hill Proprietary Mining Company (BHP).[45] These established mining businesses needed equity capital to fund long-term growth in output and represented a serious long-term investment opportunity compared to many of the highly speculative investments that have always been available in this sector. BHP was initially traded in Australia but by the 1890s about half the equity was owned by British investors and the majority of trading in the stock took place on the London Stock Exchange.[46] These were early indications that trading in securities markets was changing from bonds to equities, with ordinary shares in large established businesses being listed and traded in London. As an investing institution, the Edinburgh Investment Trust was at the forefront of these developments. By contrast, British life offices had only 3% invested in equities (ordinary shares) by 1913, while Foreign & Colonial only began investing in

---

[43] John Newlands, *The Edinburgh Investment Trust Celebrating 125 Years, 1889–2014* (pdf available on the Invescoperpetual website).

[44] John Newlands, *The Edinburgh Investment Trust Celebrating 125 Years, 1889–2014* (pdf available on the Invescoperpetual website).

[45] John Newlands, *The Edinburgh Investment Trust Celebrating 125 Years, 1889–2014* (pdf available on the Invescoperpetual website).

[46] Ranald Michie, *The Global Securities Market, A History* (Oxford University Press 2006) 106.

ordinary shares in the mid-1920s. The Edinburgh Investment Trust, therefore, as one of the earliest equity investors, led the way by investing in a range of ordinary shares in the UK and overseas. In the process, it helped to create the long-lived association between Scottish asset management companies and international equity investing.

4.4   The Power of Information: The First Scottish

The First Scottish broke completely new ground in the areas of research and analysis. Fleming in conjunction with the Trustees decided at the outset that access to good information was crucial in order to invest successfully. In turn, this meant they appreciated the importance of doing their own research and having an information advantage in comparison to other investors. The last sentence of the passage below specifically highlighted that London-based investors operated disadvantageously compared to local investors based in the USA. The thinking was explained in the 1873 Prospectus as follows:

> There is probably no field of investment wider, or combining in a greater degree the elements of security and profit than the United States, but the difficulties which individual investors in this country experience in obtaining reliable information regarding American securities prevent them availing themselves of the opportunities which they offer. . . . The investments will for the most part be made in the United States, where the securities can usually be had on much more favourable terms than in this country; and in their selection, and during the continuance of the trust, advantage will be had of the best information and advice obtainable there.[47]

Nor were these words from the Prospectus a simple marketing story written to dupe a gullible investing public. The Minute Book of the First Scottish dated 16 March 1873 recorded the following: 'It had

---

[47] *Scottish American Investment Trust Prospectus* 1 February 1873 (Dundee City Archive).

been contemplated for some time that the secretary [Fleming] should visit America in order to acquaint himself thoroughly with the United States investments…and it was thought advisable that he should make arrangements for at once proceeding to America.'[48] Apart from a major vote of confidence in the abilities of the 28 year-old Fleming, this also demonstrated unequivocally that the Trustees were serious about doing fundamental research and analysis.

The First Scottish had a more considered and also a more complex way of investing than hitherto. Fleming visited the entities in which the First Scottish would invest, and decisions on which stocks to buy were based on analysing and understanding the underlying businesses. Most English investors, such as Foreign & Colonial, tended to invest via the London Stock Exchange, buying London-quoted stocks from brokers that were denominated in sterling. The Scots however preferred to visit agents and businesses on the ground and they used local banks or brokers to execute transactions directly in foreign currency.[49] Fleming initiated this approach. He sailed to the USA on 15 March 1873 – this was his first research trip as an investor and the second of the 64 visits that he made to the USA over the next 50 years.[50] If each visits required travelling time of about 16 days, then Fleming would have spent several years of his life on ships just crossing the Atlantic. Fortunately for Fleming, the sailing time to cross the ocean fell from about 8 days in 1870, to only 5 days in 1900.[51] Fleming's March 1873 trip lasted about 2 months (his trip later in the same year would last 4 months) and he returned home on 10 May.[52] During the trip he went to Boston, Philadelphia and New

[48] *Scottish American Investment Trust Minute* Book, 16 March 1873 (Dundee City Archive).

[49] Lisa Giffen, *How Scots Financed the Modern World* (Luath 2009) 46.

[50] Jubilee speech by Robert Fleming to the 1923 (Dundee City Archive GB252/GD/EFM). He referred to crossing the Atlantic 128 times, which could be interpreted literally, but it is likely that this was 64 visits and 128 crossings.

[51] Hofstra University, *New York, Liner Transatlantic Crossing Times*, 1833–1952 (www.people. hofstra.edu/geotrans/linertransatlantic, website accessed 15 June 2016).

[52] Travelling internationally had its risks in the nineteenth century. The ship *Atlantic* sailed from Liverpool on 13 March 1873 but sank off Nova Scotia with the loss of 600 lives. According to his Jubilee speech in 1923, Fleming had nearly booked passage on the *Atlantic* but changed plans at the last minute and decided to travel to London instead.

York, meeting with Brown Brothers & Co., Kidder Peabody, and Maitland, Phelps & Co (principal brokers to the First Scottish). According to the Minutes of 20 May 1873, Fleming claimed only £80 in expenses for his entire trip of which he had received £25 cash in advance. The purpose of the trip had been to complete the investment of funds that had been subscribed in February 1873. Money for the First Scottish had been raised on a partly paid basis with £10 payable on application and allotment, with the balance of £90 payable in mid-April and mid-May 1873. Only a small number of investments had been made prior to Fleming's departure meaning that the bulk of the purchases were completed following his recommendations during this trip. The Trustees of the First Scottish were the ultimate decision-makers about what should be included in the portfolio but they and Fleming worked together closely as a team. Fleming was very influential in the search for sound investments based on detailed research into the financial health and prospects of individual companies so his knowledge of the American railroad market was very important but his judgement was probably more crucial. One of Fleming's letters, discussed at the Trustee meeting of 22 April 1873, showed the depth of knowledge that Fleming had rapidly accumulated.[53] He recommended five bonds with reasons for purchase clearly articulated. In the example of North Missouri First Mortgage 7% Bonds for example, Fleming wrote, 'This has been in trouble but is now in excellent condition. If you read carefully all through Poor's report (page 568) . . . the 1ˢᵗ Mortgage Bonds are really quite safe. Last year's net earnings were three times the amount of interest.'[54] Fleming was doing detailed research on the ground, providing thorough analysis and enabling the Trustees in Dundee to make informed discussions. This was a sound model for investment decision-making.

In the Minute Book, on 19 May 1873, it was reported that all but £40,000 (just over 10%) of the capital of the First Scottish had been invested. An outline plan would have been agreed with the Trustees prior to Fleming's departure but timing and price were largely left to Fleming's discretion. It appears there was a very good working

---

[53] *Scottish American Investment Trust Minute Book, first issue*, 22 April 1873 (Dundee City Archive).
[54] *Scottish American Investment Trust Minute Book, first issue*, 22 April 1873 (Dundee City Archive).

relationship between Fleming on the ground in the USA and the Trustees back home in Dundee. John Guild was chairman of the First Scottish and had interests in shipping and insurance. He deserves much credit for the culture and working practices that were established in Dundee with both Fleming and his fellow Trustees. Guild was ideally suited for the role, described thus: 'A man whom it was safe to follow in any undertaking or investment . . . uniting to a characteristically cautious disposition abilities of a high order in financial affairs, untiring energy and a scrupulously close attention to any interests entrusted to him'.[55] There were torrents of communications from Fleming to Dundee and the Trustees, and, according to their minute books, the Trustees, seemed to meet almost daily throughout March and April 1873. According to the first Minute Book, the Trustees met on 23 separate occasions in March 1873 alone. All these Dundonians – Fleming on the ground and the Trustees back at HQ led by John Guild – had an extremely strong work ethic and excellent attention to detail. In this respect the founders of The First Scottish thought and acted differently to the London-based grandees at Foreign & Colonial. The Dundonians were merchants, industrialists and self-made men with strong commercial backgrounds. They were not only hard working but also very interested in the day-to-day operation of their investment vehicle. Compared to Foreign & Colonial, it was managed more professionally and with greater thoroughness. In comparison, the Londoners associated with Foreign & Colonial were a patrician mixture of aristocratic politicians and professional men from legal and banking backgrounds. They created a framework at Foreign & Colonial based on a buy-and-hold approach and annual meetings but then delegated the daily activity to administrators. While Foreign & Colonial had a rational approach to investing, it would be the Scottish model of asset management, initiated by the First Scottish (and SAINTS), based on small teams working closely together making investment decisions based on detailed research, that would represent the future path of the asset management profession.

---

[55] *Dundee Yearbook 1892*, Obituary Notices, John Guild.

Following another round of fund-raising for a new vehicle, the Second Scottish American Investment Trust, Fleming was in a position to make further investments, but this time the market conditions were very different owing to a financial crash in September 1873 followed by a major depression in the USA. A similar process to that employed in the spring of 1873 was followed when investing the £400,000 of funds raised on 18 September 1873 with the launch of the Second Issue of the Scottish American Investment Trust. But this time, investing the monies was more complicated owing to the failure of America's largest bank, Jay Cooke & Co. of Philadelphia, which led to a bank run in the USA resulting in turmoil not only in the financial system but also in the US railroad industry. According to one account of the 1873 crash (Kindleberger), this is considered to be the first major international financial crisis because 'it erupted in Austria and Germany in May, spread to Italy, Holland and Belgium, leapt the Atlantic in September' when German banks withdrew money from American railroads.[56] When Jay Cooke collapsed, there was a financial panic on Wall Street which precipitated difficulties for commercial businesses more widely in the USA; of the USA's 364 railroad companies, 89 went bankrupt and by the autumn of 1874, as many as 108 railroad companies had defaulted on their bond payments.[57] Not for the first time or the last, a banking failure precipitated an economic crisis. During the Civil War, Jay Cooke had been the government's chief financier: subsequently it moved into railroad financing. The bank became over-extended with its railway loans – it was specifically involved in the financing of the second transcontinental railroad, the Northern Pacific – at a time when financing from Europe, particularly Germany, was beginning to dry up owing to a property crisis in Europe. The Northern Pacific filed for bankruptcy, which in turn brought down Jay Cooke which had lent too much at a time when market liquidity dried up. This was a classic banking failure brought on by excess credit and too little liquidity and the consequences were far-reaching. The failure of Jay Cooke sparked a

---

[56] Charles P. Kindleberger, *Manias, Panics and Crashes* (Macmillan 1978) 121.

[57] *The Panic of 1873* (www.pbs.org/wgbh/americanexperience, website accessed 29 May 2016).

financial panic in the USA resulting in the New York Stock Exchange closing for 10 days from 20 September 1873.[58] This was the first time in its history that the exchange had been unable to open its doors. *The New York Times* illustrated the scale of the problems for US finance companies – 18 banks and 73 members of the stock exchange failed.[59] Another 5,000 commercial companies collapsed, resulting in a severe recession which lasted until March 1879, 65 months from peak to trough, and high levels of unemployment. Against this challenging backdrop, capital supplied by Fleming from his Scottish investment trust would have appeared extremely attractive, even in the secondary market because this money, long-term in nature with a 10-year time horizon, was predicated on an investment mentality rather than a speculative one. This type of funding was much higher quality than equivalent money from US and continental European banks with their much shorter-term focus and need for liquidity. This is, of course, one of the main attributes of asset management; it could and should, by being patient, take a long-term view to the ultimate benefit of both investees and investors. *The New York Times* lambasted the banks at the time as follows:

> The banks have been departing from their legitimate line of business. There has been a railroad mania, and the banks have lent large sums of money on railroad bonds, to the exclusion of the merchants. If these banks had confined themselves to the transactions which come properly within their scope, we should have seen no trouble in Wall St this week. They have practically gone into the business of contractors, brokers and speculators.[60]

The pattern of investing the assets for the Second Issue of the Scottish American Investment Trust was similar to that of the First Issue. The Trustees made some initial investments from their Dundee base, though this time funds were partly invested through London owing to the problems with distressed banks in the USA, and the bulk of

---

[58] Edward Chancellor, *Devil Take the Hindmost* (Pan 1999) 185.

[59] *New York Times*, 14 October 2008, *New York and the Panic of 1873*.

[60] *New York Times*, 20 September 1873.

the money would be invested after the end of the year during Fleming's third visit to the USA. The timing was propitious because high-grade railroad bonds yields stood at 6.5% in November 1873, up from 6.2% at the beginning of the year.[61] This time Fleming was in the USA for 4 months between December 1873 and April 1874, sailing to New York but travelling far and wide, visiting St. Louis, Houston and even going as far as California because 'There is a difficulty in getting good Gold Bonds of which the Trustees are desirous of having a fair share to guard against the adverse currency legislation. It may be necessary to go across the Rocky Mountains'.[62] As noted earlier, communication in those days was by telegram – 'cable', as it was called. Fleming, as a trained book-keeper and canny Scot, created a sensible method to minimise telegram costs: 'I remember making a cable code to economise on transatlantic transmissions, cable messages cost £1 per word in those days against a shilling (£0.05) today, the word which signified the sentence, "All the coupons due this month have been duly paid" was "Miraculous"'.[63] Happily, Fleming was able to use his code word on 3 January 1874 when he confirmed to the Trustees that all the coupons due on 1 January had been paid. This was extremely reassuring following the widespread bank and railroad company failures at the end of 1873 (Fig. 4.3).

As noted, the purpose of Fleming's trip to the USA in December 1873 was to organise the latest tranche of new investment of funds from the Second Issue of the Scottish American Investment Trust. In addition, the Trustees wished to obtain some reassurance, a second opinion, that the initial investments made by the earlier First Issue of spring 1873 were performing acceptably. Fleming therefore was instructed to obtain a report from H. V. Poor, the editor of the *Railroad Manual* in the USA. Poor was commissioned to write a report on each of the securities bought in the first issue as follows: 'He (the Secretary) was also instructed

---

[61] *National Bureau of Economic Research*, Chapter 13. This bond yield of 6.5% looks to be somewhat low given the scope and impact of the financial panic.
[62] Lisa Giffen, *How Scots Financed the Modern World* (Luath 2009) 47.
[63] *Jubilee speech by Robert Fleming* to the 1923 AGM (Dundee City Archive GB252/GD/EFM). The cost of £1 per word in 1874 equates to about £75 in 2016 money, so it was still expensive to use the telegraph even though this cost had reduced rapidly since 1866.

Fig. 4.3   The 1873 Crash, cartoon, Leslie's, 1873

to furnish a list of the securities held by the Trust to Mr H V Poor- the compiler of the Railroad Manual – and to commission him to make a report on each security and on the whole direct to the Trust in Dundee, his fee for same not to exceed $100.'[64] The comments by Poor were recorded in the minutes of January 1874 as follows:

> We have carefully examined the list you handed us of securities held by the Scottish American Investment Trust and find them all to be of the highest character. They are all readily saleable in our markets (with the exception perhaps of the Marquette City Bonds). The selection [of securities] has been made with more than ordinary prudence, or perhaps we may say that it is very remarkable that in a list embracing so many securities and so large in the aggregate, there does not appear to be one about which any anxiety whatever need be felt, even in such a panic as that which the country has just passed through.[65]

This report is remarkable, less for the complimentary words than what it tells us of the thought processes of Fleming and the Trustees.[66] It was perhaps the first piece of independent research to be commissioned by an asset manager looking to extract specialist information from a knowledgeable industry source. In this case, the industry source, Poor of the *Railroad Manual*, had an independent view and no financial interest linked into the success of any particular railroad bond, which might have been the problem for a bank or a stockbroker. Incidentally, Poor's firm developed in due course to become a rating agency for corporate bonds and municipal securities (Poor's Publishing Co.), duly becoming Standard & Poors in 1941 after a merger. However, in the context of 1873 and the development

---

[64] *Scottish American Investment Trust Minute Book, First Issue* 10 December 1873 (Dundee City Archive).

[65] *Scottish American Investment Trust Minute Book, First Issue* 26 January 1874 (Dundee City Archive).

[66] In practice the report by Poor of January 1874 was somewhat optimistic. By the middle of 1875 three railroads had defaulted on the payment of interest on bonds held by the First Issue. The defaulters were St Louis and Iron Mountain, the Erie Railway and the Houston and Great Northern Railroad.

of asset management, commissioning a specialist report demonstrates unequivocally that Fleming and the Trustees were thinking deeply about the nature of investment and specifically about the collection and analysis of information. This manifested itself in several ways: in the aspirations expressed in the initial Prospectus; Fleming's visits to meet with specific businesses and obtain information; and, with the report by Poor's, specialist research sources were used to validate it. Overall, the First Scottish avoided the worst problems in America during the mid-1870s at a time when 40% of all US railroad bonds were in default; that was no mean achievement.[67]

Did any of this research, analysis and due diligence matter in the world of the 1870s? Absolutely yes because London financial institutions were often greedy and lazy whereas the evolving financial system in the USA was corrupt, embodied by the infamous 'Robber Barons'. Investing was an especially risky business in the latter part of the nineteenth century as highlighted clearly by the investigations of the Select Committee of Parliament, established in March 1875 to investigate the 'Loans to Foreign States'. This parliamentary enquiry arose directly from the financial problems in the USA and Europe from late 1873 onwards and focused particularly on a number of dubious loans that had been raised in London by central American states such as Honduras, Paraguay and Costa Rica. In July 1875, both *The Times* ('boldness and assurance . . . working in concert') and *The Economist* ('cheated the English public also – and on that upon the largest scale – those in whose name they borrowed') were scathing. Below is an extract from an interview between the parliamentary Select Committee and Samuel Herman de Zoete, chairman of the Stock Exchange which highlighted that the stockbrokers did little apart from selling their wares and certainly nothing that could be described as scrutiny:

Q. Do you make any enquiry whatever as to the probability of the State repaying the loan; does that come within the scope of your investigation?
A. No

---

[67] Alexander Nairn, *Engines That Move Markets* (Wiley 2002) 63.

Q. Neither as to the reasonableness or unreasonableness of the amount?

A. No

Q. Do you require any proofs as to the bona fides of the allotment?

A. I cannot say that we do; we take the assurance of the contractor that such and such an amount has been allotted; we do not ask for proof; we have no means of getting the proof...

Q. Am I right in assuming that if you were to make a more searching examination, you would be taking upon yourself too heavy a responsibility?

A. I'm afraid we should never get through the business.[68]

The attitude of the stock exchange – *caveat emptor* – was also highlighted in 1876 by one of its members when he described the unpleasant nature of the stock exchange. He said,

> We, the Stock Exchange, never asked you to buy a bad security. If you thought fit to venture your money and have lost it, so much the worse for you and your advisers. The [London] Stock Exchange is a channel, not a filter, it argues no faith in the construction of an aqueduct and the water it conveys is often dirty.

Using an even more colourful analogy, he asserted, 'A Stock Exchange restricted to investment business [i.e. as opposed to speculation] would be as useful and as popular as a public house [a bar] licensed only for ginger beer.'[69] From these comments it is clear that broking and raising money for loans was a speculative, murky business in the 1870s. It was invaluable therefore that Fleming and the asset management profession could begin to distinguish between rogue propositions, on the one hand, and reasonable investments, on the other, by doing their own research and analysis. But more importantly, this additional level of scrutiny and

---

[68] David Kynaston, *The City of London Vol 1, A World of Its Own 1815–1890* (Pimlico 1994) 270.

[69] David Kynaston, *The City of London Vol 1, A World of Its Own 1815–1890* (Pimlico 1994) 275. In this passage, Kynaston is referring to Charles Branch, a partner in a stockbroking firm writing in Fraser's Magazine, 1876, *A Defence of the Stock Exchange*.

professionalism created a different mind-set based on long-term capital funding for business and value creation for investors. However, this could only be achieved because Fleming had a clear understanding of the role of management and the capital structures of the companies in which his trusts were investors. He was willing to represent investors in relatively complex and detailed financial re-structuring discussions so demonstrating stewardship. This was the exercise of responsible owner-ship and investor scrutiny which introduced an additional control on the behaviour of management and their banking advisers. There were several instances of this type of behaviour by Fleming, for example, with the Erie Railroad and the Baltimore and Ohio Railroad in the 1870s.

With Erie in 1875, Fleming needed to work with (or against) an inept re-organisation committee which had superseded a fraudulent management.[70] This committee recommended Erie should go into receivership but Fleming and other British holders of the bonds fought a stout campaign on behalf of the rights of the holders of the first issue of Erie mortgage bonds. They argued for equity rather than debt to be raised and a re-structuring of the business, both financially and operationally. Fleming worked on this problem for almost a year and was given leave of absence by his Trustees to concentrate exclusively on the matter from January to March 1876. As pointed out by Fleming's biographer, 'It [Erie] involved not only an examination of the financial position and an assessment of the state of operational efficiency [by Fleming], but also detailed and protracted negotiations with members of a high-powered team, who often viewed the problem from a totally different angle.'[71] This type of engagement was taking Fleming and asset managers deeply inside the companies in which they were investing. It was also an indication that market manipulation in the USA was being tempered. Since the 1850s, The Erie Railroad had been known as 'the Scarlet Woman of Wall Street' owing to frequent manipulation of the share price based on combinations of speculators, short-sellers (whose activities were known as 'the partridge trick'), artificially

---

[70] The First Scottish sold its holdings in Erie at End-March 1875 because Fleming was concerned about possible default, which subsequently occurred. See Bill Smith, *Robert Fleming 1845–1933* (Whittingehame House 2000) page 53.
[71] Bill Smith, *Robert Fleming 1845–1933* (Whittingehame House 2000) 53.

low prices provided by fraudulent stockbrokers ('wash trades'), together with false rumours in the press and corrupt directors.[72] The market was rigged so much in favour of insiders that 'the behaviour of speculating (sic) directors corrupted the relationship between directors and shareholders (especially the British shareholders who, on the other side of the Atlantic), were unable to influence events and were led like lambs to the slaughter'.[73] Fleming and the First Scottish not only survived and made money in this environment, which was heavily skewed towards insiders, but also began the long process of beginning to improve standards. As Daniel Drew, one of the notorious market operators of the 1860s in the USA and also a director of the Erie Railroad said 'anybody who plays the stock market and is not an insider is like a man buying a cow in the moonlight'.[74] The Erie Railroad infamously created the legends of the American 'Robber Barons' which pitted Drew, Fisk and Gould against Vanderbilt. Price and ownership of the Erie Railroad were constantly being manipulated and because the company repeatedly fell into bankruptcy, 'the outside investor who bought at pretty much any time after the early 1860s had little prospect of making capital returns (owing to fraud and a dodgy balance sheet)'.[75] Fleming fought back against rigged markets on behalf of institutional investors.

In another instance, on behalf of the Baltimore and Ohio Railroad, Fleming took on the banking house of Morgan regarding the terms of a proposed new issue of bonds. Fleming was certain that the accounts were flawed based on an earlier problem he had previously identified with the Philadelphia and Reading railroad whereby a subsidiary was charged excessive loan costs in order to support an unrealistically high-dividend payout on the shares of the holding company. Fleming had asked the banker JS Morgan to clarify the situation with the company. Morgan not only failed to resolve the query, but then inflamed the situation when he told Fleming that his bank would be arranging a new bond issue out of London for

---

[72] Edward Chancellor, *Devil Take the Hindmost* (Pan 1999) 171 – a comprehensive description is provided of these dubious dealing practises.
[73] Edward Chancellor, *Devil Take the Hindmost* (Pan 1999) 173.
[74] Edward Chancellor, *Devil Take the Hindmost* (Pan 1999) 167.
[75] Alexander Nairn, *Engines that Move Markets* (Wiley 2002) 47.

Baltimore and Ohio. Fleming, deeply incensed, did two things: he threatened to write about the problem in the *Railway News,* a journal for whom he regularly wrote articles; and second, he raised the matter of his business dealings with Morgan in delicate but unambiguous terms: 'My business relations with your firm have been pleasant enough and I wish them to remain so, and, supposing you [Morgan] may be embarking on this loan [for Baltimore and Ohio] I have therefore taken this opportunity of explaining my position, confidentially, of course, in case you had any views to express.'[76] In this instance Fleming was attempting to hold to account the banking advisers. According to one observer, 'Pressure and involvement from European investors after 1877 created a more stable regime (for pricing and investors).'[77] From the outset in 1873, it appears that the Trustees of the First Scottish, and Fleming in particular, had a good grasp of the financial characteristics of the companies in which they invested and that they were prepared to spread their network in the search for information and to flex their muscles as engaged investors. This helped them avoid the worst of the defaults. Subsequently this investment approach developed into a deeper understanding about the role of company management, the behaviour of banks and the rights of investors. In each of these areas one can see important aspects of improved accountability influenced by a developing asset management profession.

4.5   Investment Performance: The First Scottish

Fleming relinquished his role as secretary of the First Scottish in 1890 following his decision to live and work in London, though he continued to maintain an office in Dundee. The Minutes record that it was however agreed that he would retain an honorary position as 'Advising Secretary' in order to maintain a connection with the company.[78] So, in assessing Fleming's success as an investor it is appropriate to evaluate the

---

[76] Bill Smith, *Robert Fleming 1845–1933* (Whittingehame House 2000) 56.

[77] Alexander Nairn, *Engines That Move Markets* (Wiley 2002) 49.

[78] *Scottish American Investment Trust, Minute Book* 5, March 1890 (Dundee City Archive).

period from 1873 to 1890 for the First Scottish, the first of three issues.[79] As of May 1890 the value of the trust company was £529,000 an appreciation of 76% on the initial capital of £300,000 producing an annualised capital growth of about 3.3% per annum. In addition, initial dividends were paid at a level of 6%, then rising to 8.25%. So, the total return (capital plus income) for investors over this 17-year period was in the region of 10% per annum. Two other trusts, the Second and Third Scottish American Trusts, produced similar returns to the First Scottish. UK government long bonds (irredeemable Consols) were yielding about 3.2% in 1873 falling to 2.9% in 1890 meaning that an equivalent UK government bond would have produced a return of a little over 3.5% (income of about 3% with a capital uplift over the 17 years of 12.1%).[80] Over these 17 years, the First Scottish produced a return that was 6.5% per annum better than the UK government bond return. These were tremendous results for investors, not only because the alternatives produced much lower returns but also given the very difficult environment in America between 1873 and 1879. Similar to Foreign & Colonial which struggled to achieve the expected level of investment returns in its first 10 years, these performance results show the benefits of thinking long-term. The First Scottish was launched just as the USA suffered one of its worst financial crises followed by its longest recession. Despite this, the investments provided excellent long-term returns to the investors, far in excess of anything available in the domestic market.

The investors in the First Scottish were also rewarded for taking risk given that both the economy and the currency of the USA were in a parlous state owing to the impact of the Civil War so the timing of these investments into the USA was courageous. The Union suspended gold payments at the end of 1861 and only resumed convertibility on 1 January 1879.[81] This return to the Gold Standard benefitted Scottish

---

[79] Bill Smith, *Robert Fleming 1845–1933* (Whittingehame House 2000) 100.

[80] *National Bureau of Economic Research, Chapter 13, Interest Rates.*

[81] *Specie Payments, Suspension and Resumption of* (www.encyclopedia.com, website accessed 26 October 2016).

investors by between 10% and 16% according to one estimate so it provided a very useful one-off boost to investment performance.[82] Compared to Foreign & Colonial which had a diversified global portfolio, the First Scottish was more risky in terms of its narrower geographic focus and its emphasis on railroad bonds, so, in theory, investors required to be rewarded for taking a higher level of risk. Following the successful completion of the Atlantic telegraphic cable link, Fleming and his colleagues were also the first organised, foreign institutional investors into this market so perhaps they gained from their ingenuity by being very early and thus able to exploit one of the great investment opportunities of the last 150 years. Finally, the First Scottish had a robust structure for making investment decisions which provided it with a distinct competitive advantage compared with many other market participants, including Foreign & Colonial. Coinciding with Fleming's move to London, November 1890 produced the Barings Bank crisis – another timely reminder that savers, with a broad choice of different investment trusts, now had a route for their savings outside of banks. Barings had lent large sums to South America during the 1880s but it was highly leveraged and a combination of a failing Argentinean banking system and unmarketable loans resulted in Barings running out of funds.[83] It was not however insolvent and the Bank of England put together a rescue package to tide Barings over its short-term difficulties.[84] It is suggested (Turner) that Barings was not systemically important but, irrespective in this instance, a major run on this bank was avoided and there was no collapse. That had to wait until 1995 when Leeson broke the bank.

Finally, it is also noteworthy that the fees for managing The First Scottish were extremely low which is entirely consistent with the reputation of the residents of Dundee for being careful with their money. According to the Prospectus for First Scottish, 'The expenses of the

---

[82] Mira Wilkins, *The History of Foreign Investment in the United States to 1914* (Harvard University Press 1989) 495.

[83] Ashraf Mahate, *Contagion Effects of Three Late Nineteenth Century British Banking Failures* (Business and Economic History 1994).

[84] John Turner, *Banking in Crisis* (Cambridge University Press 2014) 155.

management of the Trust are limited to a sum not exceeding £1,000 per annum'.[85] So, given £300,000 was raised, the annual management fee was fixed at a maximum cash sum of 0.33% of the assets. This fee was even lower than the similar fee of 0.5% per annum charged by Foreign & Colonial (again fixed as a cash charge not a percentage charge against the value of the assets). Note also that as a fixed fee in monetary terms, the actual percentage charge would have diminished if underlying values increased. So if the First Scottish achieved a return of about 10% per annum over the first 17 years of its life, about 97% of this return, or value added, was delivered to the investors with less than 3% going to the asset manager, Trustees and directors. Therefore, and quite rightly, most of the outperformance generated by the First Scottish went into the pockets of the investors rather than the asset manager.

4.6   Concluding Remarks

The First Scottish was the first British investment vehicle to identify and successfully exploit the enormous investment opportunity that was the USA, the great emerging market of the late nineteenth century and about to become the world's industrial powerhouse. The Trustees in general and Fleming in particular had an extremely clear understanding about the importance of information in the context of asset management. Fleming showed considerable energy and financial acumen in finding and then analysing potential investments. This was done at a time when the London Stock Exchange was as murky as a London sewer and American exchanges were even worse, given the behaviour of the 'robber barons'. The Trustees and Fleming introduced additional levels of research, analysis and scrutiny into the asset management process. This not only benefitted their shareholders, but it also created additional checks and balances on company directors, asset valuations and on the

---

[85] *Prospectus of the Scottish American Investment Trust*, 10 February 1873 (Dundee City Archive).

marketing of new investments by banks and stockbrokers. SAINTS also adopted a fundamental, research-based approach to investment decision-making. The Edinburgh Investment Trust was an innovative early investor into ordinary shares and all three of these investment companies had a strong ethos of international investing. This helped to give British asset management a distinctly Scottish character and further developed the idea of a profession quite distinct from banking and stockbroking. These Scottish investors also moved asset management forward, beyond the original administrative approach offered by Foreign & Colonial. At a regional level Dundee became an important financial services centre and in many ways, the hard-wording, cautious and tenacious jute merchants from Dundee were the archetypal canny Scottish investors. At a personal level, Fleming's success showed that a smart boy from an underprivileged background, with a modicum of education but possessing great drive and financial acumen could succeed in the world of asset management. Asset management is an entirely merito-cratic activity, occasionally requiring a little luck at the right time, in which the most able should flourish. Fleming showed this was indeed possible. By the time he died he was a very wealthy man and both he and his heirs, during and after his life, have been extremely generous benefactors, making gifts to charities based in Dundee, supporting education at University College Dundee and of particular note, just before Robert's death, a huge donation made to the city of Dundee itself to build almost 400 new houses in an area today still called 'Fleming Gardens'. Finally, perhaps most importantly for his own self-esteem, the University of St Andrews awarded Robert Fleming an honorary doctorate in 1928 at the age of 83.[86] This recognition by a leading academic institution must have been particularly special to the poor, local boy with a good grasp of arithmetic who had left school at 13 years of age.

---

[86] The University of St Andrews included University College, Dundee under its auspices until 1967, at which point the University of Dundee was established as a separate entity. University College, Dundee was created in 1881 owing to the generosity of the Baxter family, principally Mary Ann Baxter, sister to Edward Baxter. (www.wikivisually.com/wiki/Mary_Ann_Baxter; website accessed 15 October 2016).

Bibliography

Primary Sources

The Dundee City Council Archives and Record Centre holds information about Robert Fleming and the minute books of the Scottish American Investment Trust. These minute books are legible, comprehensive and in very good condition.

Books

Edward Chancellor, *Devil Take the Hindmost* (Pan 1999)

Francois Crouzet, *The Victorian Economy* (Routledge 2005)

Lance Davis and Robert Cull, *International Capital Markets, Domestic Capital Markets and American Economic Growth 1820–1914*, in Cambridge Economic History of the US Vol 2 ed. Engermann and Gallman (Cambridge University Press 2000)

SR Dennison and Oliver McDonagh, *Guinness 1886–1939* (Cork University Press 2000)

Albert Fishlow, Internal Transportation in the Nineteenth and Early Twentieth Centuries, in *Cambridge Economic History of the US* Vol 2 ed. Engermann and Gallman (Cambridge University Press 2000)

Lisa Giffen, *How Scots Financed the Modern World* (Luath 2009)

JC Gilbert, *A History of Investment Trusts in Dundee* (PS King & Son 1939)

K. Theodore Hoppen, *The Mid-Victorian Generation, 1846–1886* (Clarendon Press 2000)

Charles Kindleberger, *Manias, Panics and Crashes* (Macmillan 1978)

David Kynaston, *The City of London Volume 4: A World of Its Own, 1815 to 1890* (Pimlico 2002)

Ranald Michie, *The London and New York Stock Exchanges* 1850–1914 (Allen & Unwin 1987)

Ranald Michie, *The London Stock Exchange, A History* (Oxford University Press 1999)

Ranald Michie, *The Global Securities Market, A History* (Oxford University Press 2006)

Charles W. Munn, *Investing for Generations, A History of Alliance Trust* (Dundee University Press 2012)

Alexander Nairn, *Engines that Move Markets* (Wiley 2002)

John Newlands, *Put Not Your Trust in Money* (Association of Investment Trust Companies 1997)

Bill Smith, *Robert Fleming 1845–1933* (Whittingehame House 2000)

John Turner, *Banking in Crisis* (Cambridge University Press 2014)

Mira Wilkins, *The History of Foreign Investment in the United States to 1914* (Harvard University Press 1989)

Norman Watson, *Dundee: A Short History* (Black & White 2006)

Articles, Journals, Pamphlets, Websites, etc.

Graeme G. Acheson, Christopher Coyle, and John Turner, Happy Hour Followed by Hangover: Financing the UK Brewery Industry, 1880–1913 (*Business History* 58/5, 2016)

The Panic of 1873 (www.pbs.org)

Dundee Yearbook 1892, Obituary Notices, John Guild

The Economist

Education Scotland, Dundee's Jute Mills (www.educationscotland.gov.uk)

Encycopedia.com, Specie payments, suspension and resumption of (www.encyclopedia.com)

Kenneth Garbade and William Silber, Technology, Communication and the Performance of Financial Markets: 1840–1975 (*The Journal of Finance* 33/3, 1978)

Christopher Hoag, The Atlantic Telegraph Cable and Capital Market Information Flows (*The Journal of Economic History* 66/2, 2006)

New York, *Liner Transatlantic Crossing Times, 1833–1952* (www.people.hofstra.edu/geotrans/linertransatlantic)

James B. Jefferys, *Business Organisation in Great Britain 1856–1914* (Arno 1977) PhD University of London, 1938

David Luck, *Scotland's 100 Oldest Companies, The Edinburgh Investment Trust* (Business Archives Council of Scotland, May 2011)

Ashraf Mahate, Contagion Effects of Three Late Nineteenth Century British Banking Failures (*Business and Economic History* 23/1, 1994)

National Bureau for Economic Research, Chapter 13, Interest Rates (www.nber.org/databases/macrohistory/contents/chapter13)

New York Times

John Newlands, *The Edinburgh Investment Trust Celebrating 125 Years, 1889–2014* (pdf available on the Invescoperpetual website)

Paul Romer, *Why, Indeed in America?* (NBER January 1996)

Janette Rutterford, Learning from One Another's Mistakes: Investment Trusts in the UK and US, 1868–1940 (*Financial History Review 16/2*, 2009)

Claire Swan, *Dundee as a Centre of Financial Management* (PhD, University of Dundee, 2009)

University of Groningen, Madison Project (www.ggdc.net/maddison/maddison-project)

Marc Weidenmier, *Money and Finance in the Confederate States of America* (www.eh.net)

Ronald Weir, *A History of the Scottish American Investment Company, 1873–1973* (The Scottish American Investment Company 1973)

Mary Ann Baxter (www.wikivisually.com/wiki/Mary_Ann_Baxter)

5

Life Office Investment 1900–1960
and John Maynard Keynes

This chapter considers the asset management activities of life offices in
the first half of the twentieth century and within that principally the
period from 1921 to 1938 when John Maynard Keynes was chairman of
the National Mutual Life Assurance Society (the 'National Mutual'). It
continues from where Chapter 2 finished in about 1900. The intention
is to place Keynes' contribution in a wider context. Chapter 2 covered
the changes to financial markets, the growth of insurance companies and
the development of their investment policies; this one will focus much
more on asset management and its evolution. Life offices will still be the
focus owing to the size of their investment portfolios, their ability to
invest for the long-term and because this was a period of change in their
investment behaviour. Keynes, as a director of two insurance companies
during the inter-war years, challenged conventional thinking about
investment and stressed the importance of asset management as a discrete activity. Consequently, he accelerated the pace of change within
the asset management profession generally and life offices, specifically,
improved their investment capabilities. His ingenious proposition was
that life offices, particularly mutual companies, had an opportunity to

© The Author(s) 2017   **143**
N.E. Morecroft, *The Origins of Asset Management*
from 1700 to 1960, Palgrave Studies in the History of Finance,
DOI 10.1007/978-3-319-51850-3_5

become the dominant institutions responsible for middle-class savings within Britain but, to achieve this, they needed to become much more proficient at asset management. Most life offices improved their investment expertise during the 1920s and, consequently, they were better equipped to deal with the significant investment challenges thrown at them during the 1930s and 1940s. Keynes had definitely provided them with a blueprint for success; the question is how much did they follow his lead? While life offices strengthened their asset management capabilities, it is debateable whether enough of them had gone fast enough or far enough by 1960 to compete effectively with the new breed of unit trust and pension fund managers who were emerging at that juncture. The proposition is that Keynes beneficially influenced the path of asset management after 1919, particularly within life offices, but life offices could have been more successful as investing institutions had they listened to Keynes more carefully and acted more decisively.

5.1   1900–1920: Change but No Change

5.1.1   Life Office Investment: 1900–1920

The long nineteenth-century decline in government bond yields came to an end in 1897: yields bottomed at 2.4% and then rose to 5.8% shortly after the end of the First World War.[1] In 1900, life offices on average had a meagre 2% invested in government debt: this represented a major success for their asset allocation policies after 1815 as they had moved into higher yielding areas and created diversified portfolios.[2] But by 1920, owing to the impact of the 1914–1918 war, government bond holdings had risen to 32% of life office assets, back to levels seen 70 years earlier.[3] On a short-term investment view,

---

[1] *National Bureau of Economic Research, Chapter 13, Interest Rates.*
[2] Mae Baker and Michael Collins, *The Asset Composition of British Life Insurance Firms, 1900–1965* (Financial History Review 10, 2003).
[3] Mae Baker and Michael Collins, *The Asset Composition of British Life Insurance Firms, 1900–1965* (Financial History Review 10, 2003).

leaving aside overseas liabilities, this was not a problem: first, as will be explained, insurance companies had not been treated unfairly in 1915/ 1916 when obliged to buy government 5% War Loan; second, the timing of the switch out of North American railroad bonds was relatively fortuitous as prices were high; and, most importantly, government bonds performed well in the 1920s with yields of 5% in 1920 falling only to 4.3% by 1930.[4] However, by then, there was a problem looming. The depression produced more intense deflationary pressures, a governmental policy of 'cheap money' and falling yields. In the late 1920s the gross yield on life fund investments exceeded 6% but was less than 3% for 3 years in the mid-1930s – a level which made it difficult for life offices to meet the expectations of their policyholders.[5] The investment challenge for insurance companies had not yet arrived by 1920 but did after 1929. Most investors could muddle through in the 1920s with high and gently falling government bond yields, but that was no longer viable in the next decade.

During the First World War, insurance companies were forced buyers of British government stock as the National Debt mushroomed.[6] The Treasury, following a suggestion proffered by the Prudential, prepared schemes for utilising the Canadian and US investments of insurance companies to finance war spending.[7] The process of liquidating assets was decentralised so that individual insurance companies sold their North American investments, repatriated the proceeds into sterling and then lent the money to the government through immediate re-investment into government bonds. In practice, the insurance companies were cajoled into action by the government by means of a 5% surtax on dividends levied for non-cooperation with the

---

[4] *Barclays Equity Gilt Study 2012.*
[5] *Barclays Equity Gilt Study 2012.*
[6] Peter Scott, *Towards the Cult of the Equity? Insurance Companies and the Inter-war Capital Markets* (The Economic History Review Feb 2002).
[7] The idea originated from George May at the Prudential in the early part of 1915 having been seconded to the Treasury. The Prudential was paid the full market value for its dollar securities and the exercise, which completed in the summer of 1915, was adjudged a success. The scheme was then applied to other British insurance companies from January 1916 onwards. See, Laurie Dennett, *A Sense of Security* (Granta 1998), 206.

voluntary proposal.[8] Intriguingly, Keynes was at the Treasury at this juncture and participated in discussion with both Marks of the National Mutual and Dickson of Standard Life about the tax treatment of life company profits from their foreign investments.[9] Marks was chair of the English Life Offices Association and Dickson his equivalent in Scotland. Keynes, therefore, would have gained insights into life offices and their investments, while both Marks and Dickson would have got to know Keynes; this would be relevant in subsequent developments during the 1920s, when both the National Mutual and Standard Life were in the vanguard of improving their asset management capabilities. The upshot in 1916 was that the overseas investments of insurance companies were swapped into UK government bonds, so life office ownership of government bonds increased from 1% of their assets in 1913 to 32%, or £700 million, by 1920.[10] Scottish Widows conformed to this pattern of behaviour. In 1913, it held most of its investments in debentures and mortgages with less than 1% in government bonds.[11] During 1916, it sold American securities, transferred US dollars into pounds sterling and bought British government bonds on a yield of 5% which was considerably lower than the prevailing interest rate of 6% on both Bank Rate and Treasury Bills.[12] The chairman of Scottish Widows alluded to the company's patriotic behaviour in his comments to policyholders, calling it 'an unfortunate and unwise step to place British credit on a 6% basis' – implying that the government's borrowing costs were unsustainable and that the life offices had helped to keep borrowing costs lower

---

[8] Michael Moss, *Standard Life, 1825–2000* (Mainstream 2000) 178. This was referred to as 'Scheme A' and covered North American securities and represented a simple requisitioning of assets. 'Scheme B' was more successful; it covered other overseas securities and the they were treated as collateral by the government, returned to the institutions after 5 years and dividends were also paid to the underlying owner of the assets.

[9] Michael Moss, *Standard Life, 1825–2000* (Mainstream 2000) 175. Keynes worked at the UK Treasury from the beginning of 1915 until the middle of 1919.

[10] John Butt, *Standard Life*, in The Business of Insurance, ed. Oliver Westall (Manchester University Press 1984) 169.

[11] *Scottish Widows Annual Report, 1913* (Lloyds Banking Group Archives).

[12] *Scottish Widows Annual Report, 1916* (Lloyds Banking Group Archives).

than they might have been.[13] At the end of the war in 1918, Scottish Widows held almost 37% of its investment portfolio in government bonds.[14] *The Economist* pointed out that the portfolios of life offices had suffered badly, 'from the beginning of 1916 to the end of 1920 depreciation... has been enormous and unprecedented... [and] has wiped out nearly the whole of the surpluses which would otherwise have been available for bonuses to policyholders'.[15] The market falls had been devastating and many life companies cancelled payment of bonuses towards the end of and immediately after the war. Scottish Widows, for example, omitted to pay any bonuses on policies in 1918 at its quinquennial distribution: it attributed the decision partly to higher income tax and higher claims but overwhelmingly to market depreciation. While unfortunate, this turned out to be a short-term problem because the losses were not permanent and most were recouped during the 1920s as security prices recovered.[16]

In the 50 years after 1862, Bailey's investment principles (Chapter 2) had not been challenged as fundamental investment beliefs. In practice, by 1900, insurance companies had modified his principles somewhat by limited diversification into foreign securities and a reduction in mortgages but his ideas still held sway. Bailey himself had accepted that with falling yields, he was prepared to condone investment into debentures, preference shares and bonds with redemption dates.[17] But his principles based on security and stability of market values still prevailed until 1912, at which point George May, the actuary at the Prudential, gently raised other investment ideas. May was extremely circumspect, indeed deferential, in his challenge to Bailey's principles. He wrote in his paper, 'These canons

---

[13] *Scottish Widows Annual Report, 1916* (Lloyds Banking Group Archives).

[14] *Scottish Widows Annual Report, 1918* (Lloyds Banking Group Archives). During the First World War, sales of securities were left to the discretion of individual institutions so the process was not centralised. Expropriation of investment assets would be repeated during the Second World War on an even larger scale, this time orchestrated by Carlyle Gifford, the eponymous founder of Baillie Gifford, under the auspices once again of the UK Treasury. This time asset sales were centralised and done very quickly. Gifford appears later in this chapter working with both Scottish Widows and Keynes. The full story of Gifford's role in the US during the Second World War is recounted in Richard Burns' *History of Baillie Gifford, A century of Investing* (Birlinn 2008).

[15] *The Economist*, 21 May 1921.

[16] Barry Supple, *Royal Exchange Assurance* (Cambridge University Press 1970) 444.

[17] George Clayton & William Osborn, *Insurance Company Investment* (Allen & Unwin 1965) 62.

[of Bailey's] are as true today as ever they were. One is very loth (sic) to tamper with any laws that have stood the test of time.'[18] Sensibly, albeit not forcefully, May had argued in favour of holding higher yielding, or riskier assets, within the context of a diversified portfolio. He also advocated the need for better training, education and experience in investment matters for insurance company actuaries, given the increasingly specialist nature of the role. May's description of what was required from an investment specialist serves to highlight how little expertise was dedicated to asset management within insurance companies at that time. According to May,

> Whatever the principles decided upon by an office for the investment of its funds, it must be admitted that for best carrying them into effect it is necessary to have someone who has not only made a special study of the subject [investment], but above all, has had practical experience. A special training is required for the investment work of an office just as much as for the actuarial or managerial work . . . [and] there can be no doubt that the investment work not only deserves but requires the undivided attention of an expert.[19]

While broadly welcomed by his actuarial peers, his views did not lead to any re-appraisal of Bailey's investment beliefs nor did it materially change the Prudential's investment policy, either.[20] May's ideas deserved to have greater impact and perhaps they did not owing to a combination of his excessive deference to Bailey and the timing of his paper with Europe on the brink of a major war. However, May's ideas did not fall completely on deaf ears. Significantly, two particular members of the audience at May's talk to the Institute of Actuaries at Staple Inn were receptive: Geoffrey Marks, the Actuary at National Mutual and Oswald Toynbee 'Foxy' Falk, a future director of the National Mutual.[21] In due

---

[18] George May, *The Investment of Life Assurance Funds* (Journal of the Institute of Actuaries 46/2, April 1912).

[19] George May, *The Investment of Life Assurance Funds* (Journal of the Institute of Actuaries 46/2, April 1912).

[20] Laurie Dennett, *A Sense of Security: 150 Years of Prudential* (Granta 1998) 262.

[21] Marks and Falk persuaded Keynes to become a director of the National Mutual in 1919. Falk trained and qualified as an actuary at the National Mutual which he left in 1914. Falk worked with Keynes at the Treasury in 1917 and they cooperated on several investment ventures after

course, in conjunction with Keynes, they would embrace some of May's ideas during the 1920s. Post-war there were two further developments that would challenge traditional investment policy at insurance companies: first, the rapid growth of life assurance funds meant these assets needed to find investment homes; second, the expansion of equity issuance by British industrial and commercial companies broadened investment opportunities. The number of companies quoted on the London stock exchange more than trebled between 1907 and 1939 from 569 to 1712, and their market capitalisation increased fivefold to £2.5 billion.[22] Taking Scottish Widows as an example of growth in the sector, with £23 million of assets at end 1918, its net money flows from premiums were typically more than 10% of the value of existing assets in every year during the 1920s and 1930s so funds under management increased rapidly.[23] By 1938, the insurance companies were the largest group of institutional investors, responsible for 74.4% of all stock exchange securities, and new money was flowing into life offices at the rate of £60 million a year.[24] Therefore, post 1918, the time was ripe to explore new investment ideas. Who better to introduce some new investment thinking to the rather staid world of insurance than a clever mathematician-cum-economist, with no actuarial training, who possessed a healthy dislike of the City establishment?

5.1.2 Keynes' Early Investments: 1905–1920

Keynes was a fascinating polymath who flitted between different worlds straddling academia, university administration, politics, the civil service, finance and the arts where he had close connections with the Bloomsbury Group. Keynes, generally referred to by his friends as

---

1918: for example, both were directors of the National Mutual (Falk from 1918), the Provincial, the PR and the Independent Investment Company. Falk became a Partner in Buckmaster & Moore, Keynes' principal stockbroker.

[22] Peter Scott, *Towards the Cult of the Equity? Insurance Companies and the Inter-war Capital Markets* (The Economic History Review, Feb 2002).

[23] *Scottish Widows Annual Reports* (Lloyds Banking Group Archives).

[24] Peter Scott, *Towards the Cult of the Equity? Insurance Companies and the Inter-war Capital Markets* (The Economic History Review Feb 2002).

Maynard (his paternal grandmother's name), during his lifetime was primarily an economist who achieved distinction with his books. He also had a prominent media profile during the inter-war years owing to his regular critiques of the economic policies of most central bankers and leading politicians, including Winston Churchill. Despite his worries about his own physical appearance, Keynes had star appeal, particularly through the written word. He was a figure of national importance: his 1919 book 'The Economic Consequences of the Peace' sold 100,000 copies in its first 6 months and was subsequently translated into 12 languages. Married happily from the age of 40 to a Russian ballet dancer, Lydia Lopokova, he nevertheless led an unconventional life and his bisexuality has been widely covered but more importantly, as an investor he was an original and innovative thinker.[25] Similar to George Ross Goobey (Chapter 8), he was exceptionally diligent at writing things down on paper and keeping excellent records, including the names of his many lovers and his terrible golf scores together with his considered reflections about asset management, all of which was helpful for posterity (Fig. 5.1).[26]

Keynes began buying ordinary shares for his own account after graduating from Cambridge in 1905, when working at the India Office as a poorly paid civil servant. In July of that year, he bought £160 worth of shares in Marine Insurance leaving himself with a bank balance of £30.[27] Six months later he bought shares in Mather and Platt for just under £50 with money borrowed from his father.[28] Over the next 15 years he then made occasional purchases of shares, including one US stock, US Steel, bought with money borrowed from a broker, the one transaction to which Keynes himself referred as 'speculation'.[29]

---

[25] Richard Davenport-Hines, *Universal Man, The Seven Lives of John Maynard Keynes* (William Collins 2015) Chapter 5.

[26] Keynes' Collected Writings were published from 1971 and ran to 30 volumes.

[27] Richard ('Dick') Kent, *Keynes' Investment Activities While in the Treasury During World War 1* (History of Economics Review 56, Summer 2012).

[28] Richard ('Dick') Kent, *Keynes' Investment Activities While in the Treasury During World War 1* (History of Economics Review 56, Summer 2012).

[29] Richard ('Dick') Kent, *Keynes' Investment Activities While in the Treasury During World War 1* (History of Economics Review 56, Summer 2012).

Fig. 5.1   John Maynard Keynes, 1883–1946, with Lydia Lopokova, photo 1941

By December 1917, Keynes had created a piecemeal portfolio consisting of nine ordinary shares and two preference shares with a total value of nearly £6,000. With a residual balance of only £10 in his bank account he was fully invested, as he would be, or even geared, for the remainder of his investing life.[30] The largest holding was in Rio Tinto, and he also had holdings in coal with Horden Collieries and in iron and steel through Bolckow Vaughan.[31] This fascination with natural resources and commodity companies would be a recurring theme in future portfolios managed by Keynes for the next 25 years. There are two explanations

[30] Richard ('Dick') Kent, *Keynes' Investment Activities While in the Treasury During World War 1* (History of Economics Review 56, Summer 2012).

[31] Richard ('Dick') Kent, *Keynes' Investment Activities While in the Treasury During World War 1* (History of Economics Review 56, Summer 2012).

for Keynes' early fascination with equities. The first is light-hearted based on his own explanation as close friend Clive Bell wrote:

> ...according to an account [Keynes] once gave me – in a whimsical mood I must confess – Maynard, who at Cambridge and in early London days had barely glanced at 'Stock Exchange Dealings' grew so weary – this is what he told me – of reading the cricket scores in *The Times* that, while drinking his morning tea, he took to studying prices instead.[32]

The more considered explanation is that Keynes was attracted to equity investing owing to a combination of circumstance, personality and intellect. He was not wealthy and needed to make money to maintain his bohemian lifestyle and to collect art. He was also fascinated by the behaviour of financial markets, as evidenced by his interest and willingness to record his investment activity and thoughts about markets and investing. He was a natural optimist, crucial for any equity investor after the First World War, and he believed that people could shape their own destiny – his short paper on '*The economic possibilities for our grandchildren*' was perhaps one of the clearest examples of his underlying positive outlook and personality. In this paper, he forecast that economic problems would be solved and that leisure would increase substantially over the ensuing 100 years. As an iconoclast, he operated outside the traditional circles of London finance, 'he always despised the City and its stiffed-necked Establishment. . . . it cannot be said that he was ever a popular figure in the City. He would have felt very ashamed in Bloomsbury if he had been'.[33] Keynes' early and continuing interest in equities was an important part of his investment thinking and as a result he encouraged insurance companies to invest in the asset class in the 1920s, and to be adequately resourced. While in the 1930s, his excellent investment performance at Kings College, Cambridge was driven largely by holding a high percentage of its portfolio in ordinary shares in the UK and preference shares in the USA.

---

[32] Clive Bell, *Old Friends* (Harcourt Brace 1957) 45.

[33] Nicholas Davenport, *Keynes in the City* in Essays on John Maynard Keynes, ed. Milo Keynes (Cambridge University Press 1975) Chapter 20. Davenport was a director of National Mutual from 1932 to 1969.

5.2   1921–1938: Ordinary Shares and Professionalisation of Asset Management

5.2.1 Keynes in Context

Keynes was a prolific investor engaged in a broad range of asset management activities for a variety of different institutions, and he invested, and speculated, in a large number of different asset classes.[34] His biggest contribution to the development of asset management in Britain was with insurance companies because he challenged Bailey's investment principles from 60 years earlier, pushed insurance companies into equities and showed them how and why they needed to professionalise their investment activities. Personally, he enjoyed some great successes, notably with the Discretionary Fund at Kings College Cambridge but he also suffered some major failures, most publicly with the Independent Investment Company (Chapter 6). As a director, he was closely involved with the investments of two insurance companies, the National Mutual and the Provincial, and he provided investment advice to other entities and individuals. Over time, some of his own investment beliefs changed fundamentally, particularly after the Wall Street Crash when he became much more of a 'bottom-up' investor interested in income, and his personal fortunes as an investor fluctuated dramatically between virtual bankruptcy and great wealth. Owing to this breadth of activity and the range of investment outcomes, assessing Keynes' contribution to the development of asset management in Britain is particularly challenging. Some (Chambers, Wasik, Walsh) argue that Keynes was above all an innovative but also a successful investor based

---

[34] Keynes created and was a Director of two investment companies, AD and PR, which were investment vehicles for friends and family; investment advice was given to Sir Ernest Debenham and others for which he was paid; he was closely involved in managing the investment portfolios for two insurance companies – the National Mutual (Keynes was Chairman between 1921 and 1938) and the Provincial (Keynes was a Director from 1923 to 1946); at Kings College Cambridge, as Bursar, he managed the endowment for over 25 years and created a Discretionary Fund; he advised Eton; he established and was a Director of a publicly quoted investment trust, The Independent; and he managed his own money very actively.

on his long-term performance results at Kings College Cambridge.[35] Additionally, they indicate that Keynes influenced some important aspects of the model of investing practised by Yale University and popular among many university endowments today.[36] An alternative proposition (Westall and Trebilcock) is that Keynes was a dangerous maverick and wayward genius who 'provided no systematic basis for institutional development [of asset management]'.[37] In 1937, Francis Scott, managing director at the Provincial, who had placed Keynes in sole charge of investment policy, referred to Keynes' approach as 'brilliant in its originality and daring' but Scott felt it was accompanied by a level of fluctuation, or volatility, that was almost unbearable for him as a client.[38] Question marks arise too about Keynes' written work in terms of impact and timing, though not of quality. For example, he wrote extensively and perceptively about asset management, but much of this material about investor behaviour and his own investment beliefs reached a wide audience only 40 years after his death.[39] Therefore, his direct influence and contribution to the development of the asset management profession is more difficult to assess than that of the other main characters in this book. Nevertheless, despite these qualifications, Keynes deserves a place in the pantheon of the most significant British investors, because he contributed to asset management in a number of very important ways. First, Keynes identified that asset management was a complex activity which needed appropriate, skilled resources devoted to it and that asset management needed to be seen as a profession in its own right.

---

[35] David Chambers et al., *Keynes, The Stock Market Investor: A Quantitative Analysis* (Journal of Financial and Quantitative Analysis 50/4, 2015); David Chambers and Elroy Dimson, *Retrospectives: John Maynard Keynes, Investment Innovator* (Journal of Economic Perspectives 27/3, 2013).

[36] David Chambers & Elroy Dimson, *The British Origins of the US Endowment Model* (Financial Analysts Journal 71/2, 2015).

[37] Oliver Westall, *Riding the Tiger* (University of Lancaster Management School 1992).

[38] Oliver Westall, *The Provincial Insurance Company* (Manchester University Press 1992) 382.

[39] *The Collected Writings of John Maynard Keynes Volume 12* ('CW XII') was first published in 1983. In this chapter I have quoted extensively from the 2013 edition produced by the Cambridge University Press. This volume covers a range of his investment activities and writing about asset management, with particular reference to Kings College Cambridge and the Provincial Insurance Company: it is required reading for anybody interested in investment. He wrote critically about market irrationality and investing in Chapter 12 of *The General Theory of Employment, Interest and Money* published in 1936.

Specifically, he thought life assurance companies should be the principal providers of institutional saving in Britain, and to do this properly, they had an obligation to enhance their asset management capability. He was aware that securities markets had changed, offering new opportunities, particularly with equities, but also some real challenges owing to additional complexity. Second, he argues that life offices, particularly mutuals, had a huge business opportunity to be the asset managers of choice for long-term savings in Britain owing to growing middle-class affluence and the attractiveness of life assurance products such as endowment policies. From 1922 onwards, by both his actions and his words, he challenged the way in which insurance companies, particularly life assurance companies, organised and structured their asset management capabilities. As a result, many of them were much better placed, subsequently, to face the investment difficulties thrown up the 1930s and 1940s. Finally, he believed ordinary shares were a natural asset class for long-term, institutional investors and he was one of their very first advocates (as Chambers and Dimson explained in 2013).

5.2.2   Keynes, Raynes and Ordinary Shares

Keynes was a staunch believer in equities throughout his investing life and during the 1920s and 1930s he found a kindred spirit in Harold Raynes, Actuary at an insurance company, the Legal & General. Between them they changed perceptions and slowly, investment policy at other life offices, followed their lead. One of the first books, published in 1924, to extol the investment attributes of ordinary shares, or common stocks in American parlance, was Edgar Lawrence Smith's *'Common Stocks as Long Term Investments'*. This analysed the performance of US bonds and equities from 1866 to 1922. It showed that equities had produced better returns than bonds in periods of both rising and falling prices. Additionally, Smith pointed out that equities had produced a higher income than bonds. Smith provided an objective analysis of long-term returns on what was, admittedly, somewhat limited data, particularly for periods pre-1900.[40] Despite the

---

[40] For example, Smith analysed the returns and income produced on various portfolios consisting of only 10 equity holdings, equally weighted, over different time periods.

shortcomings in the data, Smith's observations on ordinary shares – essentially the Equity Risk Premium – were valuable and have since been validated by a plethora of academic economists and financial institutions. Smith's book, however, was much more than an exercise in historic arithmetic because it also contained a number of important ideas and themes: Smith wanted to change investment perceptions. He explained that ordinary shares, or common stocks, had hitherto been perceived as a 'medium for speculation' and trading but he regarded them as attractive long-term investments if held as a component within a diversified portfolio. Second, Smith argued that capital markets in the USA had experienced fundamental changes since 1900: 'The growth of our industrial corporations both in number and size, since 1900, has been the most significant factor in the economic organization of the day. Prior to 1890 there were few corporations other than railroads....'[41] Third, Smith believed that company directors had a duty to minimise the costs of running their companies by borrowing as cheaply as possible. In turn this would constrain the returns that investors could earn on corporate bonds. Management's self-interest, he argued, was for the borrowing costs to be as low as possible because 'the management of every company is on the side of the common stock and opposed to the interests of the bondholders'.[42] Thirty years later, George Ross Goobey in Britain would also address this point about the fundamental unattractiveness of fixed interest stocks, even more forcefully than Smith (Chapter 8).

'*Common Stocks as Long Term Investments*' was very popular in the USA during the 1920s and it had enjoyed three reprints by 1928. In 1930, some commentators, Professor Irving Fisher of Yale for example, even attributed equity speculation in the 1920s and the Wall Street Crash to Smith's influence.[43] In May 1925, Keynes reviewed Smith's book in *The Nation and Athenaeum*, a weekly newspaper with left of centre political leanings, and was favourably impressed by the arguments for investing in ordinary shares.

---

[41] Edgar Lawrence Smith, *Common Stocks as Long Term Investments* (Macmillan 1928) 89.

[42] Edgar Lawrence Smith, *Common Stocks as Long Term Investments* (Macmillan 1928) 85.

[43] Ali Kabiri, *The Great Crash of 1929* (Palgrave Macmillan 2015) 2.

Keynes wrote: 'This actual experience in the United States over the past 50 years affords, *prima facie*, evidence that the prejudice of investors and investing institutions in favour of bonds as being "safe" and against common stocks as having, even the best of them, a "speculative" flavour, has led to a relative over-valuation of bonds and under-valuation of common stocks.'[44] In this same review, Keynes proceeded to comment on the relevance of ordinary shares for insurance companies and forcefully disagreed with one of Smith's points. Keynes wrote, 'Mr. Smith has not, particularly, in mind such institutions as insurance companies. Indeed, rather the contrary. He points out that, since the liabilities of an insurance company are fixed in terms of money, its criteria for safe investment must be somewhat different from those of other investors, and in particular that such a company has nothing to fear from the depreciation of money.'[45] Instead, Keynes argued that, subject to the safety of meeting the contractual obligations to the policyholders, then life offices should strive for higher returns. Therefore, he was attracted to Smith's arguments in favour of ordinary shares but disagreed with Smith's statement about which type of institutions should invest in them.

Keynes finished his review of the Smith book by suggesting that similar work should be undertaken to analyse equities and bonds in the UK, though he was concerned that British ordinary shares might not appear as attractive as their US counterparts owing to lower economic growth and higher dividend distributions, and hence lower retained earnings.[46] An analysis of UK capital markets, reviewing the 15 years from March 1912 to March 1927, duly appeared in late 1927 by Harold Raynes, and was presented by him to the Institute of Actuaries in 1928.[47] Raynes had an abiding curiosity about the behaviour of security markets and a broad interest in finance and investment: he subsequently wrote several books on insurance, investment and social security. He also worked with George Ross Goobey at Legal & General between 1934 and 1936; Raynes not only

---

[44] Keynes, *An American Study of Shares Versus Bonds as Permanent Investments* (CW XII) 247–252.

[45] Keynes, *An American Study of Shares Versus Bonds as Permanent Investments* (CW XII) 251.

[46] Keynes, *An American Study of Shares Versus Bonds as Permanent Investments* (CW XII) 252.

[47] Harold Raynes, *The Place of Ordinary Stocks and Shares in the Investment of Life Assurance Funds.* (Journal of the Institute of Actuaries 59, 1928) Raynes submitted the paper in November 1927; it was discussed on 1 March 1928.

helped Keynes but would have influenced Ross Goobey's investment thinking too (Chapter 8). Raynes entered the investment debate about ordinary shares in 1927–1928 and subsequently returned to the subject during the 1930s with a second paper to the Institute of Actuaries: he deserves great credit for breaking with actuarial investment orthodoxy, much more forcefully than May had done in 1912.[48] Although the period analysed by Raynes was short, the analysis and data were more robust than Smith's work on the US equity market published in 1924. Rather than challenging Bailey's investment principles directly, Raynes was more subtle. His main proposition was that investment in ordinary shares would improve the safety of an investment portfolio and thus endorsed Bailey's hallowed first principle which stressed security. Raynes wrote in a manner that he knew would appeal to his analytical and numerate actuarial audience:

> Whether greater security to the capital of a fund is given by the investment of a proportion in ordinary stocks and shares might be considered by deductive reasoning from the principles of economics. . . . [but] a statistical investigation will, I think, prove more convincing to actuaries.[49]

Raynes' paper, the '*Place of Ordinary Shares and Stocks in the Investment of Life Assurance Funds*' submitted to the Institute of Actuaries in 1927, argued that investment in ordinary shares could combat the effects of inflation and would, in all likelihood, produce higher returns than fixed interest securities.[50] In his January 1928 speech to the annual meeting of the National Mutual (this speech is covered in detail in 5.2.3 below),

---

[48] HF Purchase, *Memoir* (Journal of the Institute of Actuaries 90, 1964). Obituary or 'memoir' to Raynes; the tone of this piece is warm and understated rather than effusive.

[49] Harold Raynes, *The place of ordinary stocks and shares in the investment of life assurance funds* (Journal of the Institute of Actuaries 59, 1928).

[50] Harold Raynes, *The place of ordinary stocks and shares in the investment of life assurance funds* (Journal of the Institute of Actuaries 59, 1928) It should also be noted that the subsequent discussion of the paper at the meeting was remarkably supportive of the analysis by Raynes. Two of those making contributions from the floor were close friends of Keynes, Recknell assistant Actuary at the National Mutual and RG Hawtrey, an influential economist and former 'Apostle' at Cambridge University and an Eton man, so the same background as Keynes. Hawtrey was firmly in the Keynes camp and they shared similar views about the nature of the depression and the importance of credit.

Keynes discussed the opportunities and challenges that ordinary shares' investment provided. An article in *The Economist* from October 1927 articulated, albeit in ironic terms, some of the prevailing suspicions about investing in equities:

> Until recently it has been held that life offices should eschew ordinary shares like the plague. Though empires fall and thrones totter, they must stick to bonds. Let them but be suspected of one ordinary share investment and the wrath of heaven will fall upon them, for they will have laid their hands on the Ark of the Covenant. But 'it is the customary fate of new truths to begin as heresies and to end as superstitions', and signs are not wanting that the sharp edge of opposition has already been turned.[51]

Increasingly these articles and speeches appeared to be components of a coordinated campaign extolling the benefits of ordinary shares. First there was *The Economist* article, above, in October 1927; then Raynes submitted his paper to the institute of Actuaries in November; Keynes addressed the National Mutual meeting in January 1928 followed by extensive newspaper coverage; and finally, Raynes delivered his paper to the Institute of Actuaries in March 1928, along with Hawtrey's (an economist and close friend of Keynes) pre-arranged participation in the actuarial debate: all of this might have been coincidental but it looked planned. Irrespective, these were loud messages that were being transmitted. In 1937, Raynes delivered an updated version of his 1927 paper to the Institute of Actuaries, partly as he explained, to cover the period of the world depression in industry and trade which had followed soon after the close of the period originally selected.[52] Once again it cast equities in a favourable light compared to fixed interest securities over the preceding 10 and 25 years. But, and this is really important owing to the chronology of events, Keynes was investing material amounts into ordinary shares before these two works by

---

[51] *The Economist, Life Office Investments, 28* October 1927.
[52] Harold Raynes, *Equities and Fixed Interest Stocks during 25 Years* (Journal of the Institute of Actuaries 68, 1937).

Smith and Raynes had been published. Helpfully, Smith and Raynes supported and reinforced Keynes' *ex ante* intuitive ideas about the attractions of equities, or as Raynes had phrased it in his paper, 'deductive reasoning from the principles of economics'. More broadly, and despite the looming crash of 1929, the work undertaken by Smith and Raynes during the 1920s was indicative that the world of investment was starting to become more data-conscious and analytical. In 1926, Standard & Poors created a 90 stock index; in 1928, Dow Jones expanded its index to include 30 industrials (up from 12 stocks in 1896); also in 1928, Benjamin Graham, the legendary US investor, began teaching his investment course at Columbia University and his seminal investment work, *Security Analysis* appeared in 1934.[53] *Security Analysis* was a very substantial piece of work of which half was devoted to the analysis of fixed income stocks so it was much more than a guide for value-based equity investors. In the UK the FT30 Index was created in 1935 while Keynes wrote his incisive 17-page essay about asset management, 'The State of Long Term Expectation' in Chapter 12 of *The General Theory* published in 1936. Unlike Graham at Columbia, and perhaps surprisingly, Keynes did not have a formal teaching role at Cambridge after 1920 owing to his administrative position as First Bursar at Kings College. The relatively small number of lectures that he delivered at Cambridge in the 1930s were generally based around draft chapters of his books on mainstream economic issues rather than investment or asset management.[54] Nevertheless, this small but growing body of information about investment and securities markets combined with better data on market indices provided a natural bridge for George Ross Goobey (Chapter 8) to develop his own investment ideas after 1945.

---

[53] Similar to Keynes, Benjamin Graham was a polymath. He was offered teaching positions in three different faculties at the University of Columbia in 1914 prior to his graduation. In addition to being a successful investor, teacher and writer he also held several US patents (one relating to the slide rule) and even wrote a Broadway play (www.c250.columbia.edu/c250_celebrates/your_Columbians/benjamin_graham, website accessed 15 October 2016).

[54] Maria Cristina Marcuzzo, *Keynes and Cambridge*, in The Cambridge Companion to Keynes, ed. Backhouse & Bateman (Cambridge University Press 2006) 122.

5.2.3 Keynes and the National Mutual Life Assurance Society

Keynes joined the board of the National Mutual in 1919, became chairman in 1921 and made his first speech in that capacity in January 1922. His annual speeches received wide coverage and were printed in full in *The Times*, generally with some additional comments in the 'City Notes' section too. *The Economist* and other papers including *The Scotsman* regularly covered the content so he had a national platform for his views. His profile at the National Mutual, a life office, was in contrast to the Provincial, where Keynes also provided investment advice. The Provincial was a small general insurance company controlled by the Scott family based in Kendal in northwest England and Keynes became the 'Scott family's principal financial adviser from 1922, taking a central role in the management of the Provincial's general insurance funds'.[55] He was a director from 1923 to 1946 and enjoyed considerable autonomy with investment policy, particularly after 1930 when Falk was removed from the investment committee owing to Falk's unabashed enthusiasm for the USA as the depression arrived. Keynes had extensive and very interesting correspondence about investment policy with the managing director of the Provincial, Francis Scott, from the 1930s onwards which is extensively documented in the Collected Writings.[56] Keynes produced high returns for the Provincial but in a volatile fashion so that 'Keynes' management of the Provincial fund was a *tour de force* but it can reasonably be asked whether it was entirely appropriate for a general insurance company'.[57] His activities at the Provincial were interesting and, anecdotally he left a rich legacy, but it is beyond the scope of this work so the remainder of this chapter will concentrate on life offices in general and the National Mutual in particular.

In his first two speeches as chairman at the National Mutual, in 1922 and 1923, Keynes laid out his inspirational ideas about life offices and

---

[55] *John Maynard Keynes* (www.sandaire.com, website accessed 4 May 2016).

[56] *Provincial Insurance Company* (CWXII) 50–88. The correspondence highlights Keynes growing interest in 'bottom-up' equity investing in particular so there is lots of correspondence about individual holdings and the exposures to mining stocks for example.

[57] Oliver Westall, *Riding the Tiger* (University of Lancaster Management School 1992).

asset management. His first proposition was that life offices were ideally placed to become the dominant savings and investing institutions in Britain. His second idea was that asset management should be viewed as a profession thus requiring specific knowledge and expertise, organised appropriately. He covered both of these items in depth in the two speeches and he argued that asset management was the biggest challenge and opportunity facing life offices in the twentieth century. In his view, it was the duty of the Board to address this issue because it would 'stand or fall' by its investment policies. Finally, he advocated that equities should be incorporated into life offices' investment portfolios although this was implicit rather than explicit in his speeches until 1928. While these may not appear to have sounded like populist ideas, they struck a chord with his audience because, according to *The Times*, Keynes was actually cheered by policyholders at the end of his first speech as chairman to the annual meeting of National Mutual in January 1922, when he said,

> If the boards of assurance societies can gain enough public confidence in their investment policies, we shall come even more than at present, to look on such societies as providing the best available organisation for looking after the savings of the middle classes . . . a well-managed mutual society where all the profits belong to the policyholders, is surely the ideal institution for the investment of small annual savings. If only the mutual societies of this country can improve their principles of investment as successfully as they have perfected actuarial science, their social usefulness will be even greater than it has been hitherto.[58]

He also made several references to 'active investment policy', 'active policy' and 'investment policy' which, he argued, if executed successfully had the potential to generate additional profits for policyholders. He subsequently defined these terms as follows:

> The management of an insurance company is almost inevitably driven, whether it likes it or not, into what has been termed lately 'an active

---

[58] *Report to the Annual Meeting of the National Mutual*, 18 January 1922 (CWXII) 121 and *The Times* 19 January 1922. Note that in the various accounts by *The Times* of Keynes' speeches over the years, they drew a distinction between 'cheers and cheering', 'applause' and general support in the form of 'here here'.

investment policy'; which after all is just another name for being alive that circumstances change. Unfortunately, it is not possible to make oneself permanently secure by any policy of inaction whatever. The idea which some people seem to entertain that an active policy involves taking more risks than an inactive policy is exactly the opposite of the truth...and an 'active' investment policy has for its object the avoidance of capital loss at least as much as the making of capital profits.[59]

The idea that asset management required specialist skills, and thus should be thought of as a profession, was an idea propagated by Keynes for the next two decades, 'The average investor must obviously be at a hopeless disadvantage in looking after his savings as compared with a well-managed mutual society. It ought to be considered as imprudent for such a man to make his own investments as to be his own doctor or lawyer,' said Keynes in 1923.[60]

His willingness to explore investment opportunities took a number of forms, one of which was to invest in ordinary shares. Ordinary shares were not mentioned explicitly in the 1922 speech, but would be covered in future speeches, and, by the end of 1923, the National Mutual had over 16% invested in the asset class.[61] In the middle years of the 1920s the National Mutual produced record surpluses and announced very high bonuses surpassing any from the previous 90 years; so early investment results under Keynes were encouraging. At the end of 1927, National Mutual had 18% of its assets in ordinary shares while the average life office had 4%, a figure that had barely changed since 1913 when it was 3%. Keynes was justified in saying 'we have been pioneers amongst the life offices in the practice of employing a substantial part of our funds in the purchase of ordinary shares'.[62]

[59] Keynes, *Investment policy for insurance companies*, May 1924 (CW XII) 240–244.
[60] *Report to the Annual Meeting of the National Mutual*, 29 January 1923 (CW XII) 125.
[61] CW XII, 155.
[62] *Report to the Annual General Meeting of the National Mutual*, 25 January 1928 (CW XII) 155.

Most of Keynes' speech to the annual meeting of the National Mutual in January 1928 dealt with investment and particularly ordinary shares. It had a number of strands, paraphrased as follows:

- Data were provided demonstrating that National Mutual had been unusual and innovative by investing significant amounts into ordinary shares.
- Life office investment strategy should contain a mixture of monetary assets and real assets.
- The growth in the number of industrial and commercial companies quoted on the stock exchange represented a new, and changing, set of investment opportunities.
- The relative undervaluation of ordinary shares provided an opportunity, potentially temporary.
- Complexities associated with investing in ordinary shares required specialist investment expertise to do it effectively.
- Investment in ordinary shares such as oil, automobiles and artificial silk, represented an ownership stake in Britain's future. He said that if British institutional investors did not invest in their own leading industries then the Americans would so his argument stressed national self-interest. He explained his ideas as follows: 'Considerations of public and private policy are in this instance happily combined. It will increase the wealth and efficiency of the country if those responsible for the investment of large funds come to consider it as part of their duty to participate as ordinary shareholders – to a moderate extent and within the due bounds of prudence – in the leading enterprises of their day and generation.'[63]

The entire speech, considered a *tour de force* by the media, received considerable attention from the press, who endorsed Keynes' position. *The Times* said the speech 'deserves to be studied . . . in a very interesting and suggestive disposition on what may be described as a comparatively new form of finance for life assurance firms'; *The Economist* asserted that

---

[63] *Report to the Annual General Meeting of the National Mutual*, 25 January 1928 (CW XII) 161.

'The suggestion – stimulating and exhilarating in the highest degree – will receive widespread attention and merits it'; *The Scotsman* called it 'an important plea' and wrote a long article about the subject but then sat on the fence.[64] *The Times*, in a commendably succinct summary, described the purpose of an active investment policy and the importance of ordinary shares. *The Times* finished by quoting Keynes, who poked fun at directors who were not up to the demands of the role in other life offices, as follows: [Keynes] pointed out that constant care and activity are needed [with investments]. Serious duties therefore devolve upon the directors, and he doubted whether it would be wise to impose burdens on directors, now elderly, who "have not performed serious duties for many years."'[65] *The Economist* was equally supportive but favoured the 'national interest' argument propounded by Keynes.[66] This was a clever speech that pulled together lots of different ideas: he used economic and financial arguments together with data from the USA (Smith) and the UK (Raynes) to support investment in ordinary shares; he teased his competitors for having aged, incompetent directors on their boards who looked to the past when they needed to consider the future; and he made an emotional appeal by linking institutional investment to Britain's national interest. Here was a powerful set of arguments which both identified asset management as an important activity and investment into ordinary shares as a particular opportunity.

Keynes was vocal addressing strategic investment matters and was also closely involved in the day-to-day management of the assets of the National Mutual. In the 1920s Keynes, in conjunction with Falk, had adopted what he called the 'credit cycle' approach to investing. This was fully explained at the beginning of 1924 in the Prospectus for the Independent Investment Company (Chapter 6). The investment process was predicated on forecasting interest rate changes and subsequently making asset allocation moves between, or within, asset classes. Consequently, equity exposure needed to be relatively liquid because trading levels were expected to be high.

---

[64] *The Times*, 26 January 1928; *The Economist* 28 January 1928; *The Scotsman* 30 January 1928.

[65] *The Times*, 26 January 1928. Keynes must have given a separate briefing to the paper because the last point about senile directors of life assurance companies was not included in his official address to the meeting in the Annual Report.

[66] *The Economist*, 28 January 1928.

Additionally, the equity portfolio was principally organised by industrial sector to enable Keynes to take sector views across the market. It appears that this process was introduced in the summer of 1924 at the National Mutual, shortly after the launch of the Independent Investment Company and that prior to this date transactions in ordinary shares were less systematic. The private minutes from 4 June 1924 clearly record the investment decisions required to restructure the existing assets and, in effect, to create a new portfolio based on what was termed an 'industrial index'. In order to establish this proposed portfolio of ordinary shares, there was an extensive list of purchases and sales so this marked a clear change from the previous investment approach.[67] In practice, the ordinary shares held by the National Mutual were entirely reasonable, certainly not esoteric, and the board had a relatively sophisticated approach to portfolio construction. Their 'industrial index' was sub-divided into 6 industrial sectors with 29 holdings so it was well diversified by stock and sector as Table 5.1 shows.[68] This emphasis on resource companies in terms of oil, coal, iron, steel and a broad range of mining companies was a continuing theme in Keynes' portfolios throughout his life, evident in his personal investments up to 1919 and also in the Kings College portfolios during the mid-1930s (Chapter 6).

The board was also alive to portfolio risk and, to take one example, it agreed to make sales of ordinary shares from three potentially vulnerable sectors during 1925 in the expectation of extended industrial action by trades unions leading up to the General Strike of 1926.[69] During 1928, after strong market gains, some reductions were made to the holdings of ordinary shares and overall therefore, in the 1920s, the investment policy of the National Mutual was prudent, innovative and successful. In January 1929 Keynes claimed that the investment strategy had earned more than 7% compound over the previous 8 years and that the society had nearly £900,000 in undistributed surplus (reserves) representing an excess of almost 21% over the liabilities.[70] So this may have been a good

---

[67] *National Mutual Private Minutes, Board & Finance Committee*, 4 June 1924 (LMA MS 34469).
[68] *National Mutual Private Minutes, Board & Finance Committee*, 4 June 1924 (LMA MS 34469).
[69] *National Mutual Private Minutes, Board & Finance Committee*, 12 August 1925 (LMA MS 34469).
[70] *Report to the Annual General Meeting of the National Mutual*, 30 January 1929 (CW XII) 161.

Table 5.1 National Mutual proposed equity portfolio 1924

Holding	£ Value	%	Sector[a]
Shell	43,000	7.5	Oil
General Electric	25,000	4.3	Engineering
Mather & Platt	25,000	4.3	Engineering
Nobel	25,000	4.3	Engineering
Burma Corp	25,000	4.3	Mines
BAT	25,000	4.3	Miscellaneous
Borax Cons. Deferred	25,000	4.3	Miscellaneous
Brunner Mond	25,000	4.3	Miscellaneous
Cements	25,000	4.3	Miscellaneous
Courtaulds	25,000	4.3	Miscellaneous
Forestal Land	25,000	4.3	Miscellaneous
James Finlay	25,000	4.3	Miscellaneous
Swedish Match	25,000	4.3	Miscellaneous
Baldwin	20,000	3.5	Coal, iron and steel
Dorman Long	20,000	3.5	Coal, iron and steel
Guest King	20,000	3.5	Coal, iron and steel
Pease & Partners	20,000	3.5	Coal, iron and steel
Cunard	20,000	3.5	Shipping
Furness Withy	20,000	3.5	Shipping
P & O	20,000	3.5	Shipping
Royal Mail	20,000	3.5	Shipping
Tintos	14,000	2.4	Mines
Zinc Preferred	10,000	1.7	Mines
Hudson Bay	10,000	1.7	Miscellaneous
Spillers	10,000	1.7	Miscellaneous
Wallpapers Deferred	10,000	1.7	Miscellaneous
Whiteaway Laidlaw	10,000	1.7	Miscellaneous
Platt Bros	5,000	0.9	Engineering
Stewarts & Lloyds	5,000	0.9	Engineering
Total	577,000	100	

[a] Sector classifications as per National Mutual definitions
Source: *National Mutual Private Minutes, Board & Finance Committee* (LMA, 34469)

start but most of Keynes' investment portfolios experienced severe difficulties at the end of the decade owing to the 1929 Crash and the National Mutual was no different. Portfolio strategy around the time of the 1929 Great Crash was particularly interesting in this instance for two reasons: first, an overly generous distribution policy combined with the fall in markets subsequently affected the ability produce an actuarial valuation and to pay policyholders' bonuses; second, there was internal discord about investment strategy on the board at the National Mutual with Falk the main troublemaker.

While there is no evidence that Keynes expected the market cataclysm that unfolded after October 1929, he was cautious in the run up to the Wall Street Crash and wished to make reductions and it was a fellow director Falk, with a passionate belief in the USA, who exacerbated investment problems.[71] A month before the crash Falk wrote to Marks, the Actuary at the National Mutual, staunchly advocating the benefits of US equities in the following terms, 'Keynes is continuing trying to get us out of American stocks... I think he is wrong. I hope his attempts will be resisted... I therefore hope that we shall continue to buy good stocks and stick to them.'[72] For good measure, Falk enclosed a memo with his letter reinforcing his point 'there does not appear to be any justification for regarding the last 8 years as a single vast bull movement [in the United States] which will be followed by a catastrophic crash'. Not only was Falk wrong in September and October 1929 but he continued to be wrong subsequently. After the crash, the stockbrokers Buckmaster & Moore, where Falk was now senior partner, continued to underestimate the effects of the market collapse, In November 1929, Buckmaster & Moore suggested that US stocks offered a buying opportunity according to their research note 'during the last 12 months American common stocks have been attractive but dangerous. In a few months time these stocks will become safe as well as attractive'.[73] Falk's position was unambiguous: he was arguing forcefully for further investment in US stocks against Keynes' desire to reduce. By the end of 1930, the implications were spelt out clearly by Marks to the board when he said that 'our mistaken refusal to sell our

---

[71] With reference to the US market in 1929, Falk adopted a similar stance at the Independent (Appendix) and at the Provincial Insurance Company where Scott removed him from the investment committee after 1930.

[72] Falk to Marks, letter 26 September 1929, *National Mutual, Investment Policy to 1930* (LMA MS 34526/1).

[73] Buckmaster & Moore research note, 13 November 1929, *National Mutual, Investment Policy to 1930* (LMA MS 34526/1).

American securities in April last year [1929], and our spasmodic incursions into the American market, have proved little short of disastrous'.[74]

In reality, despite some poor investment decisions between 1929 and 1931, it is not evident that investment results materially damaged the National Mutual over this period, reportedly suffering falls of 6% and 3.5% in 1929 and 1930 respectively, or that they were vastly worse than other life offices. The real problem was the bonus distribution policy. In January 1924, Keynes had announced that bonus payments to policyholders would be made annually rather than quinquennially and that the assets of the society would be disclosed on a marked-to-market basis.[75] The National Mutual's critical error was that annual bonus distributions were maintained after the 1929 Crash, compounded by an additional pre-promised centenary special bonus paid to policyholders in 1930. The prolonged market falls after the 1929 Crash over more than two years was incompatible with a policy of annual distributions of surplus.[76] By January 1931, the surplus of assets over liabilities was only 4.5%.[77] By January 1932, the National Mutual had a deficit of assets compared to liabilities of about £277,000 or 5%; no end-year actuarial valuation was published and the bonus declaration was postponed.[78] Keynes blamed actuarial methods 'as a sort of competition in unveracity (sic)' and while many might have sympathy with Keynes' criticism of the arcane world inhabited by actuaries, this type of flip-flopping showed poor judgement by the chairman of the Board.[79] In the following year, the National Mutual moved to

---

[74] Marks to the board, memorandum 1 December 1930, *National Mutual, Investment Policy to 1930* (LMA MS 34526/1).

[75] *Report to the Annual General Meeting of the National Mutual January 1924* (CW XII) 130–135.

[76] In the USA the market fell from October 1929 to July 1932, so a period of more than 2.5 years.

[77] Recknell to the board, memorandum 7 January 1931, *National Mutual, Private Minutes, Board and Finance Committee* (LMA MS 34469).

[78] Recknell to the board, memorandum 13 January 1932, *National Mutual Private Minutes, Board & Finance Committee* (LMA MS 34469).

[79] *The Economist*, 5 March 1932, was sympathetic to the problems at the National Mutual and reiterated its support for Keynes' innovative investment policy. The paper supported the policy of greater transparency and called the decision to postpone the valuation, 'wise and necessary'.

biennial valuations and increased the reserves by modifying its bonus procedures but this was reputationally damaging given that it had moved to annual bonus distributions as recently as 1924.[80] The events of 1932 and 1933 were a major setback for Keynes and the National Mutual and, according to one publication, this represented 'a humiliating experience that every [life] office would wish to avoid'.[81]

Keynes, always intellectually honest, explained the problems openly and frankly, at his annual address to the National Mutual policyholders in March 1932.[82] He accepted that the National Mutual may have under-performed other life offices but he also qualified it in two ways. First, he pointed out that if the depression continued then there would be no safe asset classes, anywhere. Second, he explained that it was appropriate for the National Mutual to maintain its current investment policy owing to its obligation to produce good returns over the very long-term. His emphasis therefore was on the long-term rather than the short-term implications of investment policy which was genuinely an explanation rather than an excuse because he was also prepared to discuss short-term problems. With hindsight, he explained that the asset values of the National Mutual during 1931 could have been perhaps 2% higher – 'with a little better luck or a little better management' – but overall did not feel that it was material. Recknell had worried that their problems in 1931 and 1932 might damage the National Mutual for up to 10 years into the future, but in practice the difficulties were short-term in their nature and soon passed.[83] After 1933, the National Mutual recovered so by 1938, even after a very difficult year for markets in 1937, its reserves had been rebuilt and stood at £580,000.[84] At the annual meeting in February 1938, Keynes explained that the investment return (or 'combined net earnings' as he

---

[80] *Report to the Annual General Meeting of the National Mutual March 1933* (CW XII) 199.

[81] Clive Trebilcock, *Phoenix Assurance and the Development of British Insurance: Vol 2, 1870–1984* (Cambridge University Press 1999) 599. This referred to a comment in the Bankers Magazine.

[82] *Report to the Annual General Meeting of the National Mutual,* 2 March 1932 (CW XII) 187.

[83] Recknell to the National Mutual Board, memorandum 7 January 1931 *National Mutual* (LMA MS 34469).

[84] Recknell to the National Mutual Board, memorandum 10 May 1938, *National Mutual, Investment Policy after 1930* (LMA 34526/2).

phrased it) over the previous 17 years since he became chairman had averaged 6.4% per annum (tax free) despite suffering 8% depreciation during 1937. He compared the 6.4% to actuarially calculated liabilities of 4.3% and said, 'This margin [2.1% per annum] between the rate earned on the liabilities and the rate assumed to be earned is a substantial one.'[85] Therefore, the long-term investment record was strong, particularly compared to British government bonds which yielded 4.9% in 1921 when Keynes became chairman but had fallen to 3.5% by the end of 1938.[86]

5.2.4 Life Office Investments 1921–1938

Keynes and Raynes were not the only people thinking about the world of investment after 1900 but they were the most vocal. One interesting example of an organisation gradually increasing its emphasis on asset management was Standard Life. At the turn of the twentieth century, specialist investment knowledge was sought from experienced individuals by invitation of the Board. Initially Robert Fleming, then one of his partners Charles Whigham, and finally James Ivory, the founder of the asset management company Ivory & Sime, provided investment advice.[87] This resulted in investment in the bonds of railroad companies and a significant increase in overseas holdings. Changes in the complexity of the investment portfolio were accompanied by organisational changes too. A new position of 'investment superintendent' had been created in 1911 and, subsequently in 1919, T. Dick Peat became the 'investment secretary' with control of the investment department, which began summarising investment research and compiling investment-related statistics.[88] Macnaghten, the newly appointed Manager at Standard Life from 1919, was looking to make further changes to investment policy not least because the company, owing to the exigencies of war, had more

---

[85] *The Times*, 24 February 1938.

[86] *Barclays Equity Gilt Study 2012.*

[87] Michael Moss, *Standard Life, 1825–2000* (Mainstream 2000) 117 & 387. James Ivory was a Director of Standard Life after 1906.

[88] Michael Moss, *Standard Life, 1825–2000* (Mainstream 2000) 194.

than 40% of its assets in British government bonds and UK municipal bonds with less than 1% held in ordinary shares at that date.[89] From 1922 onwards, the investment department began to meet monthly and in April 1926, the board approved a list of 55 stockbrokers to be used which marked the beginning of more widespread equity investing: by the end of that year, 6% of assets were invested in ordinary shares.[90] By 1929 Standard Life's investment in ordinary shares was almost 16% rising to over 20% by the end of 1936.[91] The first purchases were British investment companies but this was broadened out to include direct holdings of industrial shares. In due course, this included equity investments in the USA, particularly after 1933. Standard Life avoided the worst of the Wall Street Crash with the exception of one small US investment.[92] Coincidentally, two young actuaries at Standard Life, Albert King and Andrew Davidson, were supportive of Keynes' investment ideas at the National Mutual and thus encouraged Macnaghten to build up the investment department further.[93] Keynes became a director at the National Mutual at exactly the same time that Macnaghten had taken on the top job Standard Life, so they shared common problems. One imagines that Macnaghten would have pored over every word from Keynes' first speech as chairman in January 1922. Links between the two companies were further strengthened in 1923 when GH Recknell was appointed assistant Actuary at the National Mutual. Recknell and Andrew Davidson, the future Manager (chief executive) at Standard Life between 1942 and 1951, had qualified together as actuaries in Edinburgh, and allegedly, were best friends.[94] Keynes recruited Recknell and promoted him to the position of Actuary at the National Mutual in

[89] Michael Moss, *Standard Life, 1825–2000* (Mainstream 2000) 193/4 & 387.

[90] Michael Moss, *Standard Life, 1825–2000* (Mainstream 2000) 387.

[91] Peter Scott, *Towards the Cult of the Equity? Insurance Companies and the Inter-war Capital Markets* (The Economic History Review, Feb 2002).

[92] Michael Moss *Standard Life 1825–2000 (Mainstream 2000)* 194. Moss recounts the story that Macnaghten went to the Sates in the summer of 1929 and returned to Edinburgh very enthusiastic to invest in the equity market but was dissuaded from doing so by James Ivory.

[93] Michael Moss *Standard Life 1825–2000 (Mainstream 2000)* 194.

[94] *GH Recknell Personal Files*, 26 August 1975 (LMA, MS 34568). It is not clear if this document, dedicated to Recknell, was a memoir or an obituary and there was no named author.

succession to Marks, so they too enjoyed a close and long working relationship. Demonstarting the strength of the relationship, Recknell continued to correspond with Keynes on investment matters even after the latter had relinquished the chairmanship of National Mutual in 1938. It is highly likely therefore that Recknell and Davidson would have discussed Keynes' investment ideas during the 1920s and the 1930s. Standard Life, possibly with Keynes' influence, substantially strengthened its investment capability during the inter-war years and made sound investment decisions. Their considerably larger Edinburgh-based neighbours, Scottish Widows, however, were slower at organising their investment thinking.

Scottish Widows was the largest mutual life company in Britain by the time of the First World War with assets of £21.6 million.[95] An interesting addition to its board in 1921 was Carlyle Gifford, a lawyer possessing investment expertise and a founding partner of Baillie Gifford. He was welcomed to the board of Scottish Widows in the following terms, 'Well known in this City [Edinburgh] to have given great attention to the important subjects of economics and finance.'[96] From 1924 to 1931, Gifford worked with Keynes as a director of the Independent Investment Company (Chapter 6) while, at Scottish Widows, he was a member of the Committee for General Purposes with responsibility for investments.[97] The minute books are informative and highlight how little time was then spent discussing securities investments in the 1920s at Scottish Widows despite Gifford's involvement and it was only after 1929 that Scottish Widows began to document investment decisions and discussions by the designated investment committee in any real detail. There are isolated examples of investment decisions but much of the documentation covers loans, mainly to property owning aristocrats. Even at this stage in their development, life offices were operating in ways similar to banks by providing credit and loans.[98]

---

[95] *Scottish Widows Annual Report, 1913* (Lloyds Banking Group Archives).

[96] *Scottish Widows Annual Report, 1920* (Lloyds Banking Group Archives).

[97] *Scottish Widows Annual Report, 1920* (Lloyds Banking Group Archives and Minute Book XIII, 1918–1923, SW 3/2/13).

[98] Even as late as the 1930s loans were being provided by Scottish Widows. For example, in 1933, £5,000 was loaned to Gullane Golf Club for 15 years at 5% to enable the club to purchase the freehold land for courses called 'Number 1, 2 and 3' (Lloyds Banking Group Archives, SW 5/1/6 Minute Book 6).

Scottish Widows was not only slower than Standard Life to make changes to investment policy but it also got the timing of investments into ordinary shares wrong. It sold out of small, residual holdings in equities in 1922, mainly railway stocks bought before 1914, and then bought into ordinary shares in 1929, including US common stocks, just before the 1929 Crash. The decision to move into equities on 18 October 1929, only 11 days ahead of the actual Crash, was particularly unfortunate.[99] Scottish Widows agreed to buy holdings in 4 banks, 4 insurance companies, 13 commercial businesses in Britain and 3 North American railroads.[100] These decisions were taken and implemented during October and November 1929. At a time of great market turbulence, these purchases proceeded in a cautious manner but were largely complete by the beginning of 1930.[101] During February 1930, Scottish Widows added to existing ordinary shares and purchased new industrial stocks such as Turner & Newall and Guest, Keen & Nettlefolds (GKN) on yields in excess of 6%; over 7%, in the case of GKN.[102] This showed great conviction, albeit perhaps unwarranted, given that equity markets had some considerable way to fall through 1930 and 1931. In November 1930, 'Committee A' (as the finance/investment committee was now known) agreed to add further to these holdings and to broaden their equity exposure beyond railroads in the USA.[103] Decisions to add more to equities were made in 1931 with further investment into preferred shares and ordinary shares in the USA.[104] On a short-term view, the timing of these investment decisions was dreadful but the percentages were very small with only 3.9% held in ordinary shares at the end of 1931, and the directors deserve credit for showing the courage to continue investing, thus

---

[99] The Wall Street Crash occurred on 29 October 1929. These decisions by Scottish Widows to buy ordinary shares took place between 18 October and 15 November 1929. As noted, Scottish Widows continued buying steadily through the prolonged market falls.

[100] Scottish Widows Minute Book 5 SW 5/1/5, Pages 23 and 35 (Lloyds Banking Group Archives).

[101] Scottish Widows Minute Book 5 SW 5/1/5, Pages 23 and 35 (Lloyds Banking Group Archives).

[102] Scottish Widows Minute Book 5 SW 5/1/5, Page 55 (Lloyds Banking Group Archives).

[103] Scottish Widows Minute Book 5 SW 5/1/5, Page 130 (Lloyds Banking Group Archives). The proposal from the Manager that a target weighting of 6% in US equities was accepted.

[104] Scottish Widows Minute Book 5 SW 5/1/5, Page 135 and SW 5/1/6 (Lloyds Banking Group Archives). As noted previously, both preferred and ordinary shares have been treated as equity instruments throughout this narrative.

buying in at very high yields. By 1937, overall asset allocation was much better structured: exposure to ordinary shares had reached 12.5% and preference shares 16.5% (holdings had been increased gradually through the 1920s) with government bonds only 20%.[105] It had taken Scottish Widows a considerable length of time to reach this point, and the comparison with Standard Life is interesting. The latter seemed to be better organised than Scottish Widows: its move into equities was earlier and its experience during the 1929–1932 period when equity markets collapsed would have been less traumatic. It would appear, at the very least, that during the 1920s James Ivory at Standard Life made a more successful contribution than Carlyle Gifford at Scottish Widows as far as investment policy was concerned.

Standard Life and Scottish Widows were amongst several life offices that were now allocating more time and resources to investing. The Prudential, the largest of them all, under May's guidance and consistent with his paper from 1912 had begun investing in ordinary shares from the mid-1920s onwards, most notably acquiring a 15% shareholding in Marks & Spencer in 1926 when it became a public company.[106] In February 1928 the chairman of the Pearl Assurance Company said,

The effects of war in matters of finance have taught us . . . that it may be safer to have a proportion of our investments based on the trading results of great and stable corporations i.e. in first class ordinary stocks and shares, rather than entirely on a fixed monetary payment such as is given by . . . gilt-edged investments.[107]

---

[105] *Scottish Widows Annual Reports, 1922 and 1947* (Lloyds Banking Group Archives).

[106] Laurie Dennett, *A Sense of Security: 150 years of Prudential* (Granta 1998) 262. George May after retiring from the Prudential in early 1931 chaired the May Committee, which advocated government expenditure cuts in 1931. This was in direct contradiction to Keynes who argued against deflationary policies. It is unlikely that May and Keynes would have shared similar investment ideas.

[107] Peter Scott, *Towards the Cult of the Equity? Insurance Companies and the Inter-war Capital Markets* (The Economic History Review, Feb 2002).

At the same time, the Pearl announced that it was strengthening asset management by 'building up a department of men trained in economics and finance; in fact an organisation which can capably advise on and handle the statistical and economic problems involved'.[108] Also in 1928, Clerical Medical invested in ordinary shares and then went one step further in 1930 by creating its own investment trust to operate as a mechanism for gaining equity exposure for in-house funds. Equity & Law established an Investment Department in 1933, also introduced biweekly meetings of its investment committee and like Clerical Medical, created its own equity investment trust.[109] There were further indications of experimentation too by Equity & Law in 1937 when the chairman admitted to taking a 'somewhat speculative. . . . (investment approach) . . . to what might be described as hidden reserves or undisclosed profits . . . money which we could afford to lose – though we have no intention of losing it'.[110] As Murray, the Actuary at the Scottish Equitable pointed out in the same year, 'There seems to have been no period comparable with the last twenty years so far as the investment development in insurance is concerned. Most offices now do have a separate official in charge of a separate investment department and the keeping of financial and economic records of all kinds.'[111]

It is clear, therefore, that by the middle of the inter-war years asset management within life offices was changing. As chairman at the National Mutual, Keynes had argued for three things, first that asset management was a specialist activity and required particular expertise in order to conduct an effective investment policy; second, that life assurance companies should exploit wider investment opportunities with active investment policies; and third, equities should be included within portfolios. Murray's comments to the Faculty of Actuaries

[108] Peter Scott, *Towards the Cult of the Equity? Insurance companies and the Inter-war Capital Markets* (The Economic History Review, Feb 2002).

[109] Peter Scott, *Towards the Cult of the Equity? Insurance Companies and the Inter-war Capital Markets* (The Economic History Review, Feb 2002).

[110] Peter Scott, *Towards the Cult of the Equity? Insurance Companies and the Inter-war Capital Markets* (The Economic History Review, Feb 2002).

[111] AC Murray, *The Investment Policy of Life Assurance Offices* (Transactions of the Faculty of Actuaries 16/152, 1937).

in November 1937 would suggest that just about all life assurance companies had allocated greater resources to asset management, so it seems clear that the first of Keynes big ideas had been generally accepted by the mid-1930s. But had his second radical idea, particularly investing into ordinary shares, been accepted by life assurance companies in the inter-war years? Table 5.2 shows that the direction of travel was clear in that the average holdings of ordinary shares by life offices had increased significantly in the inter-war years and that by 1959 ordinary shares had become the largest individual asset class.[112] Looking back from 1975, one of Keynes' fellow directors at the National Mutual explained it as follows: 'It is certainly correct to say that it was Keynes who demonstrated to the life offices that investment in industrial and commercial ordinary shares as well as in insurance and investment trust equities was a desirable investment policy for the growth of a life fund.'[113]

While the average life office portfolio in Table 5.2 in 1913 may have reflected Bailey's investment principles, that was not the case by 1937 because exposure to mortgages, debentures and cash equivalents was much diminished. Asset allocation had changed very significantly but this was still a work in progress for many life assurance offices. The overall position with reference to ordinary shares varied significantly from institution to institution. In 1937, some life offices such as Eagle Star, Equity & Law, Brittanic, Provident Mutual and Standard Life had significant holdings in ordinary shares of more than 15% of their assets but another 44 life offices had 8% or less invested in those assets.[114] It seems that in the inter-war years, life offices were moving away from Bailey's investment principles in terms of asset allocation but there was no consensus on the role of

---

[112] Mae Baker and Michael Collins, *The asset composition of British life insurance firms, 1900–1965* (Financial History Review 10, 2003) 137–164. Note that May and Collins explain in their very informative paper that ordinary shares became the largest asset class in 1954 but that date is not shown in the table.

[113] Nicholas Davenport, *Keynes in the City*, in Essays on John Maynard Keynes, ed. Milo Keynes (Cambridge University Press 1975) Chapter 20.

[114] Mae Baker and Michael Collins, *The asset composition of British life insurance firms, 1900–1965* (Financial History Review 10, 2003). Additionally, it should be noted that two small life offices National Farmers and Friends Provident, both mutuals, had, respectively, 29% and 22% invested in ordinary shares as at 1937.

Table 5.2 Life offices asset allocation 1900–1959

	1900 allocation[a] (%)	1913 allocation (%)	1924 allocation (%)	1937 allocation (%)	1959 allocation (%)
Property	9	8	6	5	8
Mortgages	27	21	11	11	13
Loans (private)	5	6	4	3	1
Loans (public)	11	6	4	7	3
Government bonds	2	1	32	22	19
Other government bonds	9	16	16	12	6
Debentures	17	25	12	16	14
Preference shares[a]	11	6	4	8	6
Ordinary shares	n/a	3	4	10	20
Other	7	8	8	5	8
Total	98	100	101	99	98
Value £ (million)	288	396	447	881	1,657

[a] No sub-division between preference and ordinary shares in 1900; actual would have been 9/2 or 10/1
This is a simplified version of data excluding some time periods and sub-totals and has been extracted from Baker and Collins, *The Asset Composition of British Life Insurance Firms, 1900–1965* (Financial History Review 10, 2003) page 149

ordinary shares within portfolios. That the debate continued was high-lighted by an actuarial paper in 1933 from William Penman, which staunchly defended the investment principles of Bailey as follows: 'I hold very strongly the view that... where new investments are con-cerned... that the avoidance of capital loss or depreciation is more important than the rate of interest obtained.'[115] Penman dismissed invest-ing in ordinary shares because, he argued, capital loss was unacceptable.

---

[115] William Penman, *A Review of Investment Principles and Practice* (Journal of the Institute of Actuaries 64/3, 1933).

These comments received short shrift from one of the attendees at the meeting, CRV Coutts, actuary at the United Kingdom Provident Institution. Dismissively, Coutts said, 'Bailey's principles hardly touched the fringe of present investment problems. . . . he [Coutts] did not agree that the avoidance of capital loss was more important than the rate of interest obtained. The rate of interest was the main and vital thing.'[116] Coutts argued that returns achieved by the investment portfolio were more important than security and that, while Bailey's ideas may have been relevant to Britain in the 1860s, the circumstances of the 1930s were entirely different. Coutts was both correct and also talking the same language as Keynes and Raynes, and the result would be a victory by the 1950s, for more progressive thinking.

5.3   1939–1960: All Change

Inevitably the Second World War affected investment portfolios but, in some respects, the post 1945 behaviour of government was even more significant than the impact of the war itself. During the war, the British government had sent Gifford to the USA to liquidate British-owned investments in order to help with the finance of the war effort. Most of this happened during 1940 and was largely completed by 1941.[117] The government had moved much more quickly than during the First World War and rather than leaving the decisions to individual institutions, the government in the shape of Carlyle Gifford had requisitioned the assets and sold them through JP Morgan.[118] Immediately after the war in

---

[116] Coutts had trained at the National Mutual, he invested materially in ordinary shares at the National Provident where he was the Actuary, he was friendly to Keynes and he joined the Independent Investment Company in 1932 as a director. He was a natural adversary of Penman.

[117] *Scottish Widows Annual Report, 1941* (Lloyds Banking Group Archives). The report explained that the large increase in holdings of government bonds was attributable to, 'in the main from the requisitioning of the British Government of holdings of securities in the United States'.

[118] Richard Burns, *A Century of Investing: Baillie Gifford's First 100 Years* (Birlinn 2008) Chapter 4. This chapter contains a comprehensive account of Gifford's activities in the US liquidating British investments and that Keynes disagreed with the rapid pace of disposals by Gifford. It also highlights an incident in which Gifford and Keynes clashed over the valuation assigned to Viscose, an unquoted subsidiary of Courtaulds.

1945, the British government introduced a policy of 'cheap money' by massaging down bond yields to 2.5%. At the same it was nationalising what it regarded as strategically important industries such as the Bank of England, and a number of other quoted British companies, recompensing the ordinary shareholders with government bonds paying 3% (Chapter 8). For Scottish Widows, the main impact of government activity in the financial markets came in 1947 with the nationalisation of its equity holdings in electricity supply companies.[119] Consequently, but unintentionally, Scottish Widows found itself holding 31% of its assets in government bonds, back to levels held just after the First World War though on a much lower yield. However, this time it really was different because during the First World War, Scottish Widows had been willing to support the war effort by accepting lower returns on government bonds compared to prevailing market rates.[120] In 1948 on the other hand, Scottish Widows had been forced into holding bonds for political rather than patriotic considerations. Furthermore, yields were unpalatably low. Investment into ordinary shares would continue to increase at Scottish Widows, so at the end of 1948, even after nationalisation of their electricity holdings, over 20% of the portfolio was held in this asset class rising to over 40% by 1957.[121] Standard Life had a very similar approach to asset allocation with ordinary shares increasing to over 40% by 1959 and government bonds representing less than 10% of their assets. Keynes had died in April 1946 but the need for the active management of investment policy, applied by skilled practitioners and the attractions of ordinary shares, as advocated him in the 1920s, had never been clearer. The late 1940s was a key period for institutional investors in Britain who had lost trust in their own government and its handling of the equity and bond markets. By 1959, the Keynesian vision of asset management was much more prevalent than that of Bailey, as Table 5.2 shows.

---

[119] *Scottish Widows Annual Report, 1947* (Lloyds Banking Group Archives).

[120] *Scottish Widows Annual Report, 1916* (Lloyds Banking Group Archives).

[121] *Scottish Widows Annual Reports, 1948 & 1957* (Lloyds Banking Group Archives). Of note, for the first time, holdings of ordinary shares by Scottish Widows exceeded those of preference shares in 1948.

5.4   Keynes' Influence

Keynes and Raynes stimulated new thinking about life office investment that superseded the investment principles of Bailey from the mid-nineteenth century. They directly challenged Bailey's investment ideas much more effectively than the polite attempt in 1912 by May of the Prudential. In the changed conditions of post-war Britain, Keynes had an optimistic belief that asset management was important and should be better organised and resourced. Complementing Keynes' perspective as an economist, Raynes approached Bailey's principles from a more conciliatory actuarial standpoint, based on analysing capital market performance from the past. Both had a belief in the benefits of investing in ordinary shares and by the late 1930s a cohort of life offices endorsed the approach; this argument had been largely won by 1938 and had become the conventional wisdom by the 1950s. It was also evident that insurance companies had strengthened their asset management expertise, as Keynes had exhorted in 1922, though it is questionable whether many of the life companies had gone as far in this direction as he would have liked and that included his own company, the National Mutual, where Moore took over as Chairman in 1938 but did not possess the interest and vision of Keynes in investment matters.

It would be unrealistic to argue that just two men, Keynes and Raynes, were entirely responsible for changing investment thinking at life offices during the 1920s and 1930s. As noted earlier, some institutions such as Standard Life and the Prudential were gradually changing their approach to asset management in the early part of the twentieth century. Naturally, there were other personalities and forces – political, economic, financial and social – at work after 1918 which influenced the shape of capital markets and asset management. Equally, it would be nonsense to argue that Keynes and Raynes had no effect on investment thinking in the 1920s and 1930s, though one historian, Trebilcock, expressed the view that insurance companies generally resisted what he dubbed 'investment Keynesianism'.[122]

---

[122] Clive Trebilcock, *Phoenix Assurance and the Development of British Insurance: Vol 2, 1870–1984* (Cambridge University Press 1999) 598. Trebilcock argued that Keynes did not materially influence the investment policies of insurance companies during the inter-war years and that the increase in holdings of ordinary shares was not a trend but an anomaly owing to the data being

Trebilcock's assessment was probably correct in the context of general insurance companies based on Keynes' investment practices at the Provincial, and, within life offices there would have been some personal antipathy to Keynes' methods and personality. Nevertheless, particularly with life offices, Keynes' main ideas about institutional asset management were in due course, broadly adopted. In 1921, as chairman of the National Mutual, Keynes arrived like a whirlwind into the arcane actuarial world of insurance company investment and he was impossible to ignore because he was cogent and highly visible. He was prominent in the media throughout the 1920s, constantly airing his critical views on returning to the Gold Standard and subsequent monetary policy. Therefore, Keynes received much media attention, and not just through his speeches at the annual meeting of the National Mutual. He remained newsworthy and even achieved significant coverage when he wasn't being rude about his competitors or actuaries, in areas such as the announcement of annual bonuses and restricting new business. One account of his National Mutual annual speech in 1934 claimed that the government bond market rose the following day owing to his influence and reputation.[123] Keynes was the catalyst who accelerated changes to investment policy at life assurance funds: he had strong views; he aired them in the public domain; they were reported extensively, and people listened. As noted above, by 1937 investment policies were changing or had changed: most, if not all, life offices had specialist investment staff and many were comfortable with diversifying their asset allocation. This meant that in the aftermath of 1945 many insurance companies were well placed to implement an active investment policy, as Keynes explained after 1921, the following passage, probably from 1919, shows how poorly developed asset management was and that it deserved Keynes' ridicule,

On meeting Geoffrey Marks, Keynes had been told it had hitherto been actuarial practice in the life offices to distribute money at call, government

---

skewed by the actions of a small number of very large companies such as the Prudential. Subsequent work by Scott (2002) and Baker and Collins (2003) suggest that Trebilcock's analysis was incorrect.

[123] Nicholas Davenport, *Memoirs of a City Radical* (Willmer Bros 1974) 49.

bonds, loans and mortgages, debentures and reversions in more or less fixed proportions ... Maynard listened with amazement. 'Incredible!' he said 'I would have thought that the right investment policy for the National Mutual would be to hold one security only and change it every week at the Board meeting'.[124]

Keynes resigned in October 1938 as chairman of the National Mutual and according to Davenport, the reason for the resignation was that increasingly Keynes found the committee and board structure too troublesome, whereas at the Provincial and Kings College Cambridge, he had much greater freedom and autonomy.[125] He had been ill from mid-1937 having suffered a serious thrombosis. Curzon at the National Mutual, acting chairman in Keynes' absence, was unhappy with the state of the investment portfolio and that the end-1937 accounts revealed an unrealised capital loss of £641,000.[126] Clearly, the short-term performance results over the preceding year were very poor and Keynes openly acknowledged this – 'a dismal year' – at the annual meeting of policyholders in 1938.[127] Disappointingly, this was a low point on which to bow out, but over 17 years as chairman and as an investor, Keynes had achieved much with investment policy:

The measure of success of Keynes' investment policy was the pre-eminent position attained by the National Mutual.... There was a satisfactory capital surplus in hand at the end of 1938.... exceptionally high bonuses influenced the Society's position in the 'league table' for a long time afterwards [up until 1950 and beyond].... Keynes indeed revolutionized the Society's investment policy. Active dealing in gilt-edged stocks on predicted changes in the rate of interest, large scale investment in ordinary shares British and foreign (which were bought and sold on economic

---

[124] Nicholas Davenport, *Keynes in the City*, in Essays on John Maynard Keynes, ed. Milo Keynes (Cambridge, 1975) Chapter 20. It is not stated but presumably the date of this first meeting between Marks and Keynes was 1919, just after he had been appointed a director in September.

[125] Nicholas Davenport, *Keynes in the City*, in Essays on Keynes, ed. Milo Keynes (Cambridge, 1975) Chapter 20.

[126] The National Mutual Life Assurance Society, CW XII, 37.

[127] *Report to the Annual General Meeting of the National Mutual*, 20 February 1938 (CW XII) 233.

forecasts as well as on the conventional consideration of company accounts), hedging of the currency risk on foreign holdings – all these and other sophisticated techniques were introduced and vigorously practiced. Some were years ahead of their time. All are commonplace today [in 1980].[128]

He was a man ahead of his time and Ross Goobey (Chapter 8) also identified this trait of Keynes in 1957, referring to his 'astonishing foresight' when considering his own ideas about pension fund investment policy during the 1950s. As Ross Goobey said, 'In a speech of historical interest delivered at the AGM in 1928 Lord Keynes was more specific and propounded at length with eloquence and astonishing foresight the case for an active investment policy and for investment in Ordinary shares "within the due bounds of prudence."'[129] On this evidence, Keynes was about 30 years ahead of his contemporaries and, after his final annual meeting as chairman, but prior to his resignation, *The Economist* was in no doubt as to his stature within the investment community, writing, 'Mr. Keynes is regarded today as the spokesman par excellence of the institutional investor.'[130] An indication of how much Keynes' own understanding of markets and asset management had developed over the previous two decades is provided by some of his very perceptive comments in 1938, following a particularly difficult year for markets when UK equities had fallen by 17% and government bonds by 12%.[131] In his final address as Chairman, he referred to speculative markets in the following terms, '(they) are governed by doubt rather than conviction, by fear more than by forecast, by memories of last time and not by foreknowledge of next time. The level of stock exchange prices does not mean that investors know, it means they do not know'.[132] Publicly, he was

[128] Eric Street, *The National Mutual Life Assurance Society 1830–1980* (National Mutual, 1980) 35.

[129] George Ross Goobey, *Draft Review of Investment Policy for the Pension Fund*, 1 May 1957 (LMA/4481/a/01/001).

[130] *The Economist*, 26 February 1938. Chambers and Dimson make a similar point about Keynes being a generation ahead of other institutional investors in their extensive analysis of Keynes' investment activities at Kings College, Cambridge.

[131] *Barclays Equity Gilt Study 2012.*

[132] *Report to the Annual General Meeting of the National Mutual*, 20 February 1938 (CW XII) 238.

saying that markets fluctuate because they are irrational and inefficient. Privately, a month later in a letter to Curzon, he had similar observations about the psychological pressure on asset managers, and specifically directors of life companies who made investment decisions:

> I feel no shame at being found still owning a share when the bottom of the market comes. I do not think it is the business, far less the duty, of an institutional or any other serious investor to be constantly considering whether he should cut and run on a falling market, or to feel himself open to blame if shares depreciate on his hands. I would go much further than that. I should say that it is from time to time the duty of a serious investor to accept the depreciation of his holdings with equanimity without reproaching himself. Any other policy is anti-social, destructive of confidence, and incompatible with the working of the economic system. [133]

Whereas Curzon was worried about what to sell as markets tumbled, Keynes was concerned about how institutional asset management should function in the febrile world of the late 1930s, divided between different political systems and on the verge of another world war. During the 1920s and 1930s, by his words and actions, he was a visionary investment leader as the chairman of a life assurance company. Slowly, and at their own pace and in their own ways, life offices followed Keynes' encouragement to improve their investment capabilities. In terms of asset management expertise, insurance companies were in a much stronger position after the Second World War than they had been at the end of the First World War. Keynes' direct influence on the investment behaviour and thinking of life offices is difficult to quantify but several institutions – Standard Life, Scottish Widows, Legal & General, Pearl, Equity & Law, Eagle Star, Provident Mutual – adopted or adapted his ideas during the 1920s and the industry in aggregate had embraced his main thinking by the 1950s. As a bare minimum he accelerated the development of institutional asset management capabilities within life offices. More fundamentally perhaps, his underlying observation was

---

[133] Keynes to Curzon, letter 1 March 1938 (CW XII) 38.

clearly correct that the world had changed after 1918 in terms of economic leadership, government finances and securities' markets, so that asset management needed to respond to these changes, challenges and opportunities. Keynes' particular insight was to identify ordinary shares as the natural home for institutional investors with a long-term horizon. Very importantly, he also had a range of influential acquaintances within the actuarial community in both England and Scotland, of whom Raynes at the Legal & General was the most important but with further support from Coutts and Recknell. Significantly, Keynes was investing in equities at a similar point in time to some of the renowned investors in the USA and before the intellectual arguments for ordinary share investment had been articulated. He intuitively understood the huge opportunity provided by equity investing. Perhaps this is one reason why he was willing to be leveraged, or as a minimum fully invested, for most of his life. In addition, he was aware that over the long-term equities were much more likely than bonds to maintain real spending power. Certain strands of his investment thinking had appeared as chairman of the National Mutual during the 1920s and 1930s but it would take more than another 30 years for many of his other insights and achievements as an asset manager to emerge. Some life offices listened to his investment ideas and benefited. But life offices in aggregate should have paid more attention because he offered them a remarkable opportunity to establish themselves as the pre-eminent investing institutions in Britain and he gave them clear ideas about what they needed to do in order to be successful. They should have paid more attention to Keynes than they did.

Bibliography

Primary Sources

Kings College Cambridge, Archive Centre holds the extensive papers of *John Maynard Keynes*
The Lloyds Banking Group Archives contains archival material on *Scottish Widows* including their annual reports to policyholders

The London Metropolitan Archive (LMA) holds comprehensive archival material, including Board minutes and some of Keynes' correspondence, about the *National Mutual Life Assurance Society*

Books

Clive Bell, *Old Friends* (Harcourt Brace 1957)
Richard Burns, *A Century of Investing: Baillie Gifford's First 100 Years* (Birlinn 2008)
John Butt, Standard Life, in *The Historian and the Business of Insurance*, ed. Oliver Westall (Manchester University Press 1984)
George Clayton and William Osborn, *Insurance Company Investment* (Allen & Unwin 1965)
Nicholas Davenport, Keynes in the City in *Essays on John Maynard Keynes*, ed. Milo Keynes (Cambridge University Press 1975)
Nicholas Davenport, *Memoirs of a City Radical* (Willmer Bros 1974)
Richard Davenport-Hines, *Universal Man, The Seven Lives of John Maynard Keynes* (William Collins 2015)
Laurie Dennett, *A Sense of Security: 150 Years of Prudential* (Granta 1998)
Ali Kabiri, *The Great Crash of 1929* (Palgrave Macmillan 2015)
Maria Cristina Marcuzzo, Keynes and Cambridge, in *The Cambridge Companion to Keynes*, ed. Backhouse and Bateman (Cambridge University Press 2006)
Donald Moggridge ed., *The Collected Writings of John Maynard Keynes, Volume XII, Economic Articles and Correspondence: Investment and Editorial* (Cambridge University Press 2013)
Michael Moss, *Standard Life, 1825–2000* (Mainstream 2000)
Robert Skidelsky, *The Economist as Saviour 1929–1937* (Macmillan 1992)
Robert Skidelsky, *John Maynard Keynes, 1883–1946: Economist, Philosopher, Statesman* (Penguin 2003)
Edgar Lawrence Smith, *Common Stocks as Long Term Investments* (Macmillan 1928)
Eric Street, *The National Mutual Life Assurance Society 1830–1980* (self-published 1980)
Barry Supple, *The Royal Exchange Assurance: A History of British Insurance 1720–1970* (Cambridge University Press 1970)
Clive Trebilcock, *Phoenix Assurance and the Development of British Insurance: Volume 2, 1870–1984* (Cambridge University Press 1999)
John Wasik, *Keynes' Way to Wealth* (McGraw Hill 2014)
Oliver Westall, *The Provincial Insurance Company* (Manchester University Press 1992)

Articles, Journals, Pamphlets, Websites, etc.

Mae Baker and Michael Collins, The Asset Composition of British Life Insurance Firms, 1900–1965 (*Financial History Review* 10, 2003)

Barclays Equity Gilt Study, 2012

David Chambers and Elroy Dimson, Retrospectives: John Maynard Keynes, investment innovator (*Journal of Economic Perspectives* 27/3, 2013)

David Chambers and Elroy Dimson, The British Origins of the US Endowment Model (*Financial Analysts Journal* 71/2, 2015)

David Chambers, Dimson, E. and Foo, J., Keynes the Stock Market Investor: A Quantitative Analysis (*Journal of Financial and Quantitative Analysis* 50/4, 2015)

Paul Dawson, Mark Ellis, Mark Holder and Richard Kent, Keynes on Financial Markets: Why Didn't You Listen? (*Review of Futures Markets* 18, 2009)

The Economist

Benjamin Graham (www.c250.columbia.edu/c250_celebrates/your_Columbians/benjamin_graham)

Mark Holder and Dick Kent, On the Art of Investing According to Keynes (*The Journal of Portfolio Management* 37, 2011)

Homestake Mining, Record Profits on the Eve of WW 2 (www.encyclopedia.com)

Daniel Kahneman and Amos Tversky, Prospect Theory: An Analysis of Decision Under Risk. (*Econometrica* 47/2, 1979)

Richard ('Dick') Kent, Keynes' Investment Activities While in the Treasury During World War *1* (*History of Economics Review* 56, 2012)

John Maynard Keynes (www.maynardkeynes.org)

George May, The Investment of Life Assurance Funds (*Journal of the Institute of Actuaries* 46/2, 1912)

AC Murray, The Investment Policy of Life Assurance Offices (*Transactions of the Faculty of Actuaries* 16/152, 1937)

National Bureau for Economic Research, Chapter 13, Interest Rates

William Penman A Review of Investment Principles and Practice (*Journal of the Institute of Actuaries* 64/3, 1933)

HF Purchase, Memoir (*Journal of the Institute of Actuaries* 90, 1964)

Harold Raynes, The Place of Ordinary Stocks and Shares in the Investment of Life Assurance Funds (*Journal of the Institute of Actuaries* 59, 1928)

Harold Raynes, Equities and Fixed Interest Stocks During 25 Years (*Journal of the Institute of Actuaries* 68, 1937)

George Ross Goobey, *Draft Review of Investment Policy for the Pension Fund*, 1 May 1957 (LMA/4481/a/01/001)

John Maynard Keynes (www.sandaire.com)

The Scotsman

Peter Scott, Towards the cult of the equity? Insurance Companies and the Inter-war Capital Markets (*The Economic History Review* 55/1, 2002)

The Times

Oliver Westall, *Riding the Tiger* (University of Lancaster, Management School discussion paper, 1992)

6

Keynes – Flawed Investor or Genius?

This chapter explores two further aspects of Keynes' activity as an institutional investor: at a publicly quoted investment company, the Independent Investment Company (the 'Independent') and an endowment fund, the Discretionary Fund at Kings College, Cambridge (the 'Discretionary Fund'). It can be read in conjunction with Chapter 5, which discussed Keynes' asset management activities in the context of life assurance offices in general, and the National Mutual in particular so it should broaden understanding of Keynes as an investor. At a secondary level, this chapter also provides additional information about the British economy and financial markets between 1921 and 1946. Nevertheless, the emphasis remains on Keynes as an institutional investor, and with these varied asset management roles, it highlights that he operated under differing constraints with varying degrees of personal freedom.

At the National Mutual, the investment objective was to exceed the liabilities on long-term life policies and to distribute surplus profits to policyholders. At the Independent, the investment goal was to make money for shareholders and outperform other investment companies. With the Discretionary Fund, there was a requirement to meet the

© The Author(s) 2017
N.E. Morecroft, *The Origins of Asset Management*
from 1700 to 1960, Palgrave Studies in the History of Finance,
DOI 10.1007/978-3-319-51850-3_6

ongoing spending requirements of Kings College and, ideally, maintain the real value of the assets over the long-term. Of the three portfolios, Keynes had most autonomy at the Discretionary Fund and least at the National Mutual while at the Independent, Keynes and Oswald Falk were the two principal investment decision-makers with Carlyle Gifford in the background. The Prospectus of the Independent provides a very clear insight into Keynes' investment ideas at the beginning of 1924 which, in turn, influenced investment decisions that were taken at the National Mutual in the summer of that year, so his different investment activities are interconnected. Additionally, his management, over 25 years, of the Discretionary Fund shows very clearly that after the 1929 Crash, his investment beliefs changed fundamentally from 'top down' market timing to 'bottom up' stock selection (as documented extensively by Chambers and Dimson), and as a result, disappointing investment returns during the 1920s were transformed by stellar investment performance in the 1930s. Finally, the experiences at the Independent, which was a failure, and the Discretionary Fund, ultimately a success, highlight that results in asset management can be influenced by both luck and timing. Keynes learnt important lessons from the former which, in time, contributed to his success with the latter.

As an investor, Keynes' determination, strong personality, originality and willingness to take risks were often challenging for the people with whom he worked and the institutions with which he was involved. With the Provincial Insurance Company, his overconfidence was described thus, 'he foreswore any concession to the possibility that he might make mistakes'.[1] At one level his results were considered formidable owing to outstanding long-term performance returns but at another, they were questionably volatile for a general insurance company.[2] The Provincial for example, in 1938, was within a whisker of being insolvent which highlights the nature of his impact rather well.[3] Similarly, in early 1938 at the National Mutual, when Francis Curzon deputised as chairman for an incapacitated Keynes, he panicked at the unrealised losses experienced in 1937 and imposed a more conservative

---

[1] Oliver Westall, *Riding the Tiger* (University of Lancaster 1992).
[2] Oliver Westall, *Riding the Tiger* (University of Lancaster 1992).
[3] Oliver Westall, *The Provincial Insurance Company*, 1903–38 (Manchester University Press 1992) 373.

investment policy.[4] This change of policy could only be agreed in Keynes' absence because he completely dominated discussions when present in person, as one of his fellow directors at the National Mutual (Davenport) pointed out.[5] His powerful intellect, together with his overweening self-confidence, had the potential to create substantial problems and he had several investment disasters during the 1920s and 1930s in currencies and commodities as well as securities markets, though, the Independent apart, he generally recovered from his investment mishaps.[6] He was an investor, and occasional speculator, with definite weaknesses.

He was also an asset manager possessing great strengths based on his tremendous capacity for original investment thinking borne out in two areas: first, his methods of asset management at the Discretionary Fund and the outstanding performance results in the 1930s and 1940s; and, second the manner in which he described investing in his written work. He possessed and expressed remarkable insights about the nature of markets and investors, many of which remain relevant today. His thoughts and words could be categorised in various ways, three of which might be: the importance of time and long-term investing; portfolio construction with specific reference to concentrated portfolios of equities; and finally, the mass psychology of markets together with the emotional pressures on individual investors, which today would be termed 'behavioural finance'.[7] His investment ideas were years ahead of their time, maybe too far ahead which could be one reason why he did not have greater impact on other

---

[4] *National Mutual Private Minutes, Board & Finance Committee*, 9 February 1938 (LMA MS 34469).

[5] Nicholas Davenport, *Memoirs of a City Radical* (Willmer Bros 1974) 41.

[6] His principal investment disasters were as follows: 1920, he was basically insolvent and needed an emergency loan having gambled on currencies, and lost; in 1929 he lost money on commodities at a time when he was heavily geared and he was nearly wiped out; also in 1929, the PR investment company was on the brink of failing having lost 85% of its value during the 1920s and he sub-divided the assets into two parts between Falk and himself; 1932-34, the Independent; 1937–1938, the Provincial. He also suffered major losses trading commodities in 1929 and 1937/38.

[7] An interesting collection of Keynes' investment observations is summarised in Mark Holder & Dick Kent, *On the Art of Investing According to Keynes* (The Journal of Portfolio Management 37, 2011). An even wider selection of quotations by Keynes is included in a precursor to that article in Paul Dawson, Mark Ellis, Mark Holder & Richard Kent, *Keynes on Financial Markets: Why Didn't You Listen?* (Review of Futures Markets 18, 2009).

investors and investing institutions, with endowment funds for example, during his own lifetime. He produced very strong investment results over 25 years at the Discretionary Fund, and the manner in which they were achieved is instructive. Particularly in the early 1930s, Keynes displayed dexterity of thought combined with real mental toughness – essential personal attributes of all successful asset managers.

6.1   The Flawed Investor – The Independent Investment Company

The Independent was established in January 1924 as an investment company, a quoted, closed-end investment trust with paid up capital of £350,000 in shares of £10 each, partly paid. The original directors were Falk, Keynes and Carlyle Gifford.[8] The Independent had a top-down investment ethos: it intended to use the 'credit cycle' in order to make market-timing decisions based on movements between different asset classes. The investment approach was explained in the Prospectus as follows:

> Considerable profits can be made by changing from one [asset] class to another at the appropriate phase of the credit cycle . . . the course of events is sufficiently regular to enable those who are in close and constant touch with the financial situation in certain instances to anticipate impending changes in the credit cycle . . . the policy of moving from time to time from one category of investment to another will require that the funds of the Company should in the main be employed in investments which are readily marketable.[9]

Early in 1924, Falk explained, perhaps lectured would be a better description, the market-timing based 'credit cycle' investment approach to

---

[8] Carlyle Gifford was the third director involved at the Independent from 1924 until 1931 when he resigned. In practice, the two key investment decision-makers were Keynes and Falk in London; Gifford was Edinburgh based. Nevertheless, Gifford was important member of this triumvirate and generally chaired the annual meeting of shareholders.

[9] *Independent Investment Company, Prospectus* January 1924 (Guildhall Library).

Gifford when he pointed out that the Independent needed to invest in a small number of liquid, easily traded ordinary shares and not a long list of smaller holdings.[10] The intention was to pay attention to monetary conditions and hold liquid investments and then to move aggressively between different asset classes, across and within equities and bonds though other investments, such as currencies and commodities, were not excluded. The Independent intended to trade between and within asset classes at opportune times in order to make money. After the initial partly paid fund raising at the beginning of 1924, the Independent had £175,000 to invest, representing 50% of the total money raised, Table 6.1 shows the 15 largest holdings in the portfolio – by asset class the split is as follows: 65% ordinary shares, just over 5% in preferred shares and 4% in deferred shares (so 74% equity) with the balance of 26% in UK debentures (corporate bonds).[11] No government bonds were held which was a recurring theme in Keynes' portfolios. The Independent was invested in a broad cross section

Table 6.1 The Independent portfolio 1924: 15 largest holdings

Name	Type	%
Shell	Ordinary share	7.7
Underground Electric Rail Bonds	Debenture	5.5
Mather & Platt	Ordinary share	3.7
Burma Corporation	Ordinary share	3.4
Dunlop Rubber 8% Debenture	Debenture	3.1
General Electric	Ordinary share	3.0
Imperial Tobacco	Ordinary share	3.0
Royal Exchange Inscribed	Debenture	3.0
British American Tobacco	Ordinary share	2.9
Eagle Oil Transport 7% Notes	Debenture	2.9
Forestal Land	Ordinary share	2.9
Armstrong Whitworth Notes	Debenture	2.8
James Finlay	Ordinary share	2.8
Jute Industries Preference	Preference share	2.7
Furness Withy	Ordinary share	2.7

Source: Kings College Archive, JMK/IIC/2/2

---

[10] Falk to Gifford, letter 8 February 1924 (Kings College Archive, JMK/IIC/1).

[11] As noted previously, preference shares have been classified as equity instruments throughout this book.

of UK industrial businesses: Mather & Platt were mechanical engineers based in Oldham; General Electric, commercial electrical engineering, which became Marconi in due course; Furness Withy, shipbuilders and marine engineers. Stocks related to commodities also featured prominently. Shell was the Anglo/Dutch oil company created in February 1907 through the amalgamation of Shell Transport & Trading in the UK with the Royal Dutch Petroleum Company (Holland) in order to compete more effectively with Standard Oil in the USA; Burma Corporation was a mining business; James Finlay was a Glasgow-based cotton and tea specialist that had been family run for over 200 years and had been floated as a public limited company in 1924. Tobacco stocks, Imperial and British American Tobacco (BAT) also featured prominently among the largest holdings and both still survive today: Imperial Tobacco was established in 1901 with the amalgamation of 13 British tobacco companies (of which the largest was Wills) to fight the American Tobacco Company run by Buck Duke; British American Tobacco was listed on the London Stock Exchange in 1911.[12] Industrial, commercial and resource stocks dominated his portfolios. By way of contrast, established in 1868, Foreign & Colonial Investment Trust appointed its first dedicated asset manager in 1924 and started buying the ordinary shares of British industrial companies for the first time only in 1926 (Chapter 3).[13] By June 1925 the larger, fully paid-up portfolio had about 70 holdings.[14] Compared to the partly paid portfolio from March 1924, the principal new additions were US ordinary shares, namely Allied Chemical, American Smelting, Eastman Kodak, Shell Union Oil and Kennecott

---

[12] Investing in Tobacco stocks raises strong emotions and nowadays many 'ethical' investors and charitable endowments choose to shun them. But, because Tobacco companies have a capacity to survive, there is a long, continuous history of their share prices in the UK and the USA which has been analysed by Elroy Dimson, Paul Marsh and Mike Staunton in *Responsible Investing: Does it pay to be bad?* (Credit Suisse Yearbook 2015). Their analysis shows that in both countries Tobacco stocks have been among the best performing companies and that as a sector in the UK, Tobacco outperformed the broader UK market by 2.6% per annum between 1920 and 2014. A similar pattern was observed in the USA where Tobacco stocks outperformed by an even larger margin, +4.5%.

[13] John Newlands, *Put Not Your Trust in Money* (Association of Investment Trust Companies 1997) 175.

[14] John Wasik, *Keynes' Way to Wealth* (McGraw Hill 2014) 162/163.

Copper Corporation. These US stocks represented 10.5% of the portfolio and, including a holding in Swedish Match (a tobacco and match company listed in Stockholm), overseas equities represented almost 15% of the overall asset value. The large exposure to resource and commodity stocks and a continued interest in the USA were consistent features in Keynes' portfolios throughout his life.

The corporate bond holdings were small in number, only 10, but individually large and presumably relatively liquid given the willingness of the directors of the Independent to make asset allocation changes. The largest debt security, The Underground Electric Railways of London (UERL), was an interesting if not very successful business. Established in 1902, much of the initial funding to construct the London Underground came from US investors. Indicative of the growing economic influence of the USA, this represented a major reversal of capital flows given that much British money had gone into the USA to fund railroads after the 1860s. The UERL acquired a number of different transport businesses and it both operated, and also partly built three underground lines, today's Bakerloo, Northern and Piccadilly lines. It struggled financially and was taken into public ownership in 1933 under the auspices of the London Passenger Transport Board.

At the Independent, Falk had the loudest voice and Gifford the smallest with Keynes somewhere in the middle but all three were strong-willed, egocentric, driven individuals. Anecdotally, Keynes and Falk also frequently disagreed about the selection of individual securities in as much as 'Falk would buy a stock one day only for Keynes to sell it the next'.[15] But despite inevitable personality clashes and with obvious disagreements, the Independent performed well in the first five years of its existence. Gifford took the role of being the public face of the trust and he presided at the annual shareholder meetings; dividends were paid; an additional £70,000 was raised from shareholders in 1927 taking the issued

---

[15] Ewan Macpherson, telephone call, 16 July 2015. Ewan is Ian Macpherson's son. Ian was senior partner at Buckmaster & Moore and a Director of the Independent from 1931 after Gifford resigned. Scott at the Provincial also confidentially consulted Ian when doubts were harboured about the appropriateness of Keynes' investments policy in the late 1930s (see Westall, *The Provincial Insurance Company*, 373).

capital to £420,000; the market value had increased to £628,000 by 1928 but then things began to go wrong. At the end of 1928, Falk wrote to Keynes saying he planned to persuade Gifford to invest more of the Independent's assets in commodities.[16] In 1929, Falk was equally keen to re-invest into the USA: his change of view on the market directly resulted from his first visit to America that year. This marked an important disagreement with Keynes who was bearish on the US market in 1929 (Chapter 5). As the public face of the Independent, Gifford then tried to explain the thinking of the directors to the shareholders at the 5th Annual General Meeting in June 1929. Carried away perhaps by the bull market of the 1920s, or just bullied by Falk, Gifford publicly extolled the virtue of low yielding shares and explained that the Independent had been buying them for their growth potential.[17] Despite this statement of public confidence, and for reasons that were not explained, privately Gifford was harbouring doubts about what was going on at the Independent. In October 1929, just before the Wall Street Crash, Gifford wrote to Keynes saying he planned to resign from the Board because:

> The Independent has for some time been moving further away from the practice of the more normal Investment Company . . . But it has become clear to me that I cannot continue to share responsibility for the policy, without a grave risk of my personal position becoming improperly ambiguous. . . .[18]

Keynes was puzzled by Gifford's letter but persuaded him to continue as a director, writing 'indeed at recent meetings you have seemed more acquiescent in the [investment] policy which has been followed than I have'.[19] The policy in question appeared to be Falk's renewed

---

[16] Falk to Keynes, letter 5 November 1928 (Kings College Archive JMK/PR1/1).

[17] *The Times*, 18 June 1929. It is very likely that Gifford was supportive of the decision to buy ordinary shares in the USA in 1929 given that he did this for Scottish Widows just before the Crash whereas Keynes was clearly against the idea for the National Mutual (see Chapter 4). Circumstantially, therefore, Falk and Gifford outvoted Keynes on investment policy around October 1929.

[18] Gifford to Keynes, letter 26 October 1929 (King College Archive, JMK/ IIC/1).

[19] Keynes to Gifford, letter 29 October 1929 (King College Archive, JMK/ IIC/1).

enthusiasm for the USA because he had sold out of the US market in 1928, but then re-invested during the summer of 1929.[20] Entirely consistent with other descriptions, one commentator described Falk's position (albeit at the Provincial Insurance Company rather than the Independent) as follows: 'Falk became evangelically committed to the future of American securities. In June he pressed this view and British equities were sold to finance American purchases. . . . continuing to buy after the crash.'[21] Early in 1930 Falk's extreme views about British industrial failure and selling British investments in order to invest overseas had received wide coverage and Keynes even wrote to *The Times* distancing himself from Falk.[22] One of the directors at the National Mutual described Falk's broader strategic views in the following terms:

> He [Falk] was always set against British industrial equities: he had never budged from the line of his famous letter to *The Times* after the First World War when he declared that British industry was finished. In his view, American industry with its advanced technology and management skill was the only fit medium for equity investment.[23]

At the end of March 1930, the Independent had 49% of its portfolio invested in America and overall 55% was invested in equities. The Depression had barely begun; equity markets were about to get worse; and sterling would come under very serious pressure. US securities, particularly leveraged ones, were not the place to be. In March 1931, Gifford finally resigned and was replaced by Ian Macpherson from Buckmaster & Moore.[24] In that year, the Independent cut its dividend, showed asset depreciation over the year of 23% and reported that the market value of its shares stood at £154,497 less than their book value.

---

[20] Donald Moggridge, *Maynard Keynes, An Economist's Biography* (Routledge 1992) 408.

[21] Oliver Westall, *Riding the Tiger* (University of Lancaster Management School 1992).

[22] *The Times*, 13 March 1930.

[23] Nicholas Davenport, *Memoirs of a City Radical* (Willmer Bros 1974) 53.

[24] In due course at the beginning of the Second World War, Gifford and Keynes would be re-acquainted but in somewhat different circumstances – during 1940/41 Gifford was in the States selling British investments on behalf of the Churchill government to help fund the war while Keynes was back at the Treasury.

It also had a large US dollar loan, taken out in January 1931, which was about to become an even bigger debt when Britain came off the Gold Standard on 21 September 1931 resulting in sterling weakness against the US dollar. Interestingly, on 17 September 1931, Falk had proposed to Keynes that the US loan should be transferred back into sterling but Keynes refused, writing to Falk:

> What you suggest amounts in present circumstances to a frank bear speculation against Sterling...I admit that I am not clear that this would be against the national interest... [but] I am clear that an institution has no business to do such a thing at the present time...I should like to see exchange dealings controlled so as to take away the opportunity of choice.[25]

Keynes was an advocate of Britain leaving the Gold Standard and had been highly critical of Churchill's decision to go back on to Gold in 1925. Yet, in 1931 Keynes was unwilling to act in a capacity that might have helped the Independent financially at a crucial moment. It was also a strange sentiment from the man who had been very happy to short sell the war-ravaged currencies of Germany and France after 1920. Keynes must have anticipated Britain coming off Gold, and yet he refused to let Falk close the US loan. Sterling's devaluation when it came off the Gold Standard cost the Independent £40,000 at a time when its finances were already stressed.[26] It is puzzling that Keynes acted in this way. His letter, to Falk referred to above, showed a confused sense of moral responsibility; surely he had an obligation to do his best for his shareholders who had entrusted him with their money? Perhaps Keynes had inside information on which he felt unable to act or, more likely, an emotional attachment to the place of Britain and the pound in the world order. Writing in the *Sunday Express* on 27 September 1931, Keynes raised this very matter of the ethical conflict between making money and acting honourably:

> The difficult question to decide was one of honour. The City of London considered that it was under an obligation of honour to make every

---

[25] Keynes to Falk, letter 18 September 1931 (CW X11, 35).
[26] Robert Skidelsky, *The Economist as Saviour 1929–1937* (Macmillan 1992) 394.

possible effort to maintain the value of money in terms of which it had accepted large deposits from foreigners, even though the result of this was to place an intolerable strain on British industry. At what point – that was the difficult problem – were we justified in putting our own interests first?[27]

Symbolically, September 1931 formally marked the date when Britain, economically and financially, was superseded by the USA and perhaps Keynes felt he could not make financial gains from such a momentous event even though he knew it had to happen. As Keynes said, 'The great advantages to British trade and industry of our ceasing artificial efforts to maintain our currency above its real value were quickly realised.'[28] Skidelsky described Keynes as both fascinated and disgusted by money and capitalism so maybe this was an occasion when Keynes was 'fascinated' with the idea of Britain leaving Gold, but 'disgusted' at the idea of trading.[29] In practice, Keynes had written about the iniquities of the Gold Standard and thought about it deeply for more than five years. In that context, trading for the Independent at that juncture in September 1931 was just not one of Keynes' primary interests – understandably so. Honourable behaviour it may have been by Keynes in September 1931 but the value of the Independent was about to go into free-fall over the next six months: by March 1932, the market value of the securities was more than £250,000 below book value and there was a public spat with the auditors about whether the losses on the US loan should be charged to capital or revenue.[30] The point had arrived when the Independent needed extra capital meaning that the truth of the statement, allegedly by Keynes, that 'markets can stay irrational for longer than you or I can stay solvent' had indeed come to fruition.[31] During 1932, two new directors were brought onto the board of the Independent, the finance house Helbert

---

[27] *The Sunday Express*, 27 September 1931.

[28] *The Sunday Express*, 27 September 1931.

[29] Robert Skidelsky, *The Economist as Saviour 1929–1937* (Macmillan 1992) 26.

[30] *The Independent Investment Company* (Kings Col Archive, JMK/IIC/1).

[31] *John Maynard Keynes* (www.maynardkeynes.org, website accessed 2 June 2016). This famous quotation is used on the official website but in practice it appears to be apocryphal.

Wagg was appointed as the day-to-day asset manager, replacing Falk and Keynes in the management of the portfolio, and a debenture facility of £50,000 was arranged with four insurance companies to provide a safety net.[32] The lowest point for the trust was reached in March 1933 when the revenue was insufficient to pay the dividend on the preference shares and the net assets of the Independent touched £89,902. Over 9 years this represented a paper loss of 78.6% on the value of the issued share capital of £420,000 from the mid-1920s. Share prices did eventually recover so that 'by the time of Keynes's death (in 1946), the funds underlying the ordinary shares (of the Independent) had almost returned to their original issue price'.[33] That was not a much of a return for shareholders over 20 years. But, with a further twist of irony, the point when the Independent was most distressed in 1932/1933 also marked the turning point in Keynes' investment performance because this was the moment when the Discretionary Fund at Kings, Cambridge was about to enjoy a dozen years of exceptional performance.

Launched in 1924, within 10 years the Independent had all but failed, and Keynes along with Falk was one of two directors directly accountable for its demise. From 1924, Falk was chairman and, along with Keynes, the two of them were jointly responsible for establishing the company, setting investment policy and implementing day-to-day investment decisions. The Independent went badly wrong and Keynes must shoulder some of the blame even if Falk was, perhaps, the main culprit both as chairman and also owing to his excessive optimism about the US equity market in the run up to the 1929 Crash and immediately thereafter. Yet the failures at the Independent were a cathartic experience that helped Keynes become a much-improved investor during the last 15 years of his life. Keynes moved away from a market-timing approach towards stock-picking; he focused on a small

---

[32] Marks to Keynes, letter 13 June 1932 (Kings College Archive, *JMK*/IIC/1). The four insurance companies that underwrote the debenture were Eagle Star, Legal & General, National Mutual and Scottish Amicable. One of the new directors on the Independent in that year was CRV Coutts, actuary at Provident Mutual and a previous employee at the National Mutual. It is fair to say that Keynes' friends, and his colleague Marks from the National Mutual, came to his support in this moment of need in 1932.

[33] *The Independent Investment Company* (CW XII) 36.

number of preferred stock ideas, 'his pets'; he favoured higher-yielding stocks; he paid more attention to intrinsic value; his dealing activity became more muted and significantly, he kept faith with American equities through the 1930s when they recovered strongly. The timing of the change has been described as follows:

> Keynes radically switched his investment approach to a bottom-up, buy-and-hold stock-picking approach. Detailed analysis of his invest-ment correspondence as well as statistical analysis of his performance in event-time strongly suggests the choice of the early 1930s as the most likely inflection point in the evolution of his investment approach.[34]

From early 1933 onwards, Keynes' letters particularly to Scott at the Provincial are peppered with references to individual companies. This change to investment philosophy is also borne out by Keynes' speech to policyholders at the National Mutual where he was chairman. In early 1932 looking back at 1931 which was the worst year of the bear market in the UK, he argued against market-timing and explained that it would not have increased returns materially had a more active investment policy been applied. He went on to say that institutional investors with stable pools of assets needed to invest for the long-term and hold securities through the cycle (Chapter 5).[35] By early 1932, Keynes had abandoned his top down market-timing investment ideas based on the 'credit cycle' and was beginning to think as a long-term investor with a preference for stock selection within equities. Keynes learned from his investment mistakes at the Independent and he became a better asset manager during the 1930s – the Discretionary Fund was to be the main beneficiary of these changes to his invest-ment approach.

---

[34] David Chambers and Elroy Dimson *Retrospectives: John Maynard Keynes, investment innovator* (Journal of Economic Perspectives 27/3, 2013).

[35] *Report to the Annual General Meeting of the National Mutual*, 2 March 1932 (CW XII) 189.

6.2 Investment Success – The Discretionary Fund, Kings College, Cambridge

With the Discretionary Fund he enjoyed considerable autonomy as the asset manager, and reported only annually to the Estates Committee but this was a formality, and it is not apparent that his investment activities came under detailed scrutiny or challenge. The Discretionary Fund reflects the purest form of his investment ideas and was one of the first endowments to invest into equities – the subsequent high returns validated both the wisdom of the decision and the skill of Keynes.[36] He saw equities as offering a mixture of growth and higher income plus inflation protection, writing in 1925, 'an investment in common stocks is an investment in real values. An investment in bonds is an investment in money values'.[37] In an unpublished note from 1935, Keynes gave a clear indication about his thinking as an investor for the endowment assets of the college, 'the ultimate object of normal institutional investment is to purchase a reasonably secure income year by year over a moderately large number of future years'.[38] Over the 25 years to 1946, it produced a cumulative increase of more than 2500%. These were very strong returns, in both nominal and real terms, over a long time period.[39]

Initially in the 1920s relative investment performance was mediocre but it then picked up very strongly after 1930. After 8 years up to August 1929, Keynes lagged a notional index by almost 16% (geometric), so

---

[36] Keynes persuaded the Fellows at Kings to create a portfolio, the Discretionary Fund, which had investment flexibility in June 1920. It was funded by sales of agricultural land. At inception only £30,000 was allocated to it so it was much smaller than the portfolios at the Independent and the National Mutual (CW XII 89).

[37] Keynes reviewed the book by Smith, *An American Study of Shares versus Bonds as Permanent Investments*, in *The Nation and Athenaeum* in May 1925 (CW X11, 248).

[38] Keynes, *A Measuring Rod for Investment Policy*, unpublished undated note probably written in 1935 (Kings College Archive, *KCAR/3/1/1/10/32*).

[39] David Chambers *et al.*, *Keynes the Stock Market Investor: A Quantitative Analysis* (Journal of Financial and Quantitative Analysis 50/4, 2015). The performance data quoted in this section draws heavily on the detailed performance statistics compiled by Chambers and his colleagues.

that was about 2% per year.[40] Returns had been very volatile throughout the decade: strong in absolute terms but, with hindsight, disappointing relatively. In 1930 and 1931, when the equity market fell by 50%, Keynes' portfolio did less badly than the sharply falling market, by which time (August 1931) it had more than made up the relative underperformance. From 1932 onwards investment performance was exceptionally strong, particularly 1933–1936, when he outperformed the market by more than 100%.[41] These performance figures show that it took an extremely long time, more than 12 years, for Keynes to demonstrate skill as an investor, in effect over three phases of the market.

Over 25 years geometrically, the Discretionary Fund increased by 14.4% per annum, UK equities by 9% per annum; Fig. 6.1 shows the cumulative returns profile. It performed even better against inflation (Fig. 6.2), arguably a more meaningful comparator for most investors, particularly endowment funds which often have regular spending commitments. Over this 25-year period inflation was negligible as it increased by only 2.6% overall but there was deflation during the 1920s and inflation in the 1930s so it was a very unstable environment for the cost of living. The Discretionary Fund, as shown in Fig. 6.2, outperformed inflation in 18 of 21 periods, generally by very large amounts and only lagged inflation in three rolling 5-year periods around 1940. This outcome was partly achieved because Keynes had invested in equities which outperformed UK government bonds by about 3% per annum for the period from 1921 to 1946. But overall, the very high returns were achieved because Keynes outperformed the equity market, by a further 5% per annum. Keynes therefore got two major decisions right over this period: asset allocation into equities and stock selection within the asset class.

This brief resume of his investment performance over 25 years highlights impressive numbers but the more interesting aspects are the thought

---

[40] This comment about relative underperformance is slightly unfair to Keynes given that this index was not available at the time and the comparison has been made retrospectively. But, what is clear is that the pattern of returns, and their magnitude, achieved after 1932 were vastly superior to those produced beforehand.

[41] David Chambers et al., *Keynes the Stock Market Investor: A Quantitative Analysis* (JFQA 50/4, 2015). According to my calculations, Keynes cumulative outperformance between 1933 and 1936 versus UK equities was 103%.

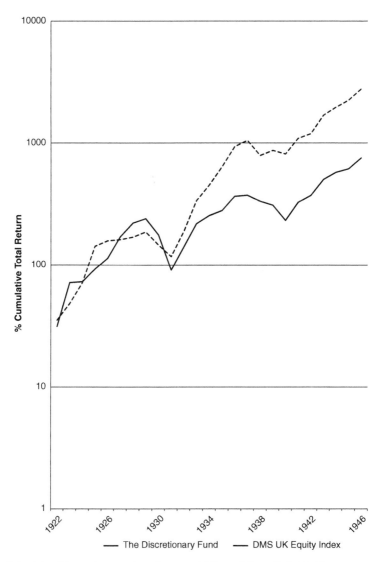

Fig. 6.1   The Discretionary Fund versus UK equities 1922–1946

All data has been taken from David Chambers et al., *Keynes the Stock Market Investor: A Quantitative Analysis* (Journal of Financial and Quantitative Analysis 50/4 2015). Annual periods begin at the end of August each year. Data has been taken for individual years which I have then compounded

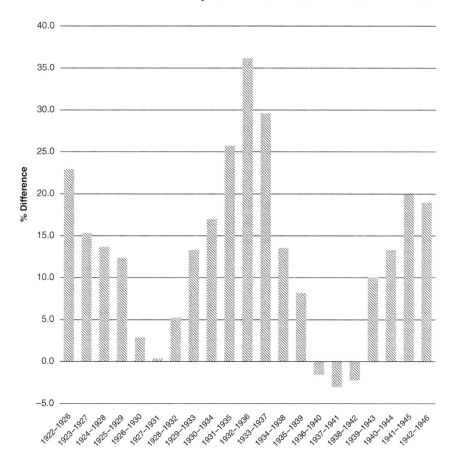

Fig. 6.2   The Discretionary Fund versus inflation 1921–1946

Data for the Discretionary Fund has been taken from David Chambers et al., *Keynes the Stock Market Investor: A Quantitative Analysis* (Journal of Financial and Quantitative Analysis 50/4 2015). Annual periods begin at the end of August each year. Data has been taken for individual years which I have then compounded. Inflation data has been taken from the Barclays Equity Gilt Study 2012 for individual calendar years which I have also compounded

processes that produced them, particularly his change of investment approach after about 1931, and his sophisticated method of portfolio construction. Keynes ascribed investment success in the 1930s to picking a small number of successful stocks, big winners, writing in 1938: 'I am convinced that the good results shown by Kings are mainly due to the large proportion of its assets held in less than 50 favourite securities.'[42] In another letter, written a couple of years later, to Scott at the Provincial he then explained with great candour how his portfolios functioned. He pointed out that most of the holdings achieved very little and that, in practice, a small number of stocks would make a huge contribution to performance, as in the case of Austin Motors (an automobile company), or what he called 'Austins':

> It is out of these big units of the small number of securities about which one feels absolutely happy that all one's profits are made. I fancy it is true that practically the whole of the appreciation of the Provincial since we started is accounted for by the profit of Austins, and the profits on Electric Power & Light and on United Gas. At any rate, I am sure I could pick out six of my pets, and that much more of our whole profit would have been made out of them. Out of the ordinary mixed bag of investments nobody ever makes anything. And if one breaks more or less even, it is the best you can possibly hope for. This has been my uniform experience in all investment connections. Exactly the same is true in the case of Kings.[43]

The investment in Austin Motors ordinary shares is a case in point where the investment value had increased by more than fivefold based on a combination of realised and unrealised gains.[44] While ultimately vindicated, Austin Motors was one holding Keynes felt he had to defend repeatedly against a number of critics. Keynes' letter to Scott highlights his justified irritation towards ill-informed colleagues who failed to appreciate the subtleties and challenges of asset management:

> The various investment accounts for which I am more or less responsible have made an aggregate profit in Austin of £350,000, most of which is realised profit. Yet . . . I have been on the defensive the whole time, being allowed to keep the shares as a courteous concession to my enthusiasm and

---

[42] Keynes to the Provincial Insurance Company Board, *Investment Results*, memorandum 7 March 1938 (CW XII) 99.

[43] Keynes to Scott, letter 10 April 1940 (CW XII) 78.

[44] Keynes *The College's Holding of Austin Motors Limited Ordinary Shares*, memorandum 29 April 1935 (Kings College Archive, KCAR/3/1/1/10/32).

the obvious bee in my bonnet...And the worst of it is that in all probability a day will come when the shares will pass their peak and my critics will point out how right they were at the end.[45]

Table 6.2 shows the 20 largest holdings of the Discretionary Fund at end August 1935.[46] At this point in the 1930s, Keynes was in the middle of a stellar period of investment performance measured in both absolute and relative terms.

This was a concentrated portfolio with the 20 largest holdings representing 61% of the assets and a committed approach in terms of country and

Table 6.2 The Discretionary Fund portfolio 1935: 20 largest holdings

Name	Type	Domicile	%
Austin Motor	Ordinary share	UK	8.4
Union Corporation	Ordinary share	South Africa	8.2
United Gas Preferred	Preference share	USA	7.1
Homestake Mining	Ordinary share	USA	5.5
Selected Industries Allot. Certs.	Ordinary share	USA	3.6
Randfontein Estates & Gold	Ordinary share	South Africa	2.7
Guaranteed 2.75%	Government bond	UK	2.6
Shell Union Preferred	Preference share	USA	2.6
US & Foreign Security Preferred	Preference share	USA	2.5
Electric Power & Light	Preference share	USA	2.3
American Metal 6% Preferred	Preference share	USA	2.2
Atlas Corp	Ordinary share	USA	1.8
Assoc. Dry Goods 7% Preferred	Preference share	USA	1.7
Consolidated Main Reef Mines	Ordinary share	South Africa	1.6
Joburg Consolidated Inv. Co.	Ordinary share	South Africa	1.6
Leyland Motors	Ordinary share	UK	1.6
Commonwealth & Southern	Preference share	USA	1.5
Yarrow & Co	Preference share	UK	1.3
Selection Trust	Ordinary share	UK	1.2
Bank of England stock	Debenture	UK	1.2

Notes: Portfolio supplied by David Chambers, Cambridge University

---

[45] Keynes to Scott, letter 1935, in Oliver Westall, *The Provincial Insurance Company* (Manchester University Press 1992) 369.

[46] *Audited Statement of Holdings by Peters, Elworthy & Moores, 1935* (Kings College Archive, KCAR/4/1/1).

sector positions. Particularly noteworthy are the large weightings of more than 5% in favoured stocks, his 'pets', such as Austin Motor, Union Corp (see below) and Homestake Mining. Homestake was a US gold stock priced at $382.5 in August 1935 which performed spectacularly well during the 1930s. It was valued at $80 in 1929 and rose in price rapidly to 1935, paying out large dividends too, during a period when the US equity market actually declined. It hit a price of $500 in 1939. Keynes' timing was good in more than one respect: first, in 1934 the US Treasury raised the price of gold from $20.67 an ounce to $35, having previously raised the price 100 years earlier (the next price rise was in 1972). [47] Second, Homestake produced record net income figures of $11.4 million in 1935 that would not be surpassed for another 40 years.[48] So, with the occasional spectacular stock such as Homestake, it is hardly surprising that Keynes attributed his investment success to a small number of big winners.

The shape of the Discretionary Fund in 1935 can be characterised as follows:

- equity-orientated;
- large holdings in a small number of favoured stocks;
- very international with a preference for the USA;
- debt exposure through corporate bonds and income via preference shares so virtually nothing in government bonds;
- a significant exposure to mining stocks, particularly gold, mainly in South Africa.

This 1935 portfolio was a mature representation of Keynes' development as an investor over the 30 years since 1905 when he bought his first equity. Throughout, he had shown an interest in investing internationally and specifically in resource- and commodity-related companies. He was comfortable investing in a wide range of different instruments across the capital structure and generally showed little interest in government securities. At this date in 1935, it was almost entirely invested in equities: 56% was invested in

---

[47] *Gold Reserve Act of 1934* (www.federalreservehistory.com, website accessed on 25 April 2016).
[48] *Homestake Mining, Record Profits on the Eve of WW 2* (www.encyclopedia.com, website accessed on 25 April 2016).

ordinary shares and 36% in preference shares with the balance of 8% invested in bonds, mainly corporate bonds. In terms of portfolio construction (Table 6.3), Keynes divided the assets between two sub-portfolios: UK-listed holdings (52%) and US-listed (48%) so by stock exchange and currency, rather than by the underlying country in which the stock operated. Within the UK-listed holdings, for example, the South African investments were all gold mining stocks, quoted and traded out of London, of which Union Corporation was the largest. With Union Corporation, Keynes was analytical and possessed a real understanding of the underlying financials of the business, giving Scott at the Provincial three clear reasons why he liked that company: breadth of activity, dividend policy and management competence. He believed that the shares could increase by threefold in the ensuing three to four years.[49] In practice, the overall portfolio was very tilted towards international investments and the main geographic exposures were the USA 48%, the UK 32% and South Africa 16%. As a sector, mining stocks were the most pronounced feature representing 27% of the assets and, in addition to the South African holdings, two other mining stocks featured prominently: Homestake (covered above) and Selection Trust, a mining finance company interested in diamond mining in Sierra Leone amongst other places. For the mid-1930s, this was a very sophisticated approach to portfolio construction

Table 6.3 The Discretionary Fund portfolio 1935: sub-portfolios

	UK-listed sub-portfolio	US-listed sub-portfolio	Combined fund
Ordinary shares	80%	30%	56%
Preference shares	10%	64%	36%
Corporate bonds + other bonds	10%	6%	8%
Largest holding	16%[a]	15%[a]	8%
Number of holdings	57	41	98
Value £	110,330	101,234	211,564

[a] % as a proportion of the sub-portfolio

---

[49] Keynes to Scott, *Union Corporation*, letter 15 August 1934 (CW XII) 57.

with a growth bias in Britain, and a strong income emphasis from the USA combined with a large thematic, exposure to mining stocks.

Within the two sub-portfolios (Table 6.3) for the UK and the USA there were significant structural differences: the UK sub-portfolio had a marked exposure towards ordinary shares (80%) and within that international mining companies in particular. Keynes probably expected most growth to be achieved from his UK-listed stocks. Whereas the US sub-portfolio had only 30% invested in ordinary shares but 64% invested in income-producing preference shares. Therefore, with its marked bias towards security of income, the US sub-portfolio was more defensive. In November 1933, Keynes was extolling the benefits of US preference shares as follows with reference to the investment company Unites States & Foreign (an investment trust or closed-end fund), 'taken at current market prices, the assets of the company cover the present price of the preferred shares twice over and the yield on them at current prices is 10%'.[50] In the same letter he also went on to say that the stock, United States & Foreign, should also perform well in the event of an inflationary increase in the USA on the back of New Deal spending by Roosevelt. This penchant for preference shares would have produced more income than an equivalent market index and is consistent with observations that Keynes' portfolios had a persistent and significant bias towards high yield between 1921 and 1946.[51] As an investor, Keynes always liked income and generally wanted income growth. One of the few defensive holdings in the UK sub-portfolio was a Bank of England debenture debt security, his twentieth largest holding; it was a quoted company at this juncture but would be nationalised in 1946.[52]

---

[50] Keynes to Scott, letter 23 November 1933 (CW XII) 62.

[51] Chambers et al., *Keynes The Stock Market Investor: A Quantitative Analysis* (JFQA 50/4, 2015), This analysis shows that Keynes' portfolio had a higher yield than the index for most of the period between 1921 and 1946 and that in 1935 the relative yield was about 150%. Much of this would have been attributable to holding preference shares as well as higher yielding ordinary shares.

[52] The Bank was founded in 1694 as a joint stock company and was still privately owned in the 1930s. In 1946 when Keynes died (coincidentally he was a director of it between 1941 and 1942), the Bank was taken into Government ownership, when it was nationalised by the post-war Labour government. After 260 years it finally became a Central Bank controlled but also guaranteed by Government. Keynes, had he been alive, would almost certainly have sold the holding (or the 3% Treasury Stock issued to pay for it), given his dislike of owning Government paper.

Although he substantially changed his investment approach, or philosophy, during the 1930s, he persevered with several of the original investment ideas from his formative years such as his thematic interest in the resources sectors and a geographic preference for the USA. Apart from investing in gold mining in the 1930s, the main change was less in the type of investments he owned and more in how he was investing: he became less interested in market-timing, paid more attention to individual companies and traded less. By around 1940, he had developed very clear ideas about how investors should think about return and risk. He identified the important attributes of a successful asset manager as follows:

> I believe now that successful investment depends on three principles: (1) a careful selection of a few investments . . . (2) a steadfast holding of these in fairly large units . . . (3) a balanced investment position i.e. a variety of risks in spite of individual holdings being large . . . [53]

He also explained his thinking about risk in terms of understanding and knowing the individual companies in which one is invested rather than simplistic diversification:

> To suppose that safety-first consists in having a small gamble in a large number of different directions . . . as compared with a substantial stake in a company where one's information is adequate, strikes me as a travesty of investment policy.[54]

At the Discretionary Fund, Keynes made two very significant contributions to investment thinking as an asset manager. First, he had an early appreciation of the importance of equities as a means to maintain the real spending power of an endowment fund. Second, he deliberately changed his own investment approach following his experience around 1929 and this enabled him to demonstrate great investment skill over the long-term.

---

[53] Keynes to the Estates Committee Kings College, *Post Mortem on Investment Policy*, memorandum 8 May 1938 (CW XII) 106/7.
[54] Keynes to Scott, letter 6 February 1942 (CW XII) 82.

He had an empirical approach to the investment world, allegedly saying 'when my information changes, I alter my conclusions – what do you do sir?', which meant he was prepared to be flexible when thinking about the process of asset management.[55] His management of the Discretionary Fund and the decisions he made, particularly after a period of adversity following the 1929 Crash, were remarkably effective. But, and this is the biggest conundrum with Keynes, it is difficult to know how and whether Keynes directly influenced broader developments in asset management, particularly with endowments and foundations. Inevitably, other Oxbridge bursars and colleges were aware of his activities including Wadham College, Oxford.[56] Alternatively, it is not obvious that other Cambridge Colleges, such as the wealthiest of them all, Trinity College followed his lead. Trinity's investment statutes were amended only in 1946 to enable equity investment while by 1953, equity exposure at Trinity stood at a meagre 3%.[57] Even Kings College, which clearly cherishes the Keynes legacy, did not appear to persevere with his investment methods after his departure from the college. At the National Mutual, Keynes enjoyed a national profile as an investor but in cloistered Cambridge it appears that his investment approach and achievements were more of a muted whisper until the publication of the Collected Writings, Volume XII in the 1980s.

6.3   Investment Insights

Keynes was ahead of his time as an investor and nothing illustrates this better than his keen understanding of an important aspect of investment behaviour, now referred to as 'Behavioural Finance': the impact of mass psychology on the market and behavioural pressures that affect an individual investor. Much of his thinking in this area was empirical, simply based on his own experiences and on the reaction and responses

---

[55] This quotation is unsourced so apocryphal. Also, more pithily paraphrased as, 'When the facts change, I change my mind – what do you do sir?'

[56] Donald Moggridge, *Maynard Keynes, An Economist's Biography* (Routledge 1992) 411.

[57] Robert Neild, *Riches and Responsibility: The Financial History of Trinity College, Cambridge* (Granta 2008) 122.

of many people with whom he had close working relationships, namely Falk, the Estates Committee at Kings, Francis Scott at the Provincial and the Board of the National Mutual. Keynes identified, intuitively, ideas that would be scientifically analysed by Kahneman and Tversky after 1979 based on their work exploring the relationship between risk and decision-making.[58] Kahneman and Tversky explained that individuals made irrational economic choices based on emotional decisions owing to behavioural biases and an inability to evaluate risk accurately. Keynes' wide-ranging comments and observations demonstrated a real awareness of these issues and showed that he was not only highly intelligent and financially astute, but also an extremely perceptive observer of people. A selection of his most relevant statements on the behavioural aspects of asset management is given below.

> ... many people were quite willing in the boom, not only to value shares on the basis of a single year's earnings, but to assume that increase in earnings would continue geometrically, so now [February 1931] they are ready to estimate capital values on today's earnings and to assume that decreases will continue geometrically.[59]

> I consider the prospects of 1931 to be extremely bad. It is indeed only too easy to feel frightened, and to find plausible reasons for one's fears. . . . But I do not draw from this conclusion that a responsible investing body should every week cast panic glances over its list of securities to find one more victim to fling to the bears. Both interest and duty point the other way.[60]

> I do not believe that selling at very low prices is a remedy for having failed to sell at high ones . . . I should say that it is from time to time the duty of a serious investor to accept the depreciation of his holdings with equanimity and without reproaching himself. Any other policy is anti-social, destructive of self-confidence, and incompatible with the working of the economic system.[61]

---

[58] Daniel Kahneman & Amos Tversky, *Prospect Theory: An Analysis of Decision Under Risk* (Econometrica 47/2, 1979).
[59] Keynes to the Board of the National Mutual, memorandum 18 February 1931 (CWXII) 17/18.
[60] Keynes to the Board of the National Mutual, memorandum 18 February 1931 (CWXII) 18.
[61] Keynes to Curzon, letter 18 March 1938 (CW XII) 37/38.

My central principle of investment is to go contrary to general opinion, on the ground that, if everyone is agreed about its merits, the investment is inevitably too dear and therefore unattractive.[62]

It [investing] is the one sphere of life and activity where victory, security and success is always to the minority and never to the majority. When you find anyone agreeing with you, change your mind. [63]

The ignorance of even the best-informed investor about the remote future is much greater than his knowledge...But if this is true of the best-informed, the vast majority of those who are concerned with the buying and selling of securities know almost nothing whatever about what they are doing. They do not possess even the rudiments of what is required for a valid judgment, and are the prey of hopes and fears easily aroused by transient events and as easily dispelled.[64]

...professional investment may be likened to those newspaper competitions in which competitors have to pick out the six prettiest faces from a hundred photographs, the prize being awarded to the competitor whose choice most nearly corresponds to the average preference of the competitor as a whole; so that each competitor has to pick, not those faces which he himself finds prettiest, but those which he thinks likeliest to catch the fancy of the competitors, all of whom are looking at the problem from the same point of view.[65]

6.4   Concluding Remarks

The Independent failed whereas the Discretionary Fund was very successful but it could have been a very different story. Owing to the volatility of returns both absolute and relative, the Fellows at Kings

---

[62] Keynes to Sir Jasper Ridley, letter March 1944 (CW XII) 111.

[63] Keynes to Labordere, letter 28 September 1937, in Robert Skidelsky, *John Maynard Keynes, 1883-1946: Economist, Philosopher, Statesman* (Penguin 2003) 521.

[64] John Maynard Keynes, *A Treatise on Money, Vol 2* (Macmillan 1930) 360.

[65] John Maynard Keynes, *The General Theory of Employment, Interest and Money* in The Collected Writings of John Maynard Keynes Vol VII, ed. Donald Moggridge (Cambridge University Press 1973) 156.

College would have been justified in asking Keynes to relinquish responsibility for investing the Discretionary Fund during the first 10 years of his stewardship, at any point up to 1931. They did not and Keynes proceeded to produce exceptional investment results between 1932 and 1946. By the 1930s, Keynes had developed his investment thinking to the point where he had a very clear idea of how to add value and he had established a sophisticated method of portfolio construction. On the other hand, the Independent failed at exactly the wrong time for both Keynes, in terms of his reputation, and its shareholders, given what could have been. In reality, the damage was done at the Independent after 1928 when Falk and Gifford went back into the equity market in the USA. The ensuing problems, for which Keynes must take some blame, meant that he lost the chance to demonstrate his investment expertise with a large portfolio in the public domain that would have been more visible than the small, private Discretionary Fund and free from the liability considerations that limited investment flexibility at the National Mutual. If only Keynes had had a free hand at the Independent and continued to manage it during the 1930s, and if his investment insights had been more widely communicated, his reputation as an asset manager might have equalled his renown as an economist. But it did not, and given his evident investment failings alongside his brilliance, that is why Keynes was less influential than some others in this history of asset management.

Bibliography

Primary Sources

Independent Investment Company, Prospectus January 1924 (Guildhall Library)
Kings College Cambridge, Archive Centre, holds the extensive papers of John Maynard Keynes
The London Metropolitan Archive (LMA) holds comprehensive archival material, including Board minutes and some of Keynes' correspondence, about the *National Mutual Life Assurance Society*

Books

Nicholas Davenport, *Memoirs of a City Radical* (Willmer Bros 1974)

John Maynard Keynes, *A Treatise on Money, Vol 2* (Macmillan 1930)

John Maynard Keynes, The General Theory of Employment, Interest and Money in *The Collected Writings of John Maynard Keynes Vol VII*, ed. Donald Moggridge (Cambridge University Press 1973) *155/156*

Donald Moggridge, *Maynard Keynes, An Economist's Biography* (Routledge 1992)

Donald Moggridge, CWXII, *The Collected Writings of John Maynard Keynes, Volume XII* (Cambridge University Press 2013)

Robert Neild, *Riches and Responsibility: The Financial History of Trinity College, Cambridge* (Granta 2008)

John Newlands, *Put Not Your Trust in Money* (Association of Investment Trust Companies 1997)

Robert Skidelsky, *The Economist as Saviour 1929–1937* (Macmillan 1992)

Robert Skidelsky, *John Maynard Keynes*, 1883–1946: *Economist, Philosopher, Statesman* (Penguin 2003)

John Wasik, *Keynes' Way to Wealth* (McGraw Hill 2014)

Oliver Westall, *The Provincial Insurance Company*, 1903–38 (Manchester University Press 1992)

Articles, Journals, Pamphlets, Websites, etc.

David Chambers and Elroy Dimson, Retrospectives: John Maynard Keynes, Investment Innovator (*Journal of Economic Perspectives* 27/3, 2013)

David Chambers, Dimson E. and Foo J., Keynes The Stock Market Investor: A Quantitative Analysis (*Journal of Financial and Quantitative Analysis* 50/4, 2015)

Paul Dawson, Mark Ellis, Mark Holder and Richard Kent, Keynes on Financial Markets: Why Didn't You Listen? (*Review of Futures Markets* 18, 2009)

Elroy Dimson, Paul Marsh and Mike Staunton, *Responsible Investing: Does It Pay to Be Bad?* (Credit Suisse Yearbook 2015)

Gold Reserve Act of 1934 (www.federalreservehistory.com)

Mark Holder and Dick Kent, On the Art of Investing According to Keynes (*The Journal of Portfolio Management* 37, 2011)

Homestake Mining, Record Profits on the Eve of WW 2 (www.encyclopedia.com)

Daniel Kahneman and Amos Tversky, *Prospect Theory: An Analysis of Decision Under Risk* (Econometrica 47/2, 1979)

John Maynard Keynes (www.maynardkeynes.org)

The Sunday Express

The Times

Oliver Westall, *Riding the Tiger* (University of Lancaster Management School 1992)

7

George Booth and Ian Fairbairn: The First Unit Trusts, 1931–1960

The Great Crash of 1929 and subsequent depression in the 1930s had a major impact on asset management in both the UK and the USA in that Benjamin Graham and Maynard Keynes substantially revised their approaches to investing: Graham incorporated a 'margin of safety' into his research and analysis, whereas Keynes moved towards fundamental 'bottom up' investing and away from market-timing. But an equally significant change occurred in the delivery of asset management services to investors at this juncture too. In the lead up to October 1929, the egregious misdemeanours of US investment companies, or investment trusts, led to the creation of different types of pooled fund vehicles in the 1930s. Unit trusts, or mutual funds, became firmly established, particularly in the USA, and this type of pooled fund structure now dominates the investment landscape by size of assets and type of vehicle. The first unit trusts were launched in Britain after 1931 by Municipal and General and, on the face of it, offered transparency in pricing, separate trusteeship and complete redeemability. Although unit trusts had a different legal structure to investment companies, in practice, the very first unit trust, the First British Fixed Trust (the 'First British'), enjoyed many similarities to the Foreign & Colonial Government

© The Author(s) 2017
N.E. Morecroft, *The Origins of Asset Management
from 1700 to 1960*, Palgrave Studies in the History of Finance,
DOI 10.1007/978-3-319-51850-3_7

Trust from 1868. Both portfolios had a small number of holdings and operated on an administrative 'buy and hold' basis so that portfolio changes would only be made in exceptional circumstances. In this respect, the First British simply updated Foreign & Colonial to the 1930s and applied the principle to ordinary shares rather than bonds, while wrapping them into a different type of pooled vehicle, the unit trust rather than the investment company. In the UK, unit trusts encouraged smaller savers, often women to invest. The vehicles were easy to understand and they contributed to a growing interest in equity investing, as demonstrated by the creation of the FT30 Index in 1935.

While welcome, the creation of the FT30 Index lagged equivalent developments in the USA, an indication perhaps that the USA was beginning to move ahead of Britain in some areas of financial markets thinking. The previous chapter explained that Smith's book about ordinary shares had appeared in 1924 and that indices of equity prices were enhanced in the USA in the 1920s. Some US institutions were also developing in interesting directions. For example, in 1920 the business-cycle economist Wesley Mitchell established the National Bureau of Economic Research (NBER) to collect better financial data in the search for improved economic policy analysis.[1] From 1921, the NBER employed, Frederick Macaulay, on a part-time basis (he also worked at Columbia University) and in 1938 he produced his paper about bond duration analysing the sensitivity of changes in bond prices based on adjusted terms to maturity.[2] After 1928, Benjamin Graham began teaching, also at Columbia, another early indication of the growing links between academia and investment practice in the USA. The rapid development of the mutual fund sector in the USA after 1930 may also have added stimulus and dynamism to their asset management profession more generally: it was about to become a serious business.

By comparison, it took much longer, until about 1960, for unit trusts to become fully established in the UK and more than 50 years before they had

[1] Geoffrey Poitras, *Frederick R. Macaulay, Frank M. Redington and the Emergence of Modern Fixed Income Analysis*, in Pioneers of Financial Economics Vol 2, ed. Poitras & Jovanovic (Edward Elgar 2007) 63.

[2] Geoffrey Poitras, *Frederick R. Macaulay, Frank M. Redington and the Emergence of Modern Fixed Income Analysis*, in Pioneers of Financial Economics Vol 2, ed. Poitras & Jovanovic (Edward Elgar 2007) 65.

grown to be larger than investment (trust) companies. Nevertheless, by 1939, when the Second World War arrested the development of British financial services, unit trusts, although still a relatively small sector, had spawned an innovative array of equity strategies, deepening and widening investment choice. George Macaulay Booth and Ian Fairbairn of Municipal and General Securities Company Limited created and nurtured unit trusts through their extended, formative period in the UK with an interest in making investment accessible to a broader cross section of society in a manner not dissimilar to Philip Rose in 1868.[3] Booth and Fairbairn demonstrated remarkable patience and resilience just to keep going. The really interesting question is why it took unit trusts as long as it did to become properly established in Britain compared to US mutual funds during the 1930s. Different regulatory environments after the 1929 Crash appears to be one of the main reasons.

7.1 US Mutual Funds: A Different Landscape

The Massachusetts Investors Trust of 1924, of Boston, is generally acknowledged as the first mutual fund, or unit trust, to invest in securities though growth was very slow and by 1929 in the USA, there were still only 19 mutual funds competing with 700 investment (trust) companies.[4] They grew rapidly after the 1929 Crash because mutual funds were seen as less prone to abuse and thus a safer alternative to investment trust companies and, 150 fixed unit trusts worth a total of $400 million were launched in the 2-year period to March 1931 mainly in the immediate aftermath of the Wall Street Crash.[5] This $400 million broadly equates to the entire amount raised by British unit trusts throughout the 1930s.[6] By 1944, the volume of assets in US mutual funds was larger than the amount invested with US investment (trust) companies so within 20 years of the

---

[3] Municipal and General was a forerunner of the M&G Group, now an autonomous fund management subsidiary of Prudential PLC.

[4] *Mutual fund history* (www.bogleheads.org website accessed 28 May 2016).

[5] Janette Rutterford, *Learning from one another's mistakes: investment trusts in the UK and US, 1868–1940* (Financial History Review 16/2, 2009).

[6] Assumed exchange rate £/$ of $4.86 in March 1931. The Gold Standard was abandoned on 21 September 1931 by the UK and sterling suffered an initial devaluation of some 25%.

first mutual fund being established, the Massachusetts Investors Trust in 1924, the junior mutual fund movement had become the senior sibling. In Britain by comparison, the value of unit trusts exceeded that of investment trusts only in 1986, 55 years after the launch of the first UK unit trust.[7] Owing to a vicious cocktail of Wall Street malpractices which included excessive gearing, price manipulation, bloated expenses – for example, one US investment trust had 45 directors – and pyramid style cross-holdings, US investment trusts collapsed spectacularly after 1929.[8] *The Economist* made the following observation: 'During the Wall Street boom many new American investment trusts were created . . . with more zeal than discretion. The ensuing slump caused much dissatisfaction, not with the trust idea itself but with the degree of skill, judgment and probity shown by the directors of some companies.'[9] More than 200 investment companies in the USA had failed by 1935.[10] For many savers in the USA, the boom and bust backdrop for investment trusts was a traumatic episode. In 1929 for example, $100 million of The Goldman Sachs Trading Corporation was sold to the public at $104, the price quickly rose to $222, a premium of more than 100% to its net assets.[11] It then dropped to $1.75 after the crash; and over a similar period, the price of the average investment trust in the USA had fallen from $1 to 5c.[12] Because investment trusts were seen as major contributors to the Crash, the authorities in the USA subsequently gave mutual funds a helping hand by creating a less favourable environment for investment (trust) companies – the US Revenue Act of 1936 introduced a surtax on undistributed profits which in turn encouraged investment companies to

---

[7] Charles Jackson, *Active Investment Management: Finding and Harnessing Investment Skill* (Wiley 2003) 18.

[8] Janette Rutterford, *Learning from one another's mistakes: investment trusts in the UK and US, 1868–1940* (Financial History Review 16/2, 2009).

[9] *The Economist*, 21 March 1931.

[10] Janette Rutterford, *Learning from one another's mistakes: investment trusts in the UK and US, 1868–1940* (Financial History Review 16/2, 2009).

[11] JK Galbraith, *The Great Crash, 1929* (Mariner 1997) 85/86.

[12] John Newlands, *Put Not Your Trust in Money* (Association of Investment Trust Companies, 1997) 178/9.

unitise (i.e. to switch from being an investment company to a mutual fund) so they could claim exemption from Federal taxes.[13] The US Investment Company Act of 1940 limited leverage and cross-holdings together with restricting the use of the name investment 'trust', requiring 'company' to be used instead.[14] Legislation in the USA killed the investment (trust) company.

Although both New York and London suffered traumatic stock market collapses after 1929, in practice, the underlying attitude to asset management was surprisingly different in the two countries. In the USA, mutual funds addressed a problem by meeting a market need that simply did not exist in Britain at that time. In Britain, the financial establishment viewed investment trusts favourably, but had reservations about unit trusts so it was a completely different landscape. During the 1930s, the majority of British investment trusts were in a much healthier financial condition than their cousins in the USA, for two reasons. First, an accumulation of hidden reserves based on capital gains from sales of securities gave many of them a big financial cushion in the region of 20% going into the crash; second, they adopted more conservative investment policies such as valuing investments at book value rather than market value.[15] Long-term investment performance over many years had been strong, the First Scottish American Investment Trust increased in value 70-fold since coming into existence in 1873 whereas most of the US investment trusts had sprung into existence only after 1918.[16] Perhaps there was a cultural difference too – people in the USA saw investment management as a high-risk game and just another way to get rich quickly in the style of *The Great Gatsby*; whereas in the UK it was more staid, asset management being something akin to using the

---

[13] Janette Rutterford, *Learning from one another's mistakes: investment trusts in the UK and US, 1868–1940* (Financial History Review 16/2, 2009).

[14] Hugh Bullock, *The Story of Investment Companies* (Columbia 1959) 12.

[15] Janette Rutterford, *Learning from one another's mistakes: investment trusts in the UK and US, 1868–1940* (Financial History Review 16/2, 2009).

[16] John Newlands, *Put Not Your Trust in Money* (Association of Investment Trust Companies 1997) 190.

services of a lawyer or doctor. According to Bullock, an American asset manager writing in 1932: 'The asset managers [in the US] should correspond to the class of men in Great Britain who devote their careers to managing funds. Investment management in Great Britain is a profession.'[17]

Unit trusts in Britain seem to have been seen as a threat to the well-established, and relatively successful, investment trust sector which had been in existence for over 60 years. Difficulties for unit trusts were compounded by the absence of a clear legal framework and proper regulation in Britain until the 1950s. This enabled dubious practices and practitioners to continue for far too long, which sullied the reputation of unit trusts in Britain for many years. In the UK therefore, unit trusts had a much harder challenge to gain acceptance and British investment companies did not suffer the same level of abuse and manipulation as their counterparts in the USA, though it should be noted that they were far from perfect. Keynes' Independent Investment Company barely survived (Chapter 6) while two other British trusts, the Glasgow American Trust and the West of Scotland Investment Trust, failed to pay their debenture holders, so there were problems in Britain too, just not as severe.[18] Very few of them openly divulged their holdings, even to shareholders and they were not obliged to publish a net asset value, the market value of the investment portfolio, until 1948.[19] There was also the occasional whiff of scandal, most notably with Clarence Hatry and his infamous investment trust, quaintly named, The (Austin) Friars, after the London address of the company secretary at 13/14 Austin Friars. Clarence Hatry was a fraudster in the Robert Maxwell mode and described by JK Galbraith as 'one of those curiously un-English figures with whom the English periodically find themselves unable to cope'.[20] Hatry's investment trusts, the Friars and

---

[17] Hugh Bullock, *The Future of the Investment Trust* in Keane's Investment Trust Monthly, written in March 1932. Re-produced by Hugh Bullock in The Story of Investment Companies (Columbia, 1959) 68/69.

[18] John Newlands, *Put Not Your Trust in Money* (Association of Investment Trust Companies 1997) 181.

[19] John Newlands, *Put Not Your Trust in Money* (Association of Investment Trust Companies 1997) 244/5.

[20] JK Galbraith, *The Great Crash, 1929* (Mariner 1997) 91.

the Dundee, collapsed in September 1929, just before the crash in the USA. During Hatry's trial at the Old Bailey it emerged that one of his investment trusts, the Friars Trust, established in 1927 had never produced an actual balance sheet.[21] Hatry was sent for trial and jailed for 12 years of which 2 years was hard labour. But out of this disarray arising from the Hatry scandal, the Association of Investment Trust Companies (AITC) was formed in 1932: JH Clifford Johnston was the first chairman with, representing the Scottish trusts, Carlyle Gifford as Deputy Chairman.[22] Unit trusts therefore, courtesy of the travails of the investment trusts, had a clear example of how both to deal with charlatans and to regulate themselves. However, most of the unit trust management groups were not interested to learn from these salutary lessons.

An entity called the Unit Trust Association had been established in March 1936 but it is not apparent that this body achieved anything and it does not appear to be recorded, or even acknowledged, in the annals of unit trust history.[23] At that time in the 1930s, only 7 of the 11 unit trust management companies were affiliated to it; and Municipal and General was not one of them.[24] It would appear that Municipal and General was underwhelmed by the idea despite being a fervent believer in treating customers fairly. The Hatry equivalent in unit trusts was Denys Colquhoun Flowerdew Lowson who became Managing Director of Security First Trust and then built up the Fifteen Moorgate Group of unit trusts. He was described thus:

> Typically he bought shares through brokers for undesignated accounts: bad performers were assigned to unit trusts…he gained control of several companies through the funds he managed in unit trusts by interlocking

---

[21] John Newlands, *Put Not Your Trust in Money* (Association of Investment Trust Companies 1997) 183.

[22] John Newlands, *Put Not Your Trust in Money* (Association of Investment Trust Companies 1997) 189, 197.

[23] For example, there is no mention of this organisation in the publication *Unit Trusts from the beginning* by Christopher Hill produced in 1984 to celebrate the 25th anniversary of the Unit Trust Association even though it covers the history of unit trusts after 1931.

[24] *The Economist,* Unit Trust Survey, 17 April 1937.

shareholdings ... he was thus able to manipulate share prices and inflate his companies' balance sheets ... as a result of Lowson's identification with unit trusts they were considered shady by the City establishment, and their development was retarded for years.[25]

According to a scathing obituary in *The Times*: 'He showed consistently that he was more concerned to turn situations to the advantage of himself and the interests he controlled than with his fiduciary duty to the companies of which he was a director.'[26] Almost 40 years after Lowson had started in the City, in July 1974, he was criticised for 'grave mismanagement' in an investigation by the Department of Trade & Industry, a government department, and received an indictment in September 1975 but he died before the case proceeded to trial.[27] In the UK many years earlier, the authorities began to raise doubts about the probity of unit trusts with a Stock Exchange report into their activities in 1935, followed by a Board of Trade investigation in 1936. Various issues were highlighted, but never resolved at the time, about unit trusts' malpractices, including fundamental points about the methodology used for the calculation of prices and yields: ' ... there was a tendency to cut corners and some trusts were criticised for manipulating their figures in an attempt to prove their success in generating income. They would, for example, set off the half-yearly management charges against capital rather than income, and buy shares just before dividends were paid and sell them directly after'.[28] A variety of factors worked against investment trusts and in favour of unit trusts in the USA in the 1930s. The converse was true in the UK.

---

[25] *Denys Colquhoun Flowerdew Lowson, Notes on a Portrait* (www.artwarefineart.com, website accessed on 28 May 2016). These interesting and detailed notes attached to the portrait of Lowson exhibited in 1951 at the Festival of Britain explain in some detail how Lowson purportedly operated.

[26] *The Times*, 11 September 1975.

[27] David Kynaston, *The City of London Volume 4: A club no more, 1945–2000* (Pimlico 2002) 477/8.

[28] Adrienne Gleeson, *People and their money: 50 years of private investment* (M&G Group, 1981) 25.

7.2 Municipal and General, Booth and Fairbairn

By contrast with many of its early unit trust competitors in Britain, Municipal and General operated with high standards of professionalism and probity and it not only created the first unit trust in the UK, but it was also the driving force behind unit trusts for the next 50, or more, years. As an organisation it was innovative and was one of the few unit trust management companies to survive into the latter part of the twentieth century, almost certainly owing to the strength of its culture and ownership structure (Annex to this chapter). Initially led by George Booth and then Ian Fairbairn, Municipal and General embodied probity, fairness, high professional standards, independence and a strong value-based investment philosophy – behaviours and beliefs which were to run deep in the organisation. The development of unit trusts in the UK will be considered through the lens of Municipal and General because it was both the original purveyor and the great survivor of the early unit trust management groups. Booth and Fairbairn worked together closely at Municipal and General for over 30 years and their influence needs to be considered in tandem. Booth was instrumental at the outset during the 1930s because he created, from nothing, a fledgling asset management business and set the direction of travel, albeit in a non-executive role because he had a range of other business interests. Fairbairn then picked up the challenge in the 1940s and 1950s as full-time executive chairman and the senior investor (Figs. 7.1 and 7.2).

7.2.1 Municipal and General Securities

Established in 1906, Municipal and General existed to supply project finance to major engineering projects by the White group of companies, an engineering and construction business with operations in New York and London. Towards the end of 1930, Booth took control of the White businesses in the UK with the explicit intention of using Municipal and General as the springboard to launch a unit trust business. Booth's role in this transaction is critical in order to understand how unit trusts came to be imported into the

Fig. 7.1   George Macaulay Booth, 1877–1971, photo c. 1930

Fig. 7.2 Ian Fairbairn, 1896–1968, photo c. 1960

UK. The key point is that Booth understood how to create a mutual fund management company because he had an intimate knowledge of the White businesses, and he understood the market for financial services in the USA, having both worked there and visited regularly on business. The story told below has obvious gaps and it is hoped that a fuller account will emerge in due course that broadens out the roles of particular individuals, notably William Burton-Baldry, Thomas Moore, George Faber and Arthur Fforde (sic) not least because this might indicate whether Booth was merely an opportunistic businessman or a far-sighted thinker about social change, savings and investments.

After 1900, White undertook major engineering works in South America with materials supplied via the Booth Shipping Line, run by George Booth after 1908. White built the famous Custom House at Manaus on the Amazon River together with tramways and electric lighting, while Booth's ships moved everything 'from paving stones to pianos'.[29] From this point onwards, George Booth developed a close, personal working relationship with the White companies in the USA and the UK. In Britain, White's projects included several iconic London buildings such as the Ritz Hotel, Selfridges and the RAC Club in Pall Mall.[30] After 1906, Municipal and General financed a number of these activities, so Municipal and General had access to the money markets in the UK. George Booth became a director of White in the USA in 1910, and, in due course, chairman of the White in the UK.[31] By 1930 White was loss making at which point George Booth and William Burton-Baldry jointly acquired the London-domiciled

---

[29] Duncan Crow, *A Man of Push and Go – the Life of George Macaulay Booth* (Rupert Hart-Davis 1965) 46.

[30] These buildings were developed by a related White company, the Waring-White Building Company according to AH John in *A Liverpool Merchant House.*

[31] Confusingly, the London-based non-US business of J G White and Co. Inc., J G White & Co. Ltd, was sold, bought back and sold again by the founder and owner Mr J G White to Booth. These transactions appeared to be driven by the fluctuating fortunes of the engineering businesses around the world outside the USA. First Mr White sold the UK subsidiary to the Booth Shipping Line in 1917 because he was worried that Britain would lose the First World War. The eponymous Mr White then bought it back in 1928 to support an ambitious engineering tender in Abyssinia. But Mr White then sold it back (he actually gave it to Booth to reduce the losses) to Booth again, privately this time, in 1930/1931 because the tender failed and of course the depression had struck.

businesses of White in a private transaction, outside the family-owned Booth businesses.[32] Booth's main rationale for acquiring the UK businesses of White in late 1930 was to make a success of Municipal and General, not the engineering business. The following comments are attributed to a stockbroker, William Burton-Baldry telling Booth:

> I don't see how I can put the idea [unit trusts] into operation unless someone like you will manage it [a fixed trust]. You've got the authority that's needed: a Director of the Bank of England and so on. I'll share the risks in J G White and Company with you [50/50] and we'll run the fixed trust [mutual funds] business through its finance company Municipal and General ... [33]

The deal occurred shortly after George Faber, based in London as managing director of Municipal and General, had visited the US parent company, J G White & Co. Inc. in New York, earlier in 1929. On that visit Faber met Thomas Moore, a Vice President. Moore was based in the States and was also a director of a US mutual fund, the All Americas Investors Corp., a Fixed Trust. Once Booth and Burton-Baldry decided to acquire the struggling London operation of White, which brought with it Municipal and General, the rationale for the deal, the launch of a unit trust then moved forward very rapidly – Burton-Baldry proposed the idea in December 1930 and it was agreed in January 1931.[34] Thomas Moore arrived in London from the States in February 1931, worked on it with lawyer Arthur Fforde of Linklaters for the next 3 months and the First British Fixed Trust was then launched on 23 April 1931. So, in terms of the timetable, the idea was probably in gestation for about 12 months beginning with the original visit of Faber to New York and then implemented very quickly within a tight 6-month timetable once the transaction was agreed.

---

[32] Duncan Crow, *A Man of Push and Go – the Life of George Macaulay Booth* (Rupert Hart-Davis 1965) 177.

[33] Duncan Crow, *A Man of Push and Go – the Life of George Macaulay Booth* (Rupert Hart-Davis 1965) 178. The initial involvement of Burton-Baldry in the early stages of this transaction is very opaque.

[34] CH Walker *Unit Trusts* (unpublished PhD LSE Library, 1938).

7.2.2 Booth and Fairbairn

Booth and Fairbairn were a strong team with complementary skills and they worked together for over 30 years. Booth was the older person, an avuncular businessman with good management and organisational skills who was well connected at various levels of society. He was a patient, paternalistic chairman of Municipal and General for the first 10 years or so but remained involved in the business for many years into his 80s so he was extremely committed to it. Fairbairn was shy, intense and very much the investment leader of the organisation and gradually took on more responsibility after the early 1940s when he became the driving force of what became M&G during the 1950s. Booth was Harrow and Cambridge while Fairbairn was Eton, Sandhurst and the Guards, but somewhat surprisingly given their upbringing, both shared similar views, not least in the area of how investment could be socially beneficial. They believed that unit trusts had a broader societal benefit and so represented a method of broadening participation in wealth creation. Booth's mother (Mary) and father (Charles) were philanthropists and campaigned against urban poverty. His father, Charles Booth, was a founding figure of social science and had published a 17-volume treatise on London poverty at the beginning of the twentieth century.[35] Charles worked on this with Beatrice Webb among others, so was closely associated with social reformers and socialists. Prior to becoming obsessively interested in London poverty, Charles had been a very successful businessman, establishing both a leather business and a shipping company with his brother Alfred. George Booth thus grew up in a privileged environment. For example, in 1906 he returned to London from an extended sojourn in New York accompanied by his three servants indicating that he was a very prosperous, wealthy man.[36] George Booth effectively lived in two different worlds: one based around international business and wealth; the other

---

[35] This huge work by Charles Booth took 17 years to compile and was published in 1902/1903 by Macmillan under the title, *Life and Labour of the People of London*.

[36] Duncan Crow, *A Man of Push and Go* (Rupert Hart-Davis 1965) 44. George Booth had worked in New York for 4 years and returned to London in January 1906. His three servants were a housemaid, a kitchenmaid and a footman.

consisted of social reform and left wing politics. Booth had several business commitments – there were two family-owned Booth companies, he was a director of the Bank of England, a director of a couple of Brazilian companies and a director of the White engineering business – which meant that his involvement with Municipal and General could not be other than non-executive. Fairbairn was also an unusual character: an Olympic rower in 1924, his great passion later in life was the strange hobby of shooting chamois.[37] His personal interests and professional focus seemed to change after he attended the London School of Economics in the 1920s and subsequently became interested in politics. On a couple of occasions in the late 1920s, he tried but failed to get elected to Parliament as the Conservative candidate for Burnley in northwest England, on a social justice platform.[38] At that time Burnley was a poor, deprived town built on the ailing cotton and coal industries. It is probable that Fairbairn's views crystallised during that period and he developed a 'determination that investments in equities, previously the preserve of the affluent, should be available to all – giving everyone the potential to own a stake in the nation's economy'.[39] John Fairbairn, Ian's nephew, explained that his uncle ardently believed in unit trusts as a method by which the disadvantaged in society could improve their lot – by the lower classes sharing in the benefits of industrial wealth as investors.[40] Booth shared similar views but probably saw unit trusts more from the perspective of increasing the pool of industrial capital for investment into Britain, as he said,

that was the idea of the unit trust idea to bring in the small investor so that British industry would depend on the support of the many rather than the few. And if you've only a little money to invest, you have no business to run the risk of putting it all into one company's shares. Whereas if your money is invested

---

[37] John Fairbairn (telephone conversations 2 December 2014 and 2 January 2015). John Fairbairn joined M&G in 1961 when they employed 29 people and he rose to the position of Deputy Chairman at the time of the sale to the Prudential in 1999. John is also a past chairman of the Esmée Fairbairn Foundation.

[38] *The Burnley News,* 6 March 1929.

[39] Esmée Fairbairn Foundation (www.esmeefairbairn.org.uk, website accessed 27 May 2016).

[40] John Fairbairn (telephone conversation, 2 January 2015).

in units which are spread over 150 shares you are running a perfectly legitimate and minimal speculative risk to take the burden of inflation.[41]

Finally, both men shared similar views about the importance of professional behaviour within financial services. Fairbairn had high ethical standards – he refused to pay commissions to sales agents and was generally reluctant to join the trade association of unit trust managers because he did not see them acting in the interests of clients.[42] 'Fairbairn was for many years the leading light in unit trusts and a great proponent of the need for control and supervision.'[43] This stance was entirely consistent with Booth's position too, and in 1942 he wrote to *The Times* advocating the need for an independent unit trust body to maintain the highest standards of professional conduct.[44] Clearly, they shared similar values, got on well, worked together for a long time and were a very interesting duo.

Booth had the original idea to make Municipal and General a unit trust management company and had the requisite management and organisational skills that enabled him to take Municipal and General from being a finance house supporting engineering projects to an asset management company. In practice he needed Fairbairn, as a day-to-day portfolio manager to manage the trusts, particularly as the remits became more complex from the mid-1930s onwards. Similarly, whilst Fairbairn was the principal portfolio manager at Municipal and General, he needed a structure around him, which Booth provided in terms of leadership and shared values. Booth recruited Ian Fairbairn, and they worked together for over three decades.[45] These two individuals appear to have been the *primus inter pares* in the unit trust world in Britain at the outset and for many years thereafter. Additionally, Booth had received neighbourly encouragement from Montagu

---

[41] Duncan Crow, *A Man of Push and Go – the Life of George Macaulay Booth* (Rupert Hart-Davis 1965) 176.

[42] John Fairbairn (telephone conversations, 2 December 2014 and 2 January 2015).

[43] Christopher Hill, *Unit Trusts from the Beginning* (Unit Trust Association 1984).

[44] *The Times*, letter, 25 August 1942.

[45] It is not entirely clear when Ian Fairbairn joined Municipal & General. His nephew John is convinced he was there from the start and he joined in 1931. Fairbairn's obituary in *The Times* (10 December 1968) placed his joining date at 1935.

Norman, Governor of the Bank of England, and possibly Keynes too who was involved with the Macmillan Committee at that juncture, to press ahead with the unit trust idea.[46] Norman and Booth were friends, literally next-door neighbours at the top of Campden Hill in London and they worked together at the Bank of England.[47] Despite Booth's undeniable influence, it was Fairbairn who subsequently became synonymous with the unit trust movement and has been seen as the driving force behind M&G.[48] Rather like Philip Rose with the Foreign and Colonial Government Trust, Booth and Fairbairn were involved right from the beginning, gradually establishing the movement and in the fullness of time, seeing it become successful. Rose needed just over 10 years for investment companies to become properly established, whereas it took Booth and Fairbairn more than 30 years with unit trusts. In some ways Booth's role was similar to that of Philip Rose during the first 15 years at Foreign & Colonial Government Trust. Both ensured their initial idea, and values, survived through a challenging period. Perhaps the main difference was that after 15 years, in 1883 at the time of Rose's death, he could be confident that his idea was solidly established; this was far from evident for unit trusts in 1946. Over time, Fairbairn became more influential and operated in an executive full-time capacity, becoming a director of Municipal and General in 1937, chairman in 1942, and finally, chairman of the holding company White Drummond in 1955. So from the 1940s onwards, Fairbairn was the key individual and the public face. Booth in 1931 and during the decade leading up to the Second World War put in place the foundations of the unit trust industry; Fairbairn went on to complete the job. Both men deserve credit for their respective contributions and each needed the other.

---

[46] Duncan Crow, *A Man of Push and Go – the Life of George Macaulay Booth* (Rupert Hart-Davis 1965) 179. Booth and Norman were literally next-door neighbours living in adjacent houses in Campden Hill London. Booth was also a Bank of England director.

[47] Duncan Crow, *A Man of Push and Go – the Life of George Macaulay Booth* (Rupert Hart-Davis 1965) 179.

[48] John Fairbairn (telephone conversations, 2 December 2014 and 2 January 2015).

7.3   The First British Fixed Trust[49]

The first unit trust, the First British, was launched on 23 April 1931. It invested in ordinary shares and at a time of deflation, with negative inflation of −7.2% in 1930 and −4.5% in 1931, this first unit trust offered investors a remarkable starting yield of 6.8%. Although this was an equity portfolio and Foreign & Colonial invested in international bonds, in other respects there were considerable similarities between the two vehicles. Both had a buy-and-hold approach; both were trusts; both were aimed at small investors; both offered a large yield premium to anything else in the market; both were concentrated portfolios; both had specific termination dates, 20 years and 24 years, respectively; and both had multiple issues of units.

The First British (Table 7.1 and Fig. 7.3) had 24 holdings of which no individual stock represented more than 6% of the total value of the fund at inception. It was conceived as a buy-and-hold ('fixed') strategy, meaning that the initial holdings could be held in perpetuity and no new holdings would be added to the initial portfolio. Stocks, however, could be sold if they failed to meet certain expectations associated with paying dividends, for example, but this was the only real method of changing the shape of the portfolio. New cash flow would be invested *pro rata* in the initial holdings. Some of the notable characteristics of this concentrated portfolio were

- Holding sizes, as a percentage of the total fund value, were roughly between 3.5% and 4.5%, so it was broadly equally weighted apart from a small number of outliers.
- The largest holdings were Midland Counties Electric Supply Co (5.6%), Harrods (5.0%), Shell (4.7%), Boots Pure Drug Company (4.7%) and the Callenders Cables & Construction Company (4.7%).[50]

---

[49] The portfolio, as shown in the original Prospectus, has been re-created as Plate 3 courtesy of Stutchbury, *The Management of Unit Trusts* (Skinner 1964).

[50] Danny O'Shea, *An Introduction to M&G, its history and its management* (M&G memorandum, 24 May 1994).

Table 7.1 First British Fixed Trust portfolio 1931

Initial %	Original securities in 1931	In 1994
5.6	Midland Counties Electric Supply Co.	Nationalised 1947
5.0	Harrods	House of Fraser
5.0	British Insulated Cables	BICC
4.7	'Shell' Transport & Trading Co.	Shell
4.7	Boots Pure Drug Co.	Boots
4.7	Callenders Cable & Construction Co.	BICC
4.6	*Savoy Hotel*	*Not known*
4.4	Rolls Royce	Receivership 1971
4.4	J & P Coats	Coats Viyella
4.4	Courtaulds	Courtaulds
4.3	Watney, Combe, Reid & Co.	Grand Met
4.3	Arthur Guinness, Son & Co.	Guinness
4.2	Yorkshire Electric	Nationalised 1947
4.1	Babcock & Wilcox	Babcock International
4.1	J Lyons & Co.	Allied Lyons
3.9	General Electric Co.	GEC
3.9	Commercial Union Assurance Co.	C.U.
3.8	Imperial Tobacco Co.	Hanson
3.6	British American Tobacco Co.	BAT Industries
3.6	Schweppes	Cadbury Schweppes
3.5	Staveley Coal & Iron	Staveley Ind.
3.4	Furness, Withy & Co.	Oetker Gruppe (Germany)
3.3	Anglo Iranian [Persian] Oil Co.	B.P.
2.5	County of London Electric Supply Co.	Nationalised 1947
100.0		

Source: Data in Table 7.1 is taken from Danny O'Shea, *An Introduction to M&G, its history and its management* (M&G memorandum, 24 May 1994). I have changed the headings and reordered the table by holding size and added in 'Savoy Hotel Limited' which was listed in the original Prospectus

– The portfolio had an emphasis on industrial and commercial stocks with very little in financials:

• Only one insurance company in the portfolio, Commercial Union; other large quoted insurance stocks at that time, Prudential and Pearl, were ignored

• No bank holdings, though Lloyds, Westminster and Midland were possible investments.

– It had a starting yield of 6.8% compared with a gilt yield of 4.5% and an equity index yield of 5.8% (at the start of 1931).

Extract from original prospectus of First British Fixed Trust

** THE TRUST consists of one or more identical Units, each Unit as now constituted comprising the 1,280 Ordinary Shares of the group of leading British Companies as set below :-

Company	Number of Shares
Anglo Persian Oil Company, Limited	50
Babcock & Wilcox, Limited	50
Boots Pure Drug Company, Limited	25
British-American Tobacco Co., Ltd.	25
British Insulated Cables, Limited	50
Callenders Cable and Construction Co., Ltd.	50
J. & P. Coats, Ltd.	50
Commercial Union Assurance Co., Ltd.	5
County of London Electric Supply Co., Ltd.	50
Courtaulds, Limited	75
Furness, Withy & Co., Limited	75
General Electric Company, Limited	50
Arthur Guinness, Son & Co., Limited	25
Harrods, Limited	50
Imperial Tobacco Company (of Great Britain & Ireland), Limited	25
J. Lyons & Company, Limited	25
Midland Counties Electric Supply Co., Ltd.	100
Rolls-Royce, Limited	75
Savoy Hotel, Limited	75
Schweppes, Limited	75
"Shell" Transport & trading Co., Ltd.	50
Staveley Coal & Iron Co., Ltd.	100
Watney, Combe, Reid & Co., Limited	50
Yorkshire Electric Power Company	75
Total	1,280

As each Unit is deposited with the Trustee, Certificates for 2,000 equal Sub-Units are issued by the Trustee in convenient denominations, each Sub-Unit representing 1/2 ,000th beneficial interest in the securities and/or other property then comprising a Unit. The Certificates are available in denominations as low as 10 (ten) Sub-Units. Based upon the Stock Exchange prices ruling on 7th April, 1931, the selling price of a Sub-Unit would have been 33s."

Fig. 7.3   The First British Prospectus, April 1931

(This page has been re-created from the document shown in Stutchbury, *The Management of Unit Trusts*, Skinner 1964, page 4)

Many of the subsequent unit trusts that were launched in the 1930s in Britain had an equity orientation. One clear indication of the increasing interest in equities, particularly ordinary shares, by the British public was the creation of the FT30 Index in July 1935 (Table 7.2). Originally known as the Financial News 30-share index, this was the brainchild of Maurice Green and Richard Clarke, respectively editor and chief leader writer of the *Financial News*. Subsequently, in 1945 the *Financial Times* acquired the *Financial News* and re-named the index. Clarke later described this index as 'a truly modern and sensitive industrial ordinary share index' and 'the [Financial News] 30 [Index] includes a great many of the most active shares in the market. In the list there is no "dead wood". It may fairly be claimed that the list is adequately representative of market activity as a whole.'[51] Clearly, this index was an attempt to capture the shape of the equity market in the UK and to provide a means of measuring the performance of companies both individually and within a composite stock market index. This first set of companies was mainly industrials though drinks were well represented in the shape of Bass, Distillers and Watney Coombe. Oddly, the index contained neither oil companies nor banks.

Table 7.2 FT30 Index 1935 – constituent stocks

Associated Portland Cement	Dunlop Rubber	Murex
Austin Motor	EMI	Patons & Baldwins
Bass Brewery	Fine Spinners & Doublers	Pinchin Johnson
BAT	**General Electric**	**Rolls Royce**
Bolsover Colliery	Guest Keen & Nettlefolds	Tate & Lyle
Callenders Cables	**Harrods**	Turner & Newall
Coats	Hawker Sidderley	United Steel
Courtaulds	ICI	Vickers
Distillers	Int'l Tea Co Stores	**Watney Coombe**
Dorman Long	London Brick	Woolworths

Source: http://stockmarketalmanac.co.uk/2015/12/ft30-index-1935-where-are-they-now/; website accessed 6 March 2017.

---

[51] *The Financial Times*, Andrew Hill, 23 July 2010.

There was only limited overlap between the new index and the First British – the names highlighted in bold were held by the First British of April 1931. Similar to the right hand side of Table 7.1, a quick glance at the list of companies in Table 7.2 shows the considerable change and dynamism which is associated with equities' ownership over time. Since 1935, the only independent survivors from the list above are BAT and Tate & Lyle. The remainder in the main have either merged or been subsumed and a few, such as Woolworths, have failed.

Booth was acquainted with two of the most important investors of the early twentieth century, namely Robert Fleming and John Maynard Keynes, who probably shaped his attitude towards ordinary shares and the bold decision to launch an equity portfolio during the depths of the depression. Flemings acted as bankers to the Alfred Booth family businesses, which were involved in shipping, engineering and leather. Booth was reportedly 'a close friend of Robert Fleming'.[52] In Booth's own words, he and Keynes were also 'in and out with each other all the time'.[53] Booth not only had a close working relationship with Keynes during the First World War (see the 'Degas' story in the footnote) when both were employed by the government, but he also had strong social ties both through family connections and mutual friends.[54] Booth and Keynes worked together on various projects

---

[52] Duncan Crow, *A Man of Push and Go – the Life of George Macaulay Booth* (Rupert Hart-Davis 1965) 176.

[53] Duncan Crow, *A Man of Push and Go – the Life of George Macaulay Booth* (Rupert Hart-Davis 1965) 183.

[54] The Degas story illustrates the closeness between Keynes and Booth. In March 1918 they were both in Paris, which at the time was under shell attack from the Germans. Booth was in Paris as a government representative and Keynes ostensibly representing the Treasury. In Booth's words: 'Maynard did nothing at all but pictures at that time . . . then all of us pushed these pictures through the streets on lorries to bring them to the ship. What excitement we had, we did enjoy ourselves. And there they are today in the National Gallery.' Over 2 days, 27 and 28 March 1918, Keynes had bought 27 paintings for Britain costing £15,000 from the Degas collection including a Cezanne still life for his own pleasure priced at £327. Charles Holmes the Director of the National Gallery (1916 to 1928) accompanied Keynes on the Paris jaunt by. But it was Keynes who had apparently raised the money for the purchases from Bonar Law, Chancellor of the Exchequer. According to Booth, Keynes had told Bonar Law, 'It'll help the French balance of payments. For heaven's sake, this is the opportunity of a lifetime.' Keynes was correct on both points of course. Recounted in Crow, *A man of Push and Go* (Rupert Hart-Davis 1965) 153.

during the First World War and subsequently from the 1920s when Booth was on the Court of the Bank of England.[55] They also shared many mutual friends such as Virginia Woolf and Vanessa Bell in the Bloomsbury Group and it is likely that some of Keynes' enthusiasm by for investing in equities rubbed off on Booth.[56] Another connection between Keynes and Booth was the Macmillan Committee that looked into the financing needs of British industry between November 1929 and June 1931. Keynes was a prominent member of this committee at the same time as Booth was a director of the Bank of England. The final reports (the main one and then the minority one) from Macmillan highlighted a number of matters close to Keynes' heart, one of which was the role, powers and ownership of the Bank of England while another was the problem of long-term capital funding in Britain for small and medium-sized enterprises. This was to become known as the 'Macmillan Gap'. Clearly, equity funding rather than bank lending was one way of bridging this gap so the ideas must have resonated with Booth too, given his role at the Bank of England, as a businessman and as a man with a strong social conscience. The Macmillan Committee's recommendations which resulted directly in the creation of the Industrial and Commercial Finance Corporation, becoming 3i in due course. The First British, with a 20-year life focused on industrial shares, was also another natural way to bridge some aspects of the Macmillan Gap.

There were four separate issues of the First British between April 1931 and February 1934: The First British, The Second British, the Third British and the Fourth British, which somewhat mirrored the five separate issues of shares from Foreign and Colonial after 1868. The reported price of a sub-unit was £1.65 (stated as 33 shillings in imperial money in the Prospectus, Fig. 7.3) and was available in certificates as small as 10 sub-units, so an initial investment could have been as little as £16.50 (£1,000 inflation adjusted to the present). Another interesting similarity to Foreign and Colonial Government Trust of 1868 was that *The Economist* also had

---

[55] Booth suggested to Norman that Keynes should join the Court of the Bank of England in 1941. The suggestion was accepted.

[56] Duncan Crow, *A Man of Push and Go – the Life of George Macaulay Booth* (Rupert Hart-Davis 1965) 183.

erroneous reservations about what was being proposed by the First British in 1931, 'the strongest among the many objections to the Fixed Trust was its fixity (sic) in a world of ever changing economic tendencies... To choose a portfolio of securities, at a purely fortuitous moment, and to lock them away in a tin box for anything up to 25 years is to court disaster'.[57] So the main objection from the esteemed newspaper was the static nature of the approach – 'it's fixity'. While the basic idea of a Fixed Trust had been adapted from the USA, in practice some of the investment guidelines had been modified and provided greater investment flexibility. For example, a typical guideline in the USA was that a mutual fund had to sell a stock if its dividend was cut in any 1 year. This was changed in the UK so that the First British would be forced to sell a stock only if 'regular dividend payments fell below the quinquennial moving average'.[58] Although the word 'regular' was not defined, nevertheless, the intention was to limit forced selling by the First British so helpfully introducing greater discretion as to what and when to sell, thus reducing administration and transaction costs. However, similar to the US Fixed Trusts, the First British continued to maintain a 'buy-and-hold' approach. Therefore, because there was no opportunity to buy new shares or re-balance the portfolio, problems would inevitably arise either with the First British holding an increasingly unbalanced and less diversified collection of holdings, or at times having too much cash before returning it to unit holders at one of the semi-annual distribution dates. So, although conceived as 'buy-and-hold', the strategy was really a 'hold until-forced-to-sell' approach, which was less than ideal.

With hindsight, Fixed Trusts were a strange creation even allowing for the Great Crash of 1929. While superficially transparent, Fixed Trusts were mainly designed to eradicate incompetence and misdemeanours by Directors of investment trusts in the USA. Unit trusts of the 'fixed' variety were a knee-jerk reaction to the excesses and failures of the financial services industry and particularly the investment management business in the USA around 1929. Fixed Trusts were not

---

[57] *The Economist*, 2 May 1931.
[58] *The Economist*, 2 May 1931.

established as a forerunner of today's passive management and indexation strategies though they clearly possessed some of those characteristics such as low transaction costs and the holding of a basket of shares as a proxy for the market. More simply, Fixed Trusts were created because fiduciary management by asset management professionals and directors had failed in 1920s America. *The Economist* explained it thus: 'The conduct of the trust being a matter of routine administration, the investor cannot lose his money through speculation, directorial irregularities or management errors.'[59] Using more colourful language, Chamberlain and Hay made a similar point about failures of investment trusts in the USA:

> Provided we are allowed the premise that the American public is not absolutely financially illiterate, it is indisputable that the success in the sale of fixed trusts must stand as one of the bitterest indictments ever launched on Wall Street. It audibly reverberates the unsavoury accusation 'we will only trust them if their hands are tied'.[60]

7.4   Unit Trusts in the 1930s

Fixed Trusts were a stepping stone to more sophisticated investment products which duly came along, after 1934, in the form of flexible trusts and became the preferred form from the mid-1930s onwards (Table 7.3). As the name suggests, flexible trusts provided more freedom – the asset manager chose from a pre-agreed list of securities and had the power to re-invest sale proceeds into alternative securities and to buy any name on the pre-agreed list, referred to as the 'permitted list' or the 'panel of allowable stocks'. Municipal and General launched two of the first flexible unit trusts: the Foreign Government Bond Trust in 1934, followed shortly thereafter by the Limited Investment Fund in 1935, a vehicle for equity

---

[59] *The Economist, Fixed Trusts,* 21 March 1931.
[60] Chamberlain and Hay, *Investment and Speculation* (1931) quoted in Janette Rutterford, Learning from one another's mistakes: investment trusts in the UK and US, 1868–1940 (Financial History Review 16/2, 2009).

Table 7.3 Unit trusts formed between 1931 and 1938

	Fixed trusts general	Fixed trusts specialist	Flexible trusts general	Flexible trusts specialist	Total
1931	1				1
1932	2				2
1933	4	1			5
1934	10	7		2	19
1935	16	2	1	2	21
1936	3		8	6	17
1937	1			5	6
1938	5		7	6	18
Total	42	10	16	21	89

Source: Compiled from *The Economist, Unit Trust Survey* 13 May 1939

investment. Save & Prosper also entered the market in June 1934 when it launched a flexible trust of mixed securities, the 'Trust of Insurance Shares'.

The Foreign Government Bond Trust of 1934 was an exciting proposition – a bond fund, designed to invest in emerging market debt. In some ways it demonstrated the growing confidence of the unit trust movement too. Allegedly the idea emanated from the Governor of the Bank of England, Montagu Norman, '[Montagu] Norman was strongly in favour of the Unit Trust idea. One day he said to Booth: "you ought to start a Busted Foreign Bond Unit Trust. You could make pots of money out of it"'.[61] The Foreign Government Bond Trust was designed to invest in high-yielding bonds overseas in a risk-controlled manner. It also had a well-written Prospectus though it sounded a little similar to the diversification story that launched Foreign & Colonial in 1868. It said, 'any one foreign bond might prove a speculation but in the aggregate they will be an investment'. The Prospectus contained a detailed matrix of 122 bonds, 'the panel', listed in 40 different countries and the investment approach was explained as follows:

Instead of a fixed unit, there will be a panel of bonds, within which a limited liberty of action in the choice of a portfolio will be allowed. Not

---

[61] Duncan Crow, *A Man of Push and Go – the Life of George Macaulay Booth* (Rupert Hart-Davis 1965) 179.

more than 5%, of the funds may be invested in any one of the bonds . . . and the normal spread would be at least 50 separate securities – there are 122 in the panel. . . . re-investment of the proceeds of sales and redemptions is permitted. . . . If at any time it should prove undesirable to invest all the funds within the panel, recourse may be had to British Government securities, and in this case the 5% limit does not apply.[62]

As the Prospectus for the Foreign Government Bond Trust explained: 'Clearly the provisions of a Fixed Trust, with its units precisely constituted of specific shares in defined proportions could not be applied to Foreign Bond markets, even if it were desirable. The varying conditions in Foreign Bond markets, together with problems of drawn bonds and redemptions, would make the fixed unit an impossibility.'[63] This statement implied that the form of unit holding changed from 'fixed' to 'flexible' because of the underlying nature of the investment portfolio, in this case bonds rather than equities. This change from fixed weights to flexible management was entirely pragmatic, rather than philosophical, at this juncture. The Foreign Government Bond Trust had considerable discretion and in practice it could invest absolutely anywhere. George Faber, Director of Municipal and General, explained this point in his letter to prospective investors which accompanied the Prospectus: 'Managerial control is with Municipal and General Securities Company Ltd, which was established in 1906. . . . (and) this management question is not unimportant. As will be realised, the freedom of action allowed within the panel is considerable. . . . .'[64] Another flexible unit trust was launched shortly thereafter in June 1934 by the Bank Insurance Group (it became Save & Prosper in 1962 and in due course part of the Flemings asset management business) which offered the 'Trust of Insurance Shares' to invest principally in shares and debt of insurance companies but with the facility to invest in

---

[62] *Prospectus Foreign Government Bond Trust*, issued by Municipal and General (Guildhall Library).

[63] *Prospectus Foreign Government Bond Trust*, issued by Municipal and General (Guildhall Library).

[64] *Prospectus Foreign Government Bond Trust*, issued by Municipal and General (Guildhall Library). 10 April 1934 letter accompanying the Prospectus from George Faber, Director.

British government bonds too. This was a flexible trust offering a mixed investment portfolio of securities: it was an odd mixture of holdings but in practical terms it represented another stepping stone towards greater investment flexibility.

Actively managed equities arrived at the end of 1935. Municipal and General created the Limited Investment Fund, launched in December. It would select stocks from a pre-agreed permitted list of 157 quoted company investments, and it expected to hold not less than 20 large UK equity stocks. Significantly, the opening lines of the Prospectus acknowledged that the original fixed trusts were perhaps overly restrictive. So this new fund was designed to be more flexible but it was also much more interesting in terms of investment ambition. It had the following attributes: '(a) The Managers have discretionary powers of investment within a list of 157 companies.... (b) Certain industries now depressed are included in the permitted investments.... (c) New industries are also included.....'[65] This language in the Prospectus showed how much investment thinking had developed in just 4 years since the First British was launched. Again, there was reassuring prose explaining the overall objective of the fund on Page 11 of the Prospectus: 'The Limited Investment Fund have framed their present policy to earn the Unit holders a yield of 4%, which in their judgment is the highest consistent with security of capital that can be envisaged in the present conditions.' Finally, there was also a change to the fee structure which more accurately charged costs to investors based on the period in which they were invested, explained as follows:

A new method has been adopted for providing preliminary expenses and continuity of management in a manner which avoids the immediate imposition of the whole of the charge on the original purchaser of a Unit. This is achieved by providing that the Trustee and the Managers (who are responsible to and replaceable by the Trustee) are together entitled to a remuneration at the total rate of one half of one per cent of

---

[65] *Prospectus, The Limited Investment Fund* issued by Municipal and General (Guildhall Library).

the average value of the deposited property throughout each year. . . . In this way, the holder of a Unit, in substance, pays only the proportion of administration charges which is incurred while he holds the Unit.[66]

By the end of 1935 therefore, the unit trust movement offered a wide range of products. Ordinary shares, global bonds and mixed funds were packaged into fixed and flexible structures. As shown above, the Municipal and General stable of unit trusts in particular was also able to describe risk, diversification and high yield in relatively sophisticated terms.

In terms of definitions, 'General Trusts' had a broad remit whereas 'Special Trusts' had a specific geographic or industrial focus (some as narrowly defined as 'Gold Shares'). General Trusts predominated though some of these had rather quirky remits. For example, Municipal and General had the 'Scottish and North Country Investment Fund' which could invest in up to 185 companies in northern Britain or in British government stocks. Of these 89 unit trusts, 72 were invested in equities and another 15 had a mixed remit to invest in equities and bonds with only 2 funds dedicated to fixed interest – overall there was a very strong focus on equity investing and particularly, ordinary shares. By 1939 there were 15 management companies offering unit trusts of which the largest were the National Group, the British Industrial Corporation, Fifteen Moorgate Securities, Municipal and General, Allied Investors and British General, with each of these groups offering between 8 and 10 unit trust products. Apart from Municipal and General, none of these unit trust management companies has survived to the present day.

Although the numbers in Table 7.3 show rapid growth in fund numbers up to the peak year for formations of 1935, the sums of money raised were not large. The First British launched by Municipal and General in April 1931 sold only £80,000 of units in its first 14 months. Admittedly the First British was attempting to sell a new concept (the unit trust) and a new investment idea (equities) to a public who would have been somewhat bruised by the heavy market falls between 1929 and 1931. Nevertheless, the comparison with the Foreign and Colonial Government Trust in the UK of 1868 is interesting. At launch Foreign & Colonial raised more than £500,000

---

[66] *Prospectus, The Limited Investment Fund* issued by Municipal and General (Guildhall Library).

(and by 1872 it had raised a total of £3.5 million) when it was created more than 60 years earlier so it had been much more successful. The largest unit trust to be launched in the 1930s was British Assets Trust in 1933 but even it raised only £7 million from 2600 investors so these were not large amounts of money.[67] The unit trust movement grew steadily and was valued at £21 million by the end of 1934, at which point *The Economist* estimated that unit trusts amounted to about 7% of the value of investment trusts and that this 'figure is a striking commentary on the success of the fixed trust during the last four years'.[68] In a similar vein, *The Times* stated: 'The popular reception given to the fixed trusts leaves no doubt whatever that they have met a genuine public demand for a means by which the small investor may spread his capital over a wide but clearly defined field.'[69] The general perception in the media was that unit trusts were an important and growing feature of the savings landscape but despite 1935 being a strong year, the reality was different. While 1935 was another year of growth as funds under management more than doubled to £46 million, thereafter the rate of growth began to slow and the money invested in unit trusts in the UK amounted to only about £84 million in value as of 1939.[70] Even 20 years later, it was barely £100 million, which in real terms was much smaller than the 1939 value. In practice, individual unit trusts were small and in aggregate they did not raise very much money from British savers between 1931 and 1959.[71]

The 1930s were difficult. There was massive economic suffering in parts of Britain during the decade, particularly in the north of England where towns may have been reliant on specific industries. Jarrow was one of those towns which had lost both its main sources of employment at the beginning of the decade, steel and shipbuilding. The problems of hardship and deprivation were highlighted by the 'Jarrow March' from the northeast of England to London in October 1936 when 200 locals walked to London over 22 days to protest to Parliament. However, despite the severe

---

[67] British Assets Trust – note this was a unit trust and is not the investment trust of the same name now called Blackrock Income Strategies and managed by Aberdeen Asset Management.

[68] *The Economist, Fixed Trust Supplement*, 6 April 1935.

[69] *The Times*, 3 March 1936.

[70] Adrienne Gleeson, *People and their money: 50 years of private investment* (M&G Group 1981) 26.

[71] Hugh Bullock and D. Corner, *Investment and unit trusts in Britain and America* (Elek 1968) 259.

depression in places like Jarrow, perhaps surprisingly but personal savings rose rapidly during the decade and British people had much more in the way of savings deposited with financial institutions at the end of the 1930s than at the start. These savings were held by entities such as insurance companies; banks, including the TSB, the Post Office Savings Bank and building societies. Deposits with the latter, for example, increased from £297 million in 1929 to £773 million by 1939 and this large increase was typical more generally with deposit-taking institutions.[72] The previous chapter highlighted that about £60 million per year was being allocated to life offices by the end of the 1930s. Therefore, some British people did have increasing reserves of cash, but they chose not to invest very much of it into unit trusts. Furthermore, as can be seen in Table 7.4, after the downmarkets from 1929 to 1931, equity markets produced very strong returns in the years to 1936, which should have made individuals receptive to stock exchange investments.

The unit trust business should have attracted more money flows than it did in the 1930s. One reason that it did not was that the unit trust

Table 7.4 UK equity and bond returns 1929–1939

Calendar year	Equity % change	Equity % yield	Bond % change	Bond % yield
1929	−19.1	5.5	−6.0	4.7
1930	−9.2	5.4	8.5	4.3
1931	−24.3	5.8	−4.7	4.5
1932	27.9	4.4	35.6	3.3
1933	20.6	3.5	−0.1	3.3
1934	9.8	3.6	24.4	2.7
1935	9.9	3.7	−5.8	2.9
1936	15.1	3.4	−2.6	2.9
1937	−16.7	4.6	−12.2	3.3
1938	−14.9	5.5	−5.4	3.5
1939	−3.1	5.4	−2.6	3.6

Source: Barclays Equity Gilt Study 2012

[72] Adrienne Gleeson, *People and their money: 50 years of private investment* (M&G Group 1981) 26/27.

management companies failed to put their own houses in order and this damaged its reputation. For example, in the advertisements of the time, income figures were manipulated by the inclusion of capital receipts or accrued income in the yield figures. According to *The Economist*, 'These problems should not be impossible of solution. . . . unit trust certificates have sold very largely on yield in the past, and in view of the movement's preponderating (sic) interest in equities, there is everything in favour of understating, rather than overstating, the return which the investor may expect.'[73] Fees and charges were an even bigger issue because there was little transparency. *The Economist* called for better information to be published within the accounts of management companies to show different sources of remuneration. Four areas of remuneration remained opaque: creating and selling units, managing the trust assets, providing a market for units already in existence and liquidating the trust.[74] One example of malpractice concerned bid/offer spreads which were far too wide. As at 31 March 1939, 77 unit trusts were analysed with bid/offer spreads that varied between 2.6% and 14.7% with an average spread of 5.0%.[75] Advertisements from 1939 by Municipal and General hinted at the problem of conflicts of interest.[76] They explained their own procedures as follows: ' . . . all money subscribed for new units, with the sole exception of the preliminary charge, must be used to buy investments for the trust. This puts the managers in the unequivocal position of being agents for the unit holders in the purchase of underlying securities and in the creation of unit'. The clear implication was that some unit trust managers acted as principals when trading – basically this meant taking additional revenue from their clients in addition to the stated asset management fees. Some unit trust managers made additional profits from both buying and selling underlying securities, and at various stages of the process when trading units for clients (creation, dealing and liquidation).

---

[73] *The Economist, Unit Trust Survey*, 13 May 1939.
[74] *The Economist, Unit Trust Survey*, 13 May 1939.
[75] *The Economist, Unit Trust Survey*, 13 May 1939.
[76] *The Economist, Unit Trust Survey*, 13 May 1939.

There was no standardisation of fees, charges and costs. Front-end charges and management fees varied and these could be shown in different ways. Given that the maximum life of trusts typically varied between 5 and 25 years with an average around 20 years, it was complicated to amortise front-end charges consistently to create like-for-like comparisons. So, for example, a front-end charge of 5%, amortised over 5 years adds 1% per annum to the quoted fee whereas if it is amortised over a 20-year life then it adds only 0.25% to the annual fee. By adding back front-end charges, *The Economist* estimated that some unit trusts charged as little as 0.30% per annum while others charged over 1.5% and that the average figure based on 28 'Flexible' trusts in 1939 was 0.59%.[77] As a headline figure 0.59% was not excessive but the real problems were lack of standardisation and no transparency. Additionally, because unit trust managers did not have to publish accounts, there was no way of knowing what the additional costs were. 'It is desirable to clear the air of controversy, that particulars of profit and cost should be given in the fullest possible detail. Whatever the precise form of the account(s) may be therefore, it would be highly advantageous if it supplied information regarding the (asset) manager's gross profits,' opined *The Economist*.[78] It was public knowledge that questionable behaviour was taking place. Clearly this was all less than ideal, but not the first time that practitioners in the financial services industry had chosen to obfuscate fees, charges and remuneration. The purveyors of unit trusts should have moved more quickly than they did to address these issues, the net effect of which resulted in a shadow hanging over the unit trust movement in the UK for the second half of the 1930s and for many years thereafter.

This self-inflicted damage was exacerbated by the outbreak of the Second World War which contributed to a postponement of scheduled legislation that would have improved standards in the unit trust industry. Despite being debated in Parliament before the war, 'The Prevention of Fraud (Investments) Act' became law only in 1958. Furthermore, owing to wartime government restriction via the Capital Controls Committee, unit

---

[77] *The Economist, Unit Trust Survey,* 13 May 1939.
[78] *The Economist, Unit Trust Survey,* 13 May 1939.

trusts were moved onto a 'care and maintenance' basis and they were prohibited from advertising their wares and competing with other, more essential money-raising activities by the government and British industry. These capital controls were lifted only in 1958. Owing to the outbreak of the Second World War, the development of unit trusts in Britain was delayed by almost 20 years. Additionally, it took until 1959 to establish a properly functioning professional body, The Association of Unit Trust Managers. This body required unit trust management companies to be authorised by the Department for Trade and Industry and to adhere to professional standards including detailed provisions covering advertising, payment of commission and the conduct of sales agents. In summary therefore, the very slow pace of development of unit trusts in Britain for more than 20 years after 1935 resulted from a combination of factors, some within the control of unit trust practitioners and some without.

Typically, holdings in unit trusts were quite small but dispersed across a large investor base. The average holding in the fixed unit trusts of Municipal and General was estimated to be £253 (£12,500 in today's money) with the majority of investors holding between £100 and £400 of units.[79] According to *The Economist*, this size and spread of holdings was typical across all UK unit trusts in the 1930s.[80] The paper went on to say, 'Gargantuan holdings do not exist in the unit trust movement where holdings of even £5,000 or more . . . are almost negligible.'[81] The First Provincial unit trust group was a small unit trust management organisation that managed three fixed trusts. In 1938, *The Daily Herald* and then *The Economist* performed some analysis into its investor base. This categorisation of its shareholders shown in Table 7.5 tells us as much about attitudes particularly towards gender, and how little they appeared to have changed from 50 years earlier. The treatment of women is more akin to how British society may have been portrayed in early-nineteenth-century *Pride and Prejudice* rather than *Brave New World* of

---

[79] *The Economist, Unit Trust Survey,* 28 May 1938.
[80] *The Economist, Unit Trust Survey,* 28 May 1938.
[81] *The Economist, Unit Trust Survey,* 28 May 1938.

Table 7.5 Unit trust holders 1938: ownership

Status/occupation	%
Spinsters	24.3
Married women	18.5
Gentlemen	17.7
Widows	11.1
Shopkeepers	4.0
Engineers	3.0
Clerks	2.9
Artists and teachers	2.3
Doctors and dentists	2.0
Manufacturers and merchants	2.0
Farmers	1.7
Clergy	1.6
Civil servants	1.4
Army and navy	1.3
Bank officials	1.2
Manual foremen	1.1
Travellers	0.9
Agents	0.9
Accountants	0.8
Builders	0.8
Solicitors	0.6
Railway employees	0.2
Total	100.0

Source: *The Economist*, Unit Trust Survey 28 May 1938

the 1930s. These categorisations were similar to those used in the register of Foreign & Colonial shareholders from 1880/1881, so despite the Suffragettes and an extension to the franchise in 1928 to include women over 21, some things had yet to change. Remarkably, the occupational grades below showing people in jobs, only granted men employment status whereas women were classified by their marital status. 'Gentlemen' are considered, in terms of the classification of the time, to be men of independent means though, as with the women, some of these gentlemen would have been in gainful employment so the data is limited. The striking fact from this data is that women owned more than 50% of the holdings. Despite the caveats, it provides an interesting snapshot of the investor base, indicating that women were the largest investor group, and demonstrates how some of the wealth may have been distributed – shopkeepers choosing to invest more money into unit trusts than solicitors for example. One presumes that solicitors were not impecunious and did have money to invest but probably favoured investment companies for their own savings.

The second part of the unitholder analysis in Table 7.6 highlights personal wealth and analyses the unit trust share holdings of deceased persons in the context of their overall financial assets based on an analysis of wills at the time of probate. The data shows that the majority of large unit trust investors had estates of more than £2,500 at death (about £125,000 inflation adjusted to today). Summarising the data, *The Economist* said, 'The average holder, reckoned in terms of wealth, is a person of some substance – "comfortable middle class" might be as good a general description as any.'[82] We can deduce that the average person holding unit trusts was quite well off and generally female, with smallish holdings of about £300 and the financial acumen to have one's own bank account

Table 7.6 Unit trust holders 1938 – wealth (at probate)

Value of estate (£)	Probates number	%
£50 or under	3	0.7
51–100	3	0.7
101–200	2	0.5
201–300	3	0.7
301–400	2	0.5
401–500	10	2.3
501–1000	35	8.0
1001–1500	37	8.4
1501–2500	59	13.5
2501–5000	86	19.7
5001–10000	87	20.0
10001–50000	98	22.5
Over 50,000	11	2.5
Total	436	100.0

Source: The Economist, Unit Trust Survey 28 May 1938

---

[82] *The Economist, Unit Trust Survey,* 28 May 1938.

in order to receive dividends. Therefore, unit trust investors of the late 1930s could be described as middle-class or professional people, investing a small amount of their disposable income. The main investors were not working class or blue-collar people discovering the world of investment for the first time.

7.5 Investment Performance

Similar to Foreign & Colonial of the 1860s and 1870s, there were several issues of the First British Fixed Trust, four to be precise, launched at different times.[83] Each had a life of 20 years and each would have had a slightly different portfolio so investors would have experienced different returns over different time periods. Similar to the Foreign & Colonial issues, the differences were marked. The four trusts were merged into a single flexible unit trust in June 1951 when the First British came to the end of its planned life. At this point, Municipal and General (or M&G as it was now known) decided to consolidate the four issues and transfer them into one trust, The M&G General Trust Fund. So, the natural period of investment performance evaluation is from 1931 to 1951. Inevitably this was a volatile period for markets and the early 1930s produced high equity returns, while another bull market in equities was about to start in the early 1950s, just as this period of evaluation is concluding. The start and end point for performance analysis is often important but highly pertinent in this particular case. These 20 years saw the 1930s Depression, the Second World War, post-war nationalisation of swathes of British industry and the devaluation of Sterling against the US dollar from $4.86 in 1931 to $2.80 in 1949. Investors were also obliged to swap some of their equity holdings for Government bonds, '3% Nationalisation Stocks', which meant that equity owners of quoted or private commercial entities were forced, and often reluctant, sellers to the Labour Government. How did the First British perform against this backdrop?

---

[83] *The Economist, Directory of Unit Trusts*, 13 May 1939.

The First British was sold to the investing public in April 1931 on the basis of 'security and marketability' and on an initial yield of 6.79%.[84] This represented a yield premium of about 20% to the market. If we assume this premium persisted over the next 4 years to end 1935 then the average yield would have been 4.8% for the initial nearly 5 years of its life. The 1951 Prospectus subsequently claimed a yield of 4.25% for the First British over its life from end December 1935 to end March 1951.[85] Stitching together these two periods we achieve an average yield over 19.9 years of 4.4% per annum. On the capital side, the First British had an issue price of £1.65 in 1931 and a conversion price in May 1951 of a little over £2.78 meaning capital appreciation of 68% or about 2.5% per annum over nearly 20 years. Over the life of the First British, investors would have earned a return of just about 7% per annum from 1931 to 1951 outperforming cash (massively), bonds (significantly) and also inflation which averaged about 3.5% per annum over the period 1932 to 1950. The launch date had been propitious but the First British deserved a bit of luck for being so courageous.

From end 1935 to March 1951 the investment performance results for the First British were acceptable but not as strong as in the first 4 years. According to the Prospectus for the M&G General Trust the yield on the First British averaged 4.25% and there was a small amount, +9.9%, of capital appreciation over the 15 years to March 1951.[86] This translates to a total annualised return of about 5% per annum. Overall, this was an acceptable outcome for investors in a remarkably turbulent period of British and world history when events exerted huge stress on political systems and economies, which in turn affected financial markets. The outcomes over both 15 and 20 years were considerably ahead of the expectations of *The Economist* back in 1931, when it had been very critical

---

[84] Hugh Bullock and D. Corner, *Investment and unit trusts in Britain and America* (Elek 1968) 254.

[85] *The Times*, 1 May 1951. The income produced was reported as follows in the Prospectus: 'Average annual income distributions (excluding all capital items) Gross % of asset value at commencement of period £4 5s 3d.' I have rounded down this figure of 4.2625% to 4.25%.

[86] *The Times*, 1 May 1951.

claiming that the First British 'courted disaster'.[87] Over most long-term periods, cash disappoints and equities thrive. In this case equities in general and those held by the First British in particular showed their resilience through a depression, a world war and a Labour government which took privately owned companies into public ownership. Three electricity supply companies owned by the First British were nationalised in 1948, namely County of London, Midland Counties and Yorkshire Electric Power. Shareholders were compensated with British government bonds in lieu of shares when these and other companies were taken into public ownership. The Chairman of Yorkshire Electric, Sir Robert Ellis, did not mince his words when he said at his final AGM in February 1948, 'This is hardly an encouragement to invest in industrial enterprise since no one knows upon whom the axe will next fall. The worst phase of the inequity lies in the fact that particular classes [of British society] are being systematically robbed instead of paying them a fair market value.'[88] As witnessed in Britain in the 1940s, when an ideological government becomes directly involved in forcibly swapping shareholder equity into government bonds, then investment risk was a lot more fundamental than technical measures of stock specific volatility that get highlighted in modern-day risk models.

7.6   Unit Trusts After 1951

As we have seen, the M&G General Trust was created in order to merge the four fixed trusts launched by Municipal and General in the early 1930s into one entity. The 1951 Prospectus referred to various aspects of the new trust, namely the terms of conversion, the opportunity for the trust to invest flexibly in quoted British companies and the new trust's stock exchange quotation.[89] There was a remarkable change of tone at this juncture from *The Economist*: the publication was gracious about the new arrangements,

---

[87] *The Economist*, 21 March 1931.
[88] *The Times*, 20 February 1948.
[89] *The Times*, 1 May 1951.

commenting favourably on a range of areas such as administration, investment objectives and the quality of the management group, saying 'At any rate, the experience is timely, the operation well-conceived, and the management highly esteemed. These are at least the right ingredients for attracting risk capital from the small saver.'[90] The Prospectus was a high quality document in its own right – not only was it scrupulous as to how past performance figures were presented, but it also emphasised commitment to probity, fairness to investors and reasonable management charges.[91] There was a maximum front-end charge of 2% and an ongoing annual management charge of only 0.375% together with an explicit statement that 'beyond these charges and the usual registration fees, no charge may be made by the Trustee or the manager for their services'. It is not possible to comment on bid/offer spreads because this was not covered in the Prospectus but given the tone of the document, it is unlikely that spreads would have been excessive. The new trust also had considerable flexibility with the only material restriction being that not more than 5% would be held in any one security.

As the 1950s progressed, unit trusts became better established. War-related restrictions were lifted, regulation was improved, a unit-linked life savings scheme was introduced by the Unicorn Group, whereby life assurance monies could be invested directly in unit trusts, and other well-managed organisations such as Flemings entered the field of unit trust management. M&G continued to innovate. In 1954, the first unit trust savings scheme was launched, the M&G Thrift Plan, and in 1957, M&G created the first unit trust exclusively for the use of company pension schemes and friendly societies, the M&G Pension Exempt.[92] The year 1958 perhaps marks the date when British unit trusts finally crossed their Rubicon owing to the behaviour of Flemings, the banking and asset management firm. As we have seen, Robert Fleming had been one of the great pioneers of investment trusts in the

---

[90] *The Economist*, 5 May 1951.

[91] *The Times*, 1 May 1951.

[92] Danny O'Shea, *An Introduction to M&G, its history and its management* (internal M&G memorandum, 24 May 1994).

late nineteenth century (Chapter 4). During 1958, Flemings, one of the largest managers of investment trusts, at the time, created a unit trust management business, Robert Fleming Trust Management Ltd., and also converted an existing investment trust, Crosby, into a unit trust. Other asset management groups were also moving into unit trust management. A consortium consisting of Atlantic Assets (an entrepreneurial investment trust managed by Ivory & Sime, an asset management firm based in Edinburgh), Flemings and Barings bought the unit trust group Bank Insurance Trust Corporation, subsequently re-branding it 'Save & Prosper' in 1962.[93] It rapidly became the largest unit trust group in Britain and, in due course, also became the brand name for Flemings' unit trusts who took complete control of Save & Prosper in 1988. By 1959, funds under management in unit trusts had reached £100 million, and after that the size of the business increased rapidly to an estimated value of £522 million in 1965.[94] Unit trusts had finally achieved scale and acceptance in Britain but it had taken a very long time.

7.7   Concluding Remarks

The First British Fixed Trust was a simple and attractive idea, launched propitiously with a very high yield given it invested in equities after an extended period of large price falls. Investment performance was reasonably good in very difficult markets and, with hindsight, demonstrated the wisdom of buying equities in 1931 after the market crash of 1929 and then holding them for the long-term, 20 years in this case. This is, or should be, one of the great lessons for all savers about investing in equities: buy low after significant market falls and always plan to hold them for as long as possible. Unit trusts also introduced a new category of savers to investment, particularly middle-class women and allowed relatively small amounts of money to be invested, typically around £300.

---

[93] Each of these three entities held 30% in Save & Prosper with the remaining 10% held by the British Linen Pension Fund.

[94] Christopher Hill, *Unit Trusts from the Beginning* (Unit Trust Association 1984).

Initially, the first unit trusts in the UK made good progress getting established in the early 1930s in challenging circumstances. Funds under management grew steadily until 1935 from a very low base and against the competing attractions of the well-established investment trusts. Subsequently, more flexible investment guidelines were introduced during the mid-1930s and the management and marketing of the newer unit trusts became more sophisticated but very little new money was raised. There was a steady stream of unit trust launches but funds raised were very small and unit trusts failed to challenge the hegemony of investment trust companies. This was partly attributable to a regulatory vacuum compounded by a lack of professionalism by some market participants which gave unit trusts a poor reputation. Then, as a consequence of the Second World War and its aftermath, unit trusts did not grow very much at all for 20 years in the UK. This was in stark contrast to the experience in the USA where unit trusts, or mutual funds, became popular quickly. The historical context, culture and regulatory environment was much more supportive towards mutual funds in the USA from the 1930s onwards compared to the UK. This only changed in Britain in the late 1950s when capital controls were lifted and the unit trust industry was properly regulated by legislation, notably by the long overdue Prevention of Fraud (Investments) Act of 1958.

For a generation, Booth at Municipal and General, in partnership with Fairbairn, were the standard-bearers for the unit trust movement. Both men showed resilience and belief and kept the ideas alive through difficult times. Fittingly, both individuals saw success in their own professional careers by the early 1960s. Instructively, sometimes even very good ideas can take a long time to become properly accepted requiring considerable perseverance to enable them to come to fruition. It took 30 years for unit trusts to achieve meaningful growth in the UK. Despite the problems and complications faced by the first unit trusts in Britain from the 1930s to the late 1950s, this was an investment idea, and movement, which deserved to succeed. This new type of pooled fund opened up new investment opportunities, particularly in terms of equity investing, for smaller savers and the strategies really were innovative with their emphasis on investing in ordinary shares and specialist remits. A new cadre of investors was introduced to the stock market, particularly women. Most importantly, between 1931 and 1951, the First British had demonstrated remarkable resilience through a depression, a world war and a government willing to take quoted companies into public ownership. If unit trusts could survive that, then they would survive anything.

Annex: The Esmée Fairbairn Foundation

Whereas the book effectively stops around 1960, this Annex moves away from the specific subject of unit trusts and briefly explains the ownership of M&G (essentially the re-branded entity that was Municipal and General) up to the end of the twentieth century. The story is unusual in that a charitable foundation preserved M&G's independence during a period when most other unit trusts groups largely disappeared and a number of independent asset manager organisations were taken over by large banks. Established in 1961 as a charitable trust, the Esmée Fairbairn Foundation (the 'EFF') had two purposes.[95] The first was to place, in trust, Fairbairn's majority shareholding in M&G, thus preserving its independence. Second, the EFF served as a memorial to Ian Fairbairn's deceased wife and reflected his own social conscience which had been a powerful influence throughout his life. Subsequently The EFF grew to become the sixth largest grant-giving family foundation in Britain,[96] It also enabled M&G to choose its own pathway because the Trustees could take an objective view of the interests of different stakeholders. In practice this meant M&G developed in a very different direction from most of its main competitors in the second half of the twentieth century. Establishing the trust had far-reaching implications so Fairbairn made a significant contribution in ways he could never have imagined, not just during his own lifetime but also for a long time

---

[95] James Wragg (email, 2 June 2016). The legal name of the 1961 trust was 'The Esmée Fairbairn Trust Fund' but the name was formally changed in 2000 to the 'Esmée Fairbairn Foundation'.
[96] *Association of Charitable Foundations, Giving Trends, Top 100 Family Foundations, 2015 Report.*

afterwards. Talking in 2015 about the years since 1961 and the effectiveness of the trust and the work of the EFF, Ian's nephew John said, 'the old boy [Ian] would have been very pleased'.[97]

Esmée Fairbairn had been killed in an air raid in 1944. Ian Fairbairn created the Esmée Fairbairn Trust in 1961, for philanthropic reasons, 'he aimed to promote a greater understanding of economic and financial issues through education. He also wanted to establish a memorial to his wife, Esmée, who had played a prominent role in developing the Women's Royal Voluntary Service and the Citizens Advice Bureau'.[98] Fairbairn, chairman and the largest shareholder, placed his personal 50.1% ownership stake into the trust which, therefore, had a controlling interest in M&G.[99] In 1961, Fairbairn was 65 years old and George Booth, the founder and previous Chairman, was 84 so they were both aware that the stewardship of the organisation had to move to the next generation and they also wished to preserve M&G's independence.[100] In its first phase, the EFF used the income from the shares to support charitable causes. One of their first decisions by the Trustees was 'to consider financing university fellowships in the field of investment matters'.[101] It was very active in supporting academic institutions and was a benefactor towards Cambridge University and the London Business School in the 1960s; and Kings College London in the 1970s by providing fellowships in Environmental Studies.[102] It was also an important donor to the privately run University of Buckingham after the 1970s, supporting various initiatives: a Department of Economics; the Esmée Fairbairn Chair in Accounting and Financial Management; the construction of the Franciscan Building; undergraduate bursaries; the Ian Fairbairn Lecture Hall; the Chandos Road Building and the History of Art department.[103] In 1999 when the EFF sold its shares in

---

[97] John Fairbairn (telephone conversation, 2 January 2015).

[98] Esmée Fairbairn Foundation (www.esmeefairbairn.org.uk, website accessed on 22 May 2016).

[99] Danny O'Shea, *An Introduction to M&G, its history and its management*, 1994 (M&G memorandum, 24 May 1994).

[100] John Fairbairn (telephone conversation, 2 December 2014).

[101] Esmée Fairbairn Foundation, *Annual Report & Accounts, 2010*.

[102] Esmée Fairbairn Foundation, *Annual Report & Accounts, 2010*.

[103] Sarah Rush, Administrator, University of Buckingham (email, 23 February 2015).

M&G, the scope of EFF's activities were transformed when the foundation received more than £600 million, which, of course, forms the basis of its endowment fund today. Celebrating 50 years of the Esmée Fairbairn Trust in 2011, it announced that had donated more than £500 million to deserving causes over its lifetime, thus making a profound impact on British society.[104] Presently, the trust distributes between £35 and £40 million each year and has broadened its activities to address four main areas – arts (and heritage), young people, social change and the environment. In 2016, the foundation was exploring different methods of operation and according to the current chairman it actively seeks interest from deserving causes in an effort to become more proactive and ever more relevant meeting societal needs.[105] As the chairman remarked, perpetuity is a very long time, but the likelihood is that this foundation will continue to exist for the foreseeable future. The Fairbairn family, and subsequent Trustees of the EFF, should be proud of this philanthropic legacy.

The other interesting aspect of EFF's ownership stake was its influence on the development of M&G after 1961. M&G was in charge of its own destiny, albeit through the Trustees of the foundation. The creation of a trust enabled M&G to remain independent for almost 40 years and during that time it rejected at least two takeover attempts, one of which was decidedly unsavoury. In 1999, when M&G finally relinquished its independence, it could do so on its own terms and choose an organisation which was a true partner who provided a good business and cultural fit. In 1961, the only other large shareholder in M&G was an investment bank, Kleinwort Benson, which held 35% of the equity.[106] This was increased to 42.5% in 1980 because M&G needed additional capital owing to financial difficulties.[107] Subsequently Kleinwort discussed purchasing M&G in the mid-1980s but the EFF Trustees

---

[104] Esmée Fairbairn Foundation, Annual Report & Accounts 2011.

[105] John Hughes-Hallett (telephone conversation, 25 May 2016).

[106] Jehanne Wake, *Kleinwort Benson, The history of two families in banking* (Oxford University Press 1997) 356. Ian Fairbairn invited Kleinwort Benson to take a stake in M&G in 1955 for £100,000.

[107] Jehanne Wake, *Kleinwort Benson The history of two families in banking* (Oxford University Press 1997) 415.

politely rebuffed this friendly approach. Kleinwort sold most of their stake in 1986 (and the EFF reduced theirs to 33.3%) when M&G had a partial public offering of their shares.[108] Despite further appreciation in M&G's value by 1999, Kleinwort would have been very happy in 1986: it had made a high return and a tremendous profit, over £50 million, on its small investment of £100,000 from 30 years earlier. In 1987, Alan Bond, the Australian entrepreneur, acquired a stake of 6.8% in M&G in a hostile attempt to buy the business.[109] Again, this suitor's approach was declined. Alan Bond would have been an unfortunate owner: he went bankrupt in 1992 and was jailed on three occasions of which the longest sentence was for 7 years in 1997 for corporate fraud.[110] Inevitably, Bond would have been a disaster for M&G but Kleinwort may not have been much better despite the cordial relations that the two organisations had enjoyed for a very long time. In practice, not choosing Kleinwort Benson in the mid-1980s was a smart move: Kleinwort, including its asset management arm, subsequently disappeared inside a large European bank whereas M&G still lives. So at this juncture, by preserving M&G's independence, the trust had behaved exactly as Fairbairn would have hoped when he established it in 1961.

With the enthusiastic agreement of both the EFF Trustees and M&G's management, Prudential bought the business in 1999 for £1.9 billion. As discussed earlier in the body of this chapter (Chapter 7), operating as the asset management arm within the Prudential and known as 'M&G Investments', M&G has retained its name and probably much of its culture. Most if not all of its direct competitors from the second half of the twentieth century have lost theirs so M&G's experience is atypical. Fairbairn found a way of dealing with the very difficult problem of inter-generational and organisational continuity by placing his shares into trust, it made M&G safe from unwanted takeovers and it preserved the essence of the entity that he had built from the beginning

---

[108] Jehanne Wake, *Kleinwort Benson, The history of two families in banking* (Oxford University Press 1997) 356 & 415.

[109] *The Times,* 23 December 1987.

[110] *Alan Bond: 10 things you need to know about the controversial tycoon* (www.abcnews.go.com, website accessed 26 May 2015).

of the 1930s. His company remained independent for 30 years after his death in 1968, and more importantly, it enabled the Trustees, in conjunction with senior management at M&G, to choose their preferred partner and, to do it at a time that suited M&G. Fairbairn made a major contribution to the development of the asset management profession in Britain and incidentally, he established this trust. Owing to the passage of time, it is inevitable that the links between Fairbairn and other members of the Fairbairn family with M&G will diminish. Indeed, a visit to the website of M&G confirms that Fairbairn is barely mentioned.[111] By comparison, the website of the EFF is very informative about Fairbairn's life, values and hopes. The moral of this particular story could be that if being remembered by posterity is important, then building a foundation and not just a business might be best.

Bibliography

Primary Sources

The Guildhall Library has limited information on Prospectuses pertaining to early Municipal & General unit trust launches in the 1930s:
– *The Foreign Government Bond Trust*
– *The Limited Investment Fund*

Books

Hugh Bullock, *The Story of Investment Companies* (Columbia 1959)
Hugh Bullock and D. Corner, *Investment and unit trusts in Britain and America* (Elek 1968)
Duncan Crow, *A Man of Push and Go – the Life of George Macaulay Booth* (Rupert Hart-Davis 1965)
John K Galbraith, *The Great Crash, 1929* (Mariner 1997)

---

[111] M&G Investments (www.mandg.co.uk, website accessed 26 May 2016).

Adrienne Gleeson, *People and their Money: 50 years of Private Investment* (M&G Group 1981)

Charles Jackson, *Active Investment Management: Finding and Harnessing Investment Skill* (Wiley 2003)

David Kynaston, *The City of London Volume 4: A Club No More, 1945–2000* (Pimlico 2002)

John Newlands, *Put Not Your Trust in Money* (Association of Investment Trust Companies 1997)

Geoffrey Poitras, Frederick R. Macaulay, Frank M. Redington and the Emergence of Modern Fixed Income Analysis, in *Pioneers of Financial Economics* Vol 2, eds. G. Poitras and F. Jovanovic (Edward Elgar 2007)

Oliver Stutchbury, *The Management of Unit Trusts* (Skinner 1964)

Jehanne Wake, *Kleinwort Benson, The History of Two Families in Banking* (Oxford University Press 1997)

Articles, Journals, Pamphlets, Websites, etc.

Alan Bond: 10 Things You Need to Know About the Controversial Tycoon (www.abcnews.go.com)

Association of Charitable Foundations, Giving Trends, Top 100 Family Foundations, 2015 Report

Barclays Equity Gilt Study, 2012

The Burnley News

The Economist, Unit Trust Surveys Appeared Regularly During the 1930s

Esmée Fairbairn Foundation, 2011 Annual Report & Accounts

Esmée Fairbairn Foundation (www.esmeefairbairn.org.uk)

The Financial Times

Christopher Hill, *Unit Trusts from the Beginning* (Unit Trust Association 1984)

Denys Colquhoun Flowerdew Lowson, Notes on a portrait (www.artwarefineart.com)

M & G Investments (www.mandg.co.uk)

Mutual Fund History (www.bogleheads.org)

National Bureau for Economic Research, Chapter 13, Interest Rates (www.nber.org)

Danny O'Shea, *An Introduction to M&G, its History and its Management* (M&G memorandum, 24 May 1994)

Janette Rutterford, Learning from One Another's Mistakes: Investment Trusts in the UK and US, 1868–1940 (*Financial History Review* 16/2, 2009)

The Times

CH Walker *Unit Trusts* (unpublished PhD, LSE Library, 1938)

8

George Ross Goobey, Revolutionising Pension Fund Investment, 1947–1960

'It is still very difficult to throw off the traditions of the past, even though one can find little or no justification for what has been done in the past,' wrote George Ross Goobey in 1953 as he tried to convince the world it was irrational for ordinary shares to yield more than government bonds in an inflationary environment. Ross Goobey's broader investment insights were similar to those of Keynes with insurance companies in the 1920s and 1930s and both of them were creative, original thinkers. Ross Goobey needed to be because the long period of falling and low interest rates that had prevailed since 1815, with no prolonged period of inflation, was about to come to an end after the Second World War. Ross Goobey's impact was more immediate and identifiable than Keynes' because he really did change investment behaviour in a material way and his ideas were widely accepted relatively quickly, within about 10 years. In practice, he was pushing on an open door because the investment behaviour of British life offices was also changing after 1945. Back in 1861, Bailey had argued that security of capital should be the first and main investment goal of all life assurance companies resulting in very cautious investment policies and avoidance of securities with fluctuating values (Chapter 2). In 1948, however, this view

© The Author(s) 2017
N.E. Morecroft, *The Origins of Asset Management
from 1700 to 1960*, Palgrave Studies in the History of Finance,
DOI 10.1007/978-3-319-51850-3_8

was vigorously challenged by Pegler, the investment actuary from the Clerical, Medical & General, when he proposed that the modified first principle could be stated as 'it should be the aim of life office investment policy to invest its funds to earn the maximum expected yield thereon'.[1] Post Keynes, therefore, the investment debate within life companies was continuing and this would have been helpful to Ross Goobey too, a fellow iconoclast. Additionally, a combination of de-stabilising government financial policies between 1945 and 1950, together with rising inflation in the early 1950s, gave credibility to his investment arguments which meant his views had immediate relevance. According to one description of him, 'George Ross-Goobey was the only truly revolutionary figure in the post-war history of British fund management'.[2] Pension fund investment was his direct sphere of activity but Ross Goobey transformed investment thinking in a number of areas and touched on very fundamental issues such as the relative valuation of asset classes, maximising returns, time horizons and volatility, and his influence was relevant to many types of investor, not just corporate pension funds. Prior to Ross Goobey shaking up the staid world of pension fund investment at Imperial Tobacco in the second half of the twentieth century, the Rowntree pension fund had been quietly effective in managing its own investments during the first half of the century; so this chapter will look at both entities. The Rowntree pension fund was innovative with its investment policies and its investment committee was well organised and very successful but, the Rowntree pension fund, while good at making money, did not shape investment thinking more generally across the pension fund community. Ross Goobey, on the other hand, had a cogent set of investment beliefs, a platform from which to air them and he was persuasive.

The man who challenged the investment establishment was an outsider, born in Poplar East London in 1911, the son of a shopkeeper and, in his spare time, his father was a 'Primitive Methodist' lay preacher.[3] This unconventional upbringing was similar perhaps to that of Robert

---

[1] JBH Pegler, *The actuarial principles of investment* (Journal of the Institute of Actuaries 74, 1948).
[2] Nicholas Faith, *The Independent*, 23 April 1999.
[3] TAB Corley, *George Henry Ross Goobey* 1911–1999, Oxford Dictionary of National Biography (Oxford University Press, 2004).

Fleming who also came from a working-class background and left school aged 13, whereas Ross Goobey was 17 when he finished his schooling. Coincidentally, Fleming and Ross Goobey each benefited from a school scholarship which gave them an early understanding of mathematics. Ross Goobey was a very well-rounded character who was not only a talented sportsman (rugby, cricket and golf) but also had a commanding presence. He was an accomplished after dinner speaker and raconteur; physically tall with a large moustache and regularly wearing a carnation in his buttonhole – he was anything but the introverted actuary depicted in the popular jokes. Somewhat bizarrely, he changed his surname from 'Goobey' to 'Ross Goobey' (not hyphenated) by incorporating one of his own Christian names, actually his mother's maiden name, into his preferred surname. He was first and foremost a mathematician who adored the arithmetic of investing in securities. His working papers are full of numbers, both handwritten and typed, analysing different aspects of markets with quadratic equations to calculate long-term yields or tabular calculations comparing the returns of high-yield stocks versus low-yield stocks over different historic 20-year periods. He was doing this work from first principles, using his own data and writing everything down. After 1947, he was based in the West Country, at the headquarters of Imperial Tobacco, in Bristol, and spent the rest of his life in that part of the world. From Bristol, Ross Goobey positively enjoyed poking fun at the London-centric City establishment and the actuarial profession. He tended to dominate both physically and intellectually and 'was a big man in every way' according to one description of him and he was both well known and highly respected in the West Country.[4] His great ability and contribution to the world of investment, very much in the face of his professional training as an actuary, was to think and act as an asset manager so he thought about investment opportunities first and liabilities second. At the time both managerially and within investment departments, actuaries were very dominant within insurance companies and, naturally, concerned

---

[4] Peter Dunscombe (telephone conversation, 6 June 2016). Peter was a portfolio manager at the Imperial Tobacco pension fund from the mid-1970s.

themselves primarily with solvency and liabilities, which in turn drove investment policy. In addition, as noted in Chapter 5, insurance companies were also the principal institutional investors at the time owing to their longevity and the size of their investment portfolios. Ross Goobey worked for a number of insurance companies after 1928 and qualified as an actuary in 1941. Between 1934 and 1936 he worked alongside Raynes at Legal & General which apparently shaped his investment thinking, According to one biographer, 'Ross Goobey's views were based on two articles by Harold Ernest Raynes, a director of Legal and General, in the Journal of the Institute of Actuaries in 1928 and 1937, which demonstrated from twenty-five years' research that company dividends tended to rise in real terms even in periods of deflation.'[5] After joining the Imperial Tobacco pension fund, Ross Goobey expressed the view that conventional actuarial thinking and an investment policy based around matching liabilities was not well suited to the new and different world of pension funds owing to inflation, the long-term nature of pension liabilities and the unimportance of short-term fluctuations in market values.[6] He rejected the investment policy of insurance companies as a suitable model for pension funds and instead preferred the more return-driven approach of investment companies so his investment philosophy owed more to the ideas of Philip Rose and Robert Fleming than to Bailey and the insurance companies (Fig. 8.1).

Traditionally most actuaries had dabbled with investment through the lens of liabilities, as shown in Chapters 2 and 5. Keynes, an economist and asset manager, challenged conventional investment wisdom as chairman of the National Mutual after 1921. By the early 1950s, investment thinking at life offices was also beginning to change as exposure to ordinary shares increased and actuarial thinking started to grapple with sharp changes in interest rates which Frank Redington referred to as 'an expanding funnel of

---

[5] TAB Corley, *George Henry Ross Goobey* 1911–1999, Oxford Dictionary of National Biography (Oxford University Press, 2004). Note that these two papers by Raynes have been discussed in Chapter 5.

[6] George Ross Goobey, *Pension Fund Investment Policy*, 4 June 1957 reprinted in *Classics, An Investors Anthology*, ed. Charles Ellis & James Vertin (Dow Jones-Irwin, 1989) 253–259.

Fig. 8.1 George Henry Ross Goobey, 1911–1999, photo c. 1972

doubt'.[7] Redington, Actuary at the Prudential formulated a theory of 'immunisation' whereby assets would be invested so that 'the existing business was immune to a general change in the rate of interest, since the value of assets and liabilities would alter to the same extent with changes in interest rates'.[8] Rather than matching cash flows, his idea was to match durations which meant considering sensitivities to changes in interest rates. This was a significant step forward in investment thinking because, as Redington said, '[it] dealt primarily with valuation, matching being a by-product'.[9] Redington at the Prudential was considering the relationship between assets and liabilities for life offices at exactly the same time as Ross Goobey was doing the same with pension funds. A memoir to Redington stated that 'he saw that the proper steering of the finances of an insurer depended on harmony between actuarial and investment policy' and that his 1952 paper on immunisation was 'recognised as a landmark in the development of actuarial thought on the relationship between assets and liabilities of a [life] office'.[10] Redington was interested in investment and shared similar thought processes to Ross Goobey – with the main difference between them being that the former was a career actuary at the Prudential thinking about insurance companies, while the latter was an asset manager with an actuarial background thinking about pension funds.

Ross Goobey, like Keynes, was different from many of his peers and willing to explore unconventional ideas: he thought primarily about investment and he was always interested in identifying investment opportunities: his starting point was not actuarial theory or liabilities but assets. He was fond of saying 'My motto is: "The best results possible"'.[11] This return-driven ethos led him to argue

---

[7] Frank Redington, *Review of the Principles of Life Office Valuations* (Journal of the Institute of Actuaries 78, 1952).

[8] Laurie Dennett, *A Sense of Security: 150 years of Prudential* (Granta 1998) 304.

[9] Massimo De Felice, *Immunisation Theory: An Actuarial Perspective on Asset Liability Management,* in Financial Risk in Insurance, ed. G. Ottaviani (Springer 2000).

[10] Ronald Skerman, *Memoir* (Journal of the Institute of Actuaries 111, 1984).

[11] George Ross-Goobey, *Address to the 1956 Conference of the ASPF, 2 November 1956* (www.pensionsarchive.org.uk/27, website accessed 16 June 2016).

that investment should not be in government bonds but other asset classes with more attractive return profiles. He correctly identified that, because pension funds at that time were very immature, with an excess of contributions over outflows, a pension fund asset manager need not worry about short-term volatility and liquidity, because fluctuations in market prices were irrelevant. Cash flow out could be met from contributions flowing in. Therefore, investment policy should aim to maximise total (income and capital) returns over the long-term. This led to the firm conviction that investment strategy should be built around a horizon that stretched beyond the 5-yearly cycle of pension fund valuations conducted by actuaries. His 'long term' was in the region of 30 years. The final piece in his investment jigsaw was inflation, 'My own view is that we will always have a measure of inflation in the long-term (even if there may be periodic flattening out of the curve, or even a downward trend for a time).'[12]

Ross Goobey had three substantive investment ideas: first, to maximise returns; second, to take a very long view and ignore short-term price fluctuations; and third, a belief that inflation would be a permanent feature of the modern world meaning that ordinary shares (and property) had attractive characteristics as real assets. These insights allowed him to identify the major investment anomaly of the time that the yield gap between ordinary shares and bonds should be reversed. This powerful observation was relevant to the economic and financial conditions which prevailed around 1950, but he also understood that markets were dynamic and so investment opportunities would change over time. Ross Goobey embraced the vibrancy of financial markets and thought about investment opportunities as the relative valuation of different asset classes. His main thoughts and subsequent investment decisions were determined by a simple idea: the search for sustainable income. Before considering his investment approach in more detail at the Imperial Tobacco pension fund, the emergence of British pension funds will be discussed together with a brief commentary on the investment activities of Rowntree, one of the first corporate pension funds.

---

[12] George Ross Goobey, *Pension Fund Investment Policy*, memorandum 4 June 1957 reprinted in *Classics, An Investors Anthology*, ed. Charles Ellis & James Vertin (Dow Jones-Irwin, 1989) 253–259.

8.1   The First British Pension Funds and Rowntree

Prior to 1850, pension fund provision in Britain was very limited. Established initially as a charity to pay benefits, to disabled seamen: the Chatham Chest of 1590 was probably the first pension fund. Some other pension arrangements emerged but they were sporadic, often quasi-governmental for specified groups of people such as Bank of England and East India Company retirees.[13] In 1743 the Church of Scotland established a fund to provide pensions to the widows of ministers of the Church of Scotland subsequently extended to professors of the four Scottish 'Ancient' universities, of Aberdeen, Edinburgh, Glasgow and St Andrews.[14] It has been claimed that The Scottish Ministers' Widows' Fund was the first 'actuarially sound pension fund in the world' and it existed for 250 years so, in that respect, it had been constructed robustly.[15] By an Act of Parliament, the directors of railway companies were obliged to establish pension funds after 1853 and, towards the end of the nineteenth century, some enlightened employers in the corporate sector began to offer pension provision to their employees: Reuters created a staff pension fund in 1882 and a number of other companies such as WH Smith (1894), Cadbury and Rowntree (both 1906) followed their lead. The state pension was established in 1908 but the major boost to private sector pension fund provision occurred in 1921 when companies were offered a large tax incentive to set up their own funds. The tax incentive 'established the principle of relieving from income tax all funds which were set aside to provide for future benefits which would themselves in due course become liable to income tax'.[16] By 1936, 6,544 private sector company pension funds had been established; public sector employees were also granted pensions around this time, including the police

---

[13] Chris Lewin, *Pensions and Insurance before 1800* (Tuckwell Press 2004) chapters 8 and 9.

[14] Chris Lewin, *Pensions and Insurance before 1800* (Tuckwell Press 2004) 361.

[15] T Sibbett, *Reviews, The Scottish Ministers' Widows' Fund, 1743–1993*, ed. Ian Dunlop, Saint Andrew Press 1992 (Journal of the Institute of Actuaries 120, 1993).

[16] Chris Lewin, *Pensions & Insurance before 1800* (Tuckwell Press 2004) 430.

(1890) and local government staff (1922).[17] The Imperial Tobacco pension fund was established in 1929 (though the company may have held some unfunded pensions obligations on its books as early as 1926).[18] One estimate (Lewin) suggests that by 1970 more than half of the entire British workforce were covered by final salary pension schemes.

Joseph Rowntree, the eponymous founder, was interested in addressing social inequality as an entrepreneur philanthropist, not dissimilar from Charles Booth in Chapter 7. In 1904, using about half of his personal fortune, Joseph Rowntree established three charitable trusts with broad-ranging aspirations to improve society.[19] He also established a pension fund. Joseph Rowntree put in £10,000 of his own money to get it started together with another £9,000 from the company and, while the company underwrote the likely cost of the future benefits, they did not forecast liabilities at this juncture.[20] This was paternalistic welfare provision, and its cost, while in the realms of the unknown, was unlikely to have been high because life expectancy was short and there was no inflation. Joining the pension fund proved to be very attractive to Rowntree's employees with a 98% take-up from eligible staff so it was clearly seen as an attractive opportunity. In 1906, the Rowntree pension fund was designed to improve the condition of its employees and it was given wide investment powers to do this. During the first half of the twentieth century, most of the newly established British pension funds invested conservatively in government bonds and had restrictive trust deeds that constrained their investment behaviour. In due course, many decided to widen their invest-ment powers but needed to modify their trusts deeds, some via the courts, but this was not required for Rowntree which had investment flexibility from the outset,: 'the investment powers given to the original Trustees were drawn with shrewd foresight...the widest possible scope was provi-ded...the Trustees could invest in...any investment or security in the

---

[17] *The History of Pensions* (www.pensionsarchive.org.uk/ 82, website accessed 16 June 2016).
[18] *The History of Pensions* (www.pensionsarchive.org.uk/ 82, website accessed 16 June 2016).
[19] The Joseph Rowntree Charitable Trust has a very ambitious social and benevolent remit with five areas of activity (see www.jrct.org/funding priorities, website accessed 15 June 2016). Two trusts address issues in the fields of housing and civil liberties.
[20] Chris Titley, *Joseph Rowntree* (Shire, 2013) 36.

United Kingdom'.[21] The culture underpinning Rowntree clearly encouraged innovative investment thinking too, as Frank Comer, secretary to the Rowntree pension fund, explained in 1956: '... it was in the tradition ruling from 1906 to this day of the Managers showing originality [with the investment portfolio] never being afraid to change their [investment] policy if advantage accrued to the Fund'.[22] These broad investment powers were also clearly utilised in practice: the pension fund started investing in ordinary shares in 1930, initially investment companies, but during the subsequent decade it broadened the exposure to include the ordinary shares of banks and insurance companies, and subsequently industrial companies.[23] In 1939, by book value (so the market value of the equity holdings would have been higher), Rowntree had 25% of its assets invested in preference and ordinary shares; only 30% in British government bonds; with the balance mainly invested in a broad cross section of debentures.[24] These investment decisions appear to have been driven by the search for higher returns rather than any intrinsic belief in the superiority of equities as an asset class which could better meet pension liabilities. The pension fund had an investment committee that met monthly under the auspices of the pension fund secretary and both William Fox (the first Secretary of the pension fund from 1906 to 1941) and Sam Clayton (1941–1956) were very active investment practitioners. About Fox it was said '...the judicious investment of the rapidly growing funds became one of his main interests' and of Clayton, with specific reference to his investment understanding, 'he had a knowledge of investment principles and a skill in applying them much above average. In many ways he proved himself an individualist and a deep thinker [on investments]'.[25] Clearly, the Rowntree pension fund viewed asset management as an important activity and valued

---

[21] Frank Comer, *Rowntree Pension Fund Golden Jubilee, Booklet 1956* (Borthwick Archive R/B6/22).

[22] Frank Comer, *Rowntree Pension Fund Golden Jubilee, Booklet 1956* (Borthwick Archive R/B6/22).

[23] Frank Comer, *Rowntree Pension Fund Golden Jubilee, Booklet 1956* (Borthwick Archive R/B6/22).

[24] *Rowntree & Co, Private Ledger, Pension Fund to 1944* (Borthwick Archive R/B6/22).

[25] *William Fox*, unattributed and undated memorandum (Borthwick Archive R/B6/22).

people who could contribute to it and they were willing to make bold investment decisions, for example between 1954 and 1956, as its secretary said, 'Our own fund had always followed the policy of trying to achieve the highest returns and two years ago we had 25% invested in equities and today we had 3%.'[26]

For 50 years after 1906, the investment policy had two beneficial outcomes: first, the pension fund produced higher investment returns than the actuarial estimates; second, owing to significant realised capital gains, made by selling and buying securities, the pension fund created a very substantial 'investment reserve' held alongside the assets of the pension fund ensuring that the pension fund had a large surplus of assets over liabilities. In estimating the liabilities, the actuary assumed a forward-looking 'rate of interest', typically between 3.5% and 4.5% (as high as 5.25% in 1931), probably based on prevailing government bond yields. Watsons, the actuarial firm, defined the 'rate of interest' in the following terms in 1948: 'When making a valuation an Actuary must assume that money invested, and new money coming into the fund which will have to be invested, will earn interest and he must estimate the rate of interest to be earned'.[27] It is not entirely clear if these were very conservative projections or if Rowntree were very good investors, but, as the report from 1953 by the investment committee showed, the pension fund had achieved a 'return' (probably based on income rather than a true total return combining income and capital gains) higher than 5% *in every year* from 1922 to 1952.[28] Even during the difficult the years after the Second World War, the pension fund continued to produce returns ahead of the actuarially projected 'rate of interest'. According to their own records, the investment committee were particularly self-congratulatory with the actual pension fund returns achieved immediately post-war, between 1946 and 1948, when British government bond yields fell to 2.6% owing to the 'cheap

---

[26] Frank Comer, *ASPF Autumn Conference Report, 1956* (London Metropolitan Archive, LMA 4494/a/4/5).

[27] *Rowntree Pension Fund Valuation at 31 October 1948*, Watsons actuarial valuation (Borthwick Archive R/B6/20).

[28] *Rowntree Pension Fund, Investment Committee Report for the year ending October 1953* (Borthwick Archive R/B6/22).

money' policy of Hugh Dalton. The Rowntree pension fund produced a return of 6.37% per annum.[29] These results maintained the pattern of returns experienced over the previous 30 years whereby the actuary demonstrated caution whereas the investment committee showed investment skill: in 1946 the actuary assumed a return of 3.5% for the next five years while the fund produced 5.25% per annum; in 1951 the actuary assumed 3.75% while the fund produced nearly 6% per annum to 1956.[30] In practical monetary terms, this was summarised in the pension fund's Golden Jubilee year of 1956 as follows: 'Income from investments amounted to £3.5 million against pensions of £1.7 million and members withdrawals of £346,000 [between 1906 and 1956]'.[31] So, there was a surplus of earned income that amounted to £1.5 million in excess of outgoings.

In 1931, the pension fund investment committee created what they referred to as an 'investment reserve' which represented realised capital gains that had been achieved by the investment committee. This was kept separate from the pension fund as 'a protection against future losses should they occur'.[32] It appears to have been accumulated by trading (selling and buying) and by some investments reaching their redemption dates, but basically it represented the transactional activity of the committee. This investment reserve became very substantial – in 1956 it was worth £490,000 while the assets of the pension fund were £4 million with estimated liabilities of £3.6 million.[33] The reported surplus of assets over liabilities was a little over 10% but the true surplus, including the investment reserve, was almost 25%. Implicitly, earned income was the main method of paying pensions while capital gains were treated as a cash buffer, which operated as a potential 'safety net', and Rowntree applied this principle with considerable prudence in the best interests of

---

[29] Frank Comer, *Comment on the 1948 Watsons actuarial valuation* (Borthwick Archive R/B6/22).

[30] *Rowntree Pension Fund, Golden Jubilee Booklet, 1956* (Borthwick Archive R/B6/22).

[31] Frank Comer, *Rowntree Pension Fund Golden Jubilee, Booklet 1956* (Borthwick Archive R/B6/22).

[32] *Rowntree Pension Fund, Watsons actuarial valuation 31 October 1948* (Borthwick Archive R/B6/22).

[33] *Rowntree Pension Fund, Golden Jubilee Booklet, 1956* (Borthwick Archive R/B6/22).

the beneficiaries. Looking back over the 50 years between 1906 and 1956, it is possible to draw out the following conclusions:

- The Rowntree pension fund adopted an active investment policy and achieved considerable success. The investment policy generated sufficient income to pay all pensions, it achieved a surplus over liabilities of between 10% and 25%, and it enabled the company to create a large 'investment reserve'.
- The investment committee invested into ordinary shares at an early stage and in 30 individual years, 1922–1952, the investment return exceeded 5%; over all quinquennial valuation periods from 1922, it produced an investment return in excess of the actuarial assumed 'rate of interest'.
- In investment terms, the Rowntree pension fund was innovative and successful with flexible investment powers from the outset in 1906 and an investment committee that was both well organised and encouraged to make decisions.

The Rowntree pension fund created a successful model for investment decision-making and it is not obvious why it was not more widely copied during the first half of the twentieth century. In that respect there were similarities with the Pelican Life Office in Chapter 2 which highlights that if asset managers are to be influential in changing attitudes and behaviours, they need to be more than 'just good at making money': they must have ideas or a set of beliefs which can be communicated effectively and applied by other organisations. In the second half of the twentieth century Ross Goobey would change pension fund investment behaviour with his ideas and, perhaps the main difference was that he wanted to more than the investors at Rowntree.

8.2 Ross Goobey and the Imperial Tobacco Pension Fund

In 1947, Ross Goobey became the portfolio manager at the Imperial Tobacco pension fund. The late 1940s was a period of macroeconomic instability and the 1950s was a period of gradually rising inflation which coloured Ross Goobey's thinking about different asset classes, particularly government bonds. Inevitably, Britain was a much poorer country in 1945 than it had been in 1939. According to one estimate, Britain had lost about 25% of its pre-war national wealth.[34] Gold and currency markets were effectively closed for 10 years after 1945, as were most other commodity markets. The government bond market was also in trouble because the 1945 Labour government continued the policy from the 1930s of 'cheap money' based on keeping interest rates as low as possible in order to avoid a post-war slump and high levels of unemployment. In 1946, the government attempted to lower nominal interest rates by swapping 3% Local Loans into 2.5% irredeemable Treasury stock. The second issue, 2.5% Treasury Stock 1975 was referred to disparagingly as 'Daltons', named after the Chancellor of the Exchequer of the time, Hugh Dalton.[35] The policy was effectively abandoned in 1947 as bond prices fell and inflationary expectations rose. Sterling became fully convertible in July 1947 but this only lasted for five weeks owing to large foreign sales of the currency. Essentially, international markets had lost faith in Britain and sold sterling Pounds to buy the US dollar instead. The 1939 value of the British pound had been set at $4.03 but the new economic reality was acknowledged in September 1949 – the currency was devalued with a new rate set at $2.80. Nor were ordinary shares exempt from government intervention – the Labour Government introduced dividend controls on companies leading to dividend payout ratios as low as 25% of earnings.[36] While this dividend restriction would have distorted corporate behaviour and may have affected prices in the short-term, this represented government tinkering rather than anything fundamental. Much more sinister for equity investors was the policy of nationalisation. This involved taking important sectors into government ownership, so most of the UK's heavy industries and public utilities were nationalised between 1946 and 1950, namely Coal (1947), the Railways (1948), Electricity (1948) and Steel

---

[34] David Kynaston, *The City of London Volume 4: A Club No More 1945–2000* (Pimlico 2002) 3.

[35] Susan Howson, *Money and monetary policy since 1945*, in the Cambridge Economic History of Modern Britain Vol 3 1939–2000, ed. Floud & Johnson (Cambridge University Press 2004) 143.

[36] Janette Rutterford, *From dividend yield to discounted cash flow: a history of UK and US equity valuation techniques* (Accounting, Business and Financial History 14/2, 2004).

(1949). Some specific companies were also nationalised for strategic reasons such as the Bank of England (1946) and Cable & Wireless (1947). Clearly, this was a challenging investment environment which only served to strengthen Ross Goobey's convictions when, in 1956, he said 'we have had dividend limitation in Gilts [British government bonds] for 200 years' meaning, in his opinion, that government bonds had always been unattractive.[37] He and Keynes were like-minded in this respect as both worried about the instability of consumer prices and, in their respective post-war environments, it is hard to see either of them voluntarily choosing to buy British government bonds. Elected in 1951, the Churchill Conservative government abandoned 'cheap money' after almost two decades of bank rate being set at 2%: it rose to 4% by April 1952; fell to 3% in 1954 and rose unsteadily to 7% by September 1957.[38] Therefore, immediately after 1945 the rate of interest, and bond yields, had been manipulated downwards only to increase very sharply during the 1950s making investment in bonds extremely unpredictable. In practice, accepting that governments were transient and that markets were dynamic, Ross Goobey took a pragmatic approach to nationalisation, dividend limitations and 'Daltons' writing in 1957 as follows: 'Hitherto nationalisation has not been on confiscatory terms . . . the experience of our Fund [Imperial Tobacco] has been quite satisfactory, especially as we did not retain the government stock which was given as compensation but sold it and re-invested it in other equities.'[39]

In terms of investment policy, immediately before and after the Second World War, the accepted approach was that the assets of 'final salary' defined benefit pension schemes should be configured to match the liabilities and avoid fluctuating capital values. For pension funds both actuarial practice and thinking was cautious albeit in what was a relatively new field of endeavour for the profession. Ross Goobey

---

[37] David Kynaston, *The City of London Volume 4: A Club No More 1945–2000* (Pimlico 2002) 100.

[38] William Allen, *Monetary Policy and Financial Repression in Britain, 1951–59* (Palgrave Macmillan 2014) 1.

[39] George Ross Goobey, *Pension Fund Investment Policy*, memorandum 4 June 1957 reprinted in *Classics, An Investors Anthology*, ed. Charles Ellis & James Vertin (Dow Jones-Irwin 1989) 253–259.

challenged the idea of stable capital values which harked back to Bailey and 1861 (Chapter 2):

> In the actuary's calculations it is assumed that the capital value of the investment is sacrosanct, but this does not necessarily mean that the value of each investment is sacrosanct. What is intended is that the capital value of the [pension] fund must not be reduced in one way or another.... How many funds, for instance, in the old days invested in Daltons at par? It will be a long while before we see them back at what they were purchased at – if ever.[40]

According to one account, 'The actuary protected the solvency of the pension fund by reducing the value of the assets or increasing the value of the liabilities' if a pension fund invested in a risky manner. This was extremely restrictive because, in principle, it penalised the more adventurous investment policies.[41] With inflation always at the forefront of his mind, actuarial thinking was, in Ross Goobey's opinion, overly simplistic because, as he pointed out 'in the past the actuarial estimates have not proved to be correct because the actuary has made no allowance for inflation in considering salary and wage levels at retirement. Up to 1949, the Company was apparently quite reconciled to repeated deficiencies arising from this omission'.[42] Consequently, the standard approach was to match liabilities in an assumed non-inflationary environment, so bonds were seen as the natural home for investments and the default asset allocation was: 50% government bonds, 25% debentures, 15% preference shares and 10% ordinary shares as reported in a publication for the Association of Superannuation & Pension Funds (ASPF) in

---

[40] William Allen, *Monetary Policy and Financial Repression in Britain, 1951–59* (Palgrave Macmillan 2014) 84.

[41] Yally Avrahampour, *Cult of Equity: actuaries and the transformation of pension fund investing, 1948–1960* (Business History Review 89/2, 2015).

[42] George Ross Goobey, *Pension Fund Investment Policy*, memorandum 30 August 1955 reprinted in *Classics, An Investors Anthology*, ed. Charles Ellis & James Vertin (Dow Jones-Irwin, 1989) 253–259.

1955.[43] Ross Goobey rejected the idea of matching and was acutely aware of the potential impact of inflation on future liabilities so his basic insight was very easy to understand and explain, as are most of the best ideas in investment. As his son Alastair said: 'Father simply observed that equity shares as a whole were on a higher current yield than bonds.'[44] In the words of the father rather than the son, the elder Ross Goobey described it in the following terms and also had his beady eye on inflation:

When I first went into the City it was traditional that if the yield on a gilt [a British government bond] security was x%...then the yield on an Ordinary share would be x+2%...I could not understand why this should be so and long ago I forecast that, before long, we would have a reverse yield gap. There is a school of thought which considers that we have come to the end of an era and that 'what goes up must come down'. I do not subscribe to this view...inflation will continue (and equities generally will do better).[45]

Ross Goobey's observation, as expressed above and with hindsight appears relatively obvious but, he thought deeply about the nature of long-term returns, yields and investment income as will be shown later in this chapter so his simple statements were built up from a deep understanding of the behaviour of financial markets. Figure 8.2 shows equities yielding about 2% more than bonds, the yield gap, after the Second World War up until 1959. After 1960 and up to the financial crisis of 2008, the relationship changed, more or less permanently and bonds have yielded more than equities, apart from the occasional equity market crash which results in a fall in values and a correspond-ing increase in yield though typically, this has been a short-term phenomenon. Market conditions after 2008, with negative interest

[43] George Ross Goobey, *Notes on Pension Fund Investment*, undated memorandum but probably late 1955 (LMA 4481/A/02/021).

[44] Alastair Ross Goobey, *Investment Practice – Full Circle?* Speech 27 October 2005 (www. pensions-institute.org/the first ross goobey lecture).

[45] George Ross Goobey, *Reverse Yield Gap*, undated memorandum (LMA 4481/A/1/21).

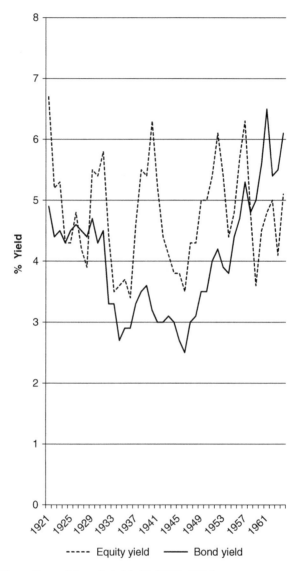

Fig. 8.2   UK equity and bond yields % 1920–1964

(*Source:* All data taken from the *Barclays Equity/Gilt Study 2012*)

rates in some countries and corresponding very low bond yields, has been atypical and one presumes, had Ross Goobey still been alive, he would be deeply shocked that UK equities have been once again yielding much more than government bonds albeit in a low inflation environment.

Established in 1929, for its first 20 years the Imperial Tobacco pension fund was almost entirely invested in British government bonds. When Ross Goobey joined it in 1947, the pension fund had 60% invested in fixed interest securities, though with 20% invested in ordinary shares compared to the typical 10%, it was a little less conservatively managed than the average pension fund.[46] In a handwritten note from 1948 he was rather critical of the pension fund pointing out that the investments had been run by the chief accountant in his spare time and that pensions was seen as a 'spending department' and a cost centre rather than a profit centre.[47] At this juncture, Ross Goobey's main role would have been the administration of the pension fund, as an actuary looking after the benefits side; there is no evidence that he was recruited for his investment capabilities. Between 1947 and 1955, investment strategy evolved only gradually, and decisions on asset allocation were made in a series of small steps, as follows: up to 1949, government bonds issued as compensation for the equity of nationalised companies were sold immediately; then, in 1949, government bond purchases ceased entirely; in 1952, ordinary shares were bought 'opportunistically'; after 1953, only ordinary shares were to be purchased with new cash inflows; and finally, in 1955, a decision was made to switch the entire portfolio into ordinary shares.[48] Given that the pension fund had strong cash flow, the 1949 decision, in itself, would have resulted in a gradual shift in asset allocation away from government bonds, and, market movements were also changing the shape of the fund too: prices of government bonds fell sharply in 1951

---

[46] Alastair Ross Goobey, *George Ross Goobey*, in Wall Street People Vol 2, ed. Charles Ellis & James Vertin (Wiley 2001) 261.

[47] George Ross Goobey, handwritten notes, undated but probably 1948 (LMA 4481/A/1/2).

[48] Yally Avrahampour, *Cult of Equity: actuaries and the transformation of pension fund investing, 1948–1960* (Business History Review 89/2, 2015).

by 13%, while ordinary shares rose by a similar amount. Between 1947 and 1952, the exposure to bonds had fallen from 60% of the assets to 30% and although several significant changes had been made to investment policy, Ross Goobey had bigger ideas.

Increasingly, he felt this was just tinkering with investment policy and by 1953, he had come to the view that the entire fund, 100% of the assets, should be invested in ordinary shares. He was convinced that ordinary shares were the natural home for pension fund investment and that, rationally therefore, the corollary should be to have all the assets invested in the most attractive asset class. His challenge was to persuade his immediate colleagues, which included the members of his investment committee as well as the in-house lawyers at Imperial Tobacco who were opposed to the proposed investment policy.[49] In 1953, Ross Goobey's note on investment policy to his investment committee argued in favour of ordinary shares owing to the higher yield, the prospect of inflation-protection, and a long-term, essentially perpetual, income stream.[50] In the same note he then asked the big question in rather gentle, rhetorical terms:

> If then Ordinary Stocks and Shares have crept into portfolios for the above-mentioned very good and compelling reasons, is it not logical that in due time the whole of a Pension Fund might be safely and advantageously invested in Ordinary Stocks and Shares? The investment committee has agreed to increase the proportion . . . I would like to see this policy followed through to its logical conclusion to the time when the Fund has 100% in Equities.

His broad arguments may have been accepted but his specific conclusion was not because in October 1953 the investment committee agreed to allocate only new cash flow contributions, to ordinary shares but not to make the radical shift Ross Goobey proposed. Despite this personal disappointment for Ross Goobey, the Imperial Tobacco

---

[49] Peter Dunscombe (telephone conversation, 15 October 2015).
[50] George Ross Goobey, *Notes on investment policy for the pension fund*, 5 October 1953 (LMA 4481/A/1/1).

pension fund was still following a more innovative path than the rest. In the quinquennial valuation of April 1954, the actuarial firm Watsons pointed out that the 'proportion invested in equities had risen to 40% [and] this policy has been pursued more vigorously in the case of this [pension] fund than has so far...been customary'.[51] There was also a minor technical victory in actuarial terms at this juncture for Ross Goobey because he persuaded Gunlake, an actuary at Watsons, to increase the assumed future rate of interest from 4% to 4.25%.[52] This higher, modified assumption about future investment returns increased the discounted value of the assets and produced a small pension fund surplus and represented another step in the right direction for Ross Goobey and his investment policy: the actuary had been obliged to agree that either Ross Goobey as the asset manager or the investment policy of this particular pension fund, would generate higher future returns than assumed previously.[53] By comparison and although the dates are slightly different, in 1951 and 1956 Watsons had assumed a future rate of interest of only 3.75% and 4.0% respectively, for the Rowntree pension fund, so lower than the equivalent assumption for the Imperial fund.[54]

In August 1955, Ross Goobey was forceful and much more direct with his proposals to the investment committee as he argued, '"The best possible result" is likely to be achieved by investment in equities as opposed to fixed interest because of inflationary tendencies'.[55] He had a point: inflation had increased sharply after 1951 averaging about 5.5% per annum during the first half of the 1950s. Market movements also made his arguments particularly persuasive: the prices of ordinary shares had risen by more than 50% in the two years since his original proposal

---

[51] *Imperial Tobacco Pension Fund, Watsons Valuation at 30 April 1954* (LMA 4481/A/1/4).

[52] *Imperial Tobacco Pension Fund, Watsons Valuation at 30 April 1954* (LMA 4481/A/1/4).

[53] Yally Avrahampour, *Cult of Equity: actuaries and the transformation of pension fund investing, 1948–1960* (Business History Review 89/2, 2015).

[54] *Rowntree Pension Fund, Golden Jubilee Booklet, 1956* (Borthwick Archive R/B6/22).

[55] George Ross Goobey, *Pension Fund Investment Policy*, memorandum 30 August 1955 reprinted in *Classics, An Investors Anthology*, ed. Charles Ellis & James Vertin (Dow Jones-Irwin, 1989) 253–259.

in August 1953, while, British government bonds had fallen by over 10% in 1955. Ross Goobey's theoretical longer-term arguments had now meshed perfectly with short-term market events at this juncture and his proposal was accepted in the late summer of 1955. Having made the decision to invest 100%, the switch was implemented gradually and left to Ross Goobey's discretion: exposure to ordinary shares increased to 68% by June 1957, to 85% by October 1958 and to 96% in April 1961.[56] In a little less than 10 years, therefore, Ross Goobey had persuaded his colleagues to accept his arguments, though in practice, it does not appear that the fund ever quite invested completely in ordinary shares, mainly because property was beginning to feature more prominently in Ross Goobey's thinking from the late 1950s onwards. The investment policy had been a success in that the actuarial valuation of 1959 explained that not only had pensions been increased but also that the pension fund was sufficiently healthy that no company guarantees to plug any shortfalls would be required before 1965.[57] Additionally, one observer estimated that the Imperial Tobacco pension fund had increased in value by 270% between 1954 and 1961, outperforming the FT30 equity index by about 70%.[58] So, equities rose strongly and Ross Goobey's portfolio did much better than the index. Whilst beating an index benchmark is useful, the broader point is that the price of British government bonds collapsed over this period, whether taking the years between 1947 and 1961 when Ross Goobey started at Imperial Tobacco, or between 1955 and 1961 when the equity-only investment policy became fully agreed. Therefore, strategically and tactically, Ross Goobey was absolutely right. His investment policy also produced quantifiable financial benefits to both Imperial Tobacco, the employer, and also to the beneficiaries of the pension fund. After the 1959 actuarial valuation, the

---

[56] Yally Avrahampour, *Cult of Equity: actuaries and the transformation of pension fund investing, 1948–1960* (Business History Review 89/2, 2015).

[57] *The Economist,* 25 March 1961, page 1236.

[58] Yally Avrahampour, *Cult of Equity: actuaries and the transformation of pension fund investing, 1948–1960* (Business History Review 89/2, 2015).

employer was able to stop making pension contributions because the fund was in surplus.[59] Additionally, benefits were also increased in three areas: final salary pension payments; death in service lump sum payments and widows' pensions.[60] In 1959, Imperial tobacco had 6,500 pensioners receiving £1.5 million in benefits so the quantum was substantial.[61] The cost of providing these benefits also plummeted: the Imperial Tobacco pension fund was non-contributory from the early 1960s until the 1970s owing to the continued success of the investment policy.[62] Thus after 12 years George Ross Goobey had not only succeeded in changing the Imperial Tobacco pension fund from a cost centre to a profit centre, and made it lots of money, but he had also increased benefits for a range of beneficiaries while reducing the costs to the employer and employees.

Within the pension fund community, Ross Goobey had a platform to explain his investment views: in 1953, he was elected to the council of the Association of ASPF and one of his first articles about investment policy appeared in *Superannuation* magazine in 1955.[63] In 1955 the ASPF allowed Ross Goobey to circulate his investment views in an official document, '*Notes on pension fund investments*', which he edited but then issued under the ASPF name.[64] This generated considerable interest, including from J T Price, a Member of Parliament associated with one of the pension funds in the retail sector for shop workers, who wrote to Ross Goobey as follows: '...my gratitude for the imaginative piece of work you have carried out in a field [pension fund investment] which is still largely uncharted territory'.[65] In November 1956, Ross Goobey had a major opportunity to influence investment thinking more widely when he delivered one of the key

[59] *The Economist*, 25 March 1961, page 1236
[60] *The Economist*, 25 March 1961, page 1236.
[61] *The Economist*, 25 March 1961, page 1236.
[62] Peter Dunscombe (email, 5 January 2016).
[63] Yally Avrahampour, *Cult of Equity: actuaries and the transformation of pension fund investing, 1948–1960* (Business History Review 89/2, 2015).
[64] *NAPF collection* (LMA 4494/A).
[65] JT Price letter to George Ross Goobey, 2 February 1956 (LMA 4481/a/2/22).

note speeches (this speech is covered in detail in 8.3 below) to the ASPF's annual pension fund conference and it included the exhortation to invest 100% in ordinary shares.[66] By 1961 the average British pension fund had almost 50% of its assets in equities, compared to about 40% for US pension funds.[67] The argument about investing in equities rather than government bonds had been won, even if there was room remaining to debate his bold recommendation of 100%. Actuarial thought was also shifting position so that by 1959, one of its Fellows was writing '. . . it is income that matters and provided that income is secure then fluctuations in the value of the portfolio do not matter, then in the author's opinion one should come down on the side of equities (or property) as the basic investment for a pension fund'.[68] Ross Goobey's relationship with the actuarial profession had its ups and downs however, partly because he was quite rude about some of his actuarial peers. He was often critical of Gunlake, the actuary to the Imperial Tobacco pension fund and in due course Watsons' senior partner, and there were allegations of a spat with the chief actuary of the Prudential in the 1950s. With pension fund investment, Ross Goobey felt that the investment policy of investment companies provided a better model than did the actuaries who worked on investment at insurance companies. More tangibly, and it is unclear whether it was personal or professional, but the Institute of Actuaries deliberately restricted Ross Goobey's influence: 'He was banned by the Institute of Actuaries from teaching students about investment. Only in 1998, at the age of 86, a year before his death, did he receive an Award of Honour', belatedly recognising his lifetime contribution.[69]

---

[66] George Ross Goobey, *Address to the 1956 Conference of the ASPF*, 2 November 1956 (www. pensionsarchive.org.uk/27, website accessed 16 June 2016).

[67] Yally Avrahampour, *Cult of Equity: actuaries and the transformation of pension fund investing, 1948–1960* (Business History Review 89/2, 2015).

[68] JG Day, *Developments in Investment Policy during the last decade* (Journal of the Institute of Actuaries 85/2. 1959).

[69] *Practical History of Financial Markets, Cult of the equity* (Pearson, 2004) 5.4.5.

8.3   Ross Goobey's Investment Beliefs

Many of Ross Goobey's beliefs about asset management revolved around the idea of income – how yields were calculated, how income had been achieved in the past, how income might grow in the future and how future inflation might influence income. For him, the chief advantage of investing in ordinary shares was that companies could increase their dividend payments over time, particularly over the very long-term. He thought about equity yields, or dividends, as a complex series of future income streams,

> In a fixed interest stock, say a British Government stock, the calculation of the yield is fairly simple. The calculation of the yield of an Ordinary stock and share is not a simple matter, but a very simple device is used, and, unfortunately, I think it gives a very wrong impression; as you know, we take the dividend yield last year and divide it by the price and take that as our dividend yield. That is a completely wrong conception of the yield on an Ordinary share. To my mind, calculating the yield on an Ordinary share one must endeavour to estimate the varying income over the next 30 to 40 years equating this to a level annual income and divide by the price. It is appreciated that this involves many assumptions as to what the future holds.[70]

This interesting passage addressed two very significant matters: first, indirectly it challenged the actuaries to re-consider their investment assumptions about their projected future rates of interest which he thought too low; second, and more importantly, it highlighted Ross Goobey's very long-term perspective – 'over the next 30 to 40 years'. His speech in November 1956 to the ASPF summarised his main views. His first point was that pension funds should be more focused on seeking returns rather than matching liabilities and, 'we in the pension fund world would do much better by following the practice of ... investment

---

[70] George Ross Goobey, *Address to the 1956 Conference of the ASPF*, 2 November 1956 (www.pensionsarchive.org.uk/27, website accessed 16 June 2016).

trusts [companies]' rather than following the investment practices of insurance companies.[71] He said,

> There are vital differences between insurance company requirements and pension fund requirements. Only the other day I had the privilege at dinner of sitting next to one of the big men in the insurance world . . . and he agreed with me that they, by sheer laziness or lack of thought, buy something for the insurance fund and allocate a small part of it to the pension fund even though it is quite unsuitable for the pension fund. . . . the important thing about insurance company contracts is that they are money contracts; they are only concerned with money, whereas our contracts should be geared to inflation. They are to depend upon the wage at retirement, and therefore we have to endeavour to frame our policy with a view to keeping up with inflation. . . . the second point is the long-term nature of our liabilities compared with those of an insurance company.[72]

His second, and main point in this speech about investment policy, addressed the advantages of pension fund investment in ordinary shares owing to the following features of the asset class, paraphrased as follows:

- Real growth: 'Common stocks are a convenient method of obtaining a diversified equity in the nation's future productive capacity'.
- Diversification: An investor can afford to suffer losses in individual equity investments because the asset class as a whole should still perform well. His point was that individually stocks are risky but collectively, as an asset class, they are not.
- 'The long-term yield of a pension fund is the important factor' so pension funds should invest for the very long-term on a total return basis: 'principal and income can be treated as one'.
- Investors, particularly cash flow positive pension funds, should exploit volatility rather than worry about it. He was unconcerned

---

[71] George Ross Goobey, *Address to the 1956 Conference of the ASPF* 2 November 1956 (www.pensionsarchive.org.uk/27, website accessed 16 June 2016).

[72] George Ross Goobey, *Address to the 1956 Conference of the ASPF*, 2 November 1956 (www.pensionsarchive.org.uk/27, website accessed 16 June 2016).

about fluctuating market values saying that 'liquidity is of minor importance'.

- Historical data showed that government bond returns had been disappointing but equities had produced inflation-adjusted growth of about 4–5%. He had a detailed understanding of long-term returns based on an analysis of capital market history dating back to 1800.[73]

This important speech mapped out the building blocks of Ross Goobey's investment beliefs: first, investment was a very long-term activity and needed to look 30 or more years into the future; second, the investment ethos of an insurance company with their monetary liabilities was inappropriate for investing pension fund assets which had real liabilities; third, ordinary shares were the natural home for pension fund investments. By 1953, certainly by 1956 at the latest, Ross Goobey had come to the view that he wished to maximise investment returns rather than just improve the efficiency of asset allocation. In 1958 he wrote:

> Basically all we are interested in as <u>investors</u> is whether the type of investment we make at any particular time will, in the long run, prove to be a more profitable investment than any other type of investment . . . In fact at no time can I visualise an <u>investment</u> in gilt-edged proving more profitable in the long run than an investment in equities.[74]

He underlined the words 'investors' and 'investment' to indicate that this was his own personal starting point when making judgements about the merits of different asset classes unconstrained by liabilities or other considerations. He possessed a strong belief in the benefits of equity investing in the 1950s owing to the yield gap, which he saw as anomalous but he was not immune to thinking about the relative valuations of different asset classes. In an interesting note from January 1958 he considered the possibility of investing in a form of consumer credit

---

[73] George Ross Goobey, *Address to the 1956 Conference of the ASPF*, 2 November 1956 (www.pensionsarchive.org.uk/27, website accessed 16 June 2016).

[74] George Ross Goobey, *Investment policy for the pension fund at the present time*, memorandum 27 January 1958 (LMA 4481/A/1/21).

(referred to as 'hire purchase' agreements and different from today's use of credit) on a prospective return of 8.5% net of expenses.[75] The same note highlighted the attractions of property, and, during the 1960s, he built up substantial holdings in the asset class; while, in the early 1970s when British government bond yields hit 17% and had become relatively less unattractive, he would only allow an ordinary share to be purchased if their yield exceeded 6%.[76] Ross Goobey was a restless investor, always thinking about the next opportunities and the future. By the end of the 1950s, when he had largely won the intellectual argument about the benefits of pension funds investing in ordinary shares, he was already considering the next investment opportunity, property, in the following terms:

> There is no doubt in my mind that investment in real property is eminently suitable for a pension fund portfolio. The chief reasons could be broadly stated thus:
> a) Such investments are very long-term (in fact generally undated) which fits in with the liabilities of the majority of pension funds
> b) They will benefit... from any continuing inflation which I am convinced will continue
> c) Even if there is no inflation this will, I am sure, lead to a growth in the economy and.... allow margins for increased rents.[77]

He made his first direct property investment in Leicester in 1953, had about 4% invested in the asset class at the end of the 1950s and increased exposure to the asset class slowly thereafter. Ross Goobey worked out quite quickly that he could increase his returns from the asset class by participating in property development rather than just owning direct property by purchasing it in the secondary market. Subsequent property investments during the 1960s were often undertaken in conjunction with property developers where Ross Goobey

---

[75] George Ross Goobey, *Investment policy for the pension fund at the present time*, memorandum 27 January 1958 (LMA 4481/A/1/21).

[76] Peter Dunscombe (email, 25 October 2015).

[77] George Ross Goobey, *Property*, undated memorandum but probably 1959 (LMA 4481/a/2/21).

could negotiate terms and acquire equity in the projects. Additionally, Ross Goobey, along with the Gilbey Pension Fund, established one of the first specialist property trusts, The Wyvern Property Unit Trust, so including this unit trust as one of his investment options, he had three potential routes by which he could invest into the asset class during the 1960s.[78] Imperial Tobacco along with the pension funds of ICI and Unilever were among the first pension investors to explore this avenue of investment.[79] By 1971, at Imperial Tobacco, property exposure had risen to almost 30% of the pension fund assets.[80] According to Peter Dunscombe property was a natural extension of his views about maximising returns, identifying a yield premium and investing in real assets:

> I do not think that Ross Goobey moved into property for diversification reasons. He just saw [property] as a real asset class with significant attractions – very long leases, upward only rent reviews and an undiscovered area for investment. He also quickly mixed with some of the big names in the development world. For example, Charles Clore was looking for investors to acquire the developments he was creating. Ross Goobey saw an opportunity to agree to buy these investments in advance on beneficial terms (an additional 0.5–1.0% on the market yield) thus producing yields well above those available on equities with long-term inflation-protected growth. Hence it was really only an extension of what he had been doing in moving into equities in the first place.[81]

By the early 1970s, Ross Goobey wrote to one of his friends as follows: 'You refer in your letter to having quoted me many years ago when I was plugging equities 100%. You probably know that I have been off equities for the past two or three years, and we are investing practically all our money now in Property.'[82] Still a great believer in yield, he

---

[78] Yally Avrahampour & Mike Young, *Comment on the George Ross Goobey papers* (www.pension sarchive.org.uk/26, website accessed 8 September 2015).

[79] Brian Whitehouse, *Partners in Property* (Birn Shaw 1964) 108.

[80] *Imperial Tobacco Pension Fund Reports* (LMA 4481/1/1/8).

[81] Peter Dunscombe (email, 5 January 2016).

[82] George Ross Goobey to Basil Hoole, letter 22 October 1973 (LMA 4481/a/1/10) l.

pointed out to another acquaintance shortly before his retirement in 1975: 'I am afraid my [golf] game is beginning to disintegrate and I am finding the greatest difficulty in keeping my golf handicap below the yield of our Fund – my handicap is 10 and our yield is 11.5%.'[83] Asset management was an activity with very long horizons for Ross Goobey. He thought about the yield on ordinary shares as a series of payments going out beyond 30 years but he also had an instinctive dislike of trading and an inclination to be fully invested with a buy-and-hold mentality. He considered himself a long-term investor and disapproved of 'market operators' in which he included the stockbroking fraternity. He wrote, 'For long term investors I would recommend them to buy good stocks and stay with them.'[84] He wrote,

> I sometimes think that the best test of whether a man is an investor or a market operator is when he picks up his *Financial Times* in the morning whether he turns to the back page containing the list of prices and fluctuations since the day before or whether he immediately turns to the middle page which contains announcements of the latest profits and dividends.[85]

More seriously, he had little interest in timing asset allocation decisions which he considered to be 'in the nature of "speculations"' because 'buying equities is not so much going into the market and getting them but rather waiting until they are available, and this fits much more readily into the picture of buying equities steadily'.[86] More explicitly, he said,

> as a long term investor my philosophy is entirely simple as I visualise that the long term trend of equity prices is upwards. I therefore, generally speaking, make my investments as soon as the funds to be invested are

---

[83] George Ross Goobey to Rob Irving, letter 15 October 1973 (LMA 4481/a/1/10).

[84] George Ross Goobey, *Running Profits and Cutting Losers*, undated memorandum (LMA 4481/A/01/21).

[85] George Ross Goobey, *Where to obtain advice*, undated memorandum (LMA 4481/A/02/28).

[86] George Ross Goobey, *Investment policy for the pension fund at the present time*, memorandum 27 January 1958 (LMA 4481/A/01/21).

available, or even before they are available. This is why in answer to the question often put to me, 'how much of your fund is invested in equities', I give the answer '105%'. We inevitably have an overdraft.[87]

He believed in fundamental analysis of businesses based on meeting management and analysing reports and accounts, 'the success or otherwise of an investment depends entirely on the skill with which the investment manager can judge the future trend of profits in the particular company'.[88] He was also aware of behavioural pressures that affect asset managers, such as 'anchoring' on a particular number when considering whether or not one should sell (or buy) an investment:

> There is one statistic which I maintain should be completely ignored and forgotten. I refer to the price that one has paid for that particular investment.... It is one of the great misfortunes of accountancy that when a stock is purchased it is entered in the books at the cost price and that figure pursues one throughout the whole ultimate life of the investment.[89]

> In considering whether one should sell an investment it is much better to ignore the price paid and to endeavour to judge the future of the Company on the facts of the situation in which the original cost of your particular investment plays no part whatsoever. Unfortunately, human nature being what it is this cost factor seems to play the most important part.[90]

In addition to investment policy and behavioural issues, he had a practical and detailed grasp of many day-to-day aspects of portfolio management. While best known for his ideas about pension fund investment policy, asset allocation and the equity-bond yield gap, Ross

---

[87] George Ross Goobey, *Running Profits and Cutting Losers*, undated memorandum (LMA 4481/A/01/21).

[88] George Ross Goobey, *Speech to the Royal Statistical Society* (Bristol Group), 17 February 1955 (LMA 4481/a/01/020).

[89] George Ross Goobey, *Speech to the Royal Statistical Society* (Bristol Group), 17 February 1955 (LMA 4481/a/01/020).

[90] George Ross Goobey, *Human Foibles*, unpublished memorandum 1963 in The Investors Anthology, ed. Charles Ellis & James Vertin (Wiley, 2001) 77/8.

Goobey thought deeply about the practicalities of asset management and was knowledgeable on a broad range of matters. As an indication, his archive contains papers on the following subjects: market timing, smaller companies, underwriting, rights issues, running profits and cutting losses, investment 'fads', company management, growth stocks, high versus low yield stocks, and at a more detailed level, how to arbitrage opportunities by switching between Shell (the London arm) and Royal Dutch (the Dutch arm) which owned 40% and 60% respectively of the holding company. Taking this as an example, he wrote about Shell as follows in 1955: 'The capital structures are very different and there is the 2 to 3 (ratio) of sharing profits to be allowed for so that a straight comparison of market process may not be appropriate. After making adjustments . . . we plot these adjusted values on a graph . . . (and) there is no reason why these intrinsic differences should diverge at all. We did this switch twice last year.'[91]

Finally, within equities, Ross Goobey had very unusual ideas about portfolio construction which highlights an interesting component of his investment thinking. Even his son Alastair, an accomplished investment professional in his own right, freely admitted that his father was strange: 'The portfolio which [George] Ross Goobey built up in the next ten years [during the 1950s] would give a modern portfolio manager the vapours; he bought shares in virtually every company quoted at the time.'[92] Consequently, portfolio construction of equity portfolios was one area where George Ross Goobey did not walk a clear path that subsequent asset managers could happily follow. He had many commendable attributes as an asset manager but also had idiosyncratic ideas about diversification, which meant that his investment portfolios contained a very large number of holdings, albeit with a large proportion in smaller companies. His penchant was buying stocks and not really selling very much at all. He had a bias towards higher yielding companies: in the late 1950s to early 1960s his portfolio had a yield premium producing about 35%

---

[91] George Ross Goobey, *Speech to the Royal Statistical Society* (Bristol Group), 17 February 1955 (LMA 4481/a/01/020).

[92] Alastair Ross Goobey, *George Ross Goobey*, in Wall Street People Vol 2, ed. Charles Ellis & James Vertin (Wiley 2001) 261/2.

more income than the FT-A 500 Index.[93] As we have seen, higher yield and income growth over the long-term were critical components in his thinking about ordinary shares. His approach was described as follows: 'He would not pick winners as such because if a stock did not have a prescribed yield then it was not on the radar screen. He would however analyse stocks that had high yields – but I get the impression that most high yield stocks were actually purchased. He was going for yield plus growth plus inflation.'[94] In a talk from 1955, Ross Goobey's portfolios contained hundreds of names and he referred to holding 514 UK companies.[95] At this time, this portfolio was invested in ordinary shares across all sectors of the UK market including very small ones, for example, a meagre 0.1% was invested in 'Tramways & Omnibus' while the largest sector exposure was 'Engineering non-Electrical' at only 6.3%. This meant he had investments in virtually every sector of the market, some in very small unit sizes. The number of stocks continued to grow and one of his successors at the Imperial Tobacco pension fund remembered a portfolio of about 800 holdings.[96] There is little evidence of Ross Goobey having what could be described as a 'sell discipline'. This predilection for holding a huge number of stocks was based on his rather unusual idea about diversification, or as he termed it 'spread'. He described his thinking as follows: 'One of the inherent principles, however, in deciding to invest one's funds in Ordinary Stocks and Shares in view of the fluctuations that do take place from time to time between industry (sic), which of course one cannot always foresee, is to maintain a "spread" of investments....'[97] In an undated memo titled 'Wide Spread', he explained his thinking as follows:

You can only be sure of experience of the past [historic equity returns] being repeated in the future if you 'buy the index'. This means that to be certain of

---

[93] George Ross Goobey, *Yields/Income*, undated notes but probably 1965 (*LMA* 4481/a/2/28)

[94] Peter Dunscombe (telephone call, 15 October 2015).

[95] George Ross Goobey, *Speech to the Royal Statistical Society* (Bristol Group), 17 February 1955 (LMA 4481/a/01/020).

[96] Peter Dunscombe (telephone call, 15 October 2015).

[97] George Ross Goobey, *Speech to the Royal Statistical Society* (Bristol Group), 17 February 1955 (LMA 4481/a/01/020).

making a success of your equity investment you must have a wide spread . . . inevitably in the minds of each Trustee some tremendous investment stumour (sic) in the past which has had the unfortunate effect of damning the whole idea of future investment in equities. There will undoubtedly be stumours (sic) in the future: do not therefore put 'all your eggs in one basket'.[98]

Apart from his use of the strange word 'stumour' and slightly odd sentence construction, the confusion arising from this statement, is that given his high yield bias and preference for smaller companies, he did not 'buy the index', rather he just bought a lot of companies which met his thematic requirements.[99] In practice, he wanted to capture the broad equity market return rather than simply replicate it and he also wished to minimise the impact of any problem holdings. There was no evidence that he invested passively because he had a complex way of thinking about selecting stocks and analysing his own investment performance against the market benchmark. 'I do not consider that spread of investments should include spread of those securities which one considers, good, bad or indifferent . . . you will have gathered from my investment policy that I do not overlook the possibility or indeed the probability that certain of my investments will prove in the long run to be unfortunate, but I feel amply compensated by those that turn out well.'[100] Ross Goobey was aware that individual companies may be risky but in aggregate the asset class was not so he wanted to obtain a broad exposure to the asset class. Most active asset managers focus on the stocks they own and attempt to pick winners, for example, Keynes and his favoured stocks that he referred to as his 'pets',

---

[98] George Ross Goobey, *Wide Spread*, undated memorandum (LMA 4481/A/1/21).

[99] The word 'stumour' is not part of my vocabulary and I had assumed, incorrectly, that the word had been made up by Ross Goobey. I am informed however that the word is used and refers to a mistake or a disappointing outcome. The specific context of a 'stumour' was given as a word used by London taxi drivers to describe their disappointment on arriving to collect somebody for a pre-booked taxi ride only to discover that the individual had made alternative arrangements. Coincidentally, Keynes also used the word 'stumer' (sic) in his private correspondence with Scott about investments in 1938 (CW X11 67) but there is no indication that Ross Goobey was aware of Keynes' thinking in this area. While Keynes wrote about avoiding stumers, in practice, most of his portfolios appeared to emphasise stocks that were either cheap and had a high yield or stocks that could grow rapidly, such as resource companies or mining stocks.

[100] George Ross Goobey to JT Price, letter 14 February 1956 (LMA 4481/1/2/22).

whereas Ross Goobey wanted to avoid the prospect of having any big individual investment losers.

As mentioned earlier, he had a strong preference for investing in small companies and would simply add new holdings, without selling existing ones when he came across new ideas.[101] 'One of the benefits I derived from going to work in Bristol was the discovery of so many excellent local companies... This prompted me to make contacts in all the other big provincial cities so that I could learn about similar local gems.'[102] The other side of this coin was that he was reluctant to invest in over-priced large companies because, 'a natural tendency when one is investing in equities for the first time to incline towards the "blue chip" companies... but.... Such shares have already achieved their status and... required to buy them on what appears to be a ridiculously low yield basis'.[103] Smaller companies could have represented as much as 45% of his equity exposure according to one estimate which would have given him a huge size bias away from the market.[104] Overall, the impression gained is that Ross Goobey was not particularly interested in portfolio construction and that he was much better at buying companies than selling them. It reinforces the view that his major skill was in the investment assessment of different asset categories: he was hugely insightful in his understanding of relative value between asset classes while within asset classes, he had a very good grasp of the fundamental drivers of long-term returns. That was how Ross Goobey made money and how he changed thinking about asset management. His greatest attribute was the ability to see the 'big picture' and to think to the 'left of the decimal point'. Nevertheless, his attitude to diversification was an important component of his belief system in terms of both his words and actions. Perhaps one way of understanding his penchant for holding hundreds of stocks is that he wanted to capture market performance from equities and he also had thematic biases. He had a permanent liking for higher yield and over

---

[101] Peter Dunscombe (telephone call, 15 October 2015).
[102] George Ross Goobey, *Lesser known companies*, undated memorandum (LMA 4481/A/1/21).
[103] George Ross Goobey, *Lesser known companies*, undated memorandum (LMA 4481/A/1/21).
[104] Peter Dunscombe (telephone call, 15 October 2015).

time, he developed a strong preference for smaller companies. His equity portfolio of ordinary shares was constructed to capture these two themes and perhaps he was more concerned with exposure to the theme than individual stock selection. In this sense, he was getting exposure to aspects of the market return that he thought was important. Today's jargon might refer to this as 'smart Beta' whereas Ross Goobey used much more down-to-earth language, 'wide spread'. Perhaps his approach to portfolio construction was more sophisticated than even his son Alastair thought. He was not interested in relative return but wanted to capture as much of the overall market return as possible over the very-long-term, and he achieved this by building a very diversified portfolio that incorporated his thematic preference for yield and smaller companies.

8.4   Contribution

Ross Goobey was to pension funds what Keynes was to insurance companies. Both men re-imagined investment policy and created investment strategies that were much better aligned with the securities markets of their day and the investment obligations of their respective institutions. Although, having said that, and for clarity, Ross Goobey completely rejected the idea of insurance companies as asset managers of pension portfolios arguing that the nature of the liabilities was entirely different. Ross Goobey's great insight was to identify the anomaly of the equity-bond yield gap. Beyond that he understood that final salary pension funds that were cash flow positive should take an aggressive and very long-term view with their investment strategy. He not only favoured ordinary shares but also wished to maximise returns by adopting an equity-only strategy in the 1950s. In turn this meant that he was willing to ignore short-term market fluctuations which he regarded as irrelevant. He was one of the first people to identify the potential problem of persistent inflation and its deleterious effects on savings in the post-1945 world. These were very powerful insights and he materially changed how British pension funds invested. In addition, he was a highly able asset management professional possessing a good understanding of many aspects of the asset management process, in particular the long-term nature of equity investing, including the attractions of smaller companies.

Many of his investment ideas are extremely relevant today, particularly for investors who are not constrained by matching liabilities or meeting cash-flow obligations. Unfortunately, today few defined benefit pension funds could follow his lead given they are cash flow negative and are required to institute recovery plans in the event of actuarial deficits.

His eccentric view of diversification and holding up to 1,000 companies would be seen as costly and rather inefficient by investors today. But, in the context of the 1950s and 1960s his 'wide spread' idea was a method by which he could get thematic exposure to the market. He wanted to capture the equity market return, he liked gaining diversified exposure to higher yield and he held a huge proportion of his assets in smaller companies. So, buying a lot of companies to diversify stock-specific risk while at the same time capturing the premium return available from equities had much logic. It has been described as a 'deep-value, income-oriented strategy' which reduced stock-specific risk.[105] Unquestionably, he held too many stocks in his portfolios but this should not obscure his overall contribution to asset management. This was a man who understood and explained fundamental truths about financial markets and asset management based around relative returns from asset classes, the value of long-term investing, the insidious impact of inflation and the irrelevance of short-term market volatility. By his own behaviour, Ross Goobey highlighted the dynamic behaviour of markets and that investment opportunities change over time, moving as he did from bonds to equities to property. Essentially he had a long-term view of the relative valuation of different asset classes and was willing to back his judgement and make significant asset allocation decisions. There was nothing short-term about Ross Goobey: over almost three decades he made, two, perhaps three, major asset allocations so he was very much in the camp of thinking about the long-term and investing accordingly. His mind was always searching for the next major investment opportunity, he had a restless investment imagination and his contribution was more substantial than just identifying the illogicality of the yield gap in an inflationary

---

[105] Peter Dunscombe (telephone call, 15 October 2015).

environment. His influence extended beyond the theory and practice of asset management. Final salary pension funds became both more affordable to employers and highly attractive to beneficiaries owing to improved benefits, during a period of rising inflation. His idea that pension fund investment could make a material financial contribution to the business, rather than operate as a cost centre, was fundamental because it led to a long-term aspiration based around maximising returns so that ethos was investment-led rather than liability-driven. The subsequent surpluses on pension funds thus increased corporate profitability, by reducing employer contributions, in turn increasing the potential attractiveness of equities as an asset class. Additionally, high investment returns raised benefits to pensioners and spouses ushering in a 'golden age' for final salary pensioners, which lasted into the 1990s for many pension fund beneficiaries. Ross Goobey, therefore, was not only one of the most influential asset management professionals in Britain in the twentieth century but by materially improving various aspects of pension fund investing, he also boosted living standards for countless people.

Bibliography

Primary Sources

Borthwick Institute for Archives at the University of York for information on the *Rowntree pension fund* and other archival information on Rowntree.

The London Metropolitan Archive *(LMA)* holds information about pension funds within *The Pensions Archive Trust* which in turn houses *The Papers of the George Ross Goobey Collection.*

Books

William Allen, *Monetary Policy and Financial Repression in Britain, 1951–59* (Palgrave Macmillan 2014)

Massimo De Felice, Immunisation Theory: An Actuarial Perspective on Asset Liability Management, in *Financial Risk in Insurance*, ed. G. Ottaviani (Springer 2000)

Laurie Dennett, *A Sense of Security: 150 Years of Prudential* (Granta 1998)

Susan Howson, Money and Monetary Policy Since 1945, in *The Cambridge Economic History of Modern Britain* Vol 3, 1939–2000, eds. R. Floud and P. Johnson (Cambridge University Press 2004)

David Kynaston, *The City of London Volume 4: A Club No More 1815 to 2000* (Pimlico 2002)

Chris Lewin, *Pensions & Insurance Before 1800* (Tuckwell Press 2004)

Alastair Ross Goobey, George Ross Goobey, in *Wall Street People* Vol 2, eds. Charles Ellis and James Vertin (Wiley 2001)

George Ross Goobey, Human Foibles, Unpublished Memorandum 1963, in *The Investors Anthology*, eds. Charles Ellis and James Vertin (Wiley 2001)

George Ross Goobey, Pension Fund Investment Policy, memorandum 4 June 1957 reprinted in *Classics, An Investors Anthology*, eds. Charles Ellis and James Vertin (Dow Jones-Irwin 1989)

Chris Titley, *Joseph Rowntree* (Shire 2013)

Brian Whitehouse, *Partners in Property* (Birn Shaw 1964)

Articles, Journals, Pamphlets, Websites, etc.

Yally Avrahampour, Cult of Equity: Actuaries and the Transformation of Pension Fund Investing, 1948–1960 (*Business History Review* 89/2, 2015)

Yally Avrahampour and Mike Young, *Comment on the George Ross Goobey Papers* (www.pensionsarchive.org.uk/26)

Barclays Equity Gilt Study, 2012

TAB Corley, *George Henry Ross Goobey* 1911–1999, Oxford Dictionary of National Biography (Oxford University Press 2004)

JG Day, Developments in Investment Policy During the Last Decade (*Journal of the Institute of Actuaries* 85/2, 1959)

The Economist

George Ross-Goobey, *Address to the* 1956 *Conference of the Association of Superannuation & Pension Funds*, 2 November 1956 (www.pensionsarc hive.org.uk/27)

The Independent

The History of Pensions (www.pensonsarchive.org.uk/82)

JBH Pegler, The Actuarial Principles of Investment (*Journal of the Institute of Actuaries* 74, 1948)

Frank Redington, Review of the Principles of Life Office Valuations (*Journal of the Institute of Actuaries* 78, 1952)

The Joseph Rowntree Charitable Trust (www.jrct.org/funding priorities)

Practical History of Financial Markets (Pearson 2004)

Alastair Ross Goobey, *Investment Practice – Full Circle?* Speech 27 October 2005 (www.pensions-institute.org/the first ross goobey lecture)

George Ross-Goobey, *Address to the* 1956 *Conference of the Association of Superannuation & Pension Funds* (www.pensionsarchivetrust.org.uk/27)

Janette Rutterford, From Dividend Yield to Discounted Cash Flow: A History of UK and US Equity Valuation Techniques (*Accounting, Business and Financial History* 14/2, 2004)

T Sibbett, Reviews, The Scottish Ministers' Widows' Fund, 1743–1993, ed. Ian Dunlop, Saint Andrew Press 1992 (*Journal of the Institute of Actuaries* 120, 1993)

Ronald Skerman, Memoir (*Journal of the Institute of Actuaries* 111, 1984)

9

Observations from the Past

From the early eighteenth century to the middle of the twentieth, the people and institutions described in this book created and shaped the asset management profession and they demonstrated how asset management could operate effectively, practically and accessibly. Since 1960, asset management has grown at an exponential rate and become a huge business in its own right. Assets managed, or funds under management by the profession, could reach $100 trillion by 2020. In turn, this raises important questions about the role of asset management in today's world, as the Bank of England recently observed:

> Academics, practitioners and regulators have been studying banks, their behaviour and failure, for several centuries, Analysing and managing the behaviour of asset managers is, by contrast, a green-field site. The risks and opportunities asset management poses, while

© The Author(s) 2017   **309**
N.E. Morecroft, *The Origins of Asset Management
from 1700 to 1960*, Palgrave Studies in the History of Finance,
DOI 10.1007/978-3-319-51850-3_9

different, could be every bit as important. To avoid the pitfalls of the banks, this greenfield site will need to be cultivated carefully.[1]

While banking and asset management are very different activities, the point above is apposite: asset management is not well understood but, in the main it is a relatively simple and transparent activity. Asset management is based around trying to satisfy savers' expectations in an uncertain future and it is very rich in historical data, so it fits neatly into Soren Kierkegaard's observation that 'life can only be understood backwards but it must be lived forwards'. Financial services generally, and asset management in particular, has an excellent opportunity to learn from the past in order to be better in the future.[2] In that vein, this chapter reviews the investment strategies covered earlier and draws together common threads. It is subdivided into two sections: first, decision-making observations that are specific to the activity of investing: portfolio structures, time horizons, the importance of income and benchmarks; while the second section comments on broader, or perhaps less tangible, aspects of the asset management profession in terms of people, culture, longevity and the social usefulness of this area of finance. As an *aide memoire*, the main entities discussed earlier were

- Insurance companies in the eighteenth and nineteenth centuries which built up assets and invested primarily to meet liabilities.
- Foreign & Colonial: A pooled fund invested in global bonds, aimed at the middle-class saver by a financially literate lawyer, Philip Rose (1868–1883).
- Robert Fleming (1873–1890) and the First Scottish invested in American corporate bonds, mainly railroad securities, it was structured as an investment trust company similar to Foreign & Colonial.

---

[1] Andrew Haldane, *The Age of Asset Management?* 4 April 2014 (www.bankofengland.co.uk/publications/Documents/speeches/2014/speech723).

[2] The Library of Mistakes in Edinburgh exists to help people learn from financial follies. It is an admirable institution and has been established with the specific aim, according to its website, 'to allow students, professionals and members of the general public to study financial history to understand how finance has worked, rather than how it should work if key unrealistic assumptions are made'.

- John Maynard Keynes at the National Mutual (1921–1938), an insurance company where he was chairman. Chapter 6 also considers his investment activities at the Independent Investment Company (1924–1934) and the Discretionary Fund (1921–1946) at Kings College, Cambridge, an endowment fund.
- The unit trusts (1931–1960) of George Booth and Ian Fairbairn at Municipal & General, specifically the First British established in 1931. This pooled fund invested in ordinary shares and was targeted at smaller investors.
- Pension fund investment and George Ross Goobey from 1947 to 1960 at Imperial Tobacco.

9.1   Investment Observations

9.1.1 Portfolio Construction

Portfolio construction is the methodology by which securities are combined together to form a coherent portfolio. Choice, number of holdings, percentage weights and various other factors, such as thematic exposures, are all important components of portfolio construction and, therefore, drivers of future returns. The portfolios underpinning the investment strategies examined in this book covered a range of asset classes and geographies and naturally very different methods of portfolio construction were employed. One simple way to ride out market volatility, or to ignore it, is to build and maintain a 'buy and hold' strategy with very low portfolio turnover. Foreign & Colonial and the First British were both conceived as having an initial portfolio that would be largely unchanged, or fixed, and merely maintained in an administrative capacity. In principle, changes to the initial portfolio would only be made in exceptional circumstances. There was no theoretical underpinning, such as the concept of passive management or tracking the market, to these approaches: Foreign & Colonial's was purely based on simplicity, combined with sensible diversification; the First British modified the 'fixed' idea from mutual funds in the USA, which was intended to curtail the influence of the greedy, dishonest or incompetent investment directors of investment companies after the 1929 Crash. Each of these portfolios was reasonably well diversified though both were also very concentrated containing less than 25 securities. Foreign & Colonial and the First British produced acceptable returns of about 7% per annum over their first 15 and 20 years, respectively, thus demonstrating that this quasi-passive approach was effective. Buy-and-hold was a sensible, low-cost, administratively simple investment idea which had merit but is not widely available today; maybe it should be?

The First Scottish invested in a narrow asset class, mainly US railroad bonds, and was constructed by a small team working together undertaking fundamental research and analysis. It was the model for active asset management that is widely practised today and has become perhaps the norm. The First Scottish held about 30 securities initially and erred towards caution and quality in its securities' selection which enabled it to weather the worst of the economic and financial problems after 1873: it had very few defaults and the longer-term performance record over 18 years was in the region of 10% per annum. Having bought into a relatively risky, cheap asset class in 1873, investing conservatively in order to avoid defaults was a major part of the success of First Scottish.

Under Keynes, the National Mutual had an active investment policy and was innovative of its time because it was prepared to look beyond simply meeting liabilities as an early investor into ordinary shares. In 1924, the National Mutual constructed its equity portfolio around an 'industrial index' – essentially a diversified set of holdings by stock and sector which were liquid, large capitalisation companies. This provided general exposure to the UK equity market and, because stocks were liquid, it enabled changes in asset allocation to be made relatively easily. The Independent Investment Company also utilised this approach which was referred to as the 'credit cycle' method. In these two cases, portfolio construction was organised in order to be subservient to market-timing decisions. With the Discretionary Fund (mainly equities), Keynes changed this investment philosophy materially after 1930 when he decided that buying and holding equities was a better way of investing. By the mid-1930s, the portfolio was constructed in a sophisticated 'bottom-up' manner with growth and income components. Keynes had a large amount of money in his favoured stocks, his 'pets' and confidently believed this was largely responsible for his good performance during the 1930s.

Ross Goobey had a very different approach and built portfolios with an exceptionally high number of holdings, over 500, with a significant allocation to the ordinary shares of smaller companies. One of his objectives was to capture broad market factor exposure – high yield and small cap – so he was willing to buy stocks and sell very little. Ross Goobey wanted to avoid 'stumours' – a big stock going wrong – so he expected to outperform by not losing, something Charley Ellis has written about in his book, *The Loser's Game*. Ross Goobey's very diversified approach to portfolio construction was more or less the antithesis of Keynes', who expected to pick a small number of big winners. But this did not mean that Ross Goobey was risk averse because one of his mantras was 'the best possible result'; he wanted to achieve high returns and thought his method was the best way to do it. In that respect his approach to portfolio construction had similarities with the First Scottish. Ross Goobey also made decisions between asset classes based on relative attractiveness so he switched from bonds to equities in the 1950s and moved into property during the 1960s with a preference for real assets given his concerns about inflation. In this respect he and Keynes were like-minded as both were prepared to modify their investment ideas in the light of experience and market developments.

With the exception of the Independent Investment Company which essentially failed, none of the investment approaches covered in this book favoured market-timing based on shorter-term asset allocation moves between different asset classes. Keynes had an asset allocation-driven style in the 1920s based on his 'credit cycle' idea but he moved away from it, partly one suspects because he not only failed to see the 1929 Crash coming but his partner Falk who, also a 'credit cycle' disciple, was actually buying ordinary shares a month before the tumultuous events of October 1929. By the 1930s, Keynes was essentially a bottom-up investor with a penchant for holding his favoured stocks for the long-term in large unit sizes. His investment performance results were much stronger after 1930, with his emphasis on 'bottom-up' stock selection. Ross Goobey switched between asset classes over three decades but this was driven by his continuing search for income, and his investment policy changed as relative yields changed. This can hardly be regarded as market timing – he made only two – ordinary shares and property – large asset allocation decisions over 25 years.

Asset management and investing operate under conditions of great uncertainty, always; the true skill in investing is not to spot these uncertainties in advance but to hold a portfolio of securities that will be resilient when unexpected events happen. The period between 1868 and 1960 had its fair share of excitements proving beyond doubt that markets are inherently turbulent and unstable. At many points over these 90 years there were justifiable reasons not to invest. In practice, most of the investment strategies considered earlier achieved investment returns that were either acceptable or outstanding.[3] Foreign & Colonial, the National Mutual and the First British would be placed in the 'acceptable category' having earned returns of about 6–7% per annum; the First Scottish, the Discretionary Fund at Kings College and the Imperial Tobacco pension fund achieved outstanding returns. Six of the seven investment strategies reviewed earlier in this book performed well, irrespective of difficult market conditions, owing to soundly constructed portfolios, with time and income also working to their advantage.[4] Sir John Templeton, the legendary twentieth-century investor, gave short shrift to market timing when he said, allegedly: 'The best time to invest is when you have money. This is because history suggests it is not timing which matters but time.'[5]

9.1.2 Time

All of these successful investment strategies had long-term horizons. Foreign & Colonial was established with a 24-year life, the First British of 1931 had a 20-year life. Ross Goobey, perhaps the most long-term of all these investors, was deeply aware of the relationship between time and investing: he looked forward more than 30 years and back into history over 150 years. He was unconcerned about stock market fluctuations or volatility and became an

---

[3] This is not a statistically robust sample and 'survivor bias' is a factor with the small selection of investment funds that form the basis of this analysis. Inevitably, luck or good fortune, may also have played a part in allowing these particular investment strategies to succeed when others, equally worthy, may have failed.

[4] The seventh investment strategy is the Independent Investment Company (Appendix, section A1) which did not perform well.

[5] This quotation is widely attributed to Sir John Templeton but I was unable to reference it.

articulate and passionate advocate of long-term thinking, specifically for pension fund investment, with real liabilities stretching a long way into the future, as he wrote 'as a long-term investor my philosophy is entirely simple as I visualise that the long-term trend of equity prices is upwards . . . for long-term investors I would recommend them to buy good stocks and stay with them'.[6] Despite the long-term horizon of these investment strategies, all of them invested in relatively liquid asset classes. In principle they could have invested in less marketable securities but generally they chose not to pursue this particular route. Perhaps the exception was the insurance companies in Chapter 2 who, during the nineteenth century, were willing to invest in illiquid debentures and mortgages. But these insurance companies had a very clear grasp of their liabilities and these types of investments were balanced by other holdings in more marketable, near-cash securities. In investment, as John Bogle said 'time is your friend, impulse is your enemy' but patience, taking things slowly and favouring the long view are important aspects of successful investing which are ever harder to accomplish in today's online world of immediate information.[7] Increasingly, disciplines and techniques are needed to avoid getting sucked into noisy news and dubious data, all of which is now available instantaneously.

Importantly, Keynes' experience and the results at Foreign & Colonial showed that judging success, or investment skill, over periods of less than 10 years is foolish. At the Discretionary Fund, Keynes' investment performance was very good over 25 years but also highly variable. Performance was volatile and a little modest during the 1920s: but he outperformed by about 100% in the mid-1930s and overall the Discretionary Fund returned about 2500% under his stewardship owing to the arithmetic wonders of compounding.[8] He was invested over a 25-year period from 1921 which equated to about four phases of the stock market and economic cycles. In a similar vein, with Foreign & Colonial's performance, the majority of investors enjoyed moderate to

---

[6] George Ross Goobey, *Running Profits and Cutting Losers*, undated memorandum (LMA/4481/a/2/21).

[7] John Bogle, *The Clash of the Cultures* (Wiley 2012) 310.

[8] Detailed performance figures on the Discretionary Fund are given in section A2 of the Appendix.

slightly disappointing returns during the 1870s. Foreign & Colonial performed well after 1879 so that by the time of Rose's death in 1883, the results achieved were strong. Over the 15 years between 1868 and 1883, Foreign & Colonial experienced approximately two to three phases of the business cycle. Therefore, with both the Discretionary Fund and Foreign & Colonial, up to 15 years was required to make a definitive judgement about the investment achievements covering different phases of the business cycle. The modern tendency of judging asset management performance over say periods of 3–5 years is misplaced because this time period is too short for skill to be demonstrated.

9.1.3 Income

All of the investment approaches discussed earlier had a pronounced bias towards income investing and exploited a higher yielding asset class. Foreign & Colonial offered investors an income premium of about 3% on overseas bonds compared to domestic government bonds, 6% versus 3%. The First Scottish, albeit with a niche approach, provided a similar opportunity by investing in high-yielding American railroad bonds in 1873. Keynes had an interest in growing income over time which he described as follows: 'The ultimate object of normal, institutional investment is to purchase a reasonably secure annual income year by year over a moderately large number of future years.'[9] He began investing into equities for Kings College in 1921; at this point equities had significantly higher yields than UK government bonds, 6.7% against 4.9%. Later, during the 1930s, Keynes displayed a pronounced liking for equities with higher dividend yields, particularly preference shares in the USA.

The First British was launched in 1931 when equities were yielding a handsome premium to bonds and the fund had a starting yield of 6.8% compared to about 5.8% for the UK equity market. M&G became one of the leading proponents of 'value investing' using higher yield as one

---

[9] John Maynard Keynes to the Estates Committee, *A Measuring Rod for Investment Policy,* undated memorandum but probably 1934/35 (Kings College Archive, KCAR/3/1/10/32).

indicator of potential attractiveness.[10] The insurance companies in Chapter 2 should be congratulated for their successful changes to investment policy during the nineteenth century largely based on income as their main criterion. Over that century they completely disinvested from British government bonds, which was absolutely correct, given that yields fell from over 5% to about 2%. Finally, Ross Goobey was obsessed with the idea of identifying assets with higher-yielding characteristics. The clearest example was his assessment of the equity/bond yield gap. More generally, the idea of finding higher yield, with an element of income growth, was important to him and he thought deeply about the subject as the following passage shows, 'To my mind, calculating the yield on an Ordinary share one must endeavour to estimate the varying income over the next 30 to 40 years equating this to a level annual income and divide by the price. It is appreciated that this involves many assumptions as to what the future holds.'[11] Keynes also thought deeply about yields, 'If we speak frankly, we have to admit that our basis of knowledge for estimating the yield ten years hence of a railway, a copper mine, a textile factory . . . amounts to little and sometimes to nothing.'[12] Both Keynes and Ross Goobey understood income and liked it but they also appreciated that it was a very complex area. An approach that emphasises income, or yield, is not the only method of investing successfully but, in this small number of examples between about 1868 and 1960, it worked.

9.1.4 Benchmarks

The investment strategies in this book had broad investment objectives based on simple ideas. These pioneering investors were not

---

[10] Danny O'Shea, M&G Head of Research, *An introduction to M&G, Its History and Its Management* (M&G memorandum, 24 May 1994).

[11] George Ross Goobey, *Address to the 1956 Conference of the ASPF, 2 November 1956* (www.pensionsarchive.org.uk/27, website accessed 16 June 2016).

[12] John Maynard Keynes, *The General Theory of Employment Interest and Money*, in The Collected Writings of John Maynard Keynes Vol VII, ed. Donald Moggridge (Cambridge University Press 1973) *149/150*.

constrained by restrictive benchmarks or short-term measurement of relative performance. Foreign & Colonial and the First Scottish essentially aimed to produce better returns than British government bonds; the First British invested in industrial ordinary shares in the midst of the Depression and offered investors the opportunity to buy equities at low levels. Keynes worried about international finances post 1918, so had a natural inclination to avoid government bonds and invest in equities. Instinctively he felt this was the best way to make money. For the Discretionary Fund, he viewed equity investment as a method of growing income and maintaining real spending power. Ross Goobey simply decided that equities would provide a hedge to combat inflation, thereby providing a better match for the future liabilities of the pension fund. These investment ideas were wide-ranging, easy to understand and produced handsome returns versus expectations. Essentially, there were two types of benchmarks that these early investment strategies were aiming to better either, government bonds (or cash) – in other words, a monetary objective, the risk-free rate; or, inflation with a real return goal intended to maintain or increase real spending power. Insurance companies, Foreign & Colonial, the First British and the National Mutual wanted to exceed the risk-free rate. The Discretionary Fund at Kings College and the Imperial Tobacco pension fund expected to maintain real values. Today, benchmarks and performance objectives are much more sophisticated and specific but do they serve the investment needs of clients better than these early offerings?

9.2 General Observations About Asset Management

9.2.1 People, Culture and Longevity

The investors highlighted in this book were creative, hardworking, intellectually tough, determined and often from unusual backgrounds – typically from outside establishment circles: Rose was a self-made man;

Keynes was remarkably unconventional, contrarian and anti-establishment; Fairbairn, an Olympic rower and aspiring politician; Ross Goobey, the working class son of an east end of London lay preacher. Fleming was the most extraordinary given that he had a working-class upbringing near Dundee and left school aged 13. His ability showed that a modest background and limited education were no barriers to success in the evolving world of finance. Superficially, George Booth appears to have been the most orthodox with his wealthy upbringing based on the success of the family businesses in shipping and leather, educated at Harrow and Cambridge and a director of the Bank of England. In reality, he was anything but orthodox: he was well-travelled and worked in New York as a very young man; he enjoyed mingling with the Bloomsbury Group and his own travels up the Amazon provided much of the raw material for Virginia Woolf's 1915 novel, 'The Voyage Out'.[13] Booth's father Charles was one of the great Victorian social reformers with close links to Joseph Rowntree and socialist politicians; social justice and business were intermingled in George Booth's life from the very start.

All of these individuals needed to fight hard to see their ideas succeed and had to be determined. Keynes demonstrated formidable resilience and self-belief which enabled him to recover from several investment setbacks during the 1920s and 1930s: he kept going when many would have quit. After 1931, Booth and Fairbairn were remarkably persistent, given that it took unit trusts more than 30 years to establish a firm foothold in Britain's financial services industry. Booth had other business interests that he could have happily pursued, but instead he supported Fairbairn at Municipal and General for a very long period. After 1947, Ross Goobey believed that 'real assets' were the correct asset class for pension funds, but in practice, he got to that point in small steps and it took about 10 years for his views to be fully implemented even within his own fund. Rose at Foreign & Colonial needed to change the legal structure of the company after 11 years and only at that point was the idea of the investment company on a firm footing. Success was not instantaneous for any of these people and generally they modified their propositions over time.

---

[13] Duncan Crow, *A Man of Push and Go* (Rupert Hart-Davis 1965) 55.

Fleming and the First Scottish possibly enjoyed the quickest success but also endured a very challenging first 5 years owing to the impact of the 1873 financial crash in New York and subsequent recession.

Inevitably, innovative investment professionals and their ideas need to be nurtured: they require supportive cultures in order to excel, not least because, as shown above, success generally takes time and is rarely linear. Culture is important in all organisations but crucial in asset management where independent-minded people with strong personalities need the right environment in order to achieve their potential. In most instances, the main characters in this book benefited from accommodative organisational or ownership structures, which gave the investment practitioners the time, space and opportunity for their ideas to succeed. In practice, a number of these people shaped their own organisations around them such as Rose, Booth and Fairbairn, but that was not always the case. Fleming was very much the junior, or underling, in terms of his relationship with the wealthy Dundee businessmen who were the Trustees of the First Scottish, but they showed great confidence in him as a person. Fleming was sent to the USA in 1873, aged only 28, and the Trustees generally accepted his judgement on investments. The Fellows at Kings College were prepared to back Keynes when he wished to establish a Discretionary Fund in 1921, and then they supported him through his patchy investment performance up to 1931. In contrast, at the National Mutual in 1930 and 1937, short-term investment problems led to criticism and Keynes did not receive the support he needed. During 1937/1938 when Keynes was recuperating, the acting chairman at the National Mutual changed some of Keynes' investment policies so Keynes resigned, preferring instead to devote his energies to the Provincial and Kings College. At the National Mutual, the lack of support was positively destructive. Of the organisations in the book, perhaps the most unlikely one to play a part in supporting innovative investment thinking was Imperial Tobacco. It is far from clear why a commercial business would recruit Ross Goobey in the first place and then give him the freedom to implement his innovative ideas. In 1947, he joined the pension fund department which at the time was part of the human resources function, and his responsibilities would have been largely related to pensions administration rather than investment. But

Ross Goobey not only turned pension fund investment into an important component of the company's finances, but he also rose within the organisation to become a main board director, driven there by his contribution, intellect and personality. With Ross Goobey perhaps this is a simple story about a talented individual who was empowered, shaped his own role with imagination and had the freedom to express his views, particularly as an investor. Subsequent success, perhaps with a small amount of fortuitous timing, then gave Ross Goobey status both within the company and in the west of England.[14]

It may be purely coincidental but the organisations behind these people have also shown a remarkable ability to survive for the long-term. Established in the fifteenth century by Henry VI, Kings College exudes longevity and the endowment fund exists, essentially, in perpetuity. Imperial Tobacco continues today having re-emerged from the Hanson conglomerate; so does Foreign & Colonial, now called the Foreign & Colonial Investment Trust PLC. Sadly, during the 1980s, the First Scottish American Trust changed its remit when it became part of the Dunedin stable of trust companies and, since 1990, has been called the Dunedin Income and Growth Trust, so it continues but in a different form, with a new name and with a narrower investment objective.[15] The National Mutual Life Assurance Society essentially disappeared after it was taken over in 2001 but it had enjoyed 170 years of independence beforehand. Perhaps the most interesting survivor of them all is Municipal & General (M&G). At the time when mutual funds were becoming established and successful in the latter part of the twentieth century, all of M&G's competitors fell away or were taken over and disappeared. In 1999, M&G was acquired by the Prudential with the consent of the Esmée Fairbairn Trust. Interestingly, 17 years after the deal, the M&G name has been retained so that M&G operates as the principal fund management business within the Prudential. Most

---

[14] Anecdotally, Ross Goobey was both very well known and extremely well respected in Bristol and Somerset (telephone conversation, Peter Dunscombe, 7 June 2016).

[15] 1990: the Scottish American was re-named 'Dunedin Income and Growth Trust' (DIGIT) quite reasonably because as the chairman stated in *The Glasgow Herald*, on 1 March 1990, 'The inappropriateness of the name of the company that now holds no shares in America is self-evident, and indeed for a company with a policy of income growth which is almost entirely invested in the UK the name is positively misleading'.

takeovers of asset management companies do not proceed in this direction because the name of the acquired company fades away as the entity is subsumed. At a similar time to the M&G deal, other substantial British asset management organisations, such as Mercury Asset Management, Phillip & Drew Fund Management, and even Flemings with 100 years behind it, were acquired, lost their independence and their identity.[16] M&G is very unusual having retained its name, history and, hopefully, some of its culture. Booth and Fairbairn deserve much of the credit and theirs is a reassuring success story based on the application of strong ethical values throughout their careers.

9.2.2 Social Usefulness

Keynes had a noble view of asset management believing that it had an enlightened role to play in the world of finance, 'the social object of skilled investment should be to defeat the dark forces of time and ignorance that envelop our future'.[17] He meant that asset management had a broader responsibility, a public interest, beyond maximising profits and short-term trading. The people and institutions examined in this book clearly placed investing first and their own interests second when embarking on their own asset management journeys so all had a purpose, or an idea, which was more than just commercial opportunity. While these early investors may not have expressed this aspiration in such elegant terms as Keynes, in practice, they, operated in a manner that had wide-ranging societal benefits. Specifically, from a financial perspective, asset management had an impact in a number of important areas. First and most importantly, it provided a savings channel that was quite different from banking; second, it made long-term investing available to a broad cross section of society beyond the very wealthy, thus broadening

---

[16] See Annex to Chapter 7.
[17] John Maynard Keynes, The *General Theory of Employment Interest and Money*, in The Collected Writings of John Maynard Keynes Vol VII, ed. Donald Moggridge (Cambridge University Press 1973) 155.

participation in wealth creation; and third, a process started that introduced better stewardship of assets and improved accountability within financial markets.

Insurance companies in the eighteenth and nineteenth centuries lubricated the financial system and helped the process of urbanisation for a long period of time. At a basic level, the insurance companies provided loans, mortgages and finance during a period when the banking system was very immature. More broadly, insurance companies were integral players in the 'financial revolution' that occurred in Britain after 1700. Insurance companies, and life assurance groups in particular, changed behaviours and relationships between different segments within British society because they created:

A social and economic arena in which thousands of individuals of different political persuasions and religious affiliations came together voluntarily to embark on a common enterprise of mutual benefaction and support. This social solidarity was reinforced by annual meetings to elect boards of directors, and to deliberate and vote democratically upon general business matters. The cost of life insurance policies effectively restricted membership to those landed and especially urban families who laid claim to genteel status, above all professionals.[18]

In Britain, insurance companies enhanced social stability and provided the bedrock for long-term saving and investment, important components of the capitalist system. In addition, during the eighteenth and nineteenth centuries there was a gradual shift in economic power from the aristocracy to the middle classes, with money being recycled, facilitated by the insurance companies through loans and mortgages. This enabled members of the burgeoning middle class to demonstrate their financial superiority in a manner that was mutually beneficial to the aristocratic landed gentry, and themselves. The aristocrats probably knew that the balance of power had changed around 1800 once they started to mortgage their land and property in order to take out annuity loans so they could stay afloat financially. Perhaps these socio-economic changes, driven by money and

---

[18] Geoffrey Clark, *Betting on Lives* (Manchester University Press, 1999) 200.

finance, made the subsequent transition of political power that much easier in 1832 with the passing of the Great Reform Act and the subsequent electoral legislation in 1867 and 1884. Compared to the other major European countries, social and political change in Britain was achieved relatively benignly. At the same time as the socio-political landscape was changing, so was the physical landscape. Investment was made into urban and industrial infrastructure which improved the quality of life with iconic developments such as Regent Street and very useful, but less glamorous, prisons and docks. In the latter part of the nineteenth century large amounts of capital was exported overseas and helped with the development of the USA in particular. The early investing institutions, of which the First Scottish was a good example, provided an outlet for patient long-term capital. The First Scottish began investing in the USA in early 1873 and, after the 1873 market crash, not only maintained its investments by staying fully invested, but also subsequently raised more money and added to its exposure. A genuine long-term investment approach helped market stability and rewarded investors.

After 1868, the first investment companies, Foreign & Colonial and the First Scottish, provided a channel for savings and investments that was quite distinct from the deposit channel of the banks. Banks can fail and several did in the late nineteenth century, notably Overend, Gurney in 1866, Jay Cooke in 1873 and the City of Glasgow Bank in 1878. The intrinsic nature of the two types of institution is different, particularly in how they make profits: banks take deposits, pay interest and then act in the capacity of principals, by using deposits as credit to make money for themselves; asset management companies operate as agents by investing monies, with the subsequent returns, net of fees, going directly to the client: the risks and rewards are therefore very different. The business models of a bank and an asset management company are dissimilar, so again this provides savers with choice and diversity by type of institution. Finally, the development of asset management enabled a distinction to be made between deposits and investments, respectively shorter term and longer term. Today, with more regulation of banks and with improved deposit protection schemes provided by government, savers have more protection but banks still fail: the usefulness of having an alternative channel for investments should not be underestimated.

An underlying objective of these early investors and their institutions was not only to increase wealth, but also to increase participation in order to spread that wealth. Prior to the first investment companies, investing was either a rich man's pursuit organised through stockbrokers and private banks, or the speculative domain of entrepreneurial businessmen. Organising investments into a pooled fund structure allowed the middle classes to invest in a diversified, relatively safe, cost-efficient manner. Foreign & Colonial offered 'the small investor the same advantages as the large capitalists' and by the early 1880s 'small investors' were beginning to invest; in the 1920s, Keynes believed that the life offices were ideally placed as institutional investors to dominate the middle-class savings market by offering high-quality investment products at a reasonable cost. After the 1930s, unit trusts mainly invested in ordinary shares, were simple and largely transparent vehicles, aimed at smaller investors, and women in particular, had started to invest more.[19] Fairbairn, and Booth, at Municipal & General had a lifelong ambition to make investment available to the less affluent as a means to improve their financial circumstances. With pensions, at Rowntree, owing to the personal generosity of the company owner Joseph Rowntree established an uncosted pension fund with very high participation rates by the employees. The management of the company then demonstrated considerable financial acumen and investment expertise so that by 1956 there was a huge cushion of assets over liabilities which meant that future pension payments were secure. In the latter part of the twentieth century, for members of Defined Benefit pension funds more generally, Ross Goobey helped to usher in a 'golden age' for pensioners by treating pension funds as a financial asset that could be invested to generate 'the best possible result', his ideas lowered the cost of pension provision, produced higher benefits and raised living standards. Given Ross Goobey's contribution, whereby he invested the assets very effectively and made pension funds more affordable, it is a tragedy that this pensions opportunity has been squandered by us, collectively. A combination of factors – government taxation of surpluses and dividends, increased longevity, restrictive benefits legislation,

---

[19] *Foreign & Colonial Government Trust, Prospectus 1868* (Guildhall Library).

employer abuse, imprudent Trustees – means that final salary defined benefit provision has largely disappeared.

Finally, the asset management profession made small steps towards playing a more significant role as stewards and custodians of financial assets. These institutions provided early checks and balances on the issuance and valuation of securities at a time when behaviour on both the London Stock Exchange and exchanges in the USA was verging on the fraudulent at worst, and merely manipulative at best. Fleming, in particular, had a clear sense of stewardship: he challenged the 'robber barons' and held the bankers of Morgan and railroad company managements accountable to their investors; while Rose, with the founding of the Association of Foreign Bond Holders in 1868, was instrumental in creating an organisation to safeguard the rights of international bond investors in the event of defaults. Keynes and Ross Goobey were very aware of the limitations of bankers and stockbrokers, Ross Goobey viewing the latter as 'market operators', while Keynes fired 'constant shafts of scorn aimed at stupid City bankers'.[20] Fairbairn at M&G and Ross Goobey at Imperial Tobacco visited the companies in which they invested in order to better understand their corporate strategy and management practice. These early asset managers, therefore, played the roles of custodian and steward.

9.3   Concluding Remarks

The asset management profession developed during the eighteenth and nineteenth centuries and became firmly established in Britain after 1868. By 1960 it had built firm foundations based on technical investment expertise in bonds, property and equities, and offered savers probity, security and choice. The small number of investment strategies included in this book also offered value for money. These foundations were sufficiently deep to create a professional services ethos and a branch of finance that was distinct from banking. Asset management provided savers with opportunity and choice. It also created an environment

---

[20] Nicholas Davenport, *Memoirs of a City Radical* (Willmer Bros 1974) 47.

whereby thoughtful, skilled and well-resourced organisations had the capability to invest, add value and accumulate wealth for their clients, either by producing returns greater than the risk-free rate or by investing in real assets to maintain spending power. Insurance companies in the eighteenth century, as the first institutional investors, were an integral part of a rapidly evolving financial system and developed some rudimentary investment techniques during the nineteenth century based around security of capital and growth of income. Specialist investment companies then developed investment strategies seeking excess return with a greater willingness to embrace risk; Foreign & Colonial created a vehicle that enabled savers to invest cost-effectively in a diversified manner via a pooled fund. The First Scottish advanced the process of asset management by exploiting the investment opportunity presented by the USA and sought to establish an information advantage by undertaking fundamental research. By the 1930s, these first investment companies had demonstrated their worth over an extended period and showed themselves to be much more robust and trustworthy than their equivalents in the USA. The First British, a simpler version of the Foreign & Colonial pooled fund idea, began to widen access to investment markets, particularly for women, and Municipal & General identified high-yield investing as one method of successful equity investing based on the idea of 'value'. After 1922, Keynes provided life offices with a roadmap that could have made them the pre-eminent investing institutions in Britain but he was only partially heard. Many of Keynes' insights as an asset manager only emerged after his death which limited his direct influence on the development of the asset management profession, particularly with reference to endowment funds, which was unfortunate. As Keynes had done for life offices and endowment funds, Ross Goobey revolutionised investing strategy for pension funds: in an inflationary world, he highlighted the importance of investment into real assets and articulated the case for very long-horizon thinking. By 1960, these early British investors had created an asset management profession with strong foundations and firm values based on a service ethos. In due course, asset management would change from a profession and become a business, systemically important within the current financial system, but that is another story.

Bibliography

Primary Sources

Guildhall Library, London, is an excellent source of data such as information on company prospectuses, including the following:
- *Foreign and Colonial Government Trust, Prospectus, March 1868.*
- *Foreign and Colonial Government Trust,* Plan of Consolidation, *March 1879.*

Kings College, Cambridge, Archive Centre Holds the Extensive Papers of *John Maynard Keynes.*
London Metropolitan Archive for *The Papers of the George Ross Goobey Collection.*

Books

John Bogle, *The Clash of the Cultures* (Wiley 2012)
Geoffrey Clark, *Betting on Lives* (Manchester University Press 1999)
Duncan Crow, *A Man of Push and Go, The Life of George Macaulay Booth* (Rupert Hart-Davis 1965)
Nicholas Davenport, *Memoirs of a City Radical* (Willmer Bros 1974)
John Maynard Keynes, The General Theory of Employment Interest and Money, in *The Collected Writings of John Maynard Keynes* Vol VII, ed. Donald Moggridge (Cambridge University Press 1973)

Articles, Journals, Pamphlets, Websites, etc.

Andrew Haldane, *The Age of Asset Management?* 4 April 2014 (www.bankofeng land.co.uk/publications/Documents/speeches/2014/speech723)
John Maynard Keynes to the Estates Committee, *A Measuring Rod for Investment Policy,* undated memorandum but probably 1934/1935 (Kings College Archive, KCAR/3/1/10/32)
George Ross-Goobey, *Address to the* 1956 Conference of the ASPF, 2 November 1956 (www.pensionsarchive.org.uk/27, website accessed 16 June 2016)
George Ross Goobey, *Running Profits and Cutting Losers,* Undated Memorandum (LMA 4481/A/01/21)
Danny O'Shea, *An Introduction to M&G, Its History and Its Management* (M&G memorandum, 24 May 1994)

Index

© The Author(s) 2017   **329**
N.E. Morecroft, *The Origins of Asset Management
from 1700 to 1960*, Palgrave Studies in the History of Finance,
DOI 10.1007/978-3-319-51850-3

CPSIA information can be obtained
at www.ICGtesting.com
Printed in the USA
LVOW02*1618240517

535706LV00014B/183/P